The Swamp Root Chronicle

THE SWAMP

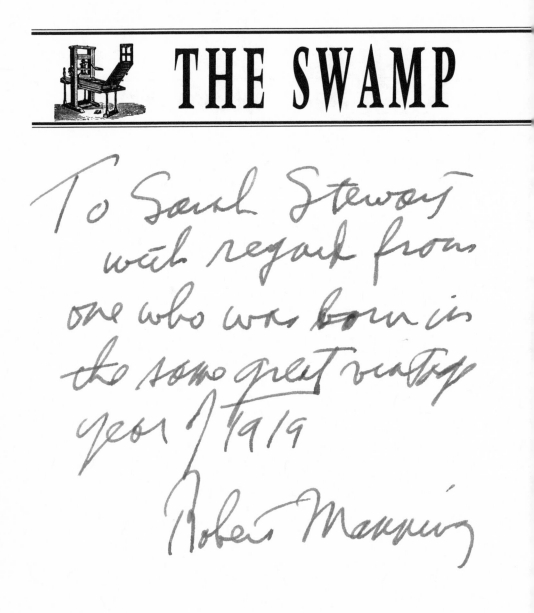

To Sarah Stewart
   with regard from
one who was born in
the same great country
year of 1919

   Robert Manning

ROOT CHRONICLE

Adventures in the Word Trade

ROBERT MANNING

W. W. NORTON & COMPANY New York London

The text of this book is composed in Times New Roman 327
with the display set in Goudy Text and Vendome Condensed.
Composition and Manufacturing by the Haddon Craftsmen, Inc.
Book design by Charlotte Staub

"Farewell to Readers" was first published in *The Atlantic* in
December 1980.

Library of Congress Cataloging-in-Publication Data

Manning, Robert, 1919–
    The swamp root chronicle : adventures in the word trade /
by Robert Manning.
    p.   cm.
1. Manning, Robert, 1919–   . 2. Journalists—United
States—Biography.   3. Editors—United States—Biography.
4. Periodicals editor—United States—Biography.
5. Atlantic (Boston, Mass. : 1932) 6. Journalism—United
States.   I. Title.
                    PN4874.M482A3 1992
                    070.4′1′092—dc20
                    [B] 92-7376

            ISBN 0-393-03090-3

W.W. Norton & Company, Inc., 500 Fifth Avenue
New York, N.Y. 10110

W.W. Norton & Company Ltd., 10 Coptic Street
London WC1A 1PU

1 2 3 4 5 6 7 8 9 0

To Maggie,

who lived and shaped so much of this story,

and to

Theresa,

who has provided the happy ending

Contents

Preface

"A newspaper writer," according to that noted friend of the press Otto von Bismarck, "is one who has failed in his calling." I am grateful that by the time I discovered this bit of Prussian wisdom I was beyond redemption.

For well over fifty years journalism has been my career and my life intermingled, one so indistingishable from the other that from the time I was seventeen years old until the present they could not be separated. Nor can they be now, as I try to recapture the excitement, the fascination, and some of the lessons learned from years of enjoying a trade that has been not just a "calling" but a passion.

I have tried to keep this story straightforward and simple, and have struggled against the temptation to exploit hindsight, especially the kind that endows the author with undeserved reputation for wisdom or prescience. I have tried to recapture events, assess policies, and present the players as they appeared to be at the time, not altered and prettified in the light of afterthought. Now and then the invitation to hindsight has proved irresistible; I have striven to isolate those occasions in footnotes of a determinedly unscholarly caste. As to the success or failure of these efforts, I throw myself on the mercy of the court (a reckless thing to do when you consider the parlous state of the American judicial system these days).

Of course I have relied heavily on memory, but for the most important stages of this journey I have been able also to draw on notes, my own abortive diary or journal entries, flaked clippings of my old newspaper, wire service, and newsmagazine stories, a reliable if fragmentary reservoir of notes and official records from my period in government service. More than that, I have had the benefit of sometimes sharper and corrective recollections of those with whom I worked and played in days past. Also, when in doubt I have been able to find ample reassurance for most of my versions of events in the writings of other journalists and historians.

Some readers will wonder, How can anyone remember precise quotations and conversations and images from long ago? I have tried to be careful and precise about this. It is astonishing how clearly the crucial moments in one's life reappear in memory—not only the words but the tone of a voice, the colors of the clothes people were wearing, the smells and sounds of the moment, the brands of cigarettes or whiskey an associate favored, the exact look on the face of a jockey driving a winner to the wire or of a president at the instant he learns of the assassination of an allied leader.

I have used quotation marks liberally, but in almost all instances I am prepared to swear an oath that I have conveyed the remarks truly, and in a few other cases I use them in the conviction that the precise spirit if not the precise wording has been captured. In other instances, where I know I am right but cannot be sure of the dialogue, I have delivered the words without quotation marks.

The word trade has undergone a revolution since the time this narrative begins, a revolution that is still going on. Television now provides the basic daily news, so daily newspapers have been obliged to be more like what the weekly newsmagazines used to be, so the newsmagazines have felt compelled to grope for ways to provide the more thoughtful (though perilously foreshortened) material that was long the provender provided by periodicals like my former magazine, *The Atlantic.* **10** This leaves those heavier periodicals groping for new relevance.

The evening newspaper on which I started is but a skim milk version of its old self and now comes out in the morning. The United Press, once the raffish training camp for a regiment of journalists, now languishes in near-bankruptcy. *Time* and *Life,* venues for some of my most challenging and rewarding years, are now lesser adjuncts of an entertainment conglomerate. The once mighty broadcasting networks are gasping for breath as they see their power, prestige, and rich profits fading.

As I began working on these memoirs the screen of my word processor would light up even before the power was turned on and flash a blunt subliminal message: Who gives a damn? (Actually the message was more vulgar than that, but this version suffices to make the point.) So I needed a lot of help and encouragement in order to keep going. Without a lot of both from many friends and former associates I would never have finished. I am deeply obliged to all of them.

First, to the happy, eager band of fellow cubs, pre–World War II vintage, at the *Binghamton Press,* some of them now gone: Patricia Quinn, Kimball Davis, Bob McManus, Dan Dickinson, Betty Burke, Steve Shields, and Bob Lovett. More recently to Dan Wakefield and Arthur Hepner for their candid chapter-by-chapter critiques. James Carroll and Ward Just for their words of encouragement just when they were needed most. Charles U. Daly for the slogan he made me post right before my eyes on my study wall: "Tell the truth or don't bother."

Richard Witkin helped with his recollections of the turbulent early days at the United Nations. Dr. Arthur Kravitz was there when I needed him. So was Robert Lescher, who combines the zeal of a good literary agent with an editor's clear-sightedness. Two of my former associates at *The Atlantic,* Emily Flint and Avril Cornel, were generous of their time and assistance as I tried to bring into focus sixteen years at 8 Arlington Street in Boston. At a time when extra concentration was needed, Judy Nies welcomed me into the placid isolation of the Boston Writers' Room; Marty Myers and Rodney Armstrong to the shelves of that gem of libraries, the Boston Atheneum, and Mario Bonello to the shelter of the St. Botolph Club. The encouragement of Donald Lamm and Eric Swenson and the help of Cecil Lyon and others at W. W. Norton have been invaluable. My **11** sons Richard, Brian, and Robert were more patient than I had reason to expect as they were subjected to anecdotes and incidents they'd already heard recited many times before, and the helpful cautions of Rick's editing pencil showed that he'd learned a few things from his father.

To all these and many more I owe the kind of thanks that implies no blame for the consequences of their help. There are two others in particular to whom I owe even more. One is Thomas Griffith. His intelligence and taste are reflected in many ways in these pages, and the entire chronicle is warmed by the glow of our long friendship. The other is my wife, Theresa. She has scanned every word with an eye not only for precision but for pomposities and assorted other character failings. Beyond that, she has stoically tolerated more than three years' worth of sinking spells, cranky moments, and all the other manic-depressive behavior that goes with the craft of writing. I will be showing her my love and gratitude for years to come.

The Swamp Root Chronicle

Chapter 1

The Happy Accident

My hometown, the small city of Binghamton, sits in upstate New York astride the junction of two rivers with musical Indian names. When I go back there, as I do now and then, I usually take a stroll alongside the Susquehanna or Chenango just to reassure myself that this is the same place I grew up in. So much has changed. I wouldn't recognize the plastic new downtown if it weren't for the rivers and the solid gray stone courthouse with its walls as thick as a county sheriff's head that still stands in the city's center, charming reminder of the past, almost unreal now like some stage set that is waiting to be dismantled and carted off. There must be scores of such relics still standing in New York State, New England, and the Midwest, hardy old structures with lawns that feature black big-mouthed cannon and cones of cannonballs sitting underneath green-encrusted likenesses of Civil War soldiers. A scattering of elms casts thin shade, and in season more starlings or sparrows than can be counted hold noisy conclave.

Standing before that old Broome County courthouse or walking close to one of the rivers I can still get my bearings in a hometown that has grown strange to me. This street in front of the soldier statues is Court Street, which arbitrarily becomes Main Street at the western end of a bridge that is so lacking in **15** character that it isn't even ugly. When I was growing up, if you crossed the bridge and went west on Main to where Binghamton stopped and Johnson City began, you would come to a stone arch bearing the boastful inscription GATEWAY TO THE VALLEY OF OPPORTUNITY. An innocent traveler was not told in which direction that Valley lay, but many of us living in that gray city in that gray time knew: Any direction, and the farther away the better.

The Depression was far from over then, in the 1930s, and for many in Binghamton and its umbilical villages, Endicott and Johnson City, the so-called Triple Cities, essentials of life were still hard to come by. The area's principal industry, the Endicott-Johnson Shoe Company, or E-J as it was usually called, was a haven of opportunity for a new generation of immigrants, especially from Eastern Europe. Upon leaving Ellis Island they made their way to the place they'd been told about in letters from America. "Which way E-J?" were the first words of English many of them learned, and they journeyed to one of the several noisy red-brick factories scattered about the Triple Cities to join earlier migrants from Ireland, Poland, Czechoslovakia, and Ukraine who had come to find new lives in the new world.

There was a new industry in town, just starting to grow into the giant it was to become. Having taken over a modest clock-making factory, the International Business Machines Company made its headquarters across the street from one of the largest of the E-J factories. The company's slogan, THINK, glowered mockingly from above IBM's entry arch toward the shoe factory across the way. The street might as well have been a wall, dividing as it did class from class. At quitting time each working day the shoeworkers in their dark shirts, raveled sweaters or team jackets, and scuffed brogans marched down their side of the street, making for nearby bowling alleys and corner saloons where they'd dally a bit before going home. As they walked, some of the E-J workers looked across at the white-collar IBM employees in their somber suits and ties or neatly tailored dresses, and chanted, "While you're thinkin', we're drinkin'!"

For several years my father worked in one of those red-brick 16 E-J factories. He had started in 1913 as an apprentice and, with time out for the World War I army, had advanced through a series of jobs in Johnson City Factory #1. By the time I was born on Christmas day in 1919 he had become an experienced treer. In those days, even inexpensive shoes like those made by Endicott-Johnson were finished by hand; the treer was the man who finished them, treating six shoes at a time on a revolving spindle, sponge-washing each and then carefully daubing on finishes "to make them beautiful," as my father proudly explained it.

He was baptized Joseph James but always called Joe, a slim, handsome man with dark curly hair who dressed like a tasteful dude and owned a smile that could turn a key in a lock. He was the next youngest of nine (eight boys and one girl) born to a pint-sized blacksmith from County Galway, and his wife, Mary. My mother was Agnes Pauline Brown, the youngest of twelve (three girls and nine boys) sired by Ellen and John Brown. John Brown was a stonemason who'd built his own wooden house along a path beside the Delaware, Lackawanna and Western Railroad tracks on Binghamton's West Side; since he was the first to settle there, he named it Brown Street. Why not? The entire batch, Browns and Mannings, were as Irish as potatoes and, when all the aunts, uncles, and cousins were counted, almost as numerous, but by the time I came along there wasn't an Irish accent among them.

Like all Irishmen, the Mannings descended from kings. An O'Mainnin or O'Maoinein, from the line of Fiacha Araidhe, twenty-seventh king of Ulster, was chief of one of the six Sodhan territories in the 1300s until he was hanged and his castle seized by a blackguard named Diarmaid O'Kelly, king of HyMany. O'Kelly is said to have died without issue, serving him right. But the remaining O'Mainnins proliferated as Mannions, O'Mannings, and Mannings, a fact for which I am usually grateful. As fast as the clan multiplied its fortunes sank, down to peasant level. My Grandfather Tom, seeing no future for himself in Galway, took off with his blacksmith tools, a derby hat, the suit on his back, and little else to upstate New York.

Tom Manning's and John Brown's families grew, but their incomes did not. Though they were among the youngest offspring, both my parents got only a few years of schooling before   **17** having to go to work and contribute to the family support. What they lacked in formal education they possessed in dignity and ambition. Joe Manning was not made for the robot-like life of a shoeworker, and Agnes wanted him to make more of himself.

He had trained as a cook in the WWI army. A few years after I was born, he put his meager savings into a small lunchroom not far from the factory where he'd worked. Mostly fellow workers patronized it until the simple short-order menu was supplemented by good beer and ale smuggled in from Canada in clanking, bulging burlap sacks, and later by Scotch whiskey imported by the same route and a quite passable rye whiskey blended from the best grain alcohol by my father and one of my uncles in the cellar. It bore their own boastful label, Cock of the Walk Rye. Joe Manning's place prospered, quickly outgrowing three successive locations until he bought a small hotel conveniently located right behind Binghamton's city hall and gave over the rear of its first floor to his new establishment. He installed a proper mahogany bar with a brass rail, beautifully etched mirrors, two pool tables, a race wire and betting book, and a pair of silver-dollar slot machines, and gave it a fancier name. The Ahwaga Club became well known as the finest speakeasy between New York City and Buffalo.

The leading lights, among them the city judge, the county DA, and the cream of what passed for local society gathered day and night for refreshment and escape from their daily rigors. If someone at headquarters was looking for the chief of police or one of his lieutenants he would usually call first at the Ahwaga Club. The same was true for the receptionists or secretaries of some of the city's finest doctors and lawyers, and for more than one churchman. Its toasty mahogony-brown interior, the click of pool balls, the convivial joking and small-talking mingled with the modulated crackle from the loudspeaker of the race-callers relaying the latest results from Belmont or Hialeah inevitably attracted travelers as well who found the place a warm oasis in which to pause in their journeys and refuel their fortitude.

Proceeds of the Ahwaga Club brought some good years to Joe and Agnes—a comfortable two-family house in a good part

18 of town with my Uncle Frank and Aunt Florence on the upper

floors, fine clothes, two shiny cars in the garage, membership in the second-best country club (the best would not admit Catholics or Jews), and trips to New York where we would put up at the Hotel McAlpin and, after my father's brief business with his suppliers was done, my parents would take me to the new musicals or for walks through the stone-and-glass canyons or rides on the Staten Island ferry. I still see my father in his golfing cap and jaunty tweed knickers, hitting a long drive off the first tee, and my mother in her jodpurs at the jumping ring or in a now-laughable swimsuit at the Oquaga Lake place we rented every summer.

It was good that they enjoyed those years because there weren't many of them. The stock market crash wiped away all the family had made from the Ahwaga Club and then some, but money still came in until the Eighteenth Amendment was repealed, bringing an end to the vicarious pleasure of illicit drink. It was as if the dastardly Diarmaid O'Kelly had materialized from centuries past and burned down the O'Mainnin castle.

My father was a soft touch; he had allowed some of the town's finest citizens to run up huge tabs at his establishment. He thought he had those many thousands to fall back on, but when he went to collect most of his debtors seemed not to know who he was. "I can always say I was stiffed by the very best people," I heard him say when, hating to do it, he telephoned one of his brothers for a short-term loan. I remember that he smiled when he said it. It wasn't until I read a Scott Fitzgerald novel many years later that I fancied that what I had been witnessing in Joe Manning's brief brush with prosperity was a little bit of Gatsby in the night.

Our family of five (a sister, Jeanette, then a brother, Thomas, had followed me) went through some very bad years, and for a while my father even lost that smile. But he and my mother had the deeply loving kind of marriage that outlasts vicissitude. For the period when Joe stumbled, Agnes was there to work in a dress shop or sell real estate to keep the family together. My father eventually recovered none of what he had lost except for the most important thing, that ready smile and its spirits-boosting effect on all around him. Much time had to pass before that would happen, though, so in the gloom of the late 1930s, I had **19** to face up to the fact that the good days were gone and I was going to have to fend for myself.

I was a senior in high school in 1937, bored with Cicero and *Silas Marner,* hoping to get to know girls who weren't nice girls. Perhaps one of those marvelously sculpted Polish girls whose father carved out leather soles at E-J's Harry F. Johnson factory, and whose appearance in a gym suit from across the exercise field aroused the yearning for promiscuity in a horny young man. Hoping, yes, but then fearful that I might thereupon be consigned forever to the furnaces of hell by Father Hannon of St. Thomas Aquinas Church. Studs Lonigan, meet Bob Manning.

I was caught in deep melancholy. It had dawned on me that a diploma from Binghamton Central High School and the ability to run fourteen consecutive balls at the Ladas Brothers pool hall were not likely to carry a fellow far beyond Binghamton's city limits. I don't know which was more compelling, being bored or being broke. In any case, I had not much prospect of the means to college and I needed a job, something to support a two-cigarette-a-day habit and a desire to go dancing once a week with a girl named Bette, who was beautiful, willowy, and wonderful even though stubbornly unpromiscuous. Nothing to alarm Father Hannon there, though not for lack of trying. (Ah, but even the *desiring* and the *trying,* we were taught at St. Thomas, were in themselves mortally sinful.)

A schoolmate suggested I might find work in the pressroom of the *Binghamton Press,* the city's afternoon newspaper. He showed me a picture of his old man, wearing a heavy apron to protect him from flying blobs of hot lead and a cocked hat made of newsprint; thanks to the stereotypers' union he'd made good money there for twenty-five years. I hastened to the *Press* in its twelve-story tower, the tallest building in all the Southern Tier of New York. The directory in the lobby of the Binghamton Press Building offered no guidance to the location of the pressroom, down in the bowels of the building where the roaring monster printing presses spewed out each day's newspapers. Envisioning these portals as my personal gateway to the Valley of Opportunity, I wandered into an alley and through a door **20** marked City Room.

How ramshackle was my Valley! Compared to what I entered, newspaper offices today are computerized, hospital-sanitary, quiet as a convent. There is little about them to equal the charming dishevelment of the daily news room in those bygone days. The smallest of them shared with the largest a chemistry of sounds, smells, and disarming clutter that could only confound an inexperienced visitor. Surely, the scene suggests, no order can be made of human affairs by men and women so raggedly preoccupied.

I was enthralled. The large *Press* city room smelled of glue-pots, pipe tobacco, cigarette and cigar smoke and, since it was shortly after lunchhour, there was also a whiff in the air of spent scotch or bourbon whiskey. Sounds as bright to me as bird calls came from the clattering of the typewriters and the clattering of teletypes, and there arose occasionally, as if uttered by an angry crow, the sharp cry of "Boy!" or "Copy!"

A dozen men and three women labored in seeming serenity and self-preoccupation over typewriters or clutters of paper. A fourth woman, this one plainly distraught, emerged suddenly from a glass-walled corner office. "What do you want?" she inquired of me.

"I've come to see about a job," I said.

"How did you know there's a job open?" she asked.

"I didn't," said I, about to explain that I was looking for the press room.

"One just opened up," she said. "Three minutes ago."

The door of the glass office burst open and a dark-haired man appeared, eyeglasses swinging from a black ribbon strung about his neck, a frock coat encasing his big frame. "Woodruff," he shouted at the woman who had been talking to me, "Goddammit, where's my sauerkraut juice?"

That was my first sight of Tom Radcliffe Hutton. He was an imposing figure, then in his mid-forties, standing about six feet or a little under, with a huge crop of black curly hair, a handsome but cloudy visage, a stocky body that moved with a smoothness suggesting strength. He was, I was to learn, a good horseman and sometime polo player, and I once saw him pick up two bushel baskets of apples, one hand grasping each basket by its slim wire handle, and carry them as if they were bunches **21** of violets. He'd already had two, perhaps three wives, and was living with one of them, or a mistress, on a farm a few miles outside town which he insisted on calling a "ranch"—and woe betide any of his underlings who called it a farm. Hutton liked to keep his origins obscure, but it was understood that he was born in upstate New York, with some brushstrokes of Indian blood in him ("Someone before him slept on the wrong side of the blanket" was a local way of saying it), and his swaggery western manner came from several years of living and newspapering in Texas.

On that autumn day in 1937, Tom Hutton had in a customary fit of rage fired one of the newspaper's five copy boys. The copy boy's offense seemed to be that he, a recent graduate of Syracuse University, had been favoring with increasingly ardent attention a new young lady reporter of somewhat limited talent but irresistable physical attributes. These attributes were the reason Tom Hutton had hired her, and in his view they were not to be enjoyed by anyone but him.

So there was an opening for one copy boy. It was Hutton's practice to hire only college graduates, but it was now October. There would not be another graduating class until spring. His secretary, the homely and warm woman who'd accosted me, and whose name I was to learn was Helen Woodruff, introduced me to her boss as a candidate for the job. I did not know what a copy boy was, what one was supposed to do, though upon observing several of them responding to the cry of "copy" as it affrighted the city room air, I deduced that their function was that of "hunkers," as Hollywood then referred to studio lackeys who were employed to be sent out for coffee and to have matches struck on them.

Tom Hutton sourly looked me over as I fidgeted in my scuffed $3.95 Thom McAn's and a rundown suit of electric-blue serge on which I still owed Harry Prew's Haberdashery some $21 of its original knock-down price of $29.50. He swung his spectacles from their black cord with a peculiar twist of the wrist that reminded me depressingly of the backhand stroke of Simon Legree.

"What are you doing out of school?" he snapped.

22   I explained that Binghamton Central High School, at which I

was a senior, was running on a split-session basis and that my schooling finished each day at noon.

"If you can get in here by 12:15 for the early stock market returns, and if you can buy a new pair of shoes (looking at my feet with distaste) and eat on $8 a week," he said, "you've got a job. Slackjaw over there"—he pointed to a sad-faced man standing like a lonesome crane in a far corner of the City Room—"will tell you the routine, and we'll soon find out whether you're to be a newspaperman or a grocery clerk."

I quickly discovered what Hutton meant by that. The five copy boys and a small band of ten to twelve young reporters stationed in Binghamton and several surrounding bureaus in the *Press*'s five-county fiefdom were considered to be trainees. We made up Tom R. Hutton's School of Applied Journalism. My admission was accidental and quite unorthodox, but thanks to Black Tom's stormy temper (it was not always unprovoked: He once fired his own son, Bud, from a reporter's job because the son threw an Underwood typewriter through his old man's glass office wall) I had an opportunity to matriculate in a college of a kind I think did not exist before and never will again, an institution that was capable of assuaging though not erasing my disappointment and sense of inferiority at not being able to move on from high school to college.

Tom Hutton was a strange man—brilliant, selfish and generous at the same time, frequently infuriating and ruthless, often charming, and capable of an arrogance that was majestic in its intensity. Later his politics became appallingly right-wing, but, at that time I came to admire him even more than I feared him, although those emotions often ran neck and neck, and I'll be forever obliged to him for having brought me into my craft.

At that time the *Binghamton Press* ranked as one of the finest small city afternoon papers in the United States. This was due in part to the drive and talent of Tom Hutton and several good men he hired, but even before he arrived in the city room, almost from its inception shortly after the turn of the century, the *Press* was an exceptionally good newspaper because the man who founded it was determined that it would be great. This determination, it must be stated, came out of no great humanitarian impulse but out of a peculiar sequence of events.

23

Before the *Press* began publishing in 1904, the one afternoon newspaper in town was the *Herald.* Old-timers remember it as a paper that served the community well. Its editor was described in *Collier*'s magazine as a man who "has never yet seriously strained himself by undue endeavors to run away from a fight." In the days when the *Herald* was enjoying its cock-of-the-walk dominance, one of the dramatic business stories in town was that of the Kilmer Company and its remarkable patent medicine, a kickapoo joy-juice sort of potion concocted by one Jonas Kilmer. Anticipating by many years the language of today's health food trade, he combined what he called "the active medicinal properties of swamp root, field herbs and healing balsams," heavily laced the potion with alcohol, and peddled it around the country as a miraculously healing elixir called Swamp Root.

Swamp Root cost very little to make and sold very well, especially in the South. But Jonas's business was a modest one until his son, Willis Sharpe Kilmer, decided he had little to learn at Cornell University, quit after his second year, and prevailed on his father to let him apply some sales promotion to the product.

Young Kilmer became one of the pioneers in patent medicine advertising. He ballyhooed Swamp Root's magical powers to heal a broad range of afflictions. There was hardly a part of the human body to which the concoction would not bring balm, but the organ that most cried out for it was the kidney. Swamp Root, claimed its makers, would erase all ravages of the kidney and guarantee to one and all who imbibed it with regularity a lifetime of happy urination.

Perhaps the label should speak for itself:

DR. KILMER'S SWAMP ROOT, KIDNEY
LIVER AND BLADDER CURE

* * *

This great remedy cures all kidney, liver, bladder and uric acid troubles, and disorders due to weak kidneys such as catarrh of the bladder, gravel, rheumatism, lumbago, and Bright's disease which is the worst form of kidney disease.

24

Readers of some of Kilmer's ads were invited, nay implored, to send samples of their urine to his Binghamton manufactory, across from the Delaware, Lackawanna and Western (subsequently known as the Delay, Linger and Wait) Railroad station and receive by return mail a urinalysis free of charge. An astonishing number of these anxious correspondents discovered by return mail that they were suffering from ominous kidney ailments that could be stemmed or cured only by copious draughts of Swamp Root. Enough of them sought the promised relief to make Jonas very well-to-do and his son Willis Sharpe very rich, the richest man in town, in fact. The younger Kilmer was comfortable with his good fortune. Once when one of his wealthy thoroughbred cronies asked him skeptically what Swamp Root was *really* good for, he replied, "About one-and-a-half to two million a year."

The editor of the *Herald,* one Guy F. Beardsley, did not care much for the Kilmers or for their product. As their wealth multiplied, so did their arrogance, their disdain for their fellow citizens. One day Willis Sharpe, driving his tandem through a busy street, became incensed at a bicyclist who failed to give way when he shouted, so he horsewhipped the man. It transpired that the poor chap was stone deaf. The *Herald* gleefully printed the story of the assaulted man's lawsuit. Kilmer retaliated by withdrawing his extensive Swamp Root advertising from the paper.

After many months, the advertising resumed, without formal explanation. The reason quickly became apparent: Kilmer's wife was suing him for divorce and he hoped that the resumption of his ads would persuade the editors to close their eyes to evidence which was, in the words of a scribe of the day, of "a most sensational and unsavory nature." The *Herald* responded with a full account of the proceeding, including a list of fourteen corespondents.

If they had stopped there, Beardsley and the newspaper might have forfended disaster. Instead, they began to attack Swamp Root.

First the paper printed a mock testimonial from a man in California who had consumed ten bottles of Dr. Jiggem's Kidney Invigorator; he died of another ailment, but his kidneys **25** survived in such a vigorous state that the undertaker had to pound them to death with a club. This in itself was enough to fire up Kilmer's unruly temper. Then the editors caused to be bruited about town the story of one of the Kilmer company's famous urinalyses. It seems that an anonymous wag had dispatched a young lad to a nearby drayman's, there to procure a pint or so of urine from an aged Percheron. It was appropriately identified as the specimen of a male Caucasian of intermediate age and sent off to Dr. Kilmer's plant for analysis. Soon thereafter the dread diagnosis arrived: Citizen Doe was on the brink of the most painful, the most debilitating kidney ravage and unless he was prepared to meet his Maker forthwith he should consume Swamp Root with diligence.

The *Herald*'s staffers did not know it, but they had signed their newspaper's death warrant. To attack Kilmer's privacy and his honor was one thing; to attack his precious elixir was an act of war. "That damned sheet won't last long after I get after it," he was quoted as saying.

Kilmer cried all the way to the offices of his lawyers. There he commanded deeds to be drawn and contracts let for construction of a building that was to be of such size that for many years to come it would be the tallest, the most imposing in that part of New York State. Inquiries went to newspaper offices in New York, Chicago, and other large cities seeking the services of editors, reporters, critics, printers, stereotypers, pressmen, advertising salesmen, and others required to produce a daily newspaper. Soon construction began on the Binghamton Press Building, whose twelve stories towered over the city and all the area around. Not long after that, one day in 1904 Binghamton's second afternoon newspaper rolled off the presses. Almost from the beginning it cast the *Herald* into shadow; the older paper survived for several years, but in a state of steady decline, and then succumbed (an affliction of the kidneys, no doubt). That left the *Press* dominant in the afternoon, and its only competition the pallid morning daily called the *Binghamton Sun*. The *Sun* gasped along for years, a sort of waif. And long, long after Willis Sharpe Kilmer had savored (and pocketed much profit from) his revenge and had passed to his reward, it was absorbed into the prosperous *Binghamton Press,* a newspaper sired, as it were, by a small bottle of horse piss.

While I had no acquaintance with Willis Sharpe Kilmer, I could claim a close friendship with one of his horses. He raced a string of some of the finest thoroughbreds in America, including Sun Beau, Sun Briar, and the great Exterminator, a horse so unimposing in appearance he was affectionately nicknamed "Old Bones." Entered as a substitute for the more highly regarded Sun Briar, Exterminator won the Kentucky Derby in 1918 and a grand total of 50 of his 100 starts before retiring to the sweet pasture abutting Kneeland Avenue. Across the street from a house in which I lived during our brief glimpse of relative prosperity were luxuriant pastures and barns that made up Kilmer's summer stables. Not far beyond them was his own half-mile racetrack encircled by an always freshly painted white fence. In those pastures Exterminator spent many of his late years, alternately frolicking and loafing near where, violating Kilmer's No Trespassing signs, we Kneeland and Rotary Avenue kids played pick-up baseball by day and ringa-levio by night. A pony named Peanuts, fat and round as a barrel, was Exterminator's constant companion and playmate. The old champion would go nowhere without Peanuts. When we clambered over the fence to pet and feed Exterminator, we had to bring two of everything, apples, sugar cubes, carrots, because he would not eat unless his mascot ate with him.

The once mighty racing champion, the pastures smelling sweet and barns washed in sun, the grazing horses and the flashes of roan, chestnut, and black that streaked around the training track—all this brought a vicarious sense of luxury, something unattainable, forbidden but so close we could almost taste it, to that plain middle-class street with its almost identical two-family houses of stucco and wood, with their almost identical garages, almost identical Fords and Chevrolets parked in the driveways, and their identical Philcos sending the voices of Amos and Andy through every screen door on a hot summer's night.

We never saw the man who owned all this but heard that it was but a fragment of his wealth, that he owned in addition not **27** only the biggest house in town, but a far more splendid horse farm in Virginia, two country estates, and a huge yacht that could take him to any port in the world, and did.

Now that I was to work for his paper, perhaps I would meet the possessor of all this. But by then, Willis Sharpe Kilmer was not much enjoying his riches. He was terminally sick and living in seclusion in his turreted stone palace on Riverside Drive or at his plush cottage on a lake fifteen miles out of town.

In my time at the *Press* he never put in an appearance. When he died on July 12, 1940, at the age of seventy-one, a deluge of prose and photos engulfed the front and several inside pages of the *Press*. A lengthy but judicious replay of Kilmer's life, clinical reports of his long illness, messages of mourning from the high and mighty including President Roosevelt and New York Governor Herbert Lehman, photographs of Kilmer in jaunty fedora with his beloved racehorses and his seagoing yacht, reminded the citizenry of what it already knew; the rascal had lived a rich life on the proceeds of those hogsheads full of dark brown juice that had irrigated the kidneys and assaulted the liver of America. Tom Hutton pulled every stop on his Wurlitzer to fill almost half the editorial page with an effusion that began, "The Commodore put out to sea last night," and got more fulsome with every one of its eighteen fat paragraphs. Every available body on the news staff was dragooned into the three-day orgy of mourning-in-print. Through all the bustle one heard ocasional expressions of concern over what might happen to the newspaper. But nary a tear was shed.

That was almost three years after I became the youngest and most unprepared student in Tom R. Hutton's School of Applied Journalism, suddenly privileged to watch and learn from men (and a couple of women) who had wandered in from the outside world to impart their talent and wisdom to this gray little manufacturing city on the banks of the Susquehanna and Chenango.

Tom Hutton fashioned his own way of weeding out those who did not soon show the talent to be a newspaperman or woman. The copy boys and all young reporters with less than two years' experience were required every six months to assem-
28 ble in the city room of an evening and submit to an overpower-

ing examination prepared by Black Tom. He assigned about three months in advance a reading list composed by whim. The examination consisted of three hours in which we were to respond to Hutton's questions about the books on that list. Then we were dispersed around the quiet of Binghamton at night to seek out some sort of news or feature story, return, and before ninety minutes in all had passed, write it as if for a real newspaper deadline. I still recall with fright the moment I was handed that first reading list. Save for the meager forays into literature that a mediocre small-city school system required, I had vented my lust for reading on *Tom Swift, The Rover Boys,* the *Poppy Ott* stories, and tattered copies of *Captain Billy's Whiz-Bang* passed surreptitiously among the boys in the Kneeland Avenue neighborhood. The deepest dips I'd taken into "literature" were Richard Halliburton's dashing travel adventures and the even more stirring adventures of *Scaramouche* and the other loveable rascals sired by Raphael Sabatini.

Suddenly my very future lurked in the pages of these works I was supposed to read, absorb, and be prepared to be queried about only a few weeks hence: *Macbeth, Hamlet,* and *King Lear;* Emerson's essay on *Compensation;* Twain's *Is Shakespeare Dead?,* the six cantos of Spenser's *Faerie Queene* (it was then that I began to realize how tiresome were some of the prescribed virtues unless honored in the breach), Malory's *Morte d'Arthur,* Kipling's *Kim,* Conrad's *Lord Jim,* and a couple of contemporary books on politics or public affairs whose titles I have forgotten. It was a list to challenge even the brightest of the dozen others who were to take the test, all of them with four years of college behind them. To me it was more like the trump of doom. Passing grade was to be fifty, as determined by Tom Hutton's personal grading system, and anyone who failed would be invited to seek other employment as soon as a replacement could be found.

What tribulation those next few weeks piled on me. Preparing for final high school exams, scurrying to prove to Hutton and the newsroom's high command that I could hustle as effectively as the college graduates, staying up late to devour that daunting pile of works on Black Tom's list, I could see but one outcome. Humiliation, a noble career nipped even before its **29** budding, dismal retreat from the Valley of Opportunity.

But weep not. The worst did not come to pass.

Hutton knew what he was doing, though we at the time did not. His reading list was conceived to find soft spots even in the best-read of the college graduates. His merciless examination questions anticipated few if any passing grades. Provocation, stimulation were his aim. He did not care, for example, whether we could extract a moral from Kipling's *Kim,* but cared instead what lesson Kipling's prose offered to a newsman. "Verbs, son, verbs!" he later thundered. "Read Kipling and you learn to use active verbs. Avoid the passive. Use the active whenever you can." Twain he thought (as did Hemingway) to be the greatest of all American writers, and also the best pricker of the pretentious and the pompous. Twain's uproarious down-river argument between the captain and his crewman over whether Shakespeare or Bacon wrote the works of Shakespeare evidenced both these attributes in the work of Mr. Clemens, attributes to be cultivated if possible in an aspiring newsman.

Fortunately, Hutton attached more importance to the second part of our ordeal than to the classroom exercise. Having failed miserably to deal with Hutton's questions about the books I had so hastily and in most instances superficially read, I plunged out into a gentle spring night to seek a newspaper story that might meet his test of being readable and somewhat plausible.

The streets were almost empty. The *Strand* and *Star* movie theaters had just let out and downtown Binghamton was going to sleep. A train whistle keened in the darkness. The sound made me think of my Uncle John, oldest of my mother's brothers. He was a trainman on the D. L. & W. who usually wore clothes that gave off a smell of wheel oil and cinders that I found romantic; thinking of him made me think of the railroad stations a few blocks away. There were two of them, the Erie on one side of a wide gauntlet of tracks and the D. L. & W. on the other. I made my way past the D. L. & W. stationhouse toward a dark tower a few yards beyond. A solitary switchman sat high above, smoking and waiting for the 10:12 from Scranton to approach. I shouted to him through an open window, asking if 30 I could climb up. He welcomed the company, and when I told him I was the nephew of a fellow railwayman, John Brown, he said, "Why John and I are old friends." Then he began recalling their times together during their first days on the railroad. Lucky Bob!

For half an hour the switchman spun railroading yarns; some of them were probably even true. I wrote assiduously into my treasured new possession, a slim stenographer's notebook purchased for 15 cents from Hamlin's Drugstore. He told me for example of a man down El Paso or San Antonio way who drew on idling freightcars a large chalk-scrawled graffiti boldly proclaiming that Bozo Texarino had been there. The switchman said that hardly a day passed that he did not see Bozo Texarino's signature on a freightcar or two passing through Binghamton. He pointed out two boxcars, one brick-red, the other a dirty brindle, on a nearby siding and I climbed down to look. Bozo's signature, big and bold, looked something like this:

Bozo had been marking cars for years, the switchman assured me, and his signature could turn up anywhere in the country where two rails ran. For years thereafter I gazed at boxcars standing in freightyards in Long Island, Chicago, in Boston and Washington, as far away as Boise, Idaho, as close as Horseheads, New York, and I watched the flanks of trains slowly passing as I waited in my car at RR crossings all over the Eastern seaboard, to see whether Bozo Texarino was alive and announcing his exuberant presence to the outside world. A friend told me many years later that he had seen what he thought was Bozo Texarino's bold mark on cars in a Seattle freight yard. I never encountered Bozo's signature again.

Was the old switchman pulling my leg? I hope not, for I tailored the anecdotes he told me into my first newspaper story. I did allow, though deep down in the story and grudgingly, that **31** some of them may have been the imaginary travels of a stationary man. The piece was never published, of course, but it softened Tom Hutton's dismay at my seeming illiteracy. The switchman and Bozo Texarino: true friends in need. They had saved my job and gotten me promoted from copy boy to cub reporter.

Chapter 2

The White Crow and Other Oddities

Hutton himself broke the news. When he summoned me into his office, the dismal results of the previous night's examination sat in plain view on his desk. He twirled that black ribbon with glasses attached as if he were Douglas Fairbanks, Sr., playing Don Q., looked at me sternly and said, "Son, after looking at your exam paper I want to make sure of one thing: Can you read at all? If you don't read you'll never write." He paused and the hint of a smile came to his face. "But that was a pretty good story you pulled out of this goddamned church pew of a town at midnight in the middle of a week, so go tell the City Desk to put you on assignment."

Next day, my salary went up to $10 a week—a 25 percent raise!—and I went to work on the Lollipop Beat, a daily round of sniffing about for news at minor offices, like the U.S. Post Office, the army and navy recruiting stations, the Weather Bureau; or assaying the goings-on at such community institutions as the local posts of the American Legion (Bingo Every Friday Night), the Veterans of Foreign Wars, the Disabled American Veterans. There were the fraternal orders—the Ancient Arabic Order, Nobles of the Mystic Shrine, and the other strangely costumed and mysterious bodies that sidled in and out of the Masonic Lodge; also the Knights of Columbus, the Order of   **33** the Eastern Star, the Loyal Order of Moose, the Benevolent and Protective Order of Elks, Woodmen of the World, and, as if to keep these childish-seeming pursuits of grown men and women in perspective, I was assigned also to the Society for the Prevention of Cruelty to Animals and the real zoo in Ross Park.

Then there were the luncheon meetings of the service clubs— the Monarch Club on Monday, Lions Club on Tuesday, Exchange Club on Wednesday, and, most demanding of all, the Kiwanis *and* Rotary Clubs convening simultaneously in different meeting rooms on Thursday. The speeches were usually as thin as the fare—fruit cup, chicken a la king, cold peas, tapioca pudding at The Arlington, the hotel that passed, alas, as Binghamton's classiest—but almost any word brought in from outside and delivered by a man who effected to know what he was talking about, whether it be the flora of far-off Fiji or Dale Carnegie–style admonitions as delivered by one of Carnegie's many lecture-circuit imitators, was sweet grist for the notebook of the *Press*'s newest and most intrepid reporter.

Thanks to the movies and in great part to their own external demeanor, journalists had gained reputations as a cynical, uncaring lot with a snarl or a cigarette or both on the lips and hearts that could fit into the navel of a gnat. I found that to be far from true. Almost to a man, and woman, the crew in the city room of the *Press* took us young apprentices under their wings. Some were surly, even combative-seeming in doing it, others so solicitous it was sometimes embarrassing. Even the toughest, least approachable of all, old Pierce Weller, the city editor and next to Tom Hutton the man who could make or break reporters, went out of his way to help the newest novice on his staff. When he was awake, that is.

Mr. Weller (we never called him anything else even in his absence) was approaching retirement age. He wore some disobedient remnants of graying hair and a face that reminded one of a very tired C. Aubrey Smith of the movies. Since ours was an afternoon paper the bulk of the newswriting and editing was done by midday, with only late-breaking news developments to be dealt with in the afternoon hours. The city editor could take a leisurely lunch, and for Pierce Weller that involved

34

a sizeable serving of eighty- or ninety-proof nourishment. If one wanted to confer with the city editor after lunch, he or she had to do so quickly. The newsroom was inordinately quiet at that time; typewriters were silent because most reporters were either themselves out to lunch or combing their beats for possible late developments.

Weller would settle with a sigh into his desk chair, pick some galley proofs off a spindle, lean back, and begin ostensibly to read. Two galley proofs usually were par for him. Suddenly the near-silence would be interrupted by the sound of a single CLICK of porcelain. The city editor's upper plate had fallen onto the lower. Mr. Weller was asleep and should not be disturbed.

This ritual was tolerated because Pierce Weller was a peerless city editor who knew his community and the people working for him. He was alert in the hours when it counted—when assignments had to be made, news opportunities sniffed out, and then when the first copy began flowing across his desk for editing and dispatch to the composing room. It was tolerated also because at Weller's right, well groomed to succeed him when Weller retired in the next few months, was a talented and hard-working young assistant city editor named Erwin C. Cronk.

There were several editors who taught me much and earned my gratitude as I groped to learn in those exciting but sometimes desperate early days—Fred Stein, who was news editor and eventual successor to Tom Hutton; Jim Stevens, Garret Rogers, Eric Tyler (the not so surreptitious lover of Black Tom's secretary), Bob Dillon, and some of the best of the reporters, particularly Ed Barrett of the police beat and Dor (for Dorrance) Smith and young Tom Cawley, the paper's best feature writer—but Cronk was the one who showed me most how to take advantage of my good luck in walking into my own valley of opportunity on that balmy October day.

Cronk's first lesson came with my very first story, an artlessly effusive report of a performance by a traveling ballet troupe. Ballet was not exactly a familiar art in Binghamton; most of us called it "toe-dancing." Anyway, I wrote as the beginning of an overly long story approximately this: "A large crowd filling the   **35**

West Junior High School auditorium last night enthusiastically appreciated the performance of the Ballet Russe de Monte Carlo, the world's greatest ballet ensemble."

Erwin Cronk looked at my crudely typed story as if it were a Chenango River bullhead rotting in the sun. "How many people does the auditorium hold?" he asked, crossing out my "large crowd" and scratching in "more than 000 persons." Said Cronk, "Call up the school and find out the auditorium's capacity." He pointed to another phrase. How did I know that everybody in the crowd "appreciated" the performance? Did I interview everyone there? Half of them, maybe more, probably didn't even know what they were watching. They might have been applauding just to be polite, or to show off to their neighbors. Cronk crossed out "enthusiastically appreciated" and substituted "warmly applauded."

"Who says it's 'the world's greatest ballet ensemble'?" Cronk asked. Said I confidently, "The poster outside the auditorium, and the advertisement in the *Binghamton Press.*" To my surprise, Cronk was unimpressed. "And I'm a one-eyed Galapagos turtle," he growled. "Shall we print that?" He crossed out "world's greatest," wrote in "well-known," then crossed that out. "If it's well-known, you don't have to say so."

He excised my two references to "sprightly toe-dancing," slashed away a couple of juicy paragraphs describing costumes, and sent my shrunken baptismal offering to the printers.

His demeanor softened. "If you've paid attention," he said, "you've just learned some lessons: be precise whenever precision is possible; don't overwrite, especially when dealing with subjects you know nothing about; don't take a pitchman's word for anything—and never, never *assume.* You'll probably break those first rules sometimes, but don't ever break the last one."

All this solicitude did not come for free. We were expected to shrug off whatever humiliations Tom Hutton heaped on us, be on call at all times, as much as any doctor or nurse, and to work fifty-, sixty-, even seventy-hour weeks—hours today's Newspaper Guild or other unions would forbid. We worked within our little worlds as if each was the big one, and indeed our beats were a microcosm of the larger outside. A young bureau chief in one of the five outlying counties would cover just about anything that happened there, from a Ladies' Grange bake-off to school board meetings, court proceedings, auto accidents, politics, rapes, and homicides. "A fellow who can cover politics well in Broome or Delaware county can cover politics in Washington or London," Hutton liked to say, and he was right—though candor demands saying that politics in Washington or London is a tad more interesting than in Oneonta or Kirkwood, New York.

The pay was niggardly. "That Kilmer feeds his racehorses foin," said the newsroom's janitor one day, "but as they say back home in Donegal, when it comes to us hoomans he's so tight he'll give ya nought but the sleeves off his vest." The company bonus at Christmas time was $1 for each year served on the paper. We all trooped off to Pitch's Oyster House for free beers on Ray Walsh one late December afternoon. He was the paper's number one photographer, who'd joined the *Press* at its founding, so long ago that he'd lost one thumb to a flash-powder explosion. His bonus for Christmas of 1938 was $34, the highest Kilmer had ever paid.

What exciting work it was, though. There were days when it seemed like being paid just to have fun. We wouldn't have traded a minute of it for anything less than a telephone call from the editor of the New York *Herald Tribune,* the only paper in the world we admired more than our own. I have long believed that newspapering could be a source of satisfaction wherever practiced, whether in the small town or the most celebrated seat of punditry in Washington or covering a war in some distant land, but something made it especially beguiling at the *Press,* and that was the unpredictability of Tom Hutton. For all his dash and brilliance he was, to put it bluntly, a mite demented. This became increasingly evident.

In the late 1930s Hutton's politics could be described as liberal moving toward illiberal Republican, a little forward of the sentiments of the predominantly Waspish leading elements of Binghamton society. Well in advance he smelled war coming in Europe, and when it did come he made the *Press* into a passionate advocate of Bundles for Britain, the psychological precursor gambit to Lend-Lease and eventual American entry into the war against Nazi Germany. As the man to displace the hated **37**

FDR he turned early to Wendell Willkie, America's next savior. When the Republican party nominating convention gathered in Philadelphia in 1940 he took an inordinately large staff of reporters and had most of them running about the Hall and shouting it up for Willkie while two reporters ground out yards of copy for the edification of *Press* readers back home. Once Willkie got the nomination, Hutton cajoled his campaign managers into scheduling their man for not one but two visits to Binghamton and vicinity.

Two days before The Great Man, as his supporters called him (or "the barefoot boy of Wall Street," as Harold Ickes called him), was to make his second campaign visit to town, there appeared in the newsroom one of those odd characters who used to visit—and I suppose still do—the newsrooms of daily papers in the hope of impressing editors with the newsworthiness of some inane cause or invention.

The oddballs could usually be discerned by peculiarities of dress—unlaced tennis shoes in winter (they were not fashionable in those days), say, or an overcoat made of old army blankets—or by the ways in which they sat waiting for an interview, hunched over mysterious-looking parcels and glancing suspiciously out of the corners of their eyes. These characters normally were reserved for me, as junior of all the reporters. Only a few days before, it had taken me more than an hour to deal with a chap who'd discovered a secret to longer life: He had become convinced that the inhaling of air was detrimental to our health, while exhaling was good for us. The secret was to minimize inhaling and maximize exhaling. "Like this," the man exclaimed. He stood up and while thrusting out his immense chest, emitted in quick succession three hoarse, rattling roars, something like the sound of a whale spouting. The entire newsroom snapped to attention. The man took in two quick, small snorts of breath, exhaled again with the same explosive rattles. Then, exhausted, he sat down. "Try it yourself. Exhale only!" the man insisted. I managed two gasping exhalations, then desperately sucked in draughts of city room air. "You'll die an early death doing that," said the visitor. For some time he harangued me with his theory, then produced a few sheets of crumpled mimeographed paper. "It's all in here," he said confidently, "phone number and all if you need more information." I thanked him graciously and ushered him to the exit, then returned to a newsroom made uproarious by a batch of baboons loudly exhaling when they weren't guffawing.

I fortunately was not present on that fall day in 1940 when a farmer from nearby Castle Creek appeared. He was a tall, spare man in overalls, with the ammoniac smell of the cow barn about him. He had found on his farm a rare bird and thought the *Press* might care to tell its readers about it. Tom Cawley won the honor of dealing with the visitor, who reached toward a large object on the floor beside him, pulled aside a canvas covering to disclose a bird cage and in it a white creature about the size of a crow.

"There she is," the farmer said. "A white crow. Never seen one before."

The reporter hadn't either. He spoke to the city editor. "Fellow here's got a white crow. Ever seen one before?" The city editor hadn't. He asked the assistant news editor, a sometime bird-watcher, and was told, "Isn't any such bird." While editors and reporters began clustering about the cage, gazing at the bedraggled, dirty-white bird with a yellow beak and hate-filled red eyes, Tom Hutton strode in.

"What's that," he said, pointing to the cage.

"Fellow says it's a white crow."

"A white crow! Great God almighty!" Hutton shouted. "That's a great good luck symbol. Ask any Indian. Bring that fellow and that bird in here." He walked into his office, the farmer, Cawley, and the bird following.

"Here's what we're going to do," said Black Tom. "Wendell Willkie needs everything he can get going for him, and he's going to get this white crow. Now, we'll go about it this way . . ." The farmer, bewildered by all this, was gently ushered away and told to come back next day, dressed in more presentable clothes so that he could be photographed with his bird. Tom Cawley was put in charge of Red-Eye the white crow, instructed first to clean out the scavenger's cage and then to protect the creature from escape or depredation, come whatever, until Candidate Willkie arrived for his speech the following night.

Next morning, bad news. Willkie had lost his voice and was canceling all campaign speeches for several days. Speaking in Willkie's behalf would be the Republican candidate for senator, the Honorable Bruce Barton, the Barton of the famous advertising firm of Batten, Barton, Durstine and Osborne, who had become a New York congressman and an inspirational speaker of the Norman Vincent Peale variety.

Hutton was not fazed. "We'll give the bird to Barton in Willkie's name," he decreed. "Bring luck to both of them."

I was assigned to meet Cawley at seven o'clock that evening and help him handle the care of the crow and other backstage details at the Central High School auditorium. I found Cawley there when I arrived and could see that something was wrong, seriously wrong. "Look at this, for God's sake." The usually taciturn, rarely demonstrative Cawley was almost sobbing. I walked to the cage. At the bottom lay a wilted, motionless array of disarranged feathers. I poked with a pencil. No return motion. I looked at Cawley. He looked at me. Together our lips silently spelled the word. D-e-a-d. The damned bird was dead.

"I don't know what happened or when," Cawley moaned. "I had the damn thing home with me all night and he seemed fine. When I went home to get him an hour ago, there he was, the dirty bastard, dead as a . . . as a white crow, for crissake!"

Hutton had chopped off heads for less than this. I was worried, but Cawley was almost frantic. He was twenty-five, with a wife and child, and Hutton was certain to blame him and probably sack him for the demise of a rare good-luck symbol.

"We'll have to go on with it," Cawley decided. He opened the door of the cage and handed me the carcass. "Here. Keep it warm on the radiator and don't let anybody, not anybody, into this room."

"What if Black Tom . . .?"

"I'll take care of Black Tom," Cawley said. When the time came for presentation of the bird, Hutton was to be standing at the rostrum. Cawley was to enter from the far side of the stage and hand the crow directly to would-be Senator Barton. The idea was for Barton to fondle the bird for a moment and then, while clearing his throat for the start of the evening's oration, to hand it fondly back to Cawley who then, in deference to any in the audience who might be members of the Broome County Humane Society, would gently, lovingly return the crow to the safety of its cage.

For many anxious minutes I kept the carcass at comfortable toast warmth on the school radiator. Then Cawley burst in, said "Pray for us all," and dashed off with the bird. I did not see the presentation but I was advised that it had gone smoothly for the most part, save for a sudden look of discomfiture on Bruce Barton's face when he heard from Black Tom's lips that he, Barton, was about to become owner of a bird. This was followed by a twitch of relief when the creature, beautifully plumped up and postured, and staring through slits at the audience while Tom Cawley handed him over, collapsed like a damp washcloth in Barton's tentative grip. At that instant, it became clear to the politician that whatever other crazy thing happened to him tonight, that ugly beak was not going to bite him.

Cawley swiftly retrieved the bird, rushed back, collected his raincoat and me, and we raced in his car to return the carcass and cage to the farmer. The farmer's reward for all this was the appearance in next afternoon's *Press* of a photograph showing him holding his discovery, then alive, next to full-blown photograph of Cawley handing the creature, now dead, to Congressman Barton while Tom Hutton, no less proud and arrogant for his ignorance of what was actually transpiring, looked on approvingly a few feet away.

"You should have fed it better," Cawley said to the farmer as he handed over the cage and its contents. We made off before he could manage a reply. Cawley hastened to a pay phone to report to his wife. "June, honey, it worked." Then he went to Pitch's and got drunk. So did I. After all, after an ordeal like that, a fellow deserves a little company.

Hutton's penchant for the peculiar and the bizarre began to take a more disturbing turn. He had a brilliant writing style and he composed all the paper's editorials himself, usually dictating them to Helen Woodruff between ten and eleven o'clock each morning as he paced the narrow width of his glassed-in office, twirling his spectacles, halting now and then to sip from a glass of sauerkraut juice. With war waging in Europe, concerns about security and sabotage began to darken the editorial page. **41**

When units of the local National Guard were called up for regular service Hutton ordered dozens of workers carrying huge kerosene torches to the roofs and balconies of buildings all along Court Street so his photographers could better capture the parade toward the D. L. & W. railroad station. The torches blazed, sputtered, leaked dangerous puddles of kerosene onto roofs, and presented downtown Binghamton with a threat only slightly less dangerous than Mrs. O'Leary's cow had presented to Chicago years before. The fire department dispatched emergency crews to put out three small fires and boot Hutton's torchbearers off their perches, but not before the *Press* photographers had captured in fiery brilliance the greatest mobilization in the region's history. Departure of the Guard was a most emotional moment for the populace, an emotion shared by me when I wrote the lead story which began: "A huge, pulsating chunk of a community's heart rode South toward sacrifice and danger today with 1,200 men of the Triple Cities National Guard." One of the best of the paper's young reporters, a taciturn, unemotional Holy Cross man named Bob McManus, thought my display of passion-in-print was "shameless slop." I took his critique with a degree of seriousness because only a short time before Bob had married my sister Jeanette and was now family, but Tom Hutton thought my piece was just dandy, "just what our heroes deserve"—and frankly, so did I.

While his top editors imposed stringent standards of accuracy, dispassion, and fairness on the *Press* news staff, Hutton was not above bending the paper to his own passions. At one point, for example, he found menace in a series of harmless American history textbooks whose author, a professor named Rugg, had somehow been singled out by the archconservative National Association of Manufacturers as a dangerous subversive. Hutton used both his editorial page and the news pages to press—unsuccessfully—for removal of the Rugg textbooks from Binghamton schools, an exercise in McCarthyism years before Senator Joseph McCarthy came onto the scene. He stormed about "security laxness" at a nearby one-track railroad tunnel through which freight trains of the dying Delaware and Hudson Railroad rattled between Binghamton and Albany. He even dispatched a reporter-photographer team to intrude into the tunnel and then tipped off the railroad police that "saboteurs" were afoot. The two men escaped as the RR police dove into view and Hutton trumpeted the "news" on the front page: RR TUNNEL EASY TARGET FOR SABOTEURS.

Meanwhile, back at the "ranch," Tom Hutton was in trouble. He had piled up a parlous amount of personal debt; creditors were serving papers on him right and left. And then, one day in 1940, the irresistible force of his arrogance and profligacy collided with the immovable object of reality. That was shortly after July 12, when Willis Sharpe Kilmer died.

The body was still warm when Tom Hutton announced to Kilmer's widow and to the executors of his estate that he, Hutton, would now run the newspaper. (It was a sort of small-town dress rehearsal for the scene in the White House some forty years later after President Reagan was shot, when the secretary of state, Alexander Haig, announced that he was now in charge of America.) None of us at the paper learned then precisely what had transpired, and the principals are long since dead, but as best as can be reconstructed, Hutton proposed to take over sole direction of the *Press* and, if it was to be sold, to determine to whom it should be sold. Kilmer's widow, a dignified and most comely lady named Jane, was not cowed.

Nor was the executor of Kilmer's estate. He was the leading lawyer in Binghamton, one of the most highly regarded in all of New York State, a man who affected the loose galluses and slow-seeming reflexes of an up-country rube but in fact could, like one of Damon Runyon's characters, squirt cider out of his left ear if you bet him he couldn't. The Executor advised Mrs. Kilmer to get rid of Tom Radcliffe Hutton forthwith.

The editor was visiting the New York State Fair at Syracuse that day, preparing projects for a lavish new Farm Page which he had perversely decided to inflict on his news staff and the *Press*'s mostly urban readers. Fred Stein, who had labored impatiently but loyally as Hutton's Number Two, exuberantly took over the editorship. Dorrance Smith, the most mild-mannered reporter on the staff, was given the forbidding role of Messenger. He was instructed to seek out Tom Hutton amid the prize livestock and home-jarred preserves at the Syracuse Fairgrounds and hand him an envelope containing a terse notice of **43** dismissal and a generous (we were later told) settlement check. Looking as if he'd almost prefer being the guest of honor at an *auto da fé,* Dor Smith carried out the most difficult assignment of his career and returned, to our relief, unharmed.

We never saw Tom Hutton again. If he returned to his office, it was during that night. He sold his "ranch," his string of polo ponies and other possessions, presumably to settle debts, and took off. Word came some time later that he was serving as a colonel in charge of public relations for General Chennault's U.S. air forces in China. A war correspondent who encountered him there wrote to a friend: "He was the craziest PR man I ever met." Next came word that he had been assigned to a remote base in the Aleutians on Rat Island. "Just the place for the bastard," said one of the many on the *Press* who had cause to dislike Hutton. I wrote to him once c/o the Aleutians base, to tell him that I too was in the service, helping to put out an army newspaper. There was no reply.

Long after World War II a brief wire service dispatch revealed that one Tom Radcliffe Hutton had organized his own political action movement, spewing out far-right manifestos, among them a proposal for impeachment of the entire Supreme Court of the United States. He was living in a small town in Washington State and, as far as I can determine, died there, apparently a lonely, embittered man, in the 1960s. I was saddened to learn that.

After Kilmer's death, the best thing that could have happened to the newspaper and to the community it served so well was to remain independent. With the volatile, increasingly eccentric Hutton gone, the paper was better than ever. Fred Stein proved to be an excellent editor in chief, briskly in command, a demanding man and stingy with praise, as I came grudgingly to believe a good editor should be. There was a coldness about his command, but that was more than compensated for by the warmth, good humor, and judgment of Erwin Cronk in the important role of city editor.

Independence was not to last. The *Press* was a money machine as well as a fine newspaper and there were several offers to buy it. Kilmer's executors took the least adventurous course

and sold it to the steadily growing chain of newspapers begun in nearby Rochester, New York, by Frank Gannett.

Thus was one of the best, sprightliest afternoon papers in America sentenced to the realm of the second-rate. By then the Gannett organization had perfected an almost foolproof process for making money by way of mediocritization. The effect was to turn whatever newspaper it acquired from black-and-white to gray. Though it competed with other newspapers in some cities, the Gannett organization favored monopoly situations and in those instances, as A. J. Liebling once explained, publishers conclude that news is "increasingly nonessential to the newspaper. . . . It is a costly and uneconomic frill, like the free lunch that saloons used to furnish to induce customers to buy beer." Even with the anemic morning *Sun* as its competition, it took the chain a long time to reduce the *Press* to the corporation's standards for dullness and unimaginativeness. The reason was that Fred Stein and Erwin Cronk, who succeeded him as chief editor, could not put out a bad newspaper. But after their reigns ended, governance-by-common-denominator soon had converted the *Press* into a pallid shadow of its former self. Perhaps my judgment of the Gannettization process is overly harsh, but I do not think so. There were, it is true, reasons for employees to welcome the sale. They could look forward to a kind of stability that had been unattainable considering the unsettling effects of Hutton's eccentricity and Kilmer's illness, and they could look forward also to more generous benefits, modest stock options, and profit-sharing—a great improvement over the Swamp Root tycoon's $1-per-year Christmas bonus.

Anyway, before the sale came about I was gone from the scene. An opportunity to join "the world's greatest news organization" had beckoned me beyond Binghamton and out into the Valley.

Chapter 3

Wire Service Blues

Amerca was now in the war. Franklin Roosevelt's challenge to make us the Arsenal of Democracy by producing 50,000 warplanes and flotillas of warships a year was, incredibly, being surpassed by American industry. More than six million American men had enlisted or been drafted into the armed forces and more were signing up every day. I was not one of them.

Most of my male friends outside the *Press* had left for military service within a few months of Pearl Harbor. I had to stand close to the eye chart in order to decipher even the big E on it; twice I had appeared before my draft board and been rejected for poor eyesight (20-over-500, or thereabouts). Work was a good amelioration, and there was more than enough of it for an eager young reporter; the more I did of it, the more confident I became that I had answered the right calling. Confident, too, that I'd learned the basics of sound journalism so assiduously drilled into me by my superiors. And for all my tendency toward the sentimental and sometimes banal, I could put words on paper that scanned even if they did not sparkle. I had long since graduated from the Lollipop Beat to more important assignments—interviews or feature stories when celebrated politicians or other movers and shakers came to town, cases brought before the city and county courts (Oh, my, there were seedy goings-on in my hometown of a sort I'd not dreamed of!), eruptions within the Board of Education, quarrels in the Broome County Board of Supervisors. There was a striking murder trial during which, for the first time, I watched some of my prose transmitted to the outside world on the wires of the Associated and United Press.

It was heady stuff, enough to make me almost forget that I was doomed to a gray life unless I somehow got myself a college education. "Bobby," Tom Cawley kept telling me with his soft, assuring, arm-around-the-shoulder voice, "You're getting that right here." He had not gotten to college either. Satisfying as it was to the ego, this progress did not much assuage the loneliness I felt at the absence of so many friends nor the guilt I felt for not being in uniform with them.

The letter from the chief of the Associated Press New York State bureau in Albany came as a dose of tonic (Swamp Root, if you will). The AP had an opening for a number three man, the lowest on that particular totem pole, in its Buffalo, New York, bureau. It was a nice coincidence, since several months before my brother-in-law, Bob McManus, had himself joined the Associated Press and was stationed in Buffalo. I would have family as company. As was customary for the AP, which was a giant cooperative jointly owned by all its newspaper "members," the bureau chief had first obtained Fred Stein's permission to recruit me. Stein took pains to say that he didn't want to lose me but that a rise to the mighty AP was an offer that should not be refused. I seized the opportunity for a change of scene.

A bleak scene it was. On surveying my new town, I thought of W. C. Fields' comment on the approach of death: On the whole, I'd rather be in Philadelphia. Buffalo caught in the final blasts of a Great Lakes winter seemed cloaked in grime and gloom. With its adjacent factory towns this cold and apparently graceless lakeport city was fiercely engaged in the war production effort, in particular steel and those newfangled craft called helicopters. The influx of workers including (I learned with what proved to be unrequited rapture) many single women, put lodging at a premium. I stumbled onto a garret room in a once-proud Delaware Avenue mansion. With a bed, a table, an easy   **47** chair that looked like a giant popover that had been too long in the oven, and a single shadeless reading lamp it went for only $4 a week. A mere bagatelle. I was prosperous now; the AP was paying me $32 a week, $6.50 more than I had been earning at the *Press*. The room came for a bargain rent because it had to be shared—with bedbugs. I quickly fled to quarters cleaner but no more lavish for the more lavish price of $6.

Bob McManus was deputy chief of the Buffalo bureau—the number two man, that is. A little more than a year before, shortly after he had married my sister, Jeanette, he had been wooed away, by more pay and the approach of a baby, from his job as the politics reporter on the *Press*. By the time I arrived in Buffalo, Mac was a seasoned wire service hand, a penetrating reporter, and he patiently guided my induction into the AP routine. More importantly, I treasured the occasional evenings when I could enjoy their company and serve as Mac's food taster for Jeanette's novitiate efforts at cooking. Such evenings were infrequent, though, because our working hours usually did not coincide, and the two of them had become increasingly preoccupied with their newborn son, the first of their nine children. In any case, not even Jeanette's great improvement in the kitchen could ameliorate the fact that work for the mighty, globe-girdling Associated Press was—in Buffalo, New York, in 1942, at least— mighty boring.

The bureau chief was a decent but hard-driving, humorless AP veteran whose ambition appeared to be to get promoted out of Buffalo as soon as possible. He and McManus once in a while ventured out to cover news-making events. Except for rare excursions outside to look into a ship collision near the docks or to watch picketing steelworkers during a strike at the Lackawanna mills, my "reporting" consisted mostly of sitting in the cell-like offices we occupied at the *Buffalo Evening News* and *Courier-Express* buildings and rewriting for the teletype wires news being published by the two local papers. Occasionally the telephone would ring and one of the two dozen "stringer" correspondents who worked on small papers within the Buffalo bureau's area would pass on news he thought worthy of the AP wire. For those stories that did make the wire, **48** stringers received at month's end a few dollars, depending on the length of the items, an inducement to much bloated prose. Very early in my stint there came one such story that rudely acquainted me with the AP's graven image, the Great God Objectivity.

The call was from the stringer in Batavia. A local bank had just been robbed by two masked men who had fled with an estimated $15,000 to $20,000 in cash. I took down the brief details, wrote a brisk dispatch, and put it onto the wire. I took care to feature in the lead paragraph what I considered to be the interesting fact that this was the second bank robbery in Batavia in two weeks. The dispatch had not been on the wire for more than five minutes before the teletype bell clanged and a message from New York tapped out: "Kill Batavia bank dispatch." The telephone rang. An irate editor in New York shouted that it was risky and a violation of objectivity to have included that information about the earlier robbery. File a new dispatch omitting that harmful information, he ordered. I meekly obeyed, puzzled though I was as to why that pertinent piece of news could be so summarily forbidden. Because it skewed the story of the moment, the bureau chief told me later, whatever that meant. These many years later, my puzzlement persists.

New York's rude interference with that innocuous Batavia dispatch may have been the extreme manifestation of the Associated Press mind-set, but the mind-set was pervasively, oppressively there. True objectivity in the writing of news, as in the telling of any story, is of course unachievable. But the somber men who ran the Associated Press affected not to believe that. The organization was in thrall to the hundreds of publishers around the country who "owned" the cooperative. Each of these men or women was an individual whose sensibility—or whose banker or lawyer or merchant friend's sensibility, for they were all members of the same country club—might be offended should something so perverse as a reporter's opinion somehow creep into a dispatch. For example, one should avoid suggesting that the banks of Batavia, New York, might have become attractive to bank robbers. That would drive away customers and bring more bank robbers to town. As to what might be "opinion" and what not, it was better to err on the side of **49** omission, to be "objective" even more stringently than in the dictionary sense—"dealing with outward things and not with thoughts or feelings; exhibiting actual facts uncolored by exhibitor's feelings or opinions." The AP's mind-set made about as much sense to me as a hydraulic device without water or, more aptly, a human circulatory system without blood.

This gains in significance when a news organization plays the role of the Associated Press. For its more than 1,400 "member" newspapers at that time, the AP was the main if not sole source of their intelligence from beyond their city and town limits. The service employed a staff of at least 7,200, amplified by an auxiliary army of newsmen working for member newspapers and other allied news services. The volume of news going out on various AP wires had come to exceed 1,000,000 words a day, spewed out over 300,000 miles of domestic wires by nearly 3,500 teletype machines. Very few newspapers then had their own correspondents in Washington, and only a tiny handful, among them the *Chicago Tribune* and Chicago *Daily News,* the *New York Times* and New York *Herald Tribune,* sent correspondents overseas. The rest of America depended upon the bloodless daily rations off the wires of the AP, and the somewhat more adventurous though smaller United Press and International News Service.

In simpler days this may have been adequate, but not for the tangled times at which we'd arrived. For example, it was such arid news-handling that helped to nurture McCarthyism in the late 1940s and early 1950s. When the senator from Wisconsin stood up before an audience in Wheeling, West Virginia, shook a sheaf of papers in one hand, and declared, "I have here in my hand" the names of 57—or 81? or 205?—certified Communists working in the U.S. Department of State. Reporters at the time did not even agree as to the number McCarthy alleged, nor did he show anyone a list. Such were the startling "objective" facts that got reported and blared their way into headlines. It was not the business of the objective reporter or news editor to question that allegation in the news report. If a denial came from the State Department or the White House, as it belatedly and sometimes tremulously did, that could be printed later—but of

50

course not with the prominence given the original charge.

In time, reality caught up with Joseph McCarthy, and fortunately it also caught up with the news trade, first as the daily newspapers grew less timorous, more sophisticated in their practices, and eventually with the wire services. More care began to be taken to distinguish between "facts" and "allegations." This was an advance, not a regression to the earlier days of "yellow" journalism and unbridled use of newspapers for private purpose. It was no longer risky for a reporter to shape his reporting into some sort of focus. Increasingly, reports of complicated political and sociological developments were amplified by interpretive comments and context-forming additives. Some of the flexibility that had long been the rule in sports reporting came to illuminate general news reporting, to the great benefit of the public at large. If it has induced some error on the side of too much opinionation, so be it. After all, isn't life the biggest game of all?

Insistence on "objectivity," even if not truly attainable, was not as altogether wrongheaded as I seem to be implying. On the contrary, a striving for dispassionate reporting was and still can be an important part of the preparation for responsible journalism. To have drilled into one an extreme respect for "just the facts" early in the game is a useful training. Like the rote learning of the Catholic catechism that characterized the teaching at my Irish-American parish in Binghamton, the AP-style addiction to objectivity was inhibiting, frustrating, increasingly difficult to credit; but just like old Father Hannon with his warnings of an eternal afterlife of scorching brimstone and shrieking pain, it installed in the conscience a lifelong warning system, urgent little flashing signals that could always be counted on hereafter to suggest that the act about to be committed or decision to be made in the name of "interpretative reporting" may be good or it may be evil, may be venial or may be mortal. Give pause, poor sinner, before you inject those words of explanation or interpretation into a news story; make certain that you are providing real focus or enlightenment and not just pushing your own prejudices or simply showing off.

(In later years I have come to favor a different analogy. **51**

Before he took to dripping paint on canvas laid on the floor below him, Jackson Pollock learned all the rudiments of his art—how to draw, to draft, and to paint the human form, still life, or landscape. That was why he was able to venture further and fashion art out of a seeming anarchy. The same was true of the other painters who brought us Abstract Expressionism in the 1940s and 1950s. Their success spawned a generation of splashers, dabbers, and drippers who took to the extreme before learning even how to sketch a nursery school house with tilted chimney. The painters who had learned the rudiments today hang in museums and celebrated collections. The imitators are forgotten. Several years after my AP experience, I found validity in this analogy as a writer and editor at *Time* magazine. Writers who graduated to *Time* from traditional journalism for the most part brought with them more accuracy, more respect for fact, more professionalism [if ours can be called a profession] than those who came straight out of college or from some little poetry magazine in Greenwich Village.)

So I was learning in Buffalo even while being mostly bored. Work with the AP was not all made up of rewriting of others' dispatches or just the relaying of livestock prices and grain and hog belly futures, though there were days when that seemed to be the case. As humble number three man, I also had the honor of operating the "pony wire," so named I have always presumed because it corresponded in mid-twentieth-century technology to the way the mail was delivered in the Old West. Today's modern network of leased wires and high-speed transmission of news had been well established by 1942, but in upstate New York, as in some other parts of the country, small daily newspapers afflicted with limited resources and/or stingy owners received the major outside news of the day by means of prearranged telephone calls. The pony wire out of Buffalo was the major connection with the outside world for small afternoon newspapers in Salamanca, Batavia, Canandaigua, Geneva, and Wellsville, New York. Every day but Sunday an editor would sit at a typewriter in each of those towns and type out news dictated to him during two daily telephone hookups with Buffalo. It fell to the number three man to assemble two bun-

52

dles of news, one of ten minutes' worth to be spoken at 10:30 A.M., a second of fifteen minutes for the 1:15 P.M. call. At the appointed time he dictated that information simultaneously to the five clients.

Time was precious. The clients paid heavily by their standards, and they wanted every second, every word to count. Since there was a war on, a great deal of important news slipped easily into a short interval. Corregidor falls. The U.S. Marines take Guadalcanal. General Doolittle's bombers hit Tokyo. But assembling the rest of the selection was far from simple. Small though they were, the "pony circuit" clients were among the AP's most demanding. Salamanca was a two-front man, but Batavia was interested only in war news from the Pacific. The lady taking down the news in Wellsville became incensed at even the mention of the names Roosevelt or Pope Pius, and her sputters of rage when one of those unmentionable names profaned the air would blot out interludes of the conference call, robbing others of precious seconds. The fellow in Canandaigua had an inordinate interest in the livestock and grain futures, and hog bellies as well. The need imposed on me by a slow-witted substitute editor in Geneva to spell out frequently used words—subpoena, Tarawa, Pétain, petit larceny, Ickes—would drive the others, particularly the Salamanca man, up the wall.

So humble number three man chose and edited with care, even, let him now confess it, with guile, for it became his consuming compulsion to impale on the spindle of those twenty-five minutes every weekday the sense of the world as it was at that instant. To forestall interruptions from Wellsville, Franklin Roosevelt became simply the President or Commander in Chief; Pius XII was the Vicar of Christ (though that didn't work for long). The idiosyncracies of the other editors were catered to with the same sort of cowardly ingenuity.

Each interlude began with a hasty roll call. Salamanca? "Here." Canandaigua? "HERE." (Feodor Chaliapin, no less). Geneva? "Aye." Wellsville? "Heeeeeere." (a voice out of the opening scene of Macbeth). Batavia? "Check." And then, carefully enunciated, paced to the typing speed of the owners of the five disembodied voices, always with regard to the eccentricities 53 and predilections at the other ends of the line, sometimes in a voice heightened by drama but mostly with a let's-get-on-with-it intensity—THE NEWS.

This daily ritual quickly became the only beguiling aspect of my soon-to-be-ended career as an AP man. To sit by the teletypes and the telephone in the scruffy cubbyhole of an office in Buffalo and know that you are wired to almost every corner of the world induced a feeling of humility but also a sense of power: How little I knew about the people and places and events out there; and how little out there knew or cared about us! And yet each day I was empowered to compose my own little world-view-in-miniature and pass it on to a few thousand readers as their only approximation of the real thing.

The routine was interrupted one dank day in November 1942. The instant I saw the envelope in my mailbox, I recognized another notification from the local draft board, this one in my Buffalo neighborhood. I welcomed it. I yearned for relief from the loneliness of wartime Buffalo, to put behind me scenes of the few hot-breathed, amateurish, spurned efforts I'd made to rise from my frustrated state of near-virginity, and, most of all I wanted an end to the mostly sterile regimen of an AP automaton.

But was relief really at hand? I was resigned to experiencing again what had happened at my draft board before—the cold waiting room, smelling of socks and male armpits; the strip-down to undershorts, the brisk application of thermometer and throat stick, a prodding finger here ("Cough") and there ("Breathe with your mouth open"), the strut before the chest X-ray machine. And then again my fatal stand before the eye chart. At this third appearance for my physical, the examining doctor could not have appeared more bored; he might have been crating Bell helicopter parts. He didn't ask me to remove my eyeglasses; I didn't offer to. That was it: 1A, fit for service in the Army of the United States.

So the time came to say good-bye to Buffalo, and to my associates at the other ends of the "pony wire." For the greater part of a year we had entwined our lives without ever meeting. **54** These were now *my* people, and I could not leave without a tug of regret. But neither could I resist the temptation that now leered before me.

Late on an autumn day I delivered the last of my "pony" calls, quickly finishing the roll call and then reciting *two* announcements by President Franklin D. Roosevelt, one item about FDR's wife Eleanor, another about his son Elliot, and even a stray item about President Roosevelt's special envoy to the Vatican, Myron Taylor, and his audience with Pope Pius XII. You couldn't hear the news for the sputtering interruptions from Wellsville. Then as I neared the end of my final recital I heard the man in Salamanca laughing. Then the fellow in Batavia. Then Geneva and Canadaigua. I have always hoped that the lady in Wellsville at least cracked a smile, but I'll never know.

I said "Good-bye" and moved on, into the Army of the United States.

That was in early 1943. Almost immediately the tide of war turned. In January in the Mediterranean Tripoli fell to the British Eighth Army and in the Pacific a month later Guadalcanal fell to the U.S. Marines. Both were turning points, strategic and psychological. On February 6, General Dwight D. Eisenhower became Supreme Allied Commander, helping to bring focus to the Western allies' effort, and beginning in July the battle in Russia turned against the Germans. From North Africa Allied forces jumped to Sicily and into Italy. By the end of that year preparations were well underway for the invasion of Europe.

I surveyed all this from my command bunker, as a private in the Anti-Aircraft Replacement Training Center at Fort Eustis, Virginia, writing for the camp newspaper and approving of my superiors' overall conduct of the war. It was, I conceded, substantially how I'd be running things if I'd been in command. As luck would have it, the opportunity for command never came. One autumn day I was ordered to take a squad on a combat intelligence exercise along the banks of the James River. At a sudden turn of the head, my eyeglasses fell into a blanket of fallen leaves. I summoned my eight men to help me find them. As we scuffed about in the leaves, we were surrounded and captured by "enemy forces." It was quickly decided at Fort **55**

Eustis headquarters that the loss of a near-blind private would not seriously jeopardize the war effort. I was handed an honorary discharge and an undeserved Good Conduct Medal and sent back to civilian life.

Fortunately for the cause of freedom, not a hint of this diminution of Allied strength reached the Axis, nor did it slow plans for the strike into Europe. Neither was there so much as a tingle of excitement in the salons of Georgetown or the corridors of power when, on a crisp, clear January day in 1944, I arrived in the nation's capital, happily astonished to be reporting for work as a Washington correspondent.

Chapter 4

War and Uneasy Peace
in Washington (1)

Though history's greatest war was still raging, Washington in early 1944 seemed a light-hearted place. The scent of victory was in the air; the capital bustled with the pursuit of it, and was beginning to think about the world *after* the war. It was smaller, warmer, cozier than today's capital, with a dogwood-scented southern sleepiness that gave ground grudgingly to a sense of urgency when all the invaders poured in. With their brisk confidence and "can-do" arrogance a civilian army of Manhattan lawyers, Ivy League academics, and Midwestern industrialists had surged into town, and they were joined by thousands of uniformed men on noncombat duty or on leave, swaggering about in goatlike pursuit among the city's bounty of single women. For all that, the place retained its southern good manners (toward whites) and small-town character.

The sheets were always warm in the District's too-few hotels. Incoming government workers felt fortunate if they could crowd three or four to a room in small apartments. A really good place to eat was a rarity. So was a native Washingtonian. Almost everybody came from somewhere else; meetings of the Iowa, Maine, or Nebraska Society or any of numerous other organizations that brought together people from back home in nostalgic, boozy reunion, were commonplace.

In one big respect it was just like the Washington of today, a company town. But beneath all the serious preoccupation with war-making, governing, and politicking, there persisted a quality that has long since been leached out of Washington: The town did not take itself more seriously than it was entitled to. In those days, the nation's capital still enjoyed a sense of humor and its inhabitants knew that the real America stretched far beyond the boundaries of the District of Columbia.

Nobody enjoyed working and living there more than the men and women in the news trade. Washington was run, it seemed, just for us; well, yes, for members of the Congress, high government officials, the civil service corps, and an ominously fecund new breed of lobbyists as well. But the town seemed to be, as perhaps it does still today, one vast pressroom, as enticing to a journalist as was that cave of hidden treasure to young Monte Cristo. Such certainly was the case for this gangly lad who checked in from the provinces with little more to serve him than an ill-fitting suit, a hunt-and-peck technique at the typewriter, and a varnish of audacity that camouflaged a world-class inferiority complex.

The wartime manpower shortage had saved me from a return to the Associated Press and further glum apprenticeship in New York State. The United Press rashly held out an offer of an immediate assignment and a salary nearly twice what the AP was offering for my return to its service—and the job was in Washington, not Buffalo or Albany, New York. I was flattered by the salary figure until I learned later that the $72.50 a week offered by the UP was not a voluntary evaluation of my worth but represented the Newspaper Guild minimum salary for one with my seven years' (counting military time) experience.

The AP's New York State bureau chief was dismayed that I would even contemplate such a change. Didn't I realize that I'd be lowering myself in class by joining those slobs at UP? Despite a series of such warnings from AP superiors I accepted the UP's offer. This made me automatically a member of the Burned Bridges Club, an informal fraternity of apostates who had defied the fiat that an employee leaving the mighty AP could never return.

58   I went with my eyes open. Like the AP and the other major wire services (International News Service, Reuters, and Agence France Presse) the UP was a news butcher to the world. Its reporters mined the great chaotic fact-mess for the momentous, the mundane, and the trivial—all without intense discrimination. Whether it was porkbelly futures, Tokyo stock returns, or a declaration of war, the teletype machines spewed it out around the clock, one great river of stew in which the big stories bobbed like meatballs in the gravy of minutiae. Their staffs boasted a few prose stylists, but style was not much required and in fact made most wire service editors and their newspaper clients nervous. Alertness and speed of delivery were more valued, and when it came to a choice between thoroughness or brevity, brevity won, often at the expense of pertinence. My favorite example is a UP dispatch filed one day in 1947 from Palestine, repeated here in its entirety: "The visit of the United Nations Palestine Commission was marred today when the delegate of the Netherlands fell into the tomb of Nicodemus." Did the poor chap ever get out?

From its founding in 1907 the UP was the Avis of news agencies. Its staffers tried harder, for longer hours and fewer dollars, knowing that AP men looked down on them but too busy to worry about that. You can readily tell a UP man from an AP man, I was advised, because AP men travel in packs to blanket a story. And where the AP had its Burned Bridges Club, the name for the UP's always-expanding roster of alumni was the Downhold Club, named in recognition of the stream of teletyped orders to all hands to "downhold expenses," downhold being a one-word way of avoiding the so-much-per-word cable costs of saying it in two words.

By coincidence, the man who first interviewed me for a UP job was also the man in New York headquarters who as overseer of expenditures gave "downhold" its currency. His name was L. B. Mickel, and "save a nickel for Mickel" was the Unipressers' sardonic watchword. An illicit accounting rarely got by him, though he did allow the UP's highly valued ace Henry McLemore to exact $5 for "repair of typewriter" in almost every expense account he filed. And with a genuflection to creativity, Mickel also approved an item from one correspondent who covered the founding of the United Nations in San Fran- **59** cisco and, unable to account for all he had spent, listed $15 under the heading, "A man ain't made of wood." ($15 was more than sufficient to the task in those days.)

I knew a lot of UP lore, enough at least to be spared surprise when I walked into Washington headquarters to report for work. The bureau was crammed into dingy quarters on the seventh floor of the National Press Building, noisy with chattering teletype machines and ringing telephones. There wasn't an uncluttered desktop in sight, nor were there enough desks or typewriters to go around. The smells were familiar, and so was the sensation that struck me as I entered the premises—the same I'd experienced seven years before on walking into the city room of the *Press:* This is the right place at the right time, a place where I belong.

"Blessed is he who has found his work," Carlyle wrote; "let him ask no other blessedness." I asked none, but I was about to be doubly blessed. It happened on my second day of work in Washington.

I was dispatched to a cavernous hive called the OWI (for Office of War Information) pressroom, which was the place that issued much of the bread-and-butter news from government agencies. Each day a battalion or more of information officers poured out a torrent of news releases from more than a score of wartime agencies, such as the War Production Board, the War Manpower Commission, the Merchant Marine, and many others whose names are beyond recall. I was surprised to see only one dusty typewriter for the four-man UP deputation. My new superior briskly explained that for a wire service that serves newspapers around the world there is always urgency ("A deadline every minute"); there usually was not time for sitting down at a typewriter and writing out dispatches.

Instead, we all had telephones linked directly to our home offices. I was instructed that when handed a snippet of news—a listing of the latest Nazi submarine depradations in the North Atlantic, a sweeping new price regulation for pine lumber, an exemption for one-inch togglebolts or domestic hard salami—I was to pick up the phone and say, "Give me dictation, please," and then dictate my news story with all possible speed. Shortly thereafter I picked up the phone for the first time. A strong yet

60

soft-timbred woman's voice came from the other end, "Ready when you are." Stage fright. Buck fever. Lockjaw. Whatever it was gripped me. This was not like reading prepared news scripts over the AP ponywire.

I tried to collect my thoughts into coherent sentences and to unknot my tongue. I managed to mumble a few words, mixed syntax, tried to start again. "Look, just talk it out as if you're talking to your typewriter. It's easier than you think. Just tell me the story," said the wonderful voice. It had the sound of a fine cello, warm and slightly vibrato, comforting and yet authoritative enough to command me into coherence.

I disposed of that first story, something so inconsequential that I can't recall its subject matter, and before that day was over communed half a dozen more times with that voice. Then I rushed to the National Press building in a fever to meet the voice's owner.

Oh Lord! A roiling strong as ocean surf still moves me as I remember the first look of her. Everything that went with it was as wondrous as the voice itself: the dark eyes with a hint of skepticism at the corners, hair of melting onyx, raised cheekbones, full lips slightly pursed to go with the look in the eyes, a pert and trimly suited shape supported by the most comely legs and with all that, a demeanor that suggested confidence without arrogance. I saw her. I met her. I was conquered. Forget it, Carlyle, you wordy prig! I *wanted* this other blessedness, the approval and the presence of this woman.

There was trouble, though. Margaret Raymond, or Maggie as almost everyone called her, had a line of suitors stretching all the way from Washington to Chicago and New York, with way stations at Princeton, Williams, and Dartmouth, and some at U.S. navy and marine outposts as well. I quickly surmised that my best strategy was to take advantage of her suitors' extended supply lines. I mounted a war of attrition, taking care to avoid the error that General William Westmoreland was to commit many years later in Vietnam; that is, I did not underestimate the enemy's numbers or determination. One by one they fell before my remorseless assault. I dared not give Maggie time to change her mind. We were married before the year was out.

Marriage to Maggie Raymond was the best kind of love af- **61** fair, a passionate partnership that was to last more than forty years. It was the start as well of my higher education. Maggie was a product of Vassar College, the same kind of Vassar, demanding and elitist, that nurtured the likes of Edna St. Vincent Millay, Mary McCarthy, Elizabeth Bishop, not the Vassar that wrong-headedly went co-ed—and downhill—many years after the war. She already had high intelligence and high character when she arrived there; she came away from the classrooms and companionships of Vassar with not just more knowledge but the seeds of wisdom as well.

What few attributes of character still survived from those my parents had tried to instill in me, Maggie heightened and added to by the example of her own high standards of ethics and intellect and by her freely expressed contempt for the cheap or spurious. That vast vacancy in my consciousness that I knew to be ignorance she diplomatically treated as mere unsatisfied curiosity, though surely a vacuum that needed filling whatever its cause. We faced a complication right off. The UP, like many other news organizations in those pre-enlightenment days, forbade husband-and-wife teams. So Maggie, who wasn't sure she wanted to be a newswoman anyway, gave up her apprenticeship as a reporter. We were already thinking about babies.

What I'd been told about the United Press proved to be true. It was a demanding employer, and a parsimonious one. Odd as it may seem, that made it a good workplace for an ambitious young person. For every one of us Unipressers there were usually three or four opposing Associated Press reporters, and that meant a UP reporter had to run faster and work harder for longer hours and less pay than most of his counterparts, thus the opportunity to learn more and to learn it faster. And the low salary provided what an economist calls maximum inducement to seek higher rewards.

Work at the OWI pressroom was mostly routine and unexciting. There were virtually no face-to-face encounters with major figures. Once in a while Elmer Davis, the much admired radio newsman who became director of the Office of War Information, would bring his amiable self and gravelly voice into the pressroom to chat with some of us fellow journalists. The influential czar of wartime price controls or some other agency chief occasionally was available for an interview. We didn't see much of the powerful chief of the War Production Board, Donald Nelson, but he crashed into the papers by courting and marrying a recently crowned Miss America. He did this without benefit of a press release; we in the press room learned about it from the gossip columnists.

Then there was Paul V. McNutt, a former governor of Indiana, whom Democratic politics and a reputation for making no waves (except in his dramatically white hair) had endowed with directorship of the War Manpower Commission. The commission had only nondescript powers and there didn't seem much for its director to do. This was provident because Governor McNutt brought little to the office except for his healthy good looks, an infectiously toothy grin, and a hunger for publicity. During his first weeks in his job he had called frequent news conferences but as attendance at them dwindled for lack of substance they had become only occasional. I was to learn why shortly after I joined the UP staff. Mr. McNutt had convened the meeting but he brought with him not one whit of news. At each question about a manpower matter, a labor dispute, an argument over the hiring of women in aircraft factories, Mr. McNutt invariably said, "I can talk about that only off-the-record." After five or six such responses, a reporter piped up from the back of the small room, "Commissioner McNutt, may we at least say on the record that we saw you?" It is my dim recollection that this was the terminal press conference by War Manpower Commissioner McNutt.

Though work at the OWI pressroom was far from glamorous, I was too excited simply by being at work in the national capital of the most powerful country in the world to realize that. Anyway, I was gone from there before I got as bored as most of the veteran newsmen were. I was assigned to be the UP's back-up reporter at both the White House and the Department of State. Only a second fiddler, but what a place to fiddle in. State was located just across the alley from the White House West Wing, in what is now called the Executive Office Building. I would shuttle back and forth depending on where the action was, whether I was needed to help Merriman Smith at the White House or R. H. Shackford at State handle the news load.   **63**

Even though it was wartime, there was nothing like the oppressive security preoccupation that now imprisons peacetime Washington in checkpoints, barriers, metal detectors, and uniformed guards. We rarely were obliged to show special credentials or ID cards. When Secretary of State Cordell Hull gave his daily, almost invariably newsless, press audiences, a handful of us reporters would belly up to his desk or gather around him in the hallway outside his huge gleaming mahogany office at precisely twelve noon. We'd ask two or three polite questions. The Secretary would respond in his soft Tennessee accent, "Well, gentlemen, you can say that we are studying all the aspects of the situation." We would thank him and then scatter to wander freely around that fine old wedding cake of a building in search of real news.

Secretary of War Henry Stimson held less frequent briefings for the press. They were usually better attended because there was always the chance that he would let loose some important battle news. Usually, though, the stern old New York Wasp had no more to offer than did his Tennessee counterpart over at State, and meetings with him were no less somber—save for one day when a chap named Croswell Bowen of the International News Service arrived breathless in the middle of Mr. Stimson's briefing. Bowen was an energetic, amiable man, and very intelligent, too, but he sometimes acted before he pondered and his hyper-eagerness often tried the patience of his editors at INS headquarters. Such was the case on this particular morning, and Bowen's chief decided to get him out of the office. "Bowen," he commanded, "hurry over to Secretary Stimson's press conference. He's going to announce the name of the Unknown Soldier." "Okay, boss," said Bowen, and rushed to the War Department.

The conference was already underway when Bowen clambered into the chamber and shouted, "I'm Bowen of the INS, Mr. Secretary. Have you announced the name of the Unknown Soldier yet?" According to one who was there, even the stern Mr. Stimson smiled. (Bowen did not stay long in Washington. If memory serves, this case of misapplied zeal was memorialized in a book by H. Allen Smith or some other chronicler of the

64 antics of journalists; I can't remember where I first read about

it. When I met him many years later in New York Croswell Bowen was feeling much more at home in the company of the many oddballs who worked on Ralph Ingersoll's newspaper, *PM*. "They have no taste for the bizarre in Washington," he said with a tolerant smile when I mentioned the Stimson incident.)

Some of the informality of those days extended into the White House itself, where FDR announced that he had transformed himself from Mr. New Deal into Dr. Win the War. Physical access to the premises was relatively easy, at least in contrast to today's precautions. When he was in town Mr. Roosevelt made himself available for two news conferences every week. As in Secretary Hull's office we newsmen—far greater in number, of course—would crowd into the Oval Room before the president's desk with its array of gimcracks, several of them in the shape of Democratic donkeys, and a sprinkling of other objects, including one or two that appeared to be Republican elephants in states of severe decrepitude. At some of these meetings the president would joke with or tease the senior correspondents who stood closest to his desk, wobble his cigarette holder, and smile greetings to us all. On one of those good days he seemed always to enjoy the show, always in full control of the proceedings. We, the press, were a giant pipe organ and he was Johann Sebastian Bach.

At the very next press conference, the president might appear gray and tired, slow of speech, dispensing with the familiar badinage, impatient to finish with the half-hour ordeal, crabbily chiding reporters for the perfidy and greed of their publishers. On these occasions we would dutifully slip into our reports references to the president's disturbing appearance. Then he would confound us next week with his comparative jauntiness, a healthier flush to his complexion, the confident jut of his cigarette holder, and we in turn would confound the public—if any of the public was paying attention—with our references to a seemingly refreshened leader. These suggestions of retained vigor were important to FDR because in those early days of 1944 he was contemplating the unthinkable: He was going to run for a fourth term.

For all the seeming informality, when it came to privacy and **65** protection from prying reporters Mr. Roosevelt was one of the most shielded of presidents, more so even than has been the case with his successors. The news conferences were his only exposure to direct inquiry. While they were a great advance over the practice of his predecessors who, if they entertained inquiries from the press at all, dealt only with written questions handed to them in advance, the FDR sessions were easily handled by such a polished manipulator, a president so limber of tongue that he could, for example, convince each of three or four presumably sophisticated veteran politicians that he was exclusively contemplating him as his vice-presidential running mate in the 1944 elections. FDR cavalierly turned aside questions he preferred not to answer; and when he did answer, reporters were prohibited from quoting him directly, they could only paraphrase his comments.

If he was displeased with something that had appeared in the papers, as he frequently was, since most of the publishers in America deplored him, he would use the next of his much listened-to radio "fireside chats" to drive home his side of the story. Photographers were forbidden to snap the president in his wheelchair, or in any posture that showed that he had been crippled by polio and was unable to make much movement without assistance. If a photographer tried, his film would be confiscated by the Secret Service and he might be barred from the White House for a while.

In contrast to today's huge White House entourages, FDR's staff was small and loyal. This was a major form of protection. A contemporary White House correspondent holds in his Rolodex file the names of probably fifty, even a hundred White House and National Security Council staffers from whom he can exact extensive, presumably confidential or even top-secret information about important policies or events; sometimes this information is even accurate. In the White House of 1944 perhaps half a dozen people—Harry Hopkins, "the gray eminence"; Steve Early, the press secretary; Grace Tully, the private secretary; Pa Watson, William Hassett, and in some instances his wife Eleanor—shared the president's confidences and any one of them (except perhaps Eleanor on occasion) would have endured hours on the rack and the insertion of

bamboo splinters under the fingernails before leaking even yesterday's weather forecast to a news reporter if The Boss didn't
want it leaked.

A reporter in search of more than the routine could pry little
out of that tightly loyal staff, and only then with the approval of
the imposing, fiercely loyal Steve Early, a former AP man
(which made him a fellow Burned Bridges Clubman) who had
served FDR from as far back as 1920. So for most newsmen,
the only access to information about what the president might
be contemplating was at the press secretary's daily briefings.
Obviously, the top priority requirement for a fledgling correspondent was to establish rapport with Mr. Early. This I failed
dismally to do.

Word had just come out that one of the president's sons,
Elliot, was to be married again. This time, in a ceremony to be
performed in a glassed-in booth overhanging the Grand Can-
yon, the bride-to-be was Faye Emerson, an exceedingly good-
looking movie star. At the morning briefing one of the reporters
asked Steve Early, "Is the president going to the wedding?"
"No," said Mr. Early. He was obviously not comfortable with
this glitzy bit of family business. Another asked, "Is Mrs.
Roosevelt going?" "No," said Mr. Early, a bit more testily.

Before I could bite my tongue I asked, "Mr. Early, who *usually* goes to Elliot's weddings?" Steve Early fixed the impertinent new boy with a gaze that could crack marble. My career as
a reporter of the news-behind-the-news at Franklin Roosevelt's
White House was over before it had begun.

It was the cool professional Steve Early who took charge in
the White House on the afternoon of April 12, 1945. The president had gone to Warm Springs, Georgia, for a rest and as
usual the chief White House reporters for the UP, AP, and INS
had traveled with the presidential party. There was a news "lid"
at the White House, meaning that nothing would be released in
our absence, and not much going on either at the State Department across the way where we were lolling at our pressroom
desks when suddenly telephones began jingling. "Hurry to the
White House," the UP's news editor shouted. The same urgent
message came to several others in the pressroom. We ran across
the alley into the West Wing.

Young secretaries and clerks stood in knots of twos and three in the lobby, its center dominated by a huge and ugly round table of mahogany, made many years before by a group of Filipino prisoners as a gift to Franklin Roosevelt. The women huddled together, embracing and softly sobbing on each other's shoulders. The door to Steve Early's office was open and we could see him at his desk, his big shoulders sunk in dejection, tears in his eyes. Just a few minutes before, he had simultaneously telephoned the headquarters of the three wire services. "I have a flash for you," he said, using the wire service term for an alarm-ringing piece of news. Franklin Roosevelt was dead.

WHAT? For all the warnings we had witnessed—the frequently diffident campaigning against Thomas E. Dewey for a fourth term, the increasingly spiritless news conferences, the fragile shadow of a man who had returned from the Yalta conference to deliver a lackluster report to Congress (an FDR speech lackluster?)—we who were up close were little more prepared for this than was the rest of the nation. Nor was the vice-president. "I feel just as if a bale of hay's fallen on me," said Harry S Truman when he learned that he was now the President of the United States.

It was presumptuous of me, I suppose, but at that time I thought I was undergoing an experience similar to Harry Truman's—the threat of being overwhelmed. World War II would end at any minute; the approach of peace was already posing great complexities and challenges for journalism. I was only twenty-four years old and not quite able to believe where that happy accident eight years before, the accident of walking into the *Binghamton Press* city room, had taken me. While incredulous, I was proud as well, and even took shameless pleasure in the thought that people back in the hometown might be impressed, even envious.

I was blissfully married. I enjoyed the heady company of a circle of newly found friends, all of them bright and amiable. Most of them were either fellow journalists or Maggie's Vassar friends, a diverse group of the most intelligent and engaging women I'd ever met. We were all young and trim as saplings.

68 Our politics were unanimously New Deal with some knee-jerk genuflections to the left of that (for example, most of us were outraged when FDR dumped Henry Wallace as vice-president, though there was one in the group who insisted Wallace was "a certified loophead"). We drank and smoked a lot and sat up late at night talking, arguing, sometimes about politics or the news trade, but mostly about writers and writing. I heard a lot about Faulkner, Fitzgerald, Hemingway, and Conrad, about Dostoyevsky and Flaubert; occasionally some show-off would try to intrude someone like Pater or Rimbaud into the dialogue, and another liked to read aloud erotic passages from Henry Miller. I could toss in a remark or two about Conrad or Twain, thanks to Tom Hutton. These were exhilarating evenings that made Binghamton seem mercifully far, far away. And when mornings came I went to a prime job in a trade I loved.

I had already been privileged to observe the great and mighty, to watch close hand—and to help tell the world about—the last days and the passing of the great FDR, and now in the months to come the spectacle of the war grinding inexorably to its end and, after six years of slaughter and carnage, the prospect of helping to describe a new era of history-in-the-making from a seat on the fifty-yard line.

So why was I so depressed?

There were disturbing reasons for that. For one, I sensed that I was not intellectually prepared to comprehend the complex economic, political, and social currents that would shape the postwar world. That was becoming evident almost at the beginning of my White House and State Department assignment. For another, while I had no doubt that journalism was the career for me I was beginning to doubt that I would ever make it as an effective, digging reporter, the kind of newsman who nurtures sources and has that special talent for persuading people to take him into their confidence, who sniffs out significant information and then is welcomed back again and again to wrest more information from official closets.

Dealing with the news in wartime rarely required this kind of reporting. There were good guys and bad guys, enemies and allies, advances and retreats, victories and defeats. All was in simple blacks and whites. Government officials provided almost all the news and we who passed it on trusted them, even to the **69** point of voluntarily censoring any material the government wanted censored. All we had to do was mark our scorecards speedily and correctly and tell the readers where the game stood. Of course a person needed a goodly amount of common sense to do the job well, but he or she could get along without much need for the kind of digging and assessing that are the marks of a good reporter. Under those conditions I could man the White House pressroom or patrol the corridors of the State Department for a major world news organization almost as handily as the next fellow. It was easy. It was glamorous. It was fun. And I got paid for it to boot.

It wasn't going to be easy anymore. We had moved into one of those times the cliché-mongers call a turning point in history. The war had caused more than death and devastation. It was as if the whole world had been tossed into God's Cuisinart and was suddenly tumbling out in new shapes and colors and human permutations.

Washington already seethed underneath with conflicts, competitions, and confusions over the making of postwar policies. People high in the government were arguing over the postwar treatment of Germany and dark clouds were already hanging over the West's wartime alliance with Communist Russia. Economists and other social scientists differed over the ways to convert from wartime to peacetime. An entirely new international monetary system had to be invented.

Even though they were—or were about to be—victors, France, Great Britain, and the other European allies were almost as badly off as defeated Germany and Italy, and the Western European governments would confront (as would American policymakers) the fear of losing power to the control of their Communist parties if they could not quickly repair their devastated economies. A new international organization that was supposed to preserve the peace was being painfully blueprinted by the Americans, Soviets, British, and French in meetings at Dumbarton Oaks, but the disclosure that they had reserved a veto power for the five so-called Great Powers was already breeding official (though not public) cynicism about the new United Nations.

70   These were deep and turbulent currents, and the challenge for

journalism after war's end would be to troll them and fish out the pertinent. Up to then I had been comfortable in the company of my fellow journalists, but now I saw them, with all their advantages, as threatening competitors. Most of them had learned, or appeared to have, their history and political science lessons in college, read the right books, knew how to use the resources of libraries, had learned how Washington worked. Some, like the AP's brilliant and handsome Flora Lewis, a competing State Department correspondent, even spoke and read several languages. They seemed always to know what questions to ask and which persons might answer them.

I watched these talented competitors spin out their discoveries of news with growing apprehension. James B. (Scotty) Reston of the *New York Times* had penetrated deep secrecy and reported the major decisions of the Dumbarton Oaks negotiations for the new United Nations Charter so cogently that he might have been sitting at the negotiating table himself. John Hightower of the AP, our talented chief competitor at the State Department, had not only ruined one of my weekends but humiliated me as well by reporting efforts by high-level officials to throttle a plan by Secretary of the Treasury Henry Morgenthau and some of his cohorts to reduce defeated Germany in perpetuity to a strictly agricultural economy. It took me two days to find an underling who knew enough to confirm that Hightower's report of the so-called Morgenthau Plan and the strenuous opposition to it within the government was essentially true. That AP story, planted by the plan's highly placed opponents, was enough to send the Morgenthau Plan down the drain. Though I didn't know it at the time, I had gotten my first lesson in the byzantine Washington art of the premeditated newsleak; it was to serve me well at a later time.

I began working longer hours, then staying up until early mornings reading books on diplomacy and history and heavy articles in heavy magazines like *Foreign Affairs*. Perceiving my young age was a disadvantage I tried, uncomfortably and with limited success, to cultivate as sources younger officials at the State Department and some of the embassies; being junior in their jobs, they usually weren't much more privy than I to the information a reporter would be seeking. I remembered how I   71 had chuckled during the most recent presidential campaign when the irascible Harold Ickes ridiculed Thomas E. Dewey's "beagle-like sniffing about for votes"; now I reflected gloomily that the description could be applied to my own scurrying about State Department corridors in search of news.

I was benefitting from the fact that I was only the back-up man at State and the White House and not as responsible as my chiefs in both places, men who could compete with the best. I did manage to scratch out some stories that were useful if secondary and I even scored one "scoop," the fact that President Truman was replacing Edward Stettinius, the amiable but ineffective secretary of state, with an old Washington hand (former congressman, senator, Supreme Court justice, and war mobilization czar) and Truman buddy, James F. Byrnes—whom I apparently offended by describing him in my news story as "bantam-like."

Though I was far more often the scooped than the scooper, my few achievements were somehow enough to keep me on a favorable footing with my superiors in the Washington bureau. Still, the negatives in my mind continued to outweigh the positives. I was certain I'd soon be found out to be the rookie I was, brought up too soon to the big leagues and pitching with a weak arm. Tom Hutton's confident assurance back in my bush-league days that "a fellow who can cover politics well in Broome or Delaware County can cover politics in Washington and London." I had glumly decided was wrong.

I could disguise my concerns in front of my bosses or friends, but I couldn't have hidden them from Maggie if I had wanted to. Late one afternoon we sat in a favorite meeting place, the bar of the old Willard Hotel across from the National Press Building. Halfway through our bourbon old-fashioneds she said, "Give me a hug and tell me all about it." I gave special obedience to the first command, then lathered my self-doubt all over the tabletop. Binghamton Central High School and the *Press* had not prepared me for this; I just didn't know enough to do the job.

Maggie was a very private woman. She kept her own concerns or pains to herself, yet attracted the confidences of others. If you sought her advice you might have to pay a price for it:

Her candor could be direct as a hammer blow. But after it hit, you usually found yourself saying, "Thank you. I needed that." To those who didn't know her, her trait of saying what she thought was discomfiting at first, and there were some who never quite recovered from it. But it was so uncommon an attribute that men and women alike quickly came to respect, even admire her for it.

She was in true form that afternoon at the Willard bar. Any time I was bothered, Maggie said, then she was bothered, too. But if I was asking for her sympathy, Sorry.

"I don't think you deserve sympathy. What you need is a sharp kick in the ass," she said. "That's the short lecture, do you want the long one?" I could only nod.

What is so important about college? Maggie asked. Vassar had been great, yes, but she'd spent four years there majoring in economics only to discover she now had almost no interest in economics. What if Hemingway had gone around whining about not going to college—or actually *had* gone to college? He'd never have written *The Sun Also Rises.* If William Dean Howells had gone to college, he'd probably never have become editor of two great magazines, *The Atlantic* and *Harper's.*

"I could go on," Maggie said.

"Think for a moment. You've already got four years on those guys who took the time to go to college. I should think that knowing that you don't know is one of the best gifts a newspaperman can have. There aren't enough who admit that to themselves. That's why there are so many satisfied mediocre ones. You've got that awareness, so why let it defeat you? And as you sift out *what* you don't know and what you *need* to know, you'll figure out how to find it—isn't that what you've been doing all along? And then you're going to be as good as anybody in the pressroom." She said all this softly but with a firmness that said, Case Closed.

I smiled, but I had to turn slightly away so she couldn't see my tears. "Maggie, I love you," I said.

Chapter 5

From the Potomac to the Charles

That bracing lecture from Maggie took the whine out of my voice and sent me back to work with improved morale. What the hell, the new President of the United States hadn't gone to college either.

Harry Truman stepped into the presidency with one tremendous advantage: most people, we in the pressroom certainly included, expected little from him. In his early days on the job he could go nowhere but up in public esteem. On the surface, at least, he didn't let this condescension bother him. He was certainly a plain and humble man, but the Truman we saw projected self-confidence to the point of cockiness. Always deferential toward the great man he had succeeded, he nevertheless quickly showed his discomfort with the Olympian aura that had come to characterize FDR's White House and most of the Roosevelt cabinet officers. It was inevitable that he drew on his old cronies on Capitol Hill for advice and on the instincts he'd honed as a part of the old Kansas City Pendergast machine. The dry martini was out; bourbon with branch water was in. A very few reporters who had entered into Truman's confidence during his days in the Senate enjoyed temporary access to him, but soon he was as protectively roped-off from the press as **74** FDR had been.

He'd been less than a month in office when on May 8, 1945, it fell to Harry Truman to announce the event to whose achievement FDR had dedicated his last few years. The new president wore a grave look, but he couldn't disguise his exuberance after he called us into the Oval Office to confirm in his clipped Missouri twang what we already knew but hungered to hear officially, that the war against Nazi Germany was over. Now it was time to finish off the Japs. (Truman didn't say "Japs," but you knew that's the word he was thinking. In certain respects he was his mother's son; when she came to visit him and Bess in the White House she indignantly refused to sleep in the Lincoln bedroom.)

At about that time, a notice appeared on the UP bureau's bulletin board inviting applicants from news organizations to apply for a year of study at Harvard University. These Nieman Fellowships, as they were called, offered to pay the equivalent of a Fellow's salary during a year's study at Harvard College and its several graduate schools. The old nagging feeling was subdued but not gone. Here, I thought, might be a cure for it—a chance to go to college after all.

The Nieman Fellowships had begun in 1937 after Agnes, widow of the Milwaukee newspaper publisher Lucius W. Nieman, had contributed one million dollars for Harvard to spend in any way it chose to "improve the standards of journalism." Each year about ten newsmen of five or more years of experience had been brought to Cambridge with stipends that were comfortable (relative, that is, to the gruel-like wages paid in our craft) and warm welcomes from the faculty to partake of Harvard's rich academic feast. To make it even more desirable, Harvard allowed the wives of Nieman Fellows free tuition and run of the place.

It seemed too good to be true. Sure enough, when I looked into the program I discovered that it probably was. Of the sixty-five or so Fellows chosen in the program's first seven years, all were college graduates except for one, and the exception was an already legendary Chicago reporter named Ed Lahey. What is more, the United Press frowned on leaves of absence, and without promise of one an applicant would not be eligible for a fellowship. If that weren't discouragement enough, I learned   75 that another UP man, a Pacific war correspondent, had already applied for one that year. He would almost certainly be chosen.

With the odds so unfavorable, the Nieman notion should have floated out of my mind. But that notice on the bulletin board kept staring back at me. When I told Maggie about it she agreed that I was an unlikely candidate, but if it would make me feel better, why not apply for a fellowship anyway? That is what I did.

The job routine was becoming familiar. The title "White House correspondent" wears a sheen of glamour, but between the occasional dramatic moments the work, then as now, can be downright boring. In fact, if you look beneath the prestige, it may be one of the worst jobs in journalism, print or television. The ladies and gentlemen of the press are captives of the president and his image-caretakers. The job is more challenging to patience and physique than to the mind, offering little or no opportunity for exploration or initiative. That was especially so for a young reporter playing second fiddle to the UP's Merriman Smith.

By then Smitty's seniority among White House correspondents gave him the privilege of ending news conferences with his "Thank you, Mr. President." He was the quintessential man for the White House wire service assignment—smart but not a deep thinker, fast-moving, aggressive, hard-driving, and hard-drinking, quick to grasp and convey the essence of a sudden newsbreak, ruthless if need be against competitors. If he'd been born a few years earlier he would have been one of the prototypes for that comedy of newspapering's earlier days, *The Front Page.**

*At Warm Springs when FDR died, Smitty stayed up half the night badgering the local telephone company to install a special phone line for him next to the railroad station, which was a mile or so down a long roadway from the Warm Springs complex. Next day the cortege made its solemn way from the president's house while hundreds of bystanders wept as the bier was placed aboard and the train moved slowly north, a scene that was Lincolnesque in its mournful majesty. Smitty, no doubt as much moved by the event as anyone, conveyed that mood in a carefully dictated play-by-play account. His AP and INS rivals had to travel all the way back to telephones at the main house before they could file their stories. At a time when even seconds counted, Smith was many minutes ahead of the opposition. He won a journalism prize for that. And it was Smith who, nearly nineteen years later, on November 22, 1963, was riding with three other reporters in a Secret

Smitty also possessed a very strong strain of the territorial imperative, so when he wasn't traveling with the president there wasn't much room around the White House for a second man (and of course, when the president was away there rarely was much to report). I liked Merriman Smith and admired his work, but I didn't like working under him.

Some days there was little to do except lounge in the capacious West Wing lobby, reading the papers, exchanging gossip or wisecracks with other reporters, waiting for the predigested rations spooned out in the press secretary's briefings or the occasional arrival or departure of a presidential visitor who had nothing but banalities to offer about the nature of his visit with the president. Little more satisfying than those daily meetings with Cordell Hull.

Fortunately, I was needed more and more across the alley. Well before the war's end the news of diplomacy and international politics had moved onto the front pages. The man I worked under at the Department of State was R. H. Shackford, at thirty-eight a UP veteran and the agency's respected chief diplomatic correspondent. He wasn't partial to his first name, Roland, or middle one, Herbert, so everyone called him Shack. He was a small, precise man with steel-rimmed spectacles and a tidy mustache that gave him the look of an academician. He had a mind that was both analytical and quick, enabling him to move speedily while being cautious, a quality much treasured in our trade. Shack escaped from a small town in Maine to Antioch, the somewhat eccentric college in Ohio, where he took advantage of some adventurous teaching and found a good wife in the bargain. In Depression days he felt lucky that after graduation he got pittance-paying work peddling cooking utensils in the Macy's New York basement, and luckier still to move from there into an only slightly better-paying job as a fledgling reporter for the United Press.

The news-pot was boiling and Shackford knew there was

Service car in President Kennedy's Dallas motorcade when the fatal shots rang out. Again he beat his competitors, this time by grabbing the one radiophone in the automobile and shouting to the Dallas UP bureau the dreadful message that President Kennedy had been wounded, perhaps fatally, by gunfire.

more than enough for him to deal with. So he welcomed me as a junior partner. He took pains to inculcate in me his methods ("I double check everything and try to triple check the big things") and even acquainted me with many of his important news sources, an act that in the news trade rates just short of offering a man the favors of your wife. In this way I got to meet such career diplomats as Charles (Chip) Bohlen and Llewellyn (Tommy) Thompson, who were rising to considerable influence within the government as two of the State Department's three outstanding experts on the Soviet Union. Outside the department, Bohlen and Thompson gained recognition and occasional publicity as the usually anonymous "official sources" who briefed the press on the twists and turns of negotiations with Moscow. I didn't get to know the third and most reflective of the Sovietologists, George Kennan, until much later. He was the broody, behind-the scenes member of that triumvirate that was to play a major role in the shaping of our government's judgments of and attitudes toward the Soviet Union and its Communist leaders.

Much of the news we passed along, too much perhaps, was glum. The wartime East-West alliance was crumbling. The Russians had made a mockery of the Yalta agreement calling for an elected government in Poland. At our end, President Truman abruptly cut off Lend-Lease aid to exhausted allies including the Soviet Union, shocking the other allies and feeding the paranoia of Soviet leaders. The war with Japan was still to be won, but to accomplish that a massive invasion with immense loss of lives on both sides seemed unavoidable. Even if one searched hard to find them there were few glints of pleasant news to lighten the gloom.

But for me one day in mid-July 1945, there came some very happy news. A telegram waiting at the UP bureau said approximately this:

YOU HAVE BEEN AWARDED A NIEMAN FELLOWSHIP IN JOURNALISM
FOR ONE YEAR BEGINNING WITH THE FALL SEMESTER. STIPEND,
$3,200. KINDLY ADVISE PROMPTLY WHETHER YOU ACCEPT.

My mind was already wandering north toward Cambridge, Massachusetts, toward a new adventure, when some three weeks later, on August 6, President Truman had another announcement to make, this one in absentia. He was on the high seas, returning from his Big Three Potsdam conference. At the White House we were handed a presidential statement. Reading as we ran to our telephones we learned:

> Sixteen hours ago an American airplane dropped one bomb on Hiroshima, an important Japanese army base. That bomb had more power than 20,000 tons of TNT.

This obviously was a momentous development, but I think it is correct to say that none of us in the pressroom had more than a dim glimmering of the immense implications of the news we were then transmitting to the world.

"It is an atomic bomb," the president's announcement said, "the harnessing of the basic power of the universe, the force from which the sun draws its power, the greatest achievement of organized science in history."

How boastful and naive those words seem in the light of forty-five years' hindsight. If it was not exactly the Second Coming, the president seemed to be saying, it surely was the coming of a great boon to mankind. In our euphoria it didn't occur to us that the opposite of what the president said could as easily be true—that perhaps "the power of the universe" had harnessed us. For better or worse, what was to be called the nuclear age had begun. Though the bomb was dramatic proof of the accuracy of his equation $E = mc^2$, Albert Einstein wasn't exactly elated. "Everything in the world has changed . . . except the way people act," he said.

Two days later, just back from Potsdam, Mr. Truman summoned us into the Oval Room for the shortest presidential press conference on record. He sat there wearing a grin as wide as the Missouri River. The official transcript:

> THE PRESIDENT: I have only a simple announcement to make. I can't hold a regular press conference today but this announcement is so important I thought I would call you in.

79

Russia has declared war on Japan. That is all.
(Much applause and laughter as the reporters raced out.) End
of transcript.

Thus did the Soviet Union, without firing a shot at the Japanese, acquire as victor's spoils the Sakhalin Islands and the Kamchatka peninsula. Next day, the second atomic bomb exploded, over Nagasaki. The day after that Japan called it quits. Every city in the country erupted with raucous joy, and Washington was not outdone by any. The White House gleamed with all its lights on and crowds surrounded it with an aimless, reckless sort of revelry that seemed somehow to combine joy at victory and sorrow at what the past five years had wrought. After hours of efforts to convey the great story on the UP wires, a bunch of us joined in the not-quite-drunken celebration through most of the night.

Next morning Maggie and I prepared for the move to Cambridge. "What a helluva send-off to college," I joked.

"Not bad," said Maggie, as we packed books into cartons. "But I guess this means you won't be writing *The Sun Also Rises.*"

Chapter 6

"I Caught This Morning's Minion . . ."

The sight of Harvard from the Boston side of the Charles River on a sunny day in September of 1945 is an instant frozen in time, much like a painting by Thomas Eakins. A lone sculler skims the shimmering water into the shadow of a gracefully arched red brick bridge. Gold gleams on the weathervanes and cupolas of the half-dozen neo-Georgian buildings in which students live. In the background the artist has raised, almost too picturesquely, a bone-white church spire. It seems to suggest not only that God is not forgotten at Harvard but that He should not be so impudent as to look unkindly on America's first college.

The scene spoke serenity, tranquillity, quiet contemplation.

Across the river in Harvard Yard, bustling reality pushed tranquillity aside. Harvard simmered with activity. The war's end had brought back to American campuses thousands of undergraduates to resume their interrupted studies. With them came a stream of students who might never have afforded college educations were it not for the GI Bill of Rights funds provided by the U.S. Government—or for the blessing of a Nieman Fellowship. I had expected to be self-conscious and uncomfortable, an aged twenty-four-year-old surrounded in freshmen classrooms by teen-agers barely rid of pimples and whispering **81** behind their hands about the old slow-wit who had taken so long to get out of high school.

I need not have worried. This was "no-nonsense" time in academia. The classrooms, lecture halls, and reading rooms held scores of men as old as I or older who had come home from the wars and were impatient to make up for lost time, to get from college whatever it was they thought would equip them for making their ways in "the real world." If any seemed out of place they were the callow, fresh-faced eighteen- and nineteen-year-olds.

Our Nieman class set some precedents. Of us eleven Fellows, two were women, the first ever awarded Niemans, and another was the first to be chosen from radio news. The rest of us were from print journalism. We all held diplomas—from ten different colleges and Binghamton Central High School. The two New Yorkers, Leon Svirsky of *Time* magazine and Ben Yablonky of Ralph Ingersoll's eccentric morning paper perversely called *PM,* were both passionate advocates of a Jewish state in Palestine while James Batal, a fellow of Lebanese descent from Fitchburg, Massachusetts, was as passionately opposed to the idea. The older couple from Louisville, the Sunday editor of the *Courier-Journal,* Cary Robertson and his wife Priscilla, played chamber music at home on Sunday afternoons and were noticeably disappointed that the rest of us were too lacking in culture to pick up a fiddle bow and join in.

The politics of most of us were too intense and leftish for the comfort of the radio man from Minneapolis, Richard Stockwell. But our politics merely bemused the fellow from Pocatello, Idaho, my UP compatriot Frank Hewlett; his war experiences had convinced him life was too precious to be wasted on political prattle. He'd not only experienced much of the war in the Pacific but for most of that time did not know whether his wife, Virginia, was living or dead until, barely recognizing her, he embraced the emaciated woman who ran toward him when the Americans liberated the Japanese-run prisoners compound in the Philippines where she'd subsisted since the fall of Bataan. Arthur Hepner was a New Yorker who'd already attended Harvard and now came back as a labor reporter (and part-time music critic) of the *St. Louis Post-Dispatch;* he could introduce the rest of us to every cranny and idiosyncrasy of the Boston region just as surely as his Irish setter knew almost every garbage can in town. Frank Kelly, a black Irishman like me, but usually a jollier one, was nurtured in Kansas City and came to Harvard by way of the AP's New York headquarters; at stagnant moments he could get events moving again by merrily reciting passages from the works of Sean O'Casey.

There were so many differences among us—in age, temperament, geography, eccentricities, political stances, and degrees of sophistication—that we might have cruised through that academic year each in his own boat on his own solitary course. Instead, we quickly blended into almost frictionless homogeneity, each eager to share in the experiences of the others. This comradeship came about in part because of the personalities of three people. One was Louis Lyons, curator of the Nieman Foundation. A laconic wry-witted Yankee, he had escaped his family's chicken farm by way of the Massachusetts Agricultural College (now the University of Massachusetts), become a star reporter for the *Boston Globe,* and in 1938 joined the first group of Nieman Fellows. At the end of that first Nieman year the program's first curator, Archibald MacLeish, decided that the program would be better run by a journalist like Louis Lyons than by a poet like himself. Somewhat rumpled in appearance, deliberate and mild-seeming when he spoke, Louis Lyons in a few years of his stewardship over the Nieman program had built a nationwide reputation as both conscience and disturber of the news trade, a shrewd judge of its practitioners and a sometime scourge of newspaper publishers. Louis viewed each Nieman class as his brood (I use that word contritely, because once he'd left the family's improvident chicken farm he never wanted to be reminded of or see a chicken again, live, broiled, fricasseed, fried, or chow-meined). He took a personal interest in the progress and welfare of each of us. For example, he was disturbed when he learned that my weekly stipend as a Nieman Fellow would amount to only $72.50 a week (my UP salary). This didn't go far in the inflationary postwar Cambridge economy. For rent alone Maggie and I had to pay $100 a month, utilities extra, for our furnished cheese-box flat in a charmless part of town. Louis got in touch with the UP's bureau manager **83** in Washington, a most estimable man named Julius Frandsen, who obligingly conjectured that if I were still in Washington at that busy time I'd be working several hours of overtime each week. Louis added enough to raise the stipend to almost $100.

The others who did so much to ensure the compatability of our group were the two woman Fellows. Charlotte Fitz-Henry had taken leave of absence from a flowering career in the AP's Chicago bureau, Mary Ellen Leary from her job as a top-flight political and state capitol reporter for the San Francisco *Examiner*. Harvard then was more of a male chauvinist institution than now, though during the war it had abandoned the practice of ghettoizing female undergraduates of its associated college, Radcliffe, in separate classrooms. As Niemans, the two ladies were welcome everywhere (as were the wives of us male Nieman Fellows) and little affected by the elements of discrimination that remained. Fitz-Henry and Leary displayed not the slightest self-consciousness about being "foreigners" in a substantially men's world; they had seen it all before on the outside. Good-looking, vivacious, and more intelligent than most of us other Fellows, they used their femininity only to good purpose, combining gentleness with veiled matriarchal authority at our gatherings, nipping most petty bickering at its inception and focusing all our eyes on the sparrow that was our opportunity at Harvard. Harvard president James Conant had betrayed some concerns about admitting the other sex into the all-male Nieman fraternity, but these must have been swept away the minute the two ladies walked up smiling to shake his hand at our welcoming reception in the Faculty Club. The wise old chemist who was guiding Harvard into the postwar nuclear age knew he'd made (or at least approved) another wise decision—and so did we.

In applying for the Fellowship, we were required to outline a credible study program. To prepare for my imagined future as, first, a trench-coated foreign correspondent, then evolution into a syndicated columnist who would become famous as the common man's Walter Lippmann, I had confidently vowed to learn the Russian language and also acquire a knowledge of high-level economics, diplomatic history, and international relations, plus some grounding in American history. "Journalism's responsibility in the world security program now being molded is certainly as vital as that of any profession or pursuit," I had portentously written in my fellowship application. "Now, if ever, is the time for intelligent, honest reporting and careful interpretive writing about the political, economic, and social relations between nations. Much of the hope for peace depends on it."

My high-minded intentions began flaking soon after arrival when I realized what this program portended; the intensive Russian course alone would require several classroom hours a week and at least as much dogged homework at night and on weekends to attain facility in a language in which just about every bloody verb was irregular. And when I surveyed the catalog of courses being offered, thirty-nine closely packed pages of them,* I realized that I had sentenced myself to a depressingly somber set of choices. Here I was, a kid with an overpowering sweet tooth invited into one of the grandest pastry shops in the world, and I was inexplicably overlooking all the goodies—the Sacher tortes, the whipped cream napoleons, the chocolate éclairs, the coconut macaroons—of academia, and choosing only the low-calorie brown rice muffins, the kind of stuff a mother insists is "good for you."

I'd come home at night with my green canvas bookbag near to bursting with impenetrable abstracts and ponderous tomes by ponderous professors while Maggie bounded in with happy excitement over classes she'd attended that day—a scintillating lecture on modern poetry, a thrilling excursion into Renaissance art, the most provocative history professor she'd ever heard.

I persisted for a few more weeks in my forbidding brown-rice diet until one morning when I took my seat for the course in Economic Analysis and Public Policy taught by Alvin Hansen, one of the greater gurus of Keynesian deficit financing. It was an advanced course, and a demanding one; the only thing that

---

*As a measure of how college curricula have expanded, not entirely for the good, the 1988–89 Harvard course catalog contained 751 pages of course listings, eight pages alone offering women's studies and several courses in African or Afro-American subjects.

gave me the comfort of familiarity was the green eyeshade worn by Professor Hansen; it was just like the one worn by Danny Ladas of the Ladas Brothers poolroom back in Binghamton. The professor plunged gleefully into his subject, scrawling figures on a blackboard and explaining in rapid speech what the figures purported to mean. When he wrote "Deficit, $2 billion," one of the graduate students interrupted: "Professor Hansen, that figure should be *$20* billion." Hansen glanced at the blackboard, shrugged, and said, "Doesn't make any difference." Reaganomics forty years ahead of its time.

That was enough for me. Obviously, I would be well advised to leave economic theory to others more qualified and seek information from them when and if I needed it. I discreetly fled that lecture hall and rushed to join Maggie in nearby Sever Hall for a course she'd been raving about, Theodore Spencer on modern English and American poetry. As I entered, a tall, elegant man was reciting in an equally elegant and warm voice,

> I caught this morning's minion,
>   kingdom of daylight's dauphin,
>   dapple-dawn-drawn Falcon, in
>   his riding . . .

These were not mere words. This was not a lecture, it was an experience. When he got to the next to final stanza of the poem, Spencer's voice rose and his gaze seemed to pierce the ceiling to the sky where the hawk was turning,

> Brute beauty and valour and act, oh, air,
>   pride, plume, here
>   Buckle! . . .

The voice boomed "Buckle!" then stopped (I swear all the eyes in the room turned upward to see that golden bird buckling, then swooping high in the sky) and Spencer resumed,

> AND the fire that breaks from
>   thee then, a billion
>   Times told lovelier, more dangerous,
>   O my chevalier! . . .

My God, how beautiful! I said to myself—an appropriate exclamation, as I was to discover. The poem was Gerard Man-ley Hopkins's *Windhover,* and it was dedicated "To Christ our Lord." In the many years since, I have read that powerful sonnet more times than I can count. That first hearing had a profound effect, for it both focused and elevated my answer to the question, What have I been missing all these years?

When I timorously told Louis Lyons that I wanted to alter the study program I'd so solemnly promised the Nieman selectors I would follow, he smiled and said in effect, Join the club. It happened every Nieman year to at least half the Fellows. Once they comprehended the enticing variety of Harvard's offerings they had second thoughts. One, a Kentucky newsman named A. B. Guthrie, had scrapped his entire planned program in order to study creative writing with one English professor, Theodore Morrison, and work on his first novel. *The Big Sky* was a monumental success.

I stuck with the Russian studies for several more weeks in order to become comfortable with the cyrillic alphabet and to absorb some bare rudiments of the language. I transferred to simpler introductory studies in economics if only to learn the vocabulary, e.g., the difference between fiscal and monetary policy, but all the heavy stuff about the workings of crass materialism—Alvin Hansen's course, John Williams on money and banking, Wassily Leontief on statistics—was for others to pursue. My new curriculum covered far more courses than I could expect to absorb, but Nieman Fellows were not required to take examinations and could spread themselves as thinly as they pleased. So, in the conviction that I'd be all the richer if even only a few tiny morsels of lots of things stuck to my ribs, I spent the rest of the academic year in an orgy of tasting and feasting.

I went back twice a week to Ted Spencer's lecture hall to move on from Hopkins to the delights and depths of contemporary poetry, from Robert Bridges through Housman and Kipling, Robinson and Frost, Amy Lowell, Pound, Eliot and Yeats to Auden; on other days he also penetrated just as tellingly the genius of Shakespeare's tragedies.

A big, bearlike professor named Carleton Coon made the study of anthropology a rollicking adventure, whether it was the Piltdowns' invention of the hand ax, the charming manlike ways of the gibbon, or Coon's own experiences with the blue- **87** eyed Berbers of the Rif or his interlude of behind-enemy-lines sabotaging of Wehrmacht tanks and trucks in North Africa. There was Perry Miller, occasionally a little tipsy but ever in command of his subject, transporting us through the evolution of American writing from the Calvinists and Transcendentalists to Twain, Howells, and Whitman into the writers of the twenties. Fred Merk's history course called "The Westward Movement" was nicknamed "Wagon Wheels" because he made his lectures so exciting you could hear the saddle leather creaking and smell the coffee bubbling over sagebrush fires. Arthur Schlesinger, Sr., was the faculty father of all Nieman Fellows during the program's first several years. Tea with the Schlesingers and a usually beguiling variety of other guests was a Sunday afternoon fixture; sometimes his son Arthur, Jr., would be there, only a year or two older than I and already famous for his superb work, *The Age of Jackson.* I thought he was just about the smartest person I'd ever met (a judgment at which I suspected he would not cavil); our paths would converge several times in the future. Arthur, Sr.'s course on the social history of America was a must for most of us Fellows. Stolid but solid, it converted the everyday preoccupations and customs of Americans through the decades into a cogent sense of how Americans had come to be the kind of people we are in the twentieth century.

I doubt there has been any teacher before or since who could transport a classroom through the period of the French Revolution with such cogency as Crane Brinton. Oscar Handlin's class on Immigration in America had already made him renowned early in what was to be a distinguished career at Harvard. Another close faculty friend of the Nieman program was Merle Fainsod. In his classroom lectures on Dictatorship and Bureaucracy and during occasional casual evenings at his home several of us imposed relentlessly on his knowledge of the Soviet Union and the workings (or nonworkings) of the system we thought the Communists intended to impose on the rest of the world. In addition to these almost invariably transfixing courses I attended almost as an afterthought a course examining the charter and the potentials of the newly formed United Nations organization.

Some professors, even those far more distinguished in their vocations than we in ours, seemed flattered that Nieman Fellows, those hardened visitors from another planet, had chosen to attend their classes, so they welcomed us outside the classrooms as well. Some of the most instructive moments came over cocktails or dinners with them and their wives, sometimes at their homes, sometimes at our knee-knocking little apartment. Ted Spencer, who somehow made room for both urbane reserve and childlike enthusiasm in the same tall and slender frame, in particular became a sort of Nieman-year mentor to Maggie and me, enthusiastically pointing us toward the works of writers and poets we should not neglect and introducing us to distinguished visitors to Cambridge. One afternoon he had us for drinks to meet his good friend W. H. Auden, whose face even then bore the deep creases and crevasses which caused someone to remark that if a fly tried to walk across that face it would break a leg. The poet rushed in with a big picture book under his arm, opened it, and said, "Look at this, Ted, my newest love!" It was a photograph of an immense dynamo. Auden was shy-seeming and not very forthcoming as he and we sat sipping more cocktails than were wise, but we were thrilled just to meet the man who wrote so tellingly about our and the world's anxieties.

For all the classroom hours, the scurrying to and from the library, and the suggested homework readings, and the socializing we did among ourselves and with newly made Harvard acquaintances, there were still a few unfilled hours; so we stuffed them with our own program of Nieman events. Every Tuesday afternoon over beer and cheese at the Faculty Club we enjoyed the company of a professor whom one of the Niemans had found particularly interesting or provocative. Svirsky with his concentration on science and medicine brought in a physicist to tell us the mysteries of the cloud chamber. Fitz-Henry in her pursuit of urban studies at MIT brought in a city planner who was devising a scheme to keep out automobiles and put all city traffic onto tracks and Dodgem-like electric buggies (an idea that looks better all the time). Batal, in his frustrating effort to convince us that there really was an Arab side to the Palestine question, introduced us to a professor of Muslim theology. My **89**

Russian teacher, a courtly, unhappy man who longed for the pre-Bolshevik days of his childhood, came to tell us what the Russia of old had been like. We held more than twenty of those informal seminars; some were a bit too esoteric, some disputatious, but if any of them was boring I can't remember it.

On alternate Friday evenings we gathered at the old Joseph's Restaurant upstairs in a townhouse in Boston's Back Bay to entertain (grill is perhaps the better word for it) over dinner an invited guest from outside, usually someone from journalism like Ralph Ingersoll or Willie Schlamm, an immigrant from Austria who was reputed (no doubt exaggeratedly) to be a reactionary *eminence gris* at Time Inc., corrupting Henry Luce's vision of the American Century. We dined and jousted with many of the most powerful and admired practitioners of our trade, among them the sharp and crusty grand dame who ran the much beloved New York *Herald Tribune,* Helen Ogden Reid; Joseph Pulitzer of the St. Louis *Post-Dispatch,* Barry Bingham of the Louisville *Courier-Journal,* and Erwin Canham of the *Christian Science Monitor.* I persuaded my mentors from the *Binghamton Press,* Fred Stein, Erwin Cronk, and Tom Cawley, to come and tell us about the exigencies of small-city newspapering for the benefit of those fellow Niemans who knew only the more detached, less intimate practices in the big cities.

Other guests came from outside our world of journalism, like Beardsley Ruml, inventor of the pay-as-you-go income tax system that was inaugurated by FDR and half a century later still chews a bite out of every American paycheck. He didn't even apologize. Another guest was Donald Ogden Stewart, the humorist and screenwriter who subsequently was vilified and his life cruelly contorted when he was deemed to be one of "the Hollywood Ten" screenwriters and directors during the postwar red-baiting aberration. A charming, gentle man, he showed himself to be about as menacing as St. Francis of Assisi, amusing us with stories of old times with Robert Benchley, Dorothy Parker, and the rest of the Algonquin Round Table crowd and his screen-writing days with Ben Hecht and Scott Fitzgerald and others. He also instructed us on how to begin writing a movie script: "Shut the door. Get pencils, papers, and typewriter ready. Stare for a while at the wall. Then pick up anything you can find to read. When it is late afternoon a sip or two of blackberry brandy is not out of order."

Several of us fellows were brash, outspoken, giving off the air of certitude that a little knowledge and a little too much wine can induce. In retrospect, I can see that those of our guests who happened to be conservative or even moderate in their politics had reason to be offended by the self-righteousness and leftish bent of our interventions. But if they were we didn't notice. Of perhaps twenty such evenings I have only bright memories—of interesting characters, informative and occasionally dazzling exchanges, exuberant argument. Those wordy, smoky dinners were valuable, too, for the reminder our guests brought with them, that there was a real world out there, less tolerant, more insistent, and we were doomed to return to it once this benign interlude in academia was over.

Over? It couldn't be. The year had just begun, or so it seemed. The vivid scene of golden autumn, with the single sculler on the Charles, flashed back to me for an instant, then gave way, as before, to reality. Undeniably it was spring. The trees and grass of Harvard Yard were brilliant green. There were now dozens of scullers on the river, in singles, fours, and eights, instead of the solitary oarsman of autumn. The Red Sox were already into their certain-to-be-disappointing season* and bird-watchers were clambering about Mount Auburn cemetery for the migration of the warblers. The professors had delivered their concluding lectures and we'd exchanged good-byes. Looseleaf notebooks now fat with some of the scribbled wisdom of the ages, and piles of books acquired during the year to be read again and never to be abandoned, barely fit into a dozen cartons. To our surprise, the deposit check came back from our greedy landlord.

Hoping that this time the rickety elevator would make it to the fourth floor, Frank Kelly and I took our last ride together to the Nieman office, a cluttered two-room suite in Holyoke House, a Harvard Square building that was slated for demolition and surely deserved it. We asked the secretary for two applications for Nieman Fellowships, filled them out, and left

*They fooled us by winning the pennant, but not the Series.   **91**

them on Louis Lyons's desk. (Sorry fellows, he wrote later, no second helpings. There are too many others out there who can use a fellowship.)

The year had brought all that a man could hope for and more, days and nights filled with excitements and insights, visions and intimations, a bounty of new friendships that were to last for decades, and the chastening but therapeutic reminder that there is more knowledge than a person can know, so do the best you can. A hundred, no, a thousand doors had been opened in my mind; perhaps most of what entered would seek the nearest exit but some gossamer bits, some useful fossil prints and potsherds would, I was sure, stay in storage for use when excavated. At a farewell dinner given by some Law School friends on the eve of our departure I found myself rhapsodizing about the Nieman year to a woman I'd just met, an obviously intelligent but somewhat forbidding and cheerless lady who had already earned two master's degrees and was about to get her Ph.D. in sociology. When I'd finished she offered a condescending smile and remarked, "But it's not the same as a college *education.*" The sniff in her voice was like an exclamation point.

"You're right," I said. "It's better."

Reluctant as our leavetaking was, we found it pleasant to be back in Washington, which had come to think of itself as the capital of the world, and was behaving accordingly, with some noble and some questionable results. Maggie and I were with our old friends again at the same table in the Willard lounge or the bar of the Old Ebbitt and I was again working with Shack, patrolling the high-ceilinged corridors of the Department of State and poking about the embassies.

I was barely back in the rhythm of it when Jay Frandsen called me to his desk one afternoon. He stood out as a true gentleman in a raffish trade, a demanding taskmaster but a thoughtful and generous one, and possessed of the unexcitability that denotes a superb wire service newsman. He had treated me especially well and I considered him to be a friend as well as boss; his warm endorsement and willingness to grant me a leave of absence were the principal reason I'd gotten a Nieman Fellowship. Usually when confronted by Jay you could sense the temperature; if the news was good, he couldn't subdue a twinkle that escaped through his eyeglasses and the involuntary hint of a smile; if bad, he'd usually be looking down at a paper on his desk and tapping a pencil. This time, I could detect neither set of signs and he didn't give me a moment to guess. He asked if I'd be interested in a new assignment. Doing what? I asked. Covering the United Nations, he said.

Jay said that New York headquarters had asked him to recommend someone and he thought that I ("With your fine college education," he said wryly) would be just the man for the job. I would get a boost in salary, of course, and I'd be chief of the United Nations bureau. Honest man that he was, he added after a pause, "But for the time being you'll be the entire bureau."

Moving to New York appealed to Maggie; during her Vassar days she'd met more dates under the Biltmore clock than could be counted on a palm tree. She welcomed the opportunity again to take in the theaters, the museums and art galleries. Save for one brief excursion to the World's Fair of 1939 I hadn't been to "Impolite Gotham," as Tom Hutton contemptuously called it, since my mother and father took me to stay in the Hotel McAlpin and to see Eddie Cantor in *Whoopee* and Will Rogers in *Three Cheers* in the 1920s. Next morning I accepted the job. It was a double opportunity: I could experience life in the big city and play a role in one of the momentous undertakings of our time, a worldwide effort to humanize—or better yet, to improve—human conduct.

Chapter 7

Onward Christian Diplomats

An abandoned gyroscope factory. That certainly was an appropriate first home for the new organization that was supposed to keep the world in peaceful balance. And it was located in a Long Island village propitiously named Lake Success. So much for the good news. In more substantive respects the United Nations had gotten off to a dreadful start.

In the first serious case brought before the Security Council the Western powers demanded that the Soviet Union withdraw its wartime military forces from northern Iran. The Soviet delegate, Andrei Gromyko, responded by stalking out of the Council chamber, the most celebrated walkout since Edward, former Prince of Wales, walked away from the British crown to marry Wallis Simpson. The Soviets countered by demanding the withdrawal of British troops from Greece and Indonesia. The Syrians and Lebanese joined in a demand that French and British forces be kicked out of their countries. The Greeks threw in charges that their three Communist-governed neighbors, the Albanians, Bulgarians, and Yugoslavs, were infiltrating guerilla bands into Greece under cover of night, some of them wearing bells around their necks and crawling on all fours to imitate wandering sheep. Nobody laughed.

94   By the time I began commuting from my newly rented apart-

ment in Manhattan to Lake Success to set up the United Press bureau the paradox was already in place: The parliament of peace was a field of combat. This—I now suppose—should not have been a surprise to a sophisticated observer and no doubt it wasn't surprising to many of the politicians and professional diplomats who had set up the machinery. By reserving for themselves a veto power over decisions of the Security Council the big powers had exempted themselves from any serious UN intervention in their affairs while reserving the right to intervene in others'. The Yalta arrangement giving the Soviet Union a couple of extra seats (by making believe that Byelorussia and Ukraine were then independent countries) seemed to mock the ideal of One Nation, One Vote. Numerically it wasn't much of a concession, though, considering that of the fifty-one original UN governments more than forty could be counted on to vote consistently with the Western powers against the six* countries of the Communist bloc.

Dean Acheson, the bright and haughty lawyer-diplomat whose guardsman's mustache and acid tongue were comple- mented by an air of boundless certitude, had become one of President Truman's principal construction superintendents for postwar foreign policy. He could barely conceal his low regard for the new world organization which the administration he represented had so assiduously cheered into being. In many respects Acheson was a loner, but he may well have been speak- ing the tacit opinion of most of the international corps of diplo- mats when he once said, "I never thought the UN was worth a damn." Yet he conceded, "to a lot of people it was a Holy Grail."

That was the point: However cynical the professionals may have been, much of the world public looked on the new organi- zation with high hopes and expectations. I was certain that this was surely the case for a majority of the American people, with their special feelings of guilt over the mortal wound America had inflicted on the League of Nations by refusing to join. Those hopes and expectations were what made the prospect of

---

*The USSR, Byelorussian Soviet Republic, Ukrainian Soviet Republic, Poland, Czechoslovakia, and Yugoslavia.

reporting the UN exciting. A large number of the fifty-odd American reporters and thirty or so foreign newsmen and women at the UN shared those sentiments (the high hopes, at least, if not the expectations; after all, we journalists were supposed to be realists, too).

An acre or so of cement-block factory shed had been partitioned into workrooms, wired and coated with paint the color of hospital-brindle to serve as the United Nations pressroom. We gathered there for eight, ten, twelve, and even more hours daily, a mixed band of men and (a few) women ranging from neophyte reporters to seasoned foreign correspondents. We were all pioneers of a sort, participants in a noble experiment. Whether we felt it outright or absorbed it subliminally the effect of this sense of high purpose was to make most of us partisans—not of one government or another, not of one "side" or ideology or other, but partisans of the United Nations *idea.*

We wanted to see the UN flourish, yet as newsmen we thrived on the conflict. This was a contradiction, to be sure. Still, one could harbor strong hopes yet dispassionately report their being assaulted. The discordance and rancor in the meeting rooms and back corridors were an unfortunate but true reflection of the postwar climate. Recording them was our job. Conflict makes news and the goings-on at the young UN were providing news aplenty, a front-page story almost every day, some days two or even three, with that name stuck right up there at the beginning: BY ROBERT MANNING, UNITED PRESS STAFF CORRESPONDENT.

Dull as it was, the course I had taken at Harvard on international organizations had been a providential afterthought, illuminating some of the subtleties of the United Nations charter and the structure and potential weaknesses of the new organization as well as the various ways big powers or canny small ones could use or obstruct the machinery. My problems lay not in understanding the UN but in covering the gushers of news it generated. Problem number one was the principal opposition, the Associated Press. The AP had sent a basketball team to Lake Success, five men to cover events that I was charged with covering all by myself. Fortunately, the five of them spent a lot of time in Mark Sennett–like bumping into each other, conferring over assignments, trying to parcel among five work enough for about three people. Even more fortunately, in those early days almost all the big stories were enacted right before us, in the debates and maneuvers in the Security Council chamber or, when the full General Assembly of fifty-one members met, in a huge improvised Assembly meeting hall salvaged from the pre-war World's Fair in nearby Flushing Meadows.

Since those confrontations enacted in public were themselves the main news, there was not great need at first for a lot of bird-dog reporting behind the scenes. I could usually hold my own against the competition simply by conveying the essence of each day's flow of cold war rhetoric and parliamentary maneuvering, taking pains to do so accurately and speedily. Each confrontation in the eleven-member Security Council of course had its denouement—usually a Soviet veto of a Western proposal or rejection by a 9-to-2 vote of a Soviet bloc proposal (by unspoken agreement, the Soviets were given the company of a second Communist bloc seat). We kept track of Soviet vetoes in the Security Council the way old movie Western gunslingers cut notches on their gun stocks. Many times one needed merely to change a number and a proper name to make one day's lead suffice for next: "The Soviet Union cast its ——th veto in the United Nations today to bar the admission of ——— to the world organization." Another front-page story.

When the full General Assembly and its several committees-of-the-whole convened, the cast was larger, the range of subjects wider; the scripts were basically the same but here no government had a veto power, so the Assembly could methodically express its majority will (though lacking any power but that of propaganda to enforce it) while applying "the tyranny of the majority" to squelch the Soviet bloc's resolutions and dull its propaganda maneuvers. Most delegates to the UN were chosen by their governments for their impassivity and their strict adherence to orders. If they indulged in emotional outbursts or displays of excitement these—except for polished performances by the consummate actors whom London, Paris, and a few lesser capitals sent to the UN—were usually transparently unspontaneous, delivered generally by rote from texts sent from the home office. Among the dozens of delegates there were inev- **97** itably some exceptions. One of these was Dmitri Manuilski, the "foreign minister" of the nonsovereign and nonindependent Republic of the Ukraine.

Some Soviet bloc delegates were relatively gregarious next to their Moscow cousins, but most took their cue from their stolid, unsmiling chief, Andrei Gromyko, who was capable of an occa-' sional display of dour wit but usually, like Mr. Bftsplk in Al Capp's *Li'l Abner* comic strip, carried his own stormcloud around with him. They indulged fulsomely in unsparingly banal, repetitious Agitprop rhetoric, sometimes sounding as if they almost believed it. Some were party dolts. Others were clever enough to exploit the fine points of parliamentary procedure in order to delay or tangle debate. When the inevitable vote came they accepted it stoically, without grimace or shrug. Not so Dmitri Manuilski.

A stocky, volatile man with a dramatic shock of white hair that seemed to have been combed with an eggbeater, Manuilski was one of Stalin's faithful old Bolsheviks. He'd spent so much time running from the czarist police that he couldn't hold any job for long, so his Communist party pseudonym was БезРабóTHNN or "Byezrobotnee" (the unemployed). These many years later he had been rewarded with an opportunity to come to Lake Success and see how the imperialists live. For this session of the Assembly, Manuilski had been designated second deputy chairman of the important First or Political Committee. This was one of the sop appointments the majority felt obliged to hand out now and then to a representative of the minority bloc, one so far down in the pecking order as to be harmless. Alas, an outbreak of flu upset the majority's plan, felling the chairman and first deputy chairman, both Westerners. So the gavel fell to Manuilski. He banged it with gusto, interrupting Western delegates in midspeech, ruling others out of order, shamelessly trying to change the agenda. Time and again, a delegate raised a point of order and Chairman Manuilski's ruling was overturned by a show of hands. After the seventh or eighth of these humiliations inflicted on him by the majority, he exploded in frustration, pounded the table, and dramatized in a few words why never the twain, East and West, would meet:

98   *"This democratic procedure must cease!"*

It didn't, of course. With the help of a sulfa drug and a stout constitution, number one chairman was back next day, red-eyed and sniffling, to resuscitate Robert's Rules of Order. Many of us were grateful to Mr. Manuilski. There were too few light moments in the parliament of nations and too little of candor; manifestations of either were to be treasured.

At this point the Lake Success experience was best symbolized by the masks of Comedy and Tragedy. The smiling face represented the professional exhilaration induced by working on a challenging and surefire news-producing assignment. The sad face signified what seemed to be happening to the United Nations idea. I had my own ample supply of banality in those days, and poured some of it into an abortive diary. "It will be another one of those days at UN," an early entry began,

> nine or ten hours of unspeakable cynicism and platitudes mixed with some of that plaintive, almost laughable sincerity that occasionally pops out of the mouth of some honest man selected by error or perhaps necessity to represent a government (almost always a small one) here. I know it is a cliché, but never have I so believed the claim that diplomats are the most deceitful of men. . . . The UN is sick and weak. Every time it gasps somebody—usually Russian, American, French, or British—gives it a new kick in the groin and then shouts that somebody else has violated the letter and spirit of the Charter.

I was struck, though, by an interesting phenomenon—"It's funny, but the weaker the damned organization seems the more it's being used"—and I took some comfort from that.

> When all the bitterness, the skepticism, the cynicism and countercynicism is poured out I still cling to that almost stupid belief that the UN's not out, and that it has a chance to grow strong and help the little guy who still thinks that a portion of common sense and decency among neighbors, or nations, is better than war. I confess to a large streak of naiveté and perhaps a dearth of that somewhat nebulous quality which diplomats around here call realism.

Slowly, almost imperceptibly, in small ways that barely attracted news notice there were hints that some of that gossamer **99** optimism might not have been altogether misplaced. There is little recognition of this in the diary, however, for it petered out after a few entries. Not, I confess, because I recognized then that it was as mawkish as its few entries now prove to be. Rather, I was becoming too busy during the long working days and too exhausted at the end of each to write down reflective comment on what was happening. The volume of activities at Lake Success had grown to the point where one man could not provide the broad coverage that a wire service required. The five AP men, all of them experienced and competent—and underextended—were filing news stories about events I'd barely become aware of.

When the big General Assembly sessions convened I got plenty of help, usually at the price of enjoying fewer of the bylines. The foreign editor, Harrison Salisbury, who was one of the UP's big stars and my immediate superior, would come out from New York with a small crew of reporters; James Roper, an experienced and versatile Unipresser, to write the "night leads" for morning papers while I and sometimes Salisbury himself covered the main running story during the day; one or two Latin American specialists for the UP's important newspaper clients to the South, and an Asian specialist for clients in the Far East, as well as one or two other reporters to range among the numerous committee and subcommittee deliberations for news possibilities.

It was during the several months when the Assembly was not in session that I had to contend on my own with a swelling array of happenings. The Security Council might be debating sanctions against Franco Spain in its chamber while in another room the Trusteeship Council discussed the future of New Guinea, Ruanda-Urundi, or Togoland and in another the new Atomic Energy Commission debated an American proposal for international control of atomic weapons. The plan had been formulated by Dean Acheson and David Lilienthal but with great fanfare had been rechristened "the Baruch Plan" for the man President Truman chose to nurture our proposals in the world arena. Bernard Baruch, after making millions in the stock market during and after World War I, had become fa-

100   mous as "adviser to presidents" and "the park bench philosopher." He must have been an impressive man in his earlier days, but by now he had become something of a windbag and publicity hound (I suppose that a man who employed Billy Rose, the nascent showman, as his stenographer might have been expected to ingest some Barnumism). When he was scheduled to appear at a commission meeting he dispatched aides to the pressroom to drum up interest and to hand out to correspondents personalized paperweights made of fragments of uranium ore encased in lucite.

The Acheson-Lilienthal Plan was in fact a far-reaching proposal for a system in which the United States would place its atomic weapons and energy capabilities under a form of international control if the Soviets would do likewise. It was a sensible and generous offer from the country that had a great dominance if not still a monopoly on nuclear weaponry, but in presenting it Americans surely knew that it was designed for a world less afflicted than this one by mistrust and suspicion. For the Soviets with their paranoic fear of scrutiny by outsiders the plan had a fatal flaw: foreigners (i.e., spies) would be permitted to make on-site inspections of Soviet atomic plants, laboratories, and—as we were to learn—that country's speedily expanding weapons capability. The Western powers pressed for the Baruch Plan while the the USSR denounced it as an imperialist plot and urged instead a simple treaty requiring all governments to renounce nuclear weapons and destroy any they possessed. "Trust us," the Russians were saying. "Not on your life," was the Western response.

The Americans knew the Russians would not accept inspection and the Russians knew the Americans would not accept a treaty without it, so insincerity virtually dripped from the ceiling of the meeting chamber as the air was rent with cries of "capitalist warmongers," "Western encirclement," and "Communist imperialism" while nuclear arsenals grew in size and in the range and precision of their threat. In the pressroom we amused ourselves with visions of the dismay and grandiose backpedaling that would ensue in Washington if Moscow suddenly opened its doors to inspection, and in Moscow should the West suddenly agree to immediate scrapping of *all* military force as the Soviets urged without any intention of dismantling **101** their huge "conventional" armies. Stalemated though it was, the debate was useful and we reported it in full because it dramatized the dangers of the nuclear age. This helped to make apparent that the menace carried within itself its own mechanism of international control: Mutual fear of a nuclear Armageddon could be as compelling a restraint as any paper treaty. To contort Franklin Roosevelt's famous phrase, the only thing we had to ease our nuclear fears was fear itself.

Meanwhile the UN was growing as other countries lined up to join the company of the charter members and the organization slowly evolved from its role as a propaganda theater for the principal cold war antagonists into one that could take on matters that did not automatically invite stalemate and might even produce some benefits for humankind. Commissions on human rights, the status of women, and international law, an emergency fund (UNICEF) to provide food and care for children around the world, a Food and Agricultural Organization. The UN picked up the work of the International Labor Organization and Commission on Narcotic Drugs from the long-dead and now dissolved (as of April 18, 1946) League of Nations. The United Nations was also becoming a staging area for that most profound and turbulent aftermath of two world wars, the dismemberment of the colonial system and the spawning of the Third World. This was generally welcomed, even by some among the colonial powers, for the war had drained them of the resources and the will they needed to hold on to their far-flung colonies. So here was another paradox: The organization envisaged by some as the eventual substitute for national sovereignty was accelerating the unbridled proliferation of sovereign nation-states.

Only a few weeks after my first despondent diary entry the UN displayed its potential for helping to bring new states into being. The two great powers acted in concert to dictate the end of the Netherlands' colonial rule of the East Indies and to create the Republic of Indonesia. As a favor to their fellow Dutch colonials the French and British held off the inevitable for a time by unscabbarding their Security Council vetoes, but they sensed that a partnership of the USSR and the U.S., tenuous as it was, would be impossible to defy. There was joy at Lake

Success. "A warm glow around the place because of the speedy action in the Indonesian case," I wrote in the diary. "The glow will disappear soon enough when the Council resumes the Balkans debate next week, so everyone (except perhaps some of the countries with colonies to lose) is enjoying it while he may. It would be a mistake to count on it as enough to beat down all the mistrust and disillusionment growing up around here, but it'll help."

As events of this sort proliferated, it no longer made sense for the UP to "save a nickel for Mickel" at the expense of its coverage of history in the making. One personal consequence of the long hours and hard work was that Maggie and I had little opportunity to enjoy many of the enticements that had drawn us to Manhattan. To make matters worse, the stress was making mischief with my stomach lining. "Slow down and give up smoking and drinking for at least a few months or you'll have ulcers," said my doctor. In return for that monumental sacrifice, I implored Harrison Salisbury for a small sacrifice from the UP in return: "Just send me one good full-time reporter."

The cure for incipient ulcers was a fellow named Richard Witkin, a New Yorker who'd broken into journalism on the yearbook put out by campers from Camp Androscoggin in Maine, a summer depositary for mostly Jewish boys who came mostly from Manhattan's "Our Crowd" families. After earning degrees from Harvard and the Columbia School of Journalism he'd gotten brief experience on a country daily in upstate New York, then a Detroit newspaper, and now was a night editor of the UP's radio news operation, a rather mundane news-packaging job, though important to the UP's never-quite-healthy revenues. In addition to his diplomas he'd earned the Distinguished Flying Cross and five Air Medals while piloting his full quota of "fifty" B-24 bombing missions over Europe (thirty-three actual sorties plus double credit for bringing his crew safely home from the deadly Ploesti oil fields and such other dangerous targets as Munich, Steyr, and Friedrichshafen).

A slim, handsome fellow about a year older than I, Witkin had a healthy sense of humor, a tankful of high-octane energy, a quick grasp of the issues and politics of the UN, and a competitor's curiosity. He wanted to find out what was happening, **103** and soon—before anyone else did. It was partnership at first sight. Putting it immodestly, if working together at the UN had been a sport, we could have played Davis Cup doubles, so instinctively did we divide the work and anticipate the flow of the game. Now it was possible to induce nervous stomach in some of our competitors.

The working partnership quickly flowered into friendship as well. Dick's wife, Katie, was a niece of the playwright George S. Kaufman (Katie was the inspiration for the little girl, Essie, in a ballet dancer's tutu who twirled mischievously about the house in Kaufman's *You Can't Take It With You,* and in fact grew up to be a dancer on Broadway). She introduced Dick into the theater world. I think it was his notion that we write a musical comedy about the United Nations. Lord knows there was enough comedy to draw upon, unintentional as most of it was. After the long days' work at Lake Success we stayed up late nights at the Manning apartment in Murray Hill concocting plot and assailing each other with scenes we found thigh-slappingly funny. This show was going to be even more hilarious than *Whoopee* or *Three Cheers,* not to mention *Oedipus Rex!* We saw no one better than Zero Mostel to play the chief Russian delegate, obviously not at all patterned after Andrei Gromyko, with Carol Channing or Elaine Stritch as the dizzy blonde from the Bronx to whom the lovestruck Communist gives a brace of Russian wolfhounds and a twelve-cylinder Zim or Zila limousine that backfires and loses a fender or two at every curtain fall. We settled on Harold Rome as the ideal composer but would as enthusiastically have embraced Frank Loesser were he willing to read the script.

We spent so much time "casting" the show and laughing at each other's recitals of boffo scenes that we got very little onto paper. The blank stares we got from some of Katie's theater friends when we recited the plot did not exactly help to keep our adrenaline running. So after a few weeks we renounced show business careers and concentrated on doing what we did best. A good thing, too, for the curtain had risen at Lake Success on a truly important drama, the creation of the state of Israel.

Great Britain, in the Balfour Declaration issued just after **104** World War I, had solemnly promised the Jews a homeland in

Palestine and at the same time the British had at least inferentially assured the Arabs that there would not be such a Jewish state. Britain now was abandoning any pretense at resolving this blatant if not perfidious contradiction on its own. The British government announced on April 2, 1947, that it intended to pull out of Palestine and was turning over its mandate to the United Nations. With violence mounting—Jewish terrorists against British occupiers, Arabs and Jews against each other— and both sides piling up armaments for the moment when the British left, the UN had no alternative but to try. So the General Assembly promptly convened in special session to deal with the Palestine question—"this most complex and tragic of historical dilemmas," as it was to be described by one of the UN's earliest and most influential civil servants, an Englishman named Brian Urquhart,*

> where two ancient peoples were in an unequal but deadly competition for a small but infinitely significant piece of territory, a struggle made critical by Hitler's annihilation of the Jews of Europe on the one hand and the emergence of Arab nationalism on the other. Britain must be enabled to relinquish the Mandate of Palestine with dignity. The Jewish refugees from World War II must be allowed to settle. The Palestinians' interests and rights must be protected. A plan must be found to accommodate the conflicting rights and demands of Arabs and Jews. The international community, through the United Nations, must restore peace and execute the plan. In our innocence none of these things seemed to us impossible.

The Assembly established a Special Committee on Palestine (UNSCOP) of eleven members to propose a solution. Britain positioned itself Pontius Pilate–like above the fray—she would endorse any proposal that satisfied *both* Jews and Arabs but would not help to enforce one. Many other UN governments had no passionate feelings about Palestine's future and many harbored Muslims among their populations; if there was a majority tendency it probably tipped toward the Arabs. Still, it was

---

*In *A Life in Peace and War* by Brian Urquhart (New York: Harper & Row, 1987; paperback edition, New York: W. W. Norton & Co., 1991).

the two main players who would determine the flow of the drama and the outcome. What we reporters knew about the two governments' postures was essentially this:

Publicly the Truman Administration favored the honoring of Britain's promise of a homeland for the Jews. Behind the scenes the government was sharply divided between those firmly dedicated to a Jewish state, mostly politicians including President Truman (in spite of his mounting irritation at pressure from American Jews), and those who expressed fear of damaging long-term American interests in the Arab world, mostly the career Foreign Service and the military, including the influential General George C. Marshall, who had become Truman's secretary of state. As for the USSR, it had long been anti-Zionist and pro-Arab, with a strong desire for a political foothold in that part of the world. But surprisingly, Andrei Gromyko stepped forward at the UN in support of partition and a Jewish state, perhaps, we speculated, in the belief that this would be a speedier way to gain that foothold or to foment long-term unrest from which Moscow could benefit.

By late summer, the Special Commission had visited Palestine (that's when the unfortunate Dutch delegate, the one memorialized in my favorite UP dispatch, tumbled into the tomb of Nicodemus, never to be heard from again, insofar as UP readers were concerned). The committee also toured the teeming Jewish refugee camps in Europe, then returned to Lake Success to deliberate. Witkin and I, dividing the labor between us, cajoled and pestered delegates on the committee and their aides, and finally found the one we were after—a delegate whose government was opposed to the committee's majority decision. Dick ascertained that on the following Monday the commission's majority would propose the partition of Palestine into separate Arab and Jewish states and got a hasty look at the text of the proposal. We rushed our story onto the wire and exulted next morning when we found it displayed in the *New York Times,* which almost never reported UN news that did not come from its own correspondents. We'd beaten out not only the AP basketball team but the rest of the UN pressroom and, most delicious of all, the usually all-encompassing ten-man bureau of the *Times.*

This biggest of all UN stories was one of twistings and turn-
ings, of deep passions and fears that the UN was moving toward decisions it had no power to enforce or control. Many
delegates were not even certain where at any given moment
their own governments stood on the issue. Those of us who had
to sort out facts from emotions found usually reliable sources
unreliable, others unapproachable. The partition proposal
needed a two-thirds majority of those voting in the General
Assembly. U.S. career diplomats, with their ambivalence verging on antipathy toward a Jewish state, did not prove to be
fervent lobbyists for their own government's policy, but there
were plenty of other Americans prepared to twist arms. For
example, as debate neared its climax Carlos Romulo, chief delegate of the Philippines, announced that the Philippines would
vote against partition. We learned later that a top presidential
adviser, ten U.S. senators, and two justices of the Supreme
Court (Frank Murphy and Felix Frankfurter) had all put pressure on Filipino officials in Washington and Manila. Mr.
Romulo's delegation voted aye. So it went with other recalci-
trants and malingerers, like Haiti and Liberia, to mention a
couple, until a majority seemed assured.

In the final vote or "showdown," as wireservice-speak would
have it, partition eked out a 33-to-13 majority. That was November 29, 1947. Most of us in the American press corps
strained to keep exultation out of our news stories. I felt that my
copy was straightforward, though I certainly reflected no
doubts about the correctness of the Assembly's decision. Personally I rejoiced. There were rueful headshakes from other
correspondents, though, especially those who had served in the
Middle East. Once the day's excitement quieted and we relaxed
over drinks at the Press bar, the Englishman who was chief
correspondent for Reuters said matter-of-factly, "Now we'll
have another war to cover."

Britain gave the UN little more than five months to figure out
how to implement its decision. On May 14, 1948, British forces
would leave and London would wash its hands of the bloody
problem, whatever its state on that day. Stalin had once asked
derisively about the Vatican, "How many divisions has the
Pope?"; the same could be asked of the United Nations. The **107**

answer, of course, was None. The Jews and all anxious champions of the Jewish homeland now had to face the question, Who is going to enforce the General Assembly's decision, and how? Washington made clear that American force could not be counted on except perhaps as a small part of an international police force. Yet such a force seemed out of the question since all the Western powers were united in their opposition to any international police force that might allow even a symbolic Soviet or Soviet bloc military presence in Palestine.

The approach of the deadline hovered darkly over the Security Council and debate grew more emotional. One day exchanges between Arab delegates and representatives of the Jewish Agency became so time-consuming and vituperative that Warren Austin, the chief American delegate, who happened to be presiding over the Council that day, sought to intervene. A gentle, portly senator from Vermont, Austin was appointed to the UN post by his admiring former Senate colleague Harry Truman. He was not a forceful man nor a polished diplomat but, given the backup of experienced aides, he was a good choice as the initial chief American delegate, one of the most decent, well-intentioned personages at the United Nations, respected for his honesty, his old New England piety, and his sweet disposition. On this rancorous afternoon his pleasant demeanor cracked. His face reddened. He pounded the gavel and said, with anguish in his voice:

"It is time for the Arabs and Jews to sit down together and settle this matter in the true Christian spirit."

Suddenly the chamber was silent; it took a moment for the incongruity of the chairman's remark to settle in. Then came a titter from someone in the gallery, followed by others, growing into what is best described as a murmur of nervous laughter. Warren Austin showed brief consternation but bravely gestured for the debate to proceed. Later, representatives from the American delegation circulated in the pressroom, urging us to refrain from embarrassing the senator by circulating his remark to the outside world. Most of us made little of the incident out of affection for Warren Austin. But it lingered in memory as the most sardonic and telling epigram ever uttered in the parliament of nations.

By late March the burning fuse was sputtering closer to the powder keg (there's that wireservice-speak again). Several members of the American delegation seemed increasingly nervous, testy. Something was going on. But what? I telephoned my mentor Shackford at the State Department and he said that he too smelled something in the air. Another few hours of buttonholing or telephoning officials brought us to a startling discovery: The United States was reconsidering its support of Palestine partition. I hadn't been able to follow Shackford's stringent formula—triple check everything—and I was short of details. But I was certain enough to write for next morning's wire that the United States, in a dramatic turnabout, was planning to withdraw its support of the partition of Palestine.

After the story went out on the morning of November 19, the U.S. delegation's press officers were deluged with inquiries and soon responded with a statement denying that the United States was renouncing its support of the creation of a Jewish state. With a gusto that only I could call unseemly, the AP and other services rushed the denial onto their wires. Excited newspaper and radio clients began peppering UP headquarters with inquiries, most of them angry, and the news editor passed them on to me, with expletives. Papers that had gone to press with the UP's "exclusive," began replating their front pages. I was humiliated. I was distraught. Distraught? Hell, I could already hear a thousand-piece brass band playing Chopin's Funeral March. My career was coming to an untimely end. I swore to New York headquarters that I was certain of my sources, but what else could I say? We had to carry the denial, too, for there it was, in cold type, the U.S. government's insistence that it still supported the partition of Palestine.

But all was not lost. The government's denial was at best only technically true if not an outright lie. It omitted one rather important detail. That was supplied only a few hours later when Warren Austin took the Security Council floor. He astonished the UN, infuriated the Jews, and delighted the Arabs by announcing that the United States, while still supporting the *principle* of a Jewish state but fearful of almost certain war in the Holy Land, now proposed to table the UN's partition decision and convene another special General Assembly session to re-   **109** consider the entire Palestine question. Meanwhile the territory should be put under a UN trusteeship. This would almost certainly kill partition for the foreseeable future and require those who favored a Jewish homeland to start all over again under less propitious circumstances. In short, my story was confirmed. I was sorry for the Jews but relieved to be vindicated.

When I later accused one of the American delegates of lying to the world, he said with an imitation smile that the denial wasn't a lie, only a carefully drafted "statement of position." After all, the United States was not abandoning its original plan, only putting it on a shelf. I thanked him for instructing me in the art of fine distinction and suggested, in terms he found vulgar, that he change careers—selling used cars, perhaps, or writing ads for something like Swamp Root, the kidney cure.

The astonishing American reversal threw into public view the conflict between President Truman and some of his close advisers on the one hand and a most powerful group of policymakers, led by Secretary of State George Marshall and including his deputy Robert Lovett and a then little-known official named Dean Rusk, who headed the State Department's office of United Nations affairs, on the other. Of course, it threw the United Nations into confusion. The Jewish Agency representative swore that any change in the partition plan "will have to be imposed on the Jewish community of Palestine by force." The confusion was compounded, to say the least, when Washington dispatches reported that President Truman himself was surprised by the American maneuver and felt he'd been betrayed by pro-Arab officials in the State Department—"the striped-pants boys," as Truman usually referred to them. A polite if not totally plausible explanation was that there was no such conspiracy by the "Arabists" to reverse the president's explicit policy, but a desperate maneuver to avert war. If so, the best that could be said of the State Department was that it had stupidly bungled communications with the White House and severely underestimated the momentum of events in Palestine.

Understandably, the General Assembly was in a general daze when it assembled again only a month before Britain's scheduled evacuation and groped for a way to prevent what now seemed an inevitable war. It was still groping on May 14 when

110

the British pulled their forces out and the Jews proclaimed the birth of the State of Israel. American delegates persisted in their efforts to persuade the powerless Assembly to bulldoze Arabs and Jews into "negotiation" (of which there had been none since the partition decision, and very little in the months before that). Late that afternoon, in the midst of this effort, word came that President Truman had just extended United States recognition to the new state. The embarrassed American delegation, still trying to rally votes for a retreat to trusteeship, learned about it from other delegates who had heard the White House announcement on radio. Soviet recognition followed in a couple of days.

Israel's decisive defeat of the invading Arab armies showed how formidable had been the Jews' preparation for the realization of their centuries-old dream, the regathering of the exiles in their homeland. Emphatic as it appeared to be, that stunning victory did not relieve the United Nations of the case. Obviously, there was more conflict, more killing to come. The Arabs and Jews had accepted the American delegate's suggestion; they were settling matters in the true Christian spirit.

Chapter 8

Breaking Out

The Palestine decision bewitched, bothered, and bewildered the young United Nations organization. It also altered the course of its development, not entirely to its detriment. Up to then the UN had been little more than a debating society, in almost all instances powerless to deal with international conflicts even though it was beginning, haltingly, to address some of the cares of lesser countries and to nourish international approaches to the common good. Suddenly it had a war on its hands, one that might have happened anyway, but which the UN had virtually mandated when it despaired (too quickly?) of achieving a negotiated solution and by majority vote imposed partition without the means to enforce it. Those means of enforcement had been envisioned in the UN charter: The five-power Military Staff Committee would develop an international force to punish aggressors and police UN decisions. But its deliberations had produced only loquacious stalemate between the Soviets and the Western powers. Now, as it groped for a way to halt the violence in Palestine, or at the least contain it, the organization nervously edged into operations of a sort that were not really contemplated in the charter. The Assembly voted to create a UN Mediator for Palestine and called on a distinguished Swedish nobleman, Count Folke Bernadotte, to take on the task, one that a UN official in a fit of understatement described as inserting a cartilage between two inflamed joints. Funds were voted to provide the Mediator with some supporting staff and an observer force made up of small contingents of military observers from assorted UN member countries, assuming that there were governments willing to volunteer some of their soldiers.

The General Assembly sent Count Bernadotte off to the war zone, genially wished him the best of luck, and adjourned for the summer—but not before voting to hold their autumn meeting in Paris. I thought it by far the best decision the UN had made to date. Seizing on accumulated vacation time, our small savings account, and some friends' tattered guidebooks, Maggie and I sailed to Europe that August. In Paris we bought a tiny Peugeot coupe and for a month before the Assembly convened went on a tour of discovery. We feasted on the sights and cuisine of southern France and sang "Sur le Pont d'Avignon" to the accompaniment of birdsongs on the balcony of an idyllic small hotel in the center of that then-fair city. We lunched at Cap d'Antibes and imagined Scott and Zelda Fitzgerald drinking there with their dashing friends the Murphys. Traveling in France was a pleasant dalliance; the love affair came in Italy— first gradual courtship in Genoa, Pisa, Rome, Assisi, and Siena and then headlong into passionate embrace with Florence.

The city was still recovering from the war. The dollar was so powerful that a pack of Lucky Strikes was a generous tip at a one-star restaurant. Hotels, restaurants, and shops were eager to please, the streets uncrowded. Erector-set replacements for the Arno River bridges that had been destroyed by the Germans were rusting eyesores, but the most beguiling of all, the Ponte Vecchio, had survived with its jostling strollers, its silversmiths' and leather workers' booths and vendors of trifles. Though scarred by war, Florence had not lost its magical way of transporting the visitor out of the present and back to the glories of its days as fountainhead of the Renaissance. All that Maggie had learned in her history and art courses at Vassar about Western civilization's arousal out of medieval darkness **113** came flowing back to her. Save for occasional help in translating Italian answers to our touristy questions, she was the only guide a novice needed.

A guest in this classroom of history learns firsthand about Giotto and his humanizing of the art of painting, Brunelleschi and his engineering of the Duomo with techniques so ingenious they still astonish architects and engineers these six centuries later. Over by that corner, when he wasn't busy inventing the Italian language young Dante used to sit on a stone pile and watch the cathedral being built. Right here in the Piazza del Duomo only yards from Donatello's magnificent David and close to Giotto's campanile was where Savonarola ranted against the excesses of the Medicis and the Pope of Rome and consigned the priceless treasures and even the clothing of rich Florentines to the bonfires of the vanities. And not far away in the Piazza Signoria was where he was hanged and burned after much torture—fourteen times on the rack on a single day; what a tiring day for his torturers!—persuaded him to confess to heresy and treason.

The windows shattered by wartime mine explosions had been replaced in the Uffizi gallery and the greatest of all collections of Italian paintings brought out of hiding (some of them from peasants' barns) and rehung there. The best of all came near the end of our two-week visit. After much inquiring, we found in an obscure street a hangar-like structure that had been conscripted as the temporary storage place for four famous sculptures, the *Captives,* that were unfinished when Michelangelo died. They are astonishing. Half-formed giants, their biceps and calves seem to ripple and swell before your eyes as they strain to break loose from their marble wombs and spring to life. Standing before them in the simple, barely lit setting I experienced a strange turbulence, a swirling, blending of the artistic with the religious and political consciousnesses. Nothing I had experienced, not even Michelangelo's Sistine Chapel Ceiling, spoke so eloquently of the act of creation and also of man's will to break free and live.

The spell cast by Florence can be overwhelming, but also misleading. It leaves the first-time visitor in dazed appreciation

114   of the splendors of the Renaissance centuries while offering lit-

tle contemporary evidence of the violence and deceits, plots and poisonings, the treacheries and other excesses, in other words the all-too familiar perversities of human conduct that were as much a part of its life as were the surviving grandeurs. One is overwhelmed into forgetting that to the Florentine princes, geniuses like Michelangelo and Massaccio were mere hirelings; it was Machiavelli who was their moral navigator.

That benign spell still gripped us when we returned to Paris, but we were quickly jolted back to the realities of human behavior: Just four days before the General Assembly was to convene, members of the Jewish terrorist Stern Gang assassinated Count Bernadotte in Jerusalem. It was a foul and outrageous deed, indicative of the deadly bitterness that was now consuming that part of the world. Identities of the assassins quickly became known but none was punished (and some of them were to rise to positions of respect and leadership in Israel).

The murder threw a shroud over the General Assembly. Fortunately, Bernadotte had chosen for his deputy a very special man, an American who was one of the few truly formidable members of the UN Secretariat. Ralph Bunche possessed intelligence, tenacity, and courage as well as the quiet patience of the ideal diplomat. These qualities would not have been enough to raise him to importance in his own country's government at that time because of the single fact that he was black. Washington's loss was the UN's good fortune. Bunche had quickly established himself as probably the most valuable member of the UN Secretariat, lower in rank but far more effective than the stolid, unimaginative Secretary General, Trygve Lie of Norway, or the deputy secretaries general chosen for their loyalties to their own governments rather than to the world organization. Out of respect for the slain Bernadotte, Bunche called himself Acting Mediator and calmly proceeded with Bernadotte's effort to impose at the least a United Nations–policed truce between Jewish and Arab forces. Out of these efforts came the UN process by which Military Observers drawn from neutral member nations serve as watchmen and honest brokers to halt conflict, to induce a truce or armistice and then to referee it. It is common UN procedure now, but it was new, dangerously, cliffhangingly new, when Bunche undertook it. His leadership **115**

of the UN intervention was sufficient to interrupt fighting between Arabs and Jews more than once—and ultimately to bring
to him the Nobel Peace Prize.

Next to the bloodletting in Palestine, the preoccupations of
the General Assembly in the charming Parisian setting of the
Trocadero and Palais de Chaillot were for the most part pallid
and dutiful. There were some high moments, though. On one
day, in an emotional memorialization of the Nazi's extermina-
tion of Jews, the Assembly formally put the word *genocide* into
the international vocabulary and asked all governments to ap-
prove a convention outlawing it.

On another day Eleanor Roosevelt, the American representative in the committee drafting a Universal Declaration of
Human Rights, went toe-to-toe in another of her memorable
confrontations with the Soviet's Andrei Vishinsky. Vishinsky's
most notable involvement in the field of human rights up to that
time had been his service as prosecutor for Joseph Stalin's purge
trials in the 1930s which sent thousands to their deaths and
other thousands to the Gulag. He looked and sounded every bit
the ruthless prosecutor, steel-rimmed eyeglasses flashing, ac-
cusatory finger puncturing the air as he delivered a long tirade
reciting the oppression of the masses by their capitalist enslav-
ers. Mrs. Roosevelt gestured for the floor. Her simple dignity
and the striking beauty of her homeliness spoke before she did.
Then, in the familiar, penetrating voice that ranged from a quiet
alto to an uncontrollable soprano quaver that Republican
women loved to parody at Fairfield County or North Shore
teas, Mrs. Roosevelt politely avoided the *ad hominem* but in
effect suggested that when it came to human rights Vishinsky
and his Kremlin associates made Attila the Hun look like Florence Nightingale. She was as brief in her remarks as she was
eloquent. The few hundred onlookers, attracted by expectation
of another Eleanor-and-Andrei collision, warmly applauded.
Vishinsky sputtered a brief rebuttal, sounding like a man who'd
just been punched in the larynx, gathered up his papers, and
stomped out. The declaration was approved without being
emasculated by Communist amendments.

There was an even more memorable moment. Early in the
116 afternoon of Wednesday, November 3, the acting president of

the Assembly, Herbert Evatt, a brash, burly man who was Australia's foreign minister, bounded to the rostrum. He rudely brushed aside the delegate who was speaking and shouted in the best Down Under accent:

"Ladies and gentlemen, I have the most wonderful news. Harry S Truman has just been reelected President of the United States!"

A mighty tumult shook the Palais. Delegates and spectators rose to their feet, some clapping, others embracing, pounding the backs of their neighbors, shouting or whistling their approval. Back in America, against all predictions, Truman had carried twenty-eight states to Thomas E. Dewey's sixteen. Outside the U.S., the demonstration suggested, Truman had done even better, carrying Europe and just about all the other member states of the United Nations. From my angle of vision I could not see whether Soviet delegates joined in the applause, but some of their East European cohorts beamed and applauded as if a huge shipment of meat had just arrived at their butcher shops. The happy uproar brought to mind that day in 1945 when the plain-looking, plain-acting man from Missouri learned that he had just become president and felt "as if a bale of hay's just landed on me." No doubt he felt better this time.

All in all, Paris had been a useful change of scene for the UN. It worked some short-term therapy on those of us who had to observe and write about its proceedings every day. Once we were back at Lake Success, though, it was the same old story. *The same old story.* Those are deadly words in the news trade. After little more than two years, the UN assignment had lost its charm. Perhaps it was only that I was jaded by the every-day sameness of events; for me, at least, either the UN story was running down or my capacity for caring passionately about it was diminishing, probably the latter.

Almost every day there were glints of progress or at least hope of progress in some areas—world health, children's relief, and the like. And there were the occasional touching vignettes that merited attention—like the sight in early 1948 of the delegate from Czechoslovakia fleeing from the Council chamber in tears, never to return, when word came of the death "by accident" of the good Czech democrat Jan Masaryk in Communist- **117** run Prague. Or the occasion when an Egyptian named Mustafa Momen, a member of an extremist group called the Muslim Brotherhood, journeyed from Cairo to demonstrate in the Security Council against British domination of his country. In a large windowless hall outside the Council chamber, he politely inquired of bystanders, "Which way is East?," removed his shoes, spread a small prayer rug, touched his forehead to it, and prayed. Then he burst into the Council chamber, shouting protests and waving a document he said was signed with his own blood. He was firmly ejected from the chamber. Months later a brief dispatch reported that young Mustafa Momen had been killed in Cairo during a Brotherhood-inspired riot against his own government.

But editors around the country seemed less and less interested in what they took to be sideshow events or "do-good" activities. The UN had become synonymous with cold war conflict and cold war rhetoric. We correspondents certainly had contributed to the syndrome by our addiction to military parlance—delegates didn't disagree, they clashed; governments didn't oppose another government's position, they blasted it; Gromyko and Austin didn't debate, they crossed swords.

Tiresome as the hyperbole became, reporters were no more successful than the diplomats in toning it down. After talking it over with Harrison Salisbury in New York, for a few days Dick Witkin and I tried to de-escalate into the milder language of the chessboard—stalemate for battlelines, gambit for counterattack, that sort of thing—but wherever these modest efforts competed with the AP or other dispatches, the stronger language was chosen by the news editors. The *New York Times* and to a lesser but more cogent extent the New York *Herald Tribune* continued to give appreciable space to UN events.

In the rest of the nation, unless it was strikingly offbeat, a dispatch from Lake Success that did not deal with big power conflict often would not even get onto the wires out of New York, and when it did it would as often be ignored by the newspaper editors who received it. As for the East-West confrontations, as each day's proceedings began to sound and read like a rerun of yesterday's or last week's or last month's, editors began to shunt the story from the front to inside pages. What was even more discouraging was to suspect that the editors might simply be reacting to a more dismal truth, that after only two years the public at large just didn't care much anymore. This did not diminish my original faith in the virtues of the United Nations concept, but the suspicion that the people it was supposed to serve did not share that faith drained much of the excitement out of each day's journey to Lake Success.

All this was disenchanting. In fact, disenchantment was the word for how I'd come to feel not just about the UN assignment but about wire service work in general. Its requirements of brevity and speed over substance and the consequent intellectual sterility; the paucity of opportunities for advancement and, oh yes! the niggardly pay—all these presented a bleak horizon, bereft of promise. I felt badly about these feelings. The United Press had been good *to* me and working for it had been good *for* me. Excellent teachers there had forced me into the beneficial discipline of compression and concision, and many of them had become warm friends in the bargain. I had been handed assignments that many more experienced newsmen had reason to envy. Most of all, working for the Avis of wire services had taught me that trying harder can indeed make one better. This was nourishing to the confidence. But I saw no prospect of an interesting career with the organization. Instead, a powerful image was haunting me: I was like one of those Michelangelo figures (smaller in stature and stringier in musculature, of course) struggling to break out of its marble prison.

I didn't know it at the time, but someone was coming my way with a sculptor's mallet in one hand and a chisel in the other.

I had met Tom Griffith during the final month of my year at Harvard, when Louis Lyons assembled the first "reunion" of past Nieman Fellows. Tom had been a reporter and then assistant city editor of the *Seattle Times* when he won his Nieman Fellowship. After finishing his Nieman year Tom got hired by *Time* magazine. He rose fast to become one of the magazine's half-dozen senior editors. He and his wife, Caroline, introduced themselves and asked Maggie and me if we would recommend a class or two that might interest them. We invited them to join us for Ted Spencer's lecture. His subject that day was the poetry of T. S. Eliot; the Griffiths were as taken with Spencer's perform-   **119** ance as we. We had never heard Eliot's poetry read as it deserved to be, only Eliot himself diffidently and indistinctly uttering it on a scratchy 78 rpm recording. After class the four of us sat down together on the spring-green ground of Harvard Yard and got acquainted. For the rest of the morning we talked—about our not altogether dissimilar origins, our Harvard experiences, and mostly about the news trade. I was impressed by Tom Griffith. He displayed a keen grasp of national politics and international affairs, and his current job at *Time* had carried him far out into the rest of the intellectual planetary system as well. As a senior editor of what *Time* called "the back of the book," he surveyed the worlds of books, music, religion, education, science, and medicine. He was plainly a man happy in his work.

It was Tom Griffith who struck mallet against chisel, shortly after New Year's Day in 1949. He had been promoted to editor of National Affairs, the lead department of *Time,* and proposed to his superiors that they hire me for his stable of writers.

When the invitation came I hesitated. Henry Luce's *Time* had a Jekyll and Hyde reputation, to put it mildly. It paid well, attracted an impressive array of talent, lavished resources on its writers, editors, and researchers, encouraged the unconventional, and ventured into important subjects that the rest of journalism neglected or treated superficially. It was especially notable for its stringent protection of editorial employees from interference by people on the business side. This ideal, the "separation of church and state," was much-bruited but all too rarely practiced by newspapers and other magazines. On top of all its attractions for one so long constrained by "objectivity" was the magazine's outspokenness on matters great and small.

Then there was the Mr. Hyde side. *Time* and to a somewhat lesser extent its sister publications were notorious for their proprietor's fixed passions (particularly the sanctity of Chiang Kaishek's China abroad and of the Republican party at home and, considerably more widely shared by the American public, "everlasting condemnation" of the Soviet Union, Communism, and Communists). Add to that *Time*'s often reckless use of poetic license and assorted other excesses. Almost everybody in

the trade knew about the exchange several years before between two of the country's most famous editors. *Time*'s sister publication *Fortune* had published a far from favorable piece about *The New Yorker* and its editor, Harold Ross, described by *Fortune* as a "small man . . . furious . . . mad . . . no taste." Ross countered with a hilarious Wolcott Gibbs parody of *Time* and Harry Luce. Luce should have known better, but he formally complained to Ross about the article. In response, Ross wrote: "You are apparently unconscious of the notorious reputation *Time* and *Fortune* have for crassness in description, for cruelty and scandalmongering and insult." I imagined that Luce by now, the year 1949, possessed a fat file of such encomiums and perhaps had even learned to enjoy them.

For better or worse the case could be made that Luce's weekly newsmagazine was in the 1940s and 1950s the most influential single publication in America. Even those who disliked it and some who despised it read it as they cursed it. Politicians and other public figures who hated it obsequiously sought its favors. Television news was in its infancy. The *New York Times* plugged only into the New York–Washington corridor. The *Wall Street Journal* was then exceedingly parochial, appealing only to those with ties to the street for which it was named. The only serious pretender to being a country-wide journal was *Newsweek,* but it ran a distant, sloppy second to *Time* in reaching into the homes and offices of news-conscious Americans. *Time,* buttressed by the strong, sometimes shrill, sometimes cultured, sometimes crass voice of its sister magazine, *Life,* was in those years the closest thing to a national press America had.

Though there were many *cons* as well as *pros* to consider, the choice wasn't all that difficult. Up to then I had been a fitful reader of the magazine, but now I studied a batch of recent copies and found them to be right-minded on far more issues than wrong-headed. Luce's Republican party orientation was Eastern Liberal and anti-antediluvian, an aberration that a New Deal Democrat could almost understand. *Time* was anti-segregation, strong on civil rights in general, curious and mostly forward-thinking and refreshingly catholic in its approach to education, medicine, science, and the arts. Though its international stance and its alarums about Communist infiltration at home crescendoed sometimes into Dantean visions, I certainly **121** shared (as I surmised did most of the country) the magazine's concern about the aggressiveness and ambitions of Stalin's Soviet Union and I shared its support of United States policy of alliances to resist Communist expansion. I savored the prospect of being able to pronounce on the bizarre and the good things of life that escaped the attention of other journals. There was, I confess, a more frivolous reason: I wanted to meet the *Time* writer who had conceived and publicized in a National Affairs section story the founding of a Society for Putting Dots in Little Orphan Annie's Eyes.

The friends I consulted in my "New Deal liberal" circles surprised me by almost unanimously saying they thought the invitation was irresistible. Among others I sought the advice of Theodore H. White, whom I'd met in Paris where, with only a few francs to his name, he was struggling to complete *Fire in the Ashes,* his book about the postwar recovery of Europe. That feisty, hard-driving former newsboy from the Boston Jewish ghetto had broken with Luce over White's coverage of what was happening in postwar China, so I was both surprised and influenced by his advice.

Take the job, Teddy White insisted. You'll probably lose more editorial fights than you win, but the victories will be sweet and you'll meet a lot of interesting people.

By this time in our lives, Maggie and I had been struck by another strong compulsion toward change. Our efforts to have children had brought disappointment and sadness—several miscarriages in our first four years of marriage for which none of the specialists we consulted could find cause or cure. Then, in mid-February our first baby was born. David came three months prematurely in the maternity ward of New York Hospital. At first I wanted to let the doctors take charge of the oh, so tiny, so helpless! boy while I stayed to offer some assurance, even if unfounded, to Maggie. But at her urging I rode with our struggling newborn son in a screaming ambulance to the premature-baby center at St. Vincent's hospital in the Village, praying—truly praying—for the first time in the several years since I had "left the church." Two nuns hovered nearby to offer comfort while nurses and a doctor hooked up oxygen and

gently placed little more than two pounds of red, wrinkled will-to-live into the sterile tube- and wire-strung incubator that was to be David's only home. I returned to help Maggie from the hospital back to our East Thirty-fifth Street apartment, and we waited in what had become a place of darkness and gloom for the word we feared would come. The Mother Superior at St. Vincent's telephoned next afternoon, gently delivering (she had had much practice at this) the news that our son had died. "He is on the way to Heaven," was the way the Mother Superior put it. We shared a flow of tears and next morning made two big decisions. We would make contact with an adoption agency forthwith, and I would change jobs.

So on St. Patrick's Day in 1949, I became Tom Griffith's newest writer in *Time*'s National Affairs department.

Chapter 9

Joining the Group

This was the high-rent district, midtown Manhattan. Compared to the windowless factory setting of the United Nations pressroom or the funky, overcrowded United Press headquarters in the New York Daily News Building, working space at *Time* was glamorous. Another NA (for National Affairs) writer and I had to ourselves an entire room on the twenty-eighth floor of the Time-Life Building, overlooking the inner plaza of Rockefeller Center, a place of bustling outdoor cafés in summer and a circus-bright ice skating rink in winter. The famous Rainbow Room was just across the way, at the top of the RCA Building. St. Patrick's Cathedral was only a block distant just in case of emergency need for succor or penance.

A few staffers wandered in to look over the new boy. One of the more affluent confided that the fabled 21 Club was only three blocks away and he knew an underground way of reaching it on a rainy day without suffering more than a brief sprinkle. This was superfluous information, but it was nice to know that if ever I could afford to eat or drink at 21 I could get there without a raincoat or umbrella, thereby depriving the restaurant's insufferably haughty checkroom attendant of her exorbitant gratuity. A more somber tip came from another writer who after introducing himself pointed out that unlike some newer skyscrapers this building had windows that could be opened when, as I almost certainly would, I became so frustrated I contemplated jumping out.

The fellow I had been eager to meet, founder of the Society for Putting Dots in Little Orphan Annie's Eyes, had the office next door. Paul O'Neil had worked on the same Seattle newspaper as Tom Griffith and had come to New York after a stint as *Time*'s Pacific Northwest correspondent. He soon established himself as the most imaginative and entertaining writer on the magazine's staff, admired and sometimes envied by his peers for the wit, novelty, and style of his work. After a cursory but apparently approving examination O'Neil gave me the first of two succinct pieces of advice for achieving the knack of writing for *Time:* "Apply the tricks of fiction to fact." Lest I misunderstand, he put extra emphasis on the last word. The second came from Tom Griffith as I sat down to write my first piece: I must say good-bye to the traditional way of composing a news story, with the important facts first and the rest in descending order so that the story may be cut wherever space dictated. "Don't attempt the beginning until you know how and where you want the story to end," Griffith said. I was to find these pieces of advice extremely useful, though much more easily remembered than followed.

It quickly became apparent that working for *Time* was going to differ from working for a daily newspaper or wire service in more ways than I had imagined—more demanding, more challenging, more rewarding (intellectually as well as materially), but far more complex and, as I'd been duly warned, frequently more frustrating. Writing for the wires was impersonal, mechanical, sexless—a "cold" business; an audience was out there somewhere in the cosmos, one supposed, but it was a dumb beast, hardly ever heard from. In contrast, because many in *Time*'s audience made their reactions strongly (sometimes nastily) clear, we who worked there had reason to know that someone was actually reading our prose; writing for *Time* was "hot."*

---

*I am not using the late Marshall McLuhan's vocabulary as he intended it in his much-discussed if less-read best-seller *Understanding Media,* but that's fair be- **125**

There was first an audience close at hand whose response was immediate and frequently emphatic: a band of women researchers fiercely dedicated to digging up useful material and correcting factual errors (and occasionally trying to put their own spin on your story); senior editors who had the power to tamper freely with the writer's prose and overrule his interpretation of events, and frequently chose to do so; a managing editor and assistant MEs who could accept, alter, or reject what you and the senior editors had wrought. And then there was Henry Robinson Luce, who was still very much in charge of the magazine that he and his Yale classmate Briton Hadden had founded in 1923.

Luce was in frequent touch with higher editors and many of the veteran writers. To the newcomer he was a felt but mostly invisible presence. The relentless curiosity, business instinct, and sense of mission that made him one of the giants of world journalism now and then manifested themselves with a crisp "How about this?" scrawled onto a newspaper clipping or a brief memo about his recent meeting with a United States senator or a European foreign minister. These were usually addressed to the managing editor, Roy Alexander, or to a senior editor and filtered down through the editorial plumbing to a writer who might be familiar with the subject matter (and if not, was plainly being importuned to become so). A rookie writer had to rise higher in the editorial hierarchy before he would get more than a glimpse of Luce—something more than the sight of him, tall, kempt in gray suit and gray hat, preoccupied, striding across the lobby into the Rockefeller Center elevator whose operator had been instructed always to close the doors instantly and zoom Mr. Luce to his aerie on the top floor of the Time-Life Building. *Aerie* seemed the appropriate word because his features and his demeanor suggested a balding eagle brooding over the many cares of the era he had personally christened "the American Century." Christened was the right word, too. Luce, the Presbyterian son of China missionaries, took his religion

---

cause McLuhan used words to mean whatever he wanted them to mean. It was he, after all, who insisted that clarity of expression betrays absence of thought.

seriously; it was said that he wanted the privacy in order to pray during the ride to the thirty-third floor. I met no one who claimed to have seen evidence of this, though sometimes two or three passengers were already in the elevator, imprisoned for an unplanned ride to the top. Luce might—or might not—look up from the newspaper or other document he was reading and raise bushy eyebrows in a gesture that could be taken to mean "good morning"; the journey would continue in silence.

In fact, during those first few months Luce seemed less of a presence than another man, who wasn't even there. T. S. (for Thomas Stanley) Matthews had been *Time*'s managing editor for several years but was now on leave of absence in hopes of recovering from the blow of his wife's death from cancer. Matthews, a slender, handsome Princeton man, was the son of an Episcopal bishop and an heiress to the Procter and Gamble fortune. He was an anomaly, an editor of a highly politicized journal who had little if any interest in politics. He cared more about *how* a *Time* story was written than what it said. He had a talent for gem-cut description (a powerful union leader "was so tough that his spit bounced") and concise characterization of a place or event. In his tenure he had brought considerable literary talent into *Time*'s pages (James Agee, Robert Fitzgerald, Irving Howe, Louis Kronenberger, to name some), and he moved the magazine a long distance if not quite all the way from the backward-running smart-aleck hyphen-prone prose that had been so easily parodied in that *New Yorker* profile. Matthews was widely respected and had done much good for *Time*. His customary manner was distant, sometimes forbidding, and his comments on a manuscript returned to a writer for reworking could be cutting. "Most of our readers don't understand Choctaw. Try it in English." He was stingy with praise (a habit I came to respect and later tried to emulate because it made the praise all the more genuine and appreciated).

Matthews had already been away for some months when I went to work and there was talk in the corridors that he might never return, or if he did would wield far less authority. A political naïf was not necessarily the right man to command the Lucean flank of the cold war nor the mission to bring a Republican back to the White House. The man filling in for him, Roy

Alexander, seemed very confidently installed in the ME's chair, but his legacy was well instilled and the memory of Matthew's patrician stare and sharp pencil persisted. Alexander was a forceful, sometimes blunt editor in his own right. In appearance he was as different from Matthews as a longshoreman from an Arrow collar model. One could not know from his earthy manners and his appearance—a bulky frame, rosy round face, large hands, a Bert Lahr look-alike—that he was fluent in Greek and Latin and could be moved to tears by the first notes of a Puccini or Verdi aria. He was seasoned by years of work on the respected St. Louis *Post-Dispatch.* Several years as a gunnery sergeant in the pre–World War II U.S. Air Corps National Guard had made him a military buff; only the arrival of the first few of his seven children kept a St. Louis warplane manufacturer from letting him fly as a test pilot during the war.

The process by which the newsmagazine was produced each week was known as "group journalism." I grope for the best word to characterize its workings. Its champions might suggest *symbiosis* or *synergism,* but either is too benign a description. The word that comes closest is *syncretism,* the attempted reconciliation or union of different or opposing principles, practices, or parties. The word is generally applied to matters of philosophy or religion, but for me it suggests the interplay of tensions within tensions that fueled the *Time* editorial operation.

There was first of all ideological tension: many—probably a considerable majority—of *Time* writers, researchers, and senior editors were liberal in their politics and generally Democratic in the voting booths while a smaller but influentially placed contingent shared Luce's Republicanism and other enthusiasms and animosities, some more fiercely than the editor in chief himself. The virtue of this was that there were always writers and editors to willingly produce stories and sincerely espouse positions that might be anathema to others—and that went for any part of the ideological spectrum. There was hierarchical tension: Women on the staff resented being confined only to jobs as researchers, deprived of opportunity to rise to writing jobs. Writers chafed under the sometimes overbearing power of the senior editors, while the senior editors bore the scars of many scuffles with the editors above them and writers beneath

128

them, some of them lost, some of them won, some of them ended in compromises that satisfied neither party. There was tension between the news-gatherers of the Time-Life News Service's elaborate and lavishly financed network of nationwide and overseas bureaus and the people back in New York who chopped, pummeled, and sometimes transformed those correspondents' dispatches into the material that appeared in print. There was tension between the staffers who had come to the magazine from newspapers or other training in the rudiments of journalism and were generally literal in their approach to facts and on the other side those who had come in straight and callow from college or from thwarted careers as novelists or poets and to whom poetic license was an invitation to uninhibited invention. Less pertinent but certainly evident was the contrast—it did not quite qualify as tension—between the numerous prep-and-Ivy-League staffers (Yale, Harvard, and Princeton predominating) and those of us who'd come from more mundane backgrounds.

With all that potential for friction compressed into a small space, one might imagine the whole Time-Life Building going up in flames from spontaneous combustion. But, as we learn in elementary physics, friction properly harnessed produces energy that can make wheels go around. I believe the business school phrase for it is "creative tension." Somehow that is the way the tensions powered the clockwork that produced the newsmagazine that sent out each week to several million readers its cocksure profile of the state of the world and arch comment on the foibles of the world's inhabitants.

The coterie of writers in the National Affairs section offered a case in point. When it came to backgrounds, save for the absence of a New York Italian, a Chicago Pole, and a Nisei or a Sioux, the bunch of us might have been assembled by central casting for a World War II movie platoon. As senior editor in charge, Tom Griffith with a round owlish face behind spectacles did not exactly fit Hollywood's conception of a platoon commander. But Griff's sharp mind, deep perception, gentle manners, and deep reservoir of tact made him an excellent leader. The oldest of us writers was Duncan Norton-Taylor, who came to *Time* from New Jersey by way of Brown University and a **129**

stint of writing for Street and Smith penny-a-word pulp magazines. He produced his crisp, workmanlike prose with such efficiency he was suspected of owning a magic self-starting Underwood typewriter that he secreted away every night. He was a
small, courtly man who viewed with amused tolerance our refusal to share his Taft Republicanism; his ambition once he
shed the travail of journalism was to write a biography of John
Calvin.

A. T. (Bobby) Baker was a Princeton man, a bright and
handsome descendant of faded wealth and a relative of the
memorable Princeton athlete and Scott Fitzgeraldean sort of
character whom *Time* frequently referred to in its sports section
as "the late, great Hobey Baker." He wrote gracefully and
could recite the works of a multitude of poets by heart. His
good friend Edward Cerf, the other Princeton man among us,
once said admiringly of Baker, "He's gone through snobbery
and come out the right end."

Cerf, a native of Portland, Oregon, was a tousled, ruggedly
good-looking fellow with a ready smile or quip and a knack for
cogent prose and candid speech. He had not been much harmed
by his exposure to the effete East; combat service in the U.S.
Marines had ripped the Ivy League leather elbow patches off his
personality while gentling his manners toward his fellow men
and women (this special capacity for gentleness, almost a sweet-
ness, I have observed in many of the civilians I've met who
served during the war in that roughest—some would say most
brutal—of the armed services).*

Louis Banks, who joined us some months after I arrived,
came to New York from California by way of UCLA, Hearst's
Los Angeles Examiner, and *Time*'s Los Angeles and Washington bureaus; he was the second among us who was pro-
nouncedly Republican in his political preference though by
Dunc Taylor's measurement he'd been severely tainted with the
debilitating "me-tooism" that distinguished East Coast Repub-

---

*Unfortunately, Ed was not gentle to himself. Transferred against his will to a
job on *Life* that was important but distasteful to him, and haunted by demons that
even close friends did not suspect, he took up his U.S. Marines service revolver
early one spring morning in 1959 and killed himself.

licans; others of us saw modest hope for his full conversion to our kind of wisdom.

Among the political neutrals, Joe David Brown from the southeastern Alabama town of Dothan, with a large head of curly hair to go with a sturdy frame and a voice flavored with molasses, was the requisite southerner; he'd already written one novel that won good reviews, satisfying sales, and conversion into a movie, and planned to write others after an interval at *Time*.

The Jewish player was Gilbert Millstein, a sometimes bouncy, sometimes moody New Yorker whose mind could vault nimbly from the works of Rimbaud or Firbank to Jack Kerouac and the Beats, then to the latest tale of rascality in New York city hall.

And there was Paul O'Neil, tall and aspen-thin, who would rather be on a trout stream than in a Manhattan skyscraper, quiet and usually as droll in his speech as in his writing. He was one of those on the staff who wanted to be writers only, with no desire to "rise" to senior editor or higher in the hierarchy. One of the first documents I was handed after joining this talented crew was a copy of a memorandum O'Neil had written to top management urging that writers at *Time* be accorded the same monetary rewards and degree of recognition and promotions that traditionally went only to those willing to clamber up the competitive ladder to senior editor rank and perhaps higher. Here are some fragments from a memo that was passed from hand to hand as an in-house classic:

> Allow me to strike a chord or so on my splintered mandolin, and sing a few stanzas about that nervous gladiator, the *Time* writer. The world knows little about him, and what it knows is generally incorrect. It is true that somebody from Corporate sometimes grabs one of him, like the owner of a mink farm seizing a prime breeder, and holds him up to the pink window of the Publisher's Letter for the readers to see. But he is always equipped with a toupee and a thick coat of panchromatic makeup, and the world is given the impression that he just got back from Yucatan with a tan, and is going off to see Churchill as soon as he has lunch with Lana Turner at the Stork Club. . . .

131

Actually he is an anxious looking fellow with thinning hair, whose stomach has assumed the knobby rigidity of a Mexican gourd from eating too much Union News food and from years of staring at the never-ending piles of research, clippings, paper clips, unsharpened pencils and old copies of government reports which fill his inbox. His shoes are often unshined, and at times, when he is in the throes, his shirts look as if they had just been done wet-wash in a Mixmaster. He spends his days crouching in the blue-tinted horror of his writing hatch, like an incorrigible in solitary, fumbling with paper and hating himself. Occasionally he swallows a pill, occasionally he glares wildly out the window. But . . . like the club fighter whose work consists of getting his ears scrambled once a fortnight at St. Nicholas Arena, the *Time* writer has his points. He is durable and cunning, and though he will probably never win the championship himself, he can, in his better moments, make the top men in his trade clinch and hold on for dear life.

. . . As a writer he must be able to produce at least the illusion of literary quality, but no craftsman has been given so small a space in which to do his stuff. He is a kind of word mechanic who must yank odd-shaped chunks of raw fact off the overhead belt, trim them to size (often with his teeth), assemble his jigsaw of conflicting information into something with a beginning, a middle and an end, bolt the whole together with adjectives, and send it off through the hopper, glittering, polished and blushing with jeweler's rouge. . . .

No overstatement there. There has never been a clearer description of the *Time* writers' weekly ordeal, endured in the knowledge that, no matter how golden, his prose would be cloaked in anonymity. It was comforting to discover that even the peerless O'Neil found it as tough a task as did the rest of us and so, I imagined, did Dunc Taylor, for all the seeming ease with which his words flowed out of the magic typewriter.

We were an amiable crew, respectful of each other's views and work. We traded tips, puns, friendly insults. On the long Saturdays and Sundays when we labored well into the night, several of us usually took lunch and dinner breaks together, frequently with more than one martini or old-fashioned to clothe the fatigue or lubricate the tongue. After the magazine went to press on Monday if it wasn't gruesomely late some of us would make time for a nightcap at one of the numerous watering places in the vicinity of Rockefeller Center. We of course strove for the approval of editors above us, the benediction of the powers-that-be, and the rapt attention of *Time*'s vast readership, but what each of us most sought was the admiration of Tom Griffith and our fellow NA writers. It usually came, when it did, in the form of sarcasm or japery. And if one had descended into preciousness—"the sound of tholepins in the night"—or pomposity—"common prudence dictates"—his punishment was a fusillade of jibes. We were proud of our output, proud to the point of arrogance, even likening ourselves to the Murderers' Row batting lineup, Ruth, Gehrig and Company of "the late, great New York Yankees."

When it came to writing assignments, most of us were utility players, taking on whatever subjects the flow of events brought our way, though Millstein and Brown gravitated toward human interest material and O'Neil in particular had a talent for avoiding the complicated political or legislative stories while securing for himself the more poetic or zany events, such as the hapless fellow who aimed a .22 rifle at a crow on a fencepost and hit a fireworks factory instead, thereby blowing up a considerable tract of New Jersey. One of the least attractive assignments was a roundup of the week's activities in the U.S. Congress, a task O'Neil had always avoided. At last Griffith was prevailed upon to throw that unwanted weekly chore O'Neil's way. The major event that week was the appearance of Secretary of State Dean Acheson before the Senate Foreign Relations Committee. Unpopular on the Hill because of his ducal demeanor and unfairly assailed by some (alas, with the Luce publications in the forefront) as one of those who had "lost China" to Communism, Acheson as usual engaged in a hostile confrontation with the senators. O'Neil's recapitulation began something like this:

> If by some act of God or nature members of the U.S. Senate's Foreign Relations committee were transmogrified into dogs, Chairman Tom Connally of Texas would be a St. Bernard, Senator George of Georgia would be a golden retriever, Senator Green of Rhode Island would be a barkless basenji, Senator

Vandenbergh of Michigan would be a German shepherd, Senator Alexander Wiley of Wisconsin would be a doberman pinscher—and Secretary of State Dean Acheson would be a cat.

Having seduced the reader into his tent and subtly encouraged sympathy for the embattled secretary of state, O'Neil then related in a few crisp paragraphs what the confrontation had been about and finished with a brief account of other matters that had preoccupied the House and the Senate during that week. It is as good an application as I can remember of O'Neil's prescription for a *Time* story—apply the tricks of fiction to fact.

We seized on all opportunities for badinage and light relief because the work was sometimes demanding to the point of exhaustion and, more pertinently, because to write in the National Affairs section for *Time* in those years—the late 1940s and early 1950s—was to be caught in a painful conflict between how we liberals saw certain crucial matters and how Luce, his managing editor Roy Alexander, and those on the staff who shared (or said they did) Luce's strong views saw them. The opportunity for outspokenness that had attracted me to *Time* was gratifying when it was aimed in the right directions, as it often was. It was satisfying to be able to speak out against racists like Senator Bilbo or Congressman Rankin of Mississippi or write stories espousing the cause of racial integration. Or to compose a lengthy (for *Time*) treatise on "the ten worst U.S. senators," half of them Republicans and all of them fair game for ridicule. Or to write scornfully about the activities of "demagogue" Joseph McCarthy and the feculent activities of his deputy character assassins, Roy Cohn and David Schine.

But *Time* was speaking out on many other matters as well. The magazine had arrogated to itself a frontline battlefield role in the cold war abroad and a Savonarolan role at home to thwart the efforts of Communists and their "dupes" to subvert America from within. This positioned our National Affairs section right in the line of fire or, as Tom Griffith once described it, in "the bloody angle." For example, Luce and hard-liners like managing editor Alexander, the aggressively conservative senior editor Max Ways, and perhaps even deputy managing editor Otto Fuerbringer, who played with seeming relish the Black

134

Hat or what the Hindus call the "budmash" (but in contemporary terms is best described as the Darth Vader role) in the *Time* hierarchy, shared the revulsion most of us felt toward Joe McCarthy and his campaign of villification and character assassination. But their revulsion was diluted when it came to some of McCarthy's intended victims, among them Dean Acheson, dedicated career foreign service figures like John Service, John Paton Davies, and John Carter Vincent, the Asian scholar Owen Lattimore, even that great and selfless patriot George Marshall. All of them, in our superiors' mistaken view, somehow engineered the "loss" of China to Communism and therefore had earned at least some of the abuse McCarthy was heaping upon them, or if not McCarthy's, abuse of some sort.

Our response to this sort of problem was devised and staunchly defended by Griffith. We would not attempt to write against the grain of higher-ranking opinion only to have our work rewritten from above or tossed into the wastebasket. Instead, we would be so rigorous, precise, and credible in our assemblage of facts that a story could not be seriously altered without unraveling the entire garment. In his years of newspapering at the St. Louis *Post-Dispatch,* Roy Alexander had grown up with this kind of reporting so he often could be persuaded, though not without misgivings and grumblings, to let the stories stand. This didn't keep the magazine from assaulting these assorted characters but the blows had to be struck elsewhere, usually in Max Ways's Foreign News section or an editorial in *Life.* In instances when the high command's animus was too strong to be denied, a trumpet solo would blare from the balcony in the form of a specially written and prominently positioned "sidebar" or "essay" that would rise above the simple facts to tell the reader what it all "really means."

Such was the case after President Truman fired General Douglas MacArthur for insubordination during the Korean war and the general's champions rose up in wrath. The firing was welcomed by most of us in NA (especially ex-Marine Cerf), but our stories of the event and the subsequent uproar were meticulously even-handed. To achieve this was especially taxing during the long and complex congressional hearings that took place after the general returned to address a joint session of the 135

Congress and to ride in a triumphal parade along Fifth Avenue before a crowd whose size MacArthur fans so exaggerated that the New York *Herald Tribune,* though sympathetic to the general, felt obliged to calculate that if this figure were true, there would have been eight or more people standing in every square foot of available space along the parade route.

However one felt about Harry Truman or Douglas MacArthur, it was a great American drama. Our reports of the hearings were written and then edited by Tom Griffith with a meticulousness that must have been maddening to Roy Alexander and even more so to his chief deputy Fuerbringer. But thanks to Griff's shuttling back and forth between his and Roy's office to defend them, our versions of the hearings made their way into the magazine substantially intact. Lest *Time* readers be deprived of the true meaning, however, there issued from Max Ways's typewriter a veritable Sousa march of indignant explanation: The firing of the great MacArthur was the worst blunder by a leader in American history, something that might be perceived in history's disaster file as equivalent, say, to Napoleon's invasion of Russia (this example of the essay's hyperbole is my own but correctly reflects the sense of the unfindable original) and it surely "brings World War III closer." To put an exclamation point to this homage to MacArthur, Luce made an emotional call on the defrocked general at his new HQ in the Waldorf Astoria and soon thereafter handed him one million dollars for the rights to publish his memoirs in *Life.*

Fortunately, there were few internal collisions as trying as the MacArthur drama. But we periodically found it necessary to use the same painstaking "just the facts, ma'am" tactics in instances where we felt constrained to prevent or blunt distortion or illegitimate bias (as contrasting with our own balanced and, of course, legitimate outspokenness) in a *Time* presentation. Now and then we even won. There were occasional instances, like *Time*'s shameful treatment of the scholar Owen Lattimore and the nuclear physicist Robert Oppenheimer for their presumed unpatriotic sympathies, where we lost outright. (Those particular transgressions, I should note, came after Griffith's and my own tenure in the National Affairs section.) Most often we came away with the sense of having achieved acceptable compromise and with integrity intact if sometimes bruised. These things mattered. We cared. That is what made *Time* such a demanding yet engaging kind of place to practice journalism.

As I rose in rank and came to know Henry Luce, at his frequent editorial lunches in *Time*'s private dining room or in occasional face-to-face meetings or exchanges of memos, I came to realize that he knowingly invited this kind of trouble for himself. He knew he couldn't find the kind of talent he wanted by seeking out only Pavlovian writers, conformists-for-hire. He seemed in fact to be uncomfortable with apostates and sycophants, those who without variation aped his thinking, though he certainly kept a few around, some of them in power positions. He respected independence and outspokenness, but there was one important thing to remember: Henry Luce was editor in chief; *Time* was his magazine. "I am the boss," he once told his assembled staff, in case we didn't already know it. If you didn't like that, work somewhere else or go start your own magazine.

Since I often fantasized the feats of journalism I would accomplish and the wisdom I was prepared to shower on my fellowman if I ran a magazine like *Time,* I found Luce's position unsurprising. After all, it was practiced in varying degrees by every press lord I'd ever heard about. Lacking the means to have my own newspaper or magazine and unaware of one that could offer employment as intriguing and as adventurous, and believing also that Emerson was correct in that essay on Compensation I'd been forced by Tom Hutton to study years before—that for something good there is inevitably a quantity of bad—I found the weekly *Sturm und Drang* an acceptable price to pay for getting to write or edit material I was proud of. The objective was to come away each week with the conviction that I had added something useful to the stream of information and had done so without writing anything I knew or suspected to be untrue or unfair. (At the end of my eleven years of writing, editing, and reporting for *Time* I felt on tough self-examination that I could say—can say—that all that I did in that time had met that test.)

In doing it, however, I managed to offend some colleagues. In   **137** those earlier tense, sometimes feverish moments of disagreement I apparently conveyed by word or gesture that I felt those writers or editors with the opposing point of view were pro forma mere mercenaries, not sincere in their convictions as I was in mine. This was an obnoxious trait that deserved comeuppance. Fortunately, I got it from one of those I'd insulted in the form of a subtle note tucked into my typewriter: "When are you going to stop being so fucking self-righteous?" Me self-righteous? "You mean you didn't know?" said Ed Cerf after I showed him the note.

I apologized to the note-writer for my unintended sanctimony. This called for some rethinking, as well as an immediate improvement in demeanor. There *were* some trimmers who cut their cloth to fit what they thought Alexander or Fuerbringer or Luce himself wanted; there were others with such overpowering family responsibilities and no financial safety net beneath them who swallowed hard and perhaps now and then bent their principles; and there were others of strongly liberal political convictions who took refuge in nonpolitical back-of-the-book redoubts like the Music, Science, Books, or People sections from which they could lob aspersions at those of us in "the bloody angle."

I came, though, to see and accept that some of the most important of the hard-liners, among them Alexander, Max Ways, Dunc Taylor, with whom I so strenuously disagreed were as sincere in their positions as I in mine. That did not mean condoning sometimes blatant notions as to what constituted fair and proper juxtaposition of facts and fancy. Still, I came to accept that however misguided I might think them to be, they deserved to be credited with believing in their politics as surely as my compatriots and I in ours. This was not an easy concession to make, but if it was a compromise I felt no guilt in making it—and less like the prig I was on the verge of becoming.

Max Ways was an interesting case. He was a large man with shaggy hair, a diffident manner of dress, and the wrinkled brow of a person perpetually preoccupied. He could be amiable in rare moments of small talk, but he was fierce in his politics. I believe his father had worked with Mencken at the Baltimore **138** *Sun* and Max got his own training on the same paper when

Mencken was still in evidence there. I disagreed with him, as did many of us, on just about every political or sociological matter that arose in those days—whether it be his interpretation of the Gnostic heresy (about A.D. 100–300), his to-me laughable proposal, since put into practice, for turning over the U.S. Postal Service to private enterprise, his apparent belief that there was really a credible threat of Communist "subversion" of American policy and enslavement of America itself. And he was one of those who wasn't above tailoring or disregarding facts to make his argument. Some saw Ways as a sort of Rasputin to Luce's Nicholas II, but I felt this to be a very long reach; Luce didn't need a monk whispering into his ear.

As I got to know him I found Max to be a charming and friendly person with a singular and obstinate mind. We were antagonists, yes, yet I enjoyed sipping a drink with him once in a while and listening to anecdotes of those Menckenesque Baltimore newspaper days. Maggie, Ways's wife, Connie, and I spent a few delightful afternoons at Belmont racetrack with Max as handicapping instructor. It was he who introduced us to an aged sprinter with wild eyes, a severe breathing problem, and a heart as big as a basketball named Jamie K, who failed only twice in more than twenty outings to provide Maggie and me with tickets to cash. The odds were invariably good because Jamie K when viewed in the paddock seemed so obviously at death's door that most bettors thought his previous win was certainly his last. It made me feel that it would be fun to own a Jamie K someday, preferably a younger and healthier one.

Those occasional afternoons on the playing field did nothing, though, to diminish the professional collisions on the battlefield, so I was appalled one day early in 1952 to learn that that Luce and Alexander had decided to reverse the two major senior editors, Ways to Griffith's job as National Affairs editor and Griffith to Ways's job as Foreign News editor. There was an all too obvious explanation.

It had been twenty years since a Republican had occupied the White House. This was the year that Americans could change all that—with a mighty nudge from Henry R. Luce and his magazines. Luce was realigning his troops for an all-or-nothing assault to help his kind of Republican win first the GOP nomi- **139** nation and then the presidency for General Dwight D. Eisenhower. *Time*'s National Affairs section was to be one of Ike's big megaphones. I had hardly begun to ponder what drastic move I might need to make in order to avoid staying in National Affairs when I was invited to join Griff. I happily moved my gear and my conscience upstairs into the Foreign News section, one floor above but not entirely away from the journalistic carnage to come.

The hassles were fewer and farther between in Foreign News, especially with the foreplay of the presidential election year to preoccupy the high command, but the change of assignments didn't take me out of domestic politics after all. *Time* always sent many more bodies than it needed to cover the national political conventions, so I went to Chicago that summer as a supernumary reporter at both conventions. First came the Republican, where the magazine made a spectacularly partisan effort to pin the "theft" of Texas Republican delegates on Senator Robert Taft and thereby assure Eisenhower's nomination. Then the Democratic, where the reluctant front-runner for the nomination was the Illinois governor, Adlai Stevenson. I'd had a fleeting acquaintance with Stevenson when he appeared at the United Nations as a member of the big U.S. delegation at General Assembly meetings. He served mostly in lesser committee debates, but with an eloquence and wit that made many wish that someone as effective as he were chief of the American delegation. Now I was assigned to help cover Stevenson's convention headquarters and had opportunity to watch him under pressure. I also got to meet several of the young, dedicated people who were helping the governor assemble a campaign organization. Like so many Democrats of my persuasion, I was excited by Stevenson's nomination and his magnificent acceptance speech. He seemed just the fellow to take on the inarticulate general whom the Republicans and some of the best Madison Avenue talent that money could buy had just lifted onto a white horse.

Shortly after the convention I got a call from another UN acquaintance. Porter McKeever had been press spokesman for the U.S. delegation at Lake Success. There he had become a friend of Stevenson. Now McKeever had been conscripted into a small group led by a smart Midwestern lawyer and Stevenson friend named George W. Ball to form an organization outside the regular Democratic party machinery to attract independents and Republicans to Stevenson. Would I come out to Springfield, Illinois, posthaste and go to work for the Volunteers for Stevenson? The call could not have come at a better time; for a Democrat *Time* was going to be an unpleasant place to work until the election was over. A disinterested appraiser might call it an invitation to a cop-out. I saw it as an opportunity. It could be fascinating to see a presidential election campaign from inside, especially one waged by a man as intelligent and eloquent as Adlai Stevenson.

Chapter 10

The People Speak

Roy Alexander agreed ever so cheerfully to grant me a leave of absence. I was pleased, but a bit disturbed that he would so readily dispense with my services. An employee far more valuable to the company also got leave to join the Stevenson campaign. He was Eric Hodgins, a former publisher and managing editor and by then a principal writer for *Fortune* magazine and author of an amusing best-seller (later a Cary Grant–Myrna Loy movie) called *Mr. Blandings Builds His Dream House.* Without benefit of inquiry I arrived at a simple explanation. Luce had already consigned to the Eisenhower campaign's inner circle two of his major employees, a key vice-president, C. D. Jackson, and one of Luce's most favored writers and resident intellectual, the precocious Emmet John Hughes. These moves had attracted considerable publicity in the trade. Now, with two of its hirelings going to work for the Stevenson camp, the company could demonstrate a gesture of evenhandedness to critics of Time Inc.'s naked marriage of journalism to partisan politics. Of course, the prospect of Manning working to defeat Eisenhower caused not the slightest fear in the *Time* hierarchy. With good reason. The company's gift to the Republicans did far more for their candidate than did its contribution to the Democrats. This was especially true in the case of Emmett

Hughes, who conceived and wrote Ike's vote-clinching speech promising that he'd go to Korea and end the bloody war there. More than any factor in the campaign (except for an incoherent but widespread American desire for "a change" in Washington), that speech induced the Eisenhower victory. In contrast, while I cannot speak for Hodgins, my contributions to the Stevenson campaign were, to put the best possible light on them, minimal.

In family terms it was not the best time to go traveling about. Our contact with an an adoption agency had been a dramatic success and our first son, Richard, had just reached his second birthday. We had moved to the suburbs, a charming Cape Cod clone in the village of Port Washington, Long Island, to accommodate what we were confident would be a larger family. In fact the second child was on the way and the obstetrician who'd encouraged us to adopt Rick was predicting confidently that he would be Rick's healthy younger brother. Maggie stoically kept to herself whatever concerns she probably had about my setting out on a mission of such doubtful prospect at that moment, and I, selfishly, accepted her loyalty as approval.

First came a sudden trip to San Francisco as a last-minute substitute for a Volunteers for Stevenson fund-raiser, a lawyer with high-powered business connections who was supposed to tap some wealthy would-be contributors. Struck down by flu, he turned over to me the suite he'd reserved at the Fairmont Hotel and a list of six prospective fat-cat contributors. I cajoled a $1,000 check out of a shipping magnate who'd been targeted for $100,000 and got nothing but vague promises from the three others whose receptionists allowed me to see them. Two did not return my calls. The hotel suite and airline tickets must have devoured all or most of the contribution. This failure bothered me, but not enough to cancel out the pleasure of visiting San Francisco for the first time. On my return to Springfield I was relieved to encounter no criticism, just a "Don't worry about it; better luck next time" attitude. This, I came to realize, was symptomatic of the loosely woven fabric of the Volunteers for Stevenson, a movement made up mostly of well-intentioned persons with excellent social credentials but not much political sophistication. Our organization was little regarded if not dis- **143** dained by Democratic party regulars in the areas where it became active.

This gap between the Volunteers amateurs and political pros became particularly evident when in Boston I was commissioned to arrange some seats for local Volunteers at the head table for a Stevenson luncheon appearance. The city and its environs were plastered with placards and huge billboards urging voters to support DEVER for GOVERNOR and KENNEDY for U.S. SENATE. Smaller letters, squeezed in like an afterthought, recommended Stevenson for President. Just in case.

I was directed to a diffident, battle-scarred Democratic pol with the requisite florid complexion and an American Legion pin in his buttonhole. He tried to suppress his laughter as I ticked off the names of a few Cambridge academicians and North Shore matrons who deserved seats of honor at the head table, but the shaking of his big belly as he savored this humorous proposal gave him away. The faces that beamed at the crowd from the head table on the appointed day were to a man—and one woman—all of either pronounced Hibernian caste or, in lesser numbers, the Neapolitan or Sicilian, in short, the visages of seasoned Boston and State House Democratic leaders, precinct captains, and party faithful. The closest the $25- or $50-per-ticket representatives of the Volunteers got to Candidate Stevenson was about twenty yards toward the rear of the giant ballroom, their view restricted by a pillar and several potted palms. That night the well-heeled Paul Dever and John F. Kennedy forces did stage a rally for Stevenson (and themselves) at Boston's old Mechanics Hall. The rally was a rousing, morale-raising rafter buster, but several of us pulled out of South Station on the campaign train with the distinct impression that Massachusetts pols did not give our candidate much of a chance to beat Eisenhower. Inspired by Stevenson's pledge to "talk sense to the American people" and by the elevated rhetoric and good humor with which he was doing so, I could not share such pessimism.

This was becoming embarrassing, though. I'd met many interesting people and seen a great deal of America by means of the campaign's chartered American Airlines plane and the railroad whistle-stop rambles, but so far I'd contributed very little to the campaign. All the unproductive traveling was not sitting well back home in Port Washington either. Maggie had tolerated my decision to join the campaign, but as her pregnancy progressed she was increasingly unhappy about being deserted for several weeks, especially since she thought the mission well-meant but Quixotic in the extreme. She admired Stevenson and what he stood for but was inclined to feel like those Boston pols, that he was not tough enough to win.

Then came an invitation to the headquarters of "the Elks Club group." Packed into one large and three small rooms rented from the Springfield chapter of The Benevolent and Protective Order of Elks was a dazzling array of intellect and literary talent that had been assembled to provide Stevenson with high-protein position papers and speech drafts. The only member of the group I'd met before was Arthur Schlesinger, Jr., now established as perhaps the most eloquent exponent of American liberalism. He had organized the group at Stevenson's request and was its intellectual straw boss, a most persuasive one.

Most of the others held impressive credentials too. They were all young, politically literate, and desirous of liberalizing Adlai Stevenson's sometimes conservative tendencies. They were united in their belief that an Eisenhower presidency would be bad for the country, with the General merely occupying the White House while Senator Robert Taft and his fellow conservatives dominated policy-making. This writing team included among others the wise and jocular Eric Hodgins from *Fortune;* John Kenneth Galbraith, the towering (in more ways than one) Harvard economist; David Bell, a bright young White House aide on loan from President Truman; John Fischer, editor in chief of *Harper's Magazine;* John Bartlow Martin, one of the best free-lance journalists then alive; Willard Wirtz, a taciturn Northwestern law professor and, at forty, the oldster of the group; David L. Cohn, a bright and charming Mississipian who was only half-joking when he championed the legalization of dueling as a means of reintroducing civility into American society.

There were even better-known figures who contributed occasionally to the Elks Club output, either sending in material from afar or wandering into Springfield now and then to lend a **145**

hand. Among them were Bernard De Voto, historian, columnist, and leading expert on the virtues of the dry martini; the
poet and playwright Archibald MacLeish, playwright Robert
E. Sherwood, and even FDR's noted speech writer Samuel Ros-
enman. The resident Elks Club crew did the high-pressure work
of churning out the final drafts of the major speeches and most
secondary ones. They sent them on to Carl McGowan, Stevenson's sternly protective lieutenant, for preliminary vetting.
Then they went to the candidate himself, sometimes only an
hour or so before speech time. Stevenson almost invariably
worked them over to fit his own rhythm and speech habits—
usually (but not always) improving them but at the expense of
too much precious time, even to the point of delaying the texts
too late for good press coverage. "Adlai would rather write
than be president," his friend George Ball once quipped.

"This is more like it!" I thought as I walked into the upstairs
quarters of the Elks Club group. They labored in a shamble of
rented typewriters, tables, and desks and towering piles of government reports, statistical abstracts, and other reference materials. The place was smaller than the old Binghamton *Press*
newsroom but reminiscent of it in its sounds and confusion.
Jack Fischer introduced himself. He looked more frazzled and
less serene than I'd expected the august editor of *Harper's* to be.
He was then serving as a desk editor for the speechwriting-in-
progress, a function usually performed by Dave Bell. But Bell
had fallen ill from overwork. Fischer told me why I was there: a
combination of simple fatigue and a raging stomach bug had
felled most of the Elks Club group and there was urgent need of
help to prepare a string of short rear-platform remarks for Governor Stevenson's "whistle-stops" as the campaign train wound
its way about the northeast between major big city speeches.
Fischer pointed to a desk and handed me some folders of "field
research" on some small towns in Pennsylvania and Maryland.
Provided by the minions of the Democratic National Committee, these described the various communities at which the campaign train would briefly stop—history, geography, population, principal sources of employment, ethnic makeup, and
special characteristics or enthusiasms—e.g. "the people of Hag-
146   erstown (or Gaithersburg or somewhere, I can't remember

which) are nuts about baseball." Fischer put me in charge of
five or six whistle stops. The instructions were: Keep them
brief—about three minutes, no more than five, for each stop—
and try to convey that the candidate knows something about
each town's needs or concerns. This wasn't exactly an opportunity to articulate a major new global foreign policy or to put
into Adlai Stevenson's mouth some proposal as brilliantly vote-
gathering as Eisenhower's "I shall go to Korea," but it was for a
change an assignment I felt I could handle. And it was a privilege to be associated even so tenuously with the high-powered
Elks Club group.

For a day and most of a night I labored over the "whistle-
stop" drafts. The prose was mostly straightforward and unmemorable, so unmemorable that I can vaguely remember only
one passage. It cited the tendency of Republicans to refuse to
see or to allocate the funds to further American foreign policy
interests and to their willingness to gamble instead that world
affairs would work themselves out without foreign entangle-
ments—"a truly dangerous form of isolationism," I wrote,
"that might be called 'Blinkers to Nevers to Chance.' " That
clever reference to baseball's great double-play combo ought to
wow those baseball nuts in Hagerstown! I thought, and passed
the draft to Jack Fischer. Fischer groaned as he slashed the
smart-aleck passage from the manuscript. The candidate had
promised to talk sense to the American people, he said, not
*non*sense. To my relief, Fischer found the rest of the texts satisfactory, given the pressure of time, and I went off with them to
rejoin the campaign train at Pittsburgh.

The campaign train and an almost full load of press, campaign staff, and celebrities (including Humphrey Bogart and
Lauren Bacall) and the briefcaseful of speeches took off on
schedule to wind its way back to New York—but, alas, without
the candidate.

Prison rioters at the the State Penitentiary at Menard in
southern Illinois had taken seven guards hostage and were
threatening to kill them if their demands for prison reform were
not met. As governor, Stevenson decided that he had to go to
the scene, even if it wiped out his last campaign appearances in
the vital East. The candidateless train made its appointed **147**

rounds. Senator William Fulbright was drafted to appear at each stop in Stevenson's stead. He rejected the prepared texts and delivered a few remarks in a distracted Arkansas drawl. The small crowds received them in similar dispiritedness. No one was more dispirited than I as I contemplated the untouched manila folder containing the entire output of my career as speech writer for a would-be president—words unspoken, unheard, unread, not even dust for the ashbin of history.

Stevenson rejoined his troops in New York for his last appeal to the East Coast. As the train trundled back to Illinois, with brief stops through Ohio and Indiana for rear-platform speeches (none of them mine), we were swept by a collective euphoria. Yes, it had been a clumsy, badly organized campaign with more downs than ups, but the ups had been glorious, high and in some instances thrilling moments in the history of American election campaigns. The odds were daunting, the "one-party press" (though not its reporters) was widely behind Eisenhower. Against all this, almost everybody aboard that train shared a feeling that Stevenson was going to win. Privileged visitors to the candidate himself in the isolation of his private Pullman car reported that he was predicting as many as 350 or more electoral votes for himself.

I have never been able since to account for that euphoria. It lasted among most of us until Election Day itself. Then, early that morning, long before the first voting results seeped in, reality struck like a schoolteacher's sharp rap on the head. Wake up, dummy! We had let our wishes rule our reason. We'd played parts in a campaign we could all be proud of, even write about in years to come, but now that all the shouting was over it was suddenly, painfully clear that Adlai Stevenson didn't have a chance against the war hero who had thrown a fatherly arm about the country's electorate, comforted Americans when they wanted to be comforted not challenged, and who, in spite of his occasional bumbling, had given Americans a complacent feeling that he would lead them without bothering them.

That night in the tacky ballroom of the Springfield's tacky Leland Hotel the buffet lay wilting, virtually untouched but the bar was swamped and bartenders sweated as the crowd pressed

148 together for the last words of the campaign. Stevenson walked in somberly and stepped to the microphone, a piece of paper in one hand. "No, no!" several people shouted. Stevenson waved for silence and began his concession speech. "No, no!" came the shouts again and then receded as he read his gracious telegram to President-elect Eisenhower and thanked the 27 million Americans who had voted for him (against nearly 34 million for Ike), then turned to thank us who had worked for him. He ended with a story that was appropriate for Lincoln country and very Stevensonian too—about the time Abraham Lincoln was asked how he felt after losing an election. "He said he felt like a little boy who had stubbed his toe in the dark. He said that he was too old to cry but it hurt too much to laugh."

That was how we all felt at that moment, teary-eyed and sad, not a little vexed with the American electorate and not ready to admit that our own efforts, including the candidate's, may have been at fault.

Had we mattered very much? Overall, I felt, the Volunteers made more of a contribution than I have here credited, I among them. Once committed, most of the people we reached out to stayed committed, unlike many of the Democratic party organizations around the country that gave only token support and the tens of thousands of regular Democrats who deserted to Eisenhower. There were many campaign stops where our work gave independents and undecided Republican voters opportunity to see, hear, and contribute to the Stevenson campaign, and on many occasions we were able to arrange for them to be better appreciated than in Boston. I had even managed to write a couple of useful speeches, not for the candidate, though, but for George Ball. They were well received by him, by his audience, and by many members of the press, and helped to seal a friendship with Ball that was to bring us together often in the future.

Many of us drank too much and stayed up too late that final night; we needed a proper Irish-style wake to soften our sense of loss. Yet I awakened before dawn, anxious now to speed north to Chicago and catch a fast plane home. As four of us drove past farmhouses, warm and comfortable-looking with their occupants just stirring for their daily chores, through the rich Illinois countryside, its black soil made to look even richer by **149** the gilding of the rising sun, I pondered the great symphony of places and people and events I'd just experienced, from sea to shining sea, as the good song goes, under spacious skies, past amber waves of grain, and so much else of the vast and varied American panorama. And I thought, "Cheer up. What a great country this is!" Bone-tired. Hungover. Reeling from the blow of an electoral landslide. Yet I felt suddenly, inexplicably serene. No bitterness. No regrets. Not a trace of cynicism. I felt good about the many new friends I'd made, the glimpses I'd had of a great human drama and the small part I'd been privileged to play in it. I had learned the hard way that I had no talent for political fund-raising or advance work, or personal politicking. And I knew that once I sorted them out I had learned a few things about human nature and about the democratic process at work. I felt proud to have been a part of it. More than that, I felt good about America.

At *Time,* even though the election was over, the aftersmell of battle hung over the staff and there were figurative bloodstains on the floor. The National Affairs section, with plenty of assists from *Life* magazine, had presented readers with a choice between a national savior riding under the Republican banner and a Democrat who was a well-spoken weakling who made too many jokes—a sort of elitist simp who was soft on Communism and had even said some kind words about Alger Hiss. The cover story summing up the pros and cons of Stevenson had been scheduled for just two weeks before Election Day with the final appraisal of Eisenhower to follow in the final week of the campaign.

Enter that well-known ironist and comic, Mr. Fickle Fate. The man assigned to write the final Stevenson cover story was none other than Otto Fuerbringer, a man whose political sympathies could be in no doubt. The editing of the story was the job of T. S. Matthews. He had returned from his long leave of absence, but instead of taking back his old managing editor's chair from Roy Alexander he had been given by Luce the loftier title but less powerful job of "editor" with his authority confined to editing each week's cover story. This was a much-reduced responsibility, but an important one nonetheless. The drama heightens. Adlai Stevenson and Tom Matthews had been classmates at Princeton and they had been friends ever since.

The nonpolitical Tom Matthews had become politicized. Fuerbringer could wield an ax with the best of the old Tower of London crew, but he was also smart and supple. Rather than striking Stevenson head-on, the writer attacked him with a technique that might be called praising-with-faint-damn, an approach that had been used with devastating effect a few years before by a writer named Roger Butterfield in a *Life* article on the perennial Republican presidential candidate Thomas E. Dewey. Fuerbringer felt admiration for that treatment and adapted it to the task at hand. For example, crediting Stevenson with great eloquence, the writer searched until he found a Stevenson quotation that suggested the opposite; crediting him with charming wit, Fuerbringer singled out examples that made the candidate sound like a third-rate Catskill comic. And so on. When Matthews saw the Fuerbringer story he found it to be "a clumsy but malign and murderously meant attack." But the writer's approach was vulnerable to a clever editor like Matthews. He accepted Fuerbringer's story structure and simply substituted for each damning example a quotation or anecdote or comment that showed Adlai Stevenson to good advantage. The result, a considerable amount of praise and far less damning than had been intended. This offended among others Fuerbringer, National Affairs editor Max Ways, and, apparently, Luce. Shortly thereafter, Luce announced that he was exercising his prerogative as editor in chief and would personally edit *Time*'s wind-up cover story on General Eisenhower. That edict took away the only responsibility that had been left to Tom Matthews and led to the end of his creatively eccentric career as *Time*'s editor.

I of course had been spared all this but was back at work in time to attend a special dinner party staged by Luce for the entire editorial staff at New York's Union Club. Many assumed that Time Inc.'s founder, concerned over reports that a substantial number of the staff were demoralized by *Time*'s unbalanced coverage of the election, would offer words of conciliation, perhaps even a hint or two of contrition. The advance word was wrong. This was the occasion when Luce made his "I am your **151** boss" speech. It was a remarkable dissertation, lasting more than an hour, encompassing Luce's views (negative) of Marx, Nietzsche, Comte, and H. G. Wells among others, reaffirming his shining optimism for the future of America and his pride in *Time*. But not a word of consolation let alone apology. "I told you I was your boss. I guess that means I can fire any of you. . . . I could fire all of you until Roy [Alexander] got hold of me and said, 'This guy is crazy' and put me in Matteawan or something. But I don't know anybody who can fire me. . . ."

The working routine at *Time* was substantially unchanged and I was welcomed back into it as if I'd never been away. No gloating by the I-Like-Ikers, no I-told-you-so's, just here's your desk, go back to work. I was happy to be writing most of the main Foreign News articles for Tom Griffith. Of course, there *had* been some change for those writers and editors who had worked so hard for an Eisenhower victory. After years of throwing every projectile they could muster at the Democratic incumbents—the linguistic equivalents of poisoned darts blown out of Amazonian blowguns, blivises,* hand grenades, strafing runs, and carpet-bombing attacks—the partisans now had to come down from their artillery positions and learn how to deliver powder puffs. From what I could see, they found writing about the new Republican administration and its newly anointed saints to be neither as easy nor as satisfying as had been the bashing of those Democratic sinners for twenty years, especially when the candidates for canonization were men like John Foster Dulles, Richard Nixon, or Charles ("What's good for GM is good for the country") Wilson. If one was accustomed to dismissing a fellow named George Allen, a steady visitor to President Truman's White House, as a court jester and "presidential crony," it must have been a mite uncomfortable to have to elevate the same George Allen into a widely respected "adviser to presidents" when it turned out that

---

*I first introduced the blivis (or blivit) into *Time*'s pages in 1949 or early 1950, in a story about the oratorical style of the labor leader John L. Lewis. It was there described as a two-pound paper bag filled with three pounds of cooked oatmeal. James Shepley, then *Time*'s Washington bureau chief, objected to this bowdlerized definition and taunted New York to print the real one: three pounds of shit in a two pound bag. He was overruled.

152

he was a welcome and even more frequent visitor to the Eisenhower White House.

At home, life had been brightened and quickened by the arrival of Rick's first brother, Brian, in February of 1953, and he was followed fourteen months later by another whom we named Robert but refrained from saddling him with Jr. by giving him a middle name different from mine.

At work, life went on with a minimum of rancor and a surprising amount of camaraderie for a staff so varied in viewpoints, temperaments, and peculiarities. Far from being hurt by my temporary defection, I was being rewarded with increasingly interesting assignments. There were cover stories on foreign leaders—Britain's Anthony Eden, France's Antoine Pinay, Japan's Ichirō Hatoyama, 1953's Man of the Year Chancellor Konrad Adenauer of West Germany, East Germany's Communist boss Walter Ulbricht, and China's Chou Enlai. The death of Joseph Stalin earned two successive cover stories, one on the tyrant himself, the other on the rise of the first of his successors, a Cossack with a shady past and porcine face named Georgi Malenkov, who before being rudely deposed did us the favor of disposing of Stalin's bestial secret police chief Lavrenty Beria, presumably in Beria's favorite execution chamber in the basement of Lubianka prison.

Clare Boothe Luce had been made Eisenhower's ambassador to Italy, so Luce had set up an office in Rome to be with the wife with a brilliant mind and tongue of titanium—and to turn his insatiable curiosity toward the politics of that charmingly confused country. Needless to say, more story suggestions poured in from Rome than from any other world capital, more than an overworked Foreign News staff could possibly handle. We handled many, though, and surely provided *Time* readers with more than they wanted or needed to know about Italy's life of controlled political chaos. My cover story on the Christian Democrat Alcide De Gasperi earned a special distinction. This most intrepid and most interesting in the parade of premiers who took office during the postwar years was of virtually no interest to Americans. My story won the dubious honor of setting the modern-day record for drawing the lowest newsstand sale by an issue of *Time,* a record achieved without any illicit **153** use of steroids. It may have been surpassed not much later by a cover story on Bao Dai, the vapid about-to-be-ex-Emperor of Vietnam. I had a hand in that one too.

When Roy Alexander called me into his office one day to tell me I was being promoted to senior editor, I was as pleased as I'd been concerned when he let me go on leave, more than pleased, in fact, even though this would take me away from writing for a while. I spent a year as acting editor of Foreign News when Tom Griffith went on leave to write a graceful, discerning book about the condition of America.* For several more months I filled in for another editor, Henry Grunwald, a brilliant and ambitious immigrant from Vienna who'd risen from copy boy to senior editor and wanted some time off to try his hand at writing plays. (He did not succeed at drama but came back to become in time wealthier and more powerful than most playwrights as editor in chief of all Time Inc. magazines, Luce's old job as reconstituted after his death.)

Editing Grunwald's sections of the magazine—Books, Medicine, Religion, Music, The Press, and TV-Radio—proved to be more varied and invigorating than any work I had done up to that time. If there was a special quotient of genius in Henry Luce's and Briton Hadden's invention of *Time,* it was their creation of "the back-of-the-book." It was not until long after *Time* came into being that newspapers, transfixed by politics, murders, fires, drownings, steamy divorce suits, and wars if they were big enough, paid much if any attention to some of the more everyday (and therefore more important) aspects of life. A dry and often incomprehensible discussion of national farm policy or a new tax bill could be found in the conventional press. Few save for some metropolitan papers carried sprightly movie, theater, or book reviews, news about music, dance, religion, science, or medicine. A midcentury appraisal of the life and legacy of Sigmund Freud, a critical exploration of the works of William Faulkner, an examination of the life and thought of Paul Tillich or Reinhold Niebuhr, an appraisal of

---

The Waist-High Culture was a brilliant and engagingly written critique, but it was somewhat ahead of its time. It got critical acclaim and far fewer sales than it deserved.

the world as perceived by Arnold Toynbee—these were a quite different kind of journalism. The magazine's energetic, always entertaining, and frequently adventurous sections in the back-of-the-book plus its catchy way of dealing with personalities—peering beyond the cosmetics to tell what the people *Time* wrote about ate and drank, what cigarettes they smoked, whether they chewed gum or betel nut, how they dressed, what their hobbies were, where or whether they worshiped—these were what attracted readership. Surveys taken at that time showed that most readers turned first to *Time*'s Medicine section and then to other back-of-the-book departments, and some did not even bother with the stories up front. Its "discovery" and presentation of the news the newspapers neglected was the key to *Time*'s rise to great success. It is fair to say that most readers bought it not for its political predilections but in spite of them.

Another secret of Luce's success was his ability to inculcate his own driving curiosity into those who worked for him and to nudge them into new fields of experience. When a marvelous racehorse, the big gray named Native Dancer, began capturing the American fancy, I was chosen to write a cover story about the horse mostly because I knew next to nothing about horseracing. I might therefore avoid the usual clichés and bring readers into sharing my own fascination at learning the anatomy of a great champion and of a popular spectator sport. Native Dancer and his milieu, I discovered, were more interesting company than premiers and foreign ministers, and the horse had a better track record than any of them.

The Native Dancer assignment was an experiment. The usual process for a *Time* cover story was to divide the work between a passel of reporters and researchers who poured material into New York and a writer who then compressed and carved the torrent of information into the final story of 2,500 to 3,500 words. In this instance I was invited to do both the reporting and the writing of the Native Dancer story on my own except for some help from a researcher who combed the libraries for lore about thoroughbred racing. I greatly enjoyed the experience and the editors apparently thought well enough of the experiment, the writer serving as his own reporter, to try it again with a different kind of champion.   **155**

One day early in 1954 word came from Uganda that the crash of a small plane in the bush had presumably killed its distinguished passengers, Ernest Hemingway and his wife Mary. Newscasts and newspapers around the world headlined the news. A few days later, the Hemingways walked out of the bush, battered but very much alive. He was carrying a bottle of gin in one hand and a bunch of bananas in the other. "My luck, she is running very good," said Hemingway. The writer returned to his small plantation outside Havana, the Finca Vigia. He was still recuperating from his severe crash injuries when word came from Stockholm that the Nobel Prize in Literature had been awarded to Ernest Hemingway for his novel *The Old Man and the Sea* and his large body of work. I was assigned to interview Hemingway, if I could, and write a cover story about his achievement.

Before trying to arrange a meeting with Hemingway himself, I talked with people who might give me some insights, some hints as to how I might approach him. I talked to the poet Archibald MacLeish, who knew him in his early Paris days, to Malcolm Cowley the critic, who also traveled with and wrote captivatingly about that "Lost Generation" crowd, and to others with some knowledge of the man. I even subjected myself to the hardship of inviting Marlene Dietrich to lunch at Manhattan's plush Pavillon restaurant in the hope of persuading her to part with some love poems Hemingway had written to her. I had grudgingly let Henry Grunwald, who was going to edit my cover story, join us. What the hell. Marlene was seductive enough for two of us and Grunwald would pick up the luncheon check. We both were charmed by the trim and still deliciously dangerous-seeming Miss Dietrich as she picked at her modest lunch, a green salad with only lemon juice for dressing, listened raptly to us while coyly plucking at the V of her bodice. Handsome and charming as Grunwald and I were, we got no love poems from her, only some happy talk about how much she adored Papa and a gift to take to him. The gift was a recording of a song that was then rocking the music world, a loud omen of an ear-splitting musical revolution to come, called "Shake, Rattle and Roll." "Tell him this comes with love from The Kraut," she said.

I spent more than an hour and $124 of *Time*'s money on the telephone urging Hemingway to let me fly to Havana and spend some time with him. He resisted. "The last time I spent time with a writer was for that dame at *The New Yorker* and she [Lillian Ross] cut me all to pieces," he said. "Goddamn little pieces." I assured him I was coming to praise Hemingway, not butcher him. I tried several avenues of persuasion, finally confiding to him that I was bringing greetings and a gift from his friend The Kraut. That expensive lunch at Pavillon paid off. "Well, okay," he said. "As long as you're coming bring me some LP records." The long-playing record was then relatively new on the market; I asked him what kind of music he preferred. "You figure it out and surprise me," he said. "And, oh yes, pick up one of those new Mount Everest expedition sweaters they're selling at Abercrombie and Fitch. It can get cold out on the water this time of year."

Chapter 11

The Life and Death of a Whittler

Veteran out of the wars before he was twenty;
  Famous at twenty-five; thirty a master
Whittled a style for his time from a walnut stick
  In a carpenter's loft in a street of that
April city.

That is how the poet Archibald Macleish described Ernest Hemingway in his early glory, back in the 1920s when it always seemed to be April in Paris. Wine-stained afternoons in the sidewalk cafés and roistering nights in Left Bank boîtes. Walking home alone in the rain. Talk of death, and scenes of it, in the Spanish sun. Treks and trophies in Tanganyika's green hills. Duck-shooting in the Venetian marshes. Experiencing and writing about two world wars. Loving and drinking and fishing out of Key West and Havana. Swaggering into Toots Shor's or posturing in *Life* magazine or talking a verbless sort of choctaw for the notebooks of Lillian Ross and the pages of *The New Yorker*.

Who in my generation of Americans was not fascinated by Hemingway the writer and by Hemingway the maker of his own legend? I certainly was. I had read everything he had written **158** and many in the stream of books and articles that had been written about him. Now I had the opportunity to meet him at the time he was savoring the high moment of his fame and moving, grudgingly, into the twilight of his life.

Late on a November afternoon I arrived at the Finca Vigia a dozen or so miles outside Havana carrying more than two dozen LP recordings, a bottle of thirty-year-old Ballantine's scotch, and the gift from his friend Marlene Dietrich. The house was a cream-colored villa made of limestone, shaggily maintained but comfortable looking. It stood among thirteen acres at the end of a long driveway bordered by palms, banana trees, and other tropical plants. Hemingway was waiting on the villa's veranda. He extended his hand and said, "Welcome."

A big man. Even after allowing for all the descriptions and photographs, the first impression of him in the flesh was size. He was barefooted and bare-legged, wearing floppy khaki shorts and a checked sport shirt, its tail tumbled outside. He squinted slightly through round silver-framed glasses. A tentative smile, the sort that could instantly turn into a sneer or snarl, showed through his clipped white beard. Idleness had turned him to paunch, and he must have weighed then about 225 pounds, but there was no other suggestion of softness in the burly, broad-shouldered frame, and he had the biceps and calves of an NFL linebacker. He was fifty-five but looked older, and was trying to mend the ruptured kidney, cracked skull, two compressed and one cracked vertebra, and bad burns suffered in that airplane crash in the Uganda bush. Those latest injuries, added to a lifetime's accumulation of wounds, including half a dozen to the head, more than two hundred shrapnel scars, a shot-off kneecap, wounds in the feet, hands, and groin, had slowed him down. The place in Cuba had become more home than any place he'd had.

"Drink?" Hemingway asked. "Is a martini on the menu?" I asked. The speed of the reply pleased him, and the smile broadened into a laugh. "We'll make that two. Thank God you're a drinking man. There was a *Life* photographer here for three days a while ago who didn't drink. He was the cruelest man I've ever met. Cruelest man in the world. Made us stand in the sun for hours at a time. And he didn't drink." With stiff caution, he sank into a large overstuffed chair which had been lined back, **159** sides, and bottom with big art and picture books to brace his injured back.

Not knowing how much of his time Hemingway would give me (or his protective wife would allow him to give me), I plunged like an earnest cub just out of journalism school into the matter at hand: Could we talk about his work? Not right away. First he wanted to know more about me, about my background, about where I lived, my family. I told him how Maggie had introduced me to the works of Ernest Hemingway by giving me a copy of *A Farewell to Arms.* "You've obviously married well," he said.

Next, a brief tour of the villa. A three-story climb led to the top of a tower where Hemingway had his study. The living room was nearly fifty feet long and high-ceilinged, with gleaming white walls that set off the Hemingways' small but choice collection of paintings (including a Miró, two by Juan Gris, a Klee, a Braque—later stolen from the villa—and five André Massons), and a few trophy heads from the African safaris. In another room, near the entrance to a large tile-floored dining room, was an oil portrait of Hemingway in his thirties, wearing a flowing striped French seaman's shirt. "It's an old-days picture of me as Kid Balzac by Waldo Pierce," said Hemingway. "Mary has it around because she likes it."

In one large corner of the living room stood a six-foot-high rack filled with dozens of magazines and newspapers from the States, London, and Paris. Books stood in casual piles, littered windowsills and tables, and spilled a trail into two large rooms adjacent. One was a thirty-by-twenty-foot library whose floor-to-ceiling shelves sagged with books. The other was Hemingway's large but crowded bedroom—strewn with correspondence in varied stages of attention or neglect. There were neat piles of opened letters together with stamped and addressed replies; cardboard boxes overflowing with the shards of correspondence that had been opened, presumably read, and one day might be filed; a couple of filing cabinets, whose mysteries probably were best known to a part-time stenographer the Hemingways brought in from Havana a day or two at a time when needed. A large lion skin lay on the floor, in the gaping mouth of which were half a dozen letters and a pair of manila

160

envelopes. "That's the Urgent in-box," Hemingway explained.

He settled back into his fortified chair and sipped his drink. "I don't mind talking tonight, because I never work at night. There's a lot of difference between night thinking and day thinking. Night thoughts are usually nothing. The work you do at night you always will have to do over again in the daytime anyhow. So let's talk. When I talk, incidentally, it's just talk. But when I write I mean it for good."

Evening sounds grew strident in the soft tropical darkness. Distant dogs yelped. Near the house, a hoot owl broke into short, sharp cries. "That's the Shitty Owl," Hemingway said. "He'll go on like that all night. He's lived here longer than we have." By now it seemed safe to pull out my notebook without risk of inhibiting him.

"I respect writing very much, the writer not at all, except as the instrument to do the writing," he said abruptly. "When a writer retires deliberately from life or is forced out of it by some defect, his writing has a tendency to atrophy, just like a man's limb when it's not used.

"I'm not advocating the strenuous life for everyone or trying to say it's the choice form of life. Anyone who's had the luck or misfortune to be an athlete has to keep his body in shape. The body and mind are closely coordinated. Fattening of the body can lead to fattening of the mind. I would be tempted to say that it can lead to fattening of the soul, but I don't know anything about the soul." He halted, broodingly, as if taking inventory of his own shortcomings, his own aches and pains, his too ample paunch, a blood pressure that was too high, and a set of muscles that were suffering from too many weeks of disuse. "However, in everyone the process of fattening or wasting away will set in, and I guess one way is as bad as the other."

He had been reading about medical discoveries which suggested to him that a diet or regimen or treatment that may work for one man does not necessarily work for another. "This was known years ago, really, by people who make proverbs. But now doctors have discovered that certain men need more exercise than others; that certain people can assimilate more punishment in many ways than others.

"Take Primo Carnera, for instance. Now he was a real nice **161** guy, but he was so big and clumsy, never should have been a boxer. It was pitiful. Or take Tom Wolfe, who just never could discipline his mind to his tongue. Or Scott Fitzgerald, who just couldn't drink." He pointed to a couch across the room. "If Scott had been drinking with us and Mary called us to dinner, Scott'd make it to his feet, all right, but then he'd probably fall down. Alcohol was just poison to him. Because all these guys had these weaknesses, it won them sympathy and favor, more sometimes than a guy without those defects would get."

For a good part of his adult life Hemingway was a notable drinker, a ten-goal player at the bar, and what he was now saying could be taken as a rationale. But he could hold his liquor well, as the old saying goes, and he was somewhat more disciplined in this regard than the legend suggests. Usually when he was working hard at writing, he would drink nothing except perhaps a glass or two of wine with meals. Rising at about daybreak or half an hour thereafter, he had put in a full and hard day's work for a writer by ten or eleven in the morning and was ready for relaxation when more mundane laborers were little more than underway.

From his earliest days as a writer Hemingway worked with painful slowness, and still did. He wrote mostly in longhand, frequently while standing at a bookcase in his bedroom or a fireplace mantel; occasionally he would typewrite ("when trying to keep up with dialogue"). For years he carefully logged each day's work. Except for occasional spurts when he was engaged in relatively unimportant efforts, his output ran between four hundred and seven hundred words a day. Mary Hemingway remembered very few occasions when it topped a thousand words.

He did not find writing to be quick or easy. "I always hurt some," he remarked.

Hemingway was capable of great interest in and generosity toward younger writers and some older ones as well, but (as was demonstrated in the posthumously published *A Moveable Feast*), he had an unbecoming compulsion to belittle the reputations of many of his literary contemporaries, particularly those whose fame might challenge his. Gertrude Stein, Sherwood Anderson, T. S. Eliot, not to mention Fitzgerald, Wolfe, Ford

Madox Ford, James Gould Cozzens, and others, were invariably good for a jab or two when their names came up. He was outraged when William Faulkner accused him of lacking "the courage to get out on a limb . . . to risk bad taste, overwriting, dullness." Faulkner later apologized for the remark, but Hemingway did not forgive. He called Faulkner a "no good son-of-a-bitch" and said he could "keep his god-damned Onomatopoeia County." As for critics, "I often feel," he said, "that there is now a rivalry between writing and criticism, rather than the feeling that one should help the other." Writers today could not learn much from the critics. "Critics should deal more with dead writers. A living writer can learn a lot from dead writers."

Did he have a simple definition of fiction-writing? I asked. "Inventing out of knowledge," he said. "To invent out of knowledge means to produce inventions that are true. Every man should have a built-in automatic shit detector operating inside him. It also should have a manual drill and a crank handle in case the machine breaks down or the power fails. If you're going to write, you have to find out what's bad for you. Part of that you learn fast, and then you learn what's good for you."

What kinds of things? "Well, take certain diseases. These diseases are not good for you. I was born before the age of antibiotics, of course. . . . Now take *The Big Sky* [the book that A. B. Guthrie wrote when he was a Nieman Fellow]. That was a very good book in many ways . . . and just about the best book ever written on the clap." Hemingway smiled.

"But back to inventing. In *The Old Man and the Sea* I knew two or three things about the situation, but I didn't know the story." He hesitated, filling the intervals with a vague movement of his hands. "I didn't even know if that big fish was going to bite for the old man when it started smelling around the bait. I had to write on, inventing out of knowledge. You reject everything that is not or can't be completely true. I didn't know what was going to happen for sure in *For Whom the Bell Tolls* or *A Farewell to Arms*. I was inventing."

Philip Young's *Ernest Hemingway,* published in 1953, had attributed much of Hemingway's inspiration or "invention" to his violent experiences as a boy and in World War I. "If you haven't read the book, don't bother," Hemingway volunteered. **163**

"How would you like it if someone said that everything you've done in your life was done because of some trauma. Young had a theory that was like—you know, the Procrustean bed, and he had to cut me to fit into it."

During dinner, Mary Hemingway joined in. As Mary Walsh she had worked for *Time* herself, as a correspondent during the war in London. There she had met Hemingway, just as his third marriage, to Martha Gellhorn, was breaking down. We traded small talk about the magazine and the few *Time* people we both knew in common, but the conversation quickly verged back to writing styles and techniques. Hemingway thought too many contemporary writers defeated themselves through addiction to symbols. "No good book has ever been written that has in it symbols arrived at beforehand and stuck in." He waved a chunk of French bread. "That kind of symbol sticks out like, like raisins in raisin bread. Raisin bread is all right, but plain bread is better."

He mentioned Santiago, his old man of the sea, in roughly these terms: Santiago was never alone because he had his friend and enemy, the sea, and the things that lived in the sea, some of which he loved and others he hated. He loved the sea, but the sea is a great whore, as the book made clear. He had tried to make everything in the story real—the boy, the sea, and the marlin and the sharks, the hope being that each would then mean many things. In that way, the parts of a story become symbols, but they are not first designed or planted as symbols.

The Shitty Owl hooted the household to sleep. I was awakened by tropical birds at the dawn of a bright and promising day. Hemingway was eager to embark on his first fishing trip on *Pilar* since long before the African crash. By six-thirty he was dressed in yesterday's floppy shorts and sport shirt, barefooted, and hunched over his *New York Times,* one of the six papers he and Mary read every day. From the record player came a mixture of Scarlatti, Beethoven, Oscar Peterson, and a remake of some 1928 Louis Armstrong—all, I was pleased to note, from the LP recordings I had brought him.

At brief intervals Hemingway popped a pill into his mouth. "Since the crash I have to take so many of them they have to fight among themselves unless I space them out," he said.

While we were breakfasting, a grizzled Canary Islander named Gregorio, who served as the *Pilar*'s first mate, chef, caretaker, and bartender, was preparing the boat for a day at sea. By nine o'clock, with a young nephew to help him, he had fueled the boat, stocked it with beer, whiskey, wine, and a bottle of tequila, a batch of fresh limes, and food for a large seafood lunch afloat. As we made out of Havana Harbor, Gregorio at the wheel and the young boy readying the deep-sea rods, reels, and fresh bait-fish, Hemingway pointed out landmarks and waved back jovially to passing skippers who greeted him, occasionally shouting "Papa." He sniffed the sharp sea air with delight and peered ahead for the dark line made by the Gulf Stream. "Watch the birds," he said. "They show us when the fish are up."

Mary Hemingway had matters to handle at the finca and in the city, so she could not come along, but out of concern for Hemingway's health she exacted a promise. In return for the long-missed fun of a fishing expedition, he agreed to take it easy and come back early, in time for a nap before an art exhibit to which he and Mary had promised their support. He was in a hurry, therefore, to reach good fishing water. Gregorio pushed the boat hard to a stretch of the Gulf Stream off Cojimar, home port of the Old Man of the novel. Hemingway relaxed into one of the two cushioned bunks in the boat's open-ended cabin.

"It's wonderful to get out on the water. I need it." He gestured toward the ocean. "It's the last free place there is, the sea. Even Africa's about gone; it's at war, and that's going to go on for a very long time."

Pilar fished two rods from its high antenna-like outriggers and two from seats at the stern, and at Hemingway's instruction, Gregorio and the boy baited two with live fish carefully wired to the hooks, and two with artificial lures. A man-o'-war bird gliding lazily off the coast pointed to the first school of the day, and within an hour *Pilar* had its first fish, a pair of bonito sounding and shivering the outrigger lines. The fishing was bountiful, with frequent good runs of bonito and dolphin intermixed with quiet interludes in which to sip drinks, to soak up the Caribbean sun, and to talk.

Sometimes moody, sometimes erupting with boyish glee at **165** the strike of a tuna or the gold and blue explosion of a hooked dolphin, and sometimes—as if to defy or outwit his wounds— pulling himself by his arms to the flying bridge to steer *Pilar* for a spell, Hemingway talked little of the present, not at all of the future, and a great deal of the past.

He recalled when Scribner's sent him first galley proofs of *For Whom the Bell Tolls*. "I remember, I spent ninety hours on the proofs of that book without once leaving the hotel room. When I finished, I thought the type was so small nobody would ever buy the book. I'd shot my eyes, you see. I had corrected the manuscript several times but still was not satisfied. I told Max Perkins about the type, and he said if I really thought it was too small, he'd have the whole book reprinted. That's a real expensive thing, you know. He was a sweet guy. But Max was right, the type was all right."

"Do you ever read any of your stuff over again?"

"Sometimes I do," he said. "When I'm feeling low. It makes you feel good to look back and see you can write."

"Is there anything you've written that you would do differently if you could do it over?"

"Not yet."

New York. "It's a very unnatural place to live. I could never live there. And there's not much fun going to the city now. Max is dead. Granny Rice is dead. He was a wonderful guy. We always used to go to the Bronx Zoo and look at the animals."

The Key West days, in the early thirties, were a good time. "There was a fighter there—he'd had one eye ruined, but he was still pretty good, and he decided to start fighting again. He wanted to be his own promoter. He asked me if I would referee his bout each week. I told him, 'Nothing doing,' he shouldn't go in the ring anymore. Any fighter who knew about his bad eye would just poke his thumb in the other one and then beat his head off.

"The fighter said, 'The guys come from somewhere else won't know 'bout my eye, and no one around here in the Keys gonna dare poke my eye.'

"So I finally agreed to referee for him. This was the Negro section, you know, and they really introduced me: 'And the referee for tonight, the world-famous millionaire, sportsman, and playboy, Mister Ernest Hemingway!' " Hemingway chuckled. "Playboy was the greatest title they thought they could give a man." Chuckle again. "How can the Nobel Prize move a man who has heard plaudits like that?"

Frequently a sharp cry from Gregorio on the flying bridge interrupted the talk. "Feesh! Papa, feesh!" Line would snap from one of the outriggers, and a reel begin to snarl. "You take him," Hemingway would say, or if two fish struck at once, as frequently happened, he would leap to one rod and I to the other.

He talked about the act of playing a fish as if it were an English sentence. "The way to do it, the style, is not just an idle concept. It is simply the way to get done what is supposed to be done; in this case it brings in the fish. The fact that the right way looks pretty or beautiful when it's done is just incidental."

Hemingway had written only one play, *The Fifth Column*. Why no others? "If you write a play, you have to stick around and fix it up," he said. "They always want to fool around with them to make them commercially successful, and you don't like to stick around that long. After I've written, I want to go home and take a shower."

Almost absently, he plucked out of the air James Joyce and their times together in Paris. "Once Joyce said to me he was afraid his writing was too suburban and that maybe he should get around a bit and see the world, the way I was doing. He was under great discipline, you know—his wife, his work, his bad eyes. And his wife said, yes, it was too suburban. 'Jim could do with a spot of that lion-hunting.' How do you like that? A *spot* of lion-hunting!

"We'd go out, and Joyce would fall into an argument or a fight. He couldn't even see the man, so he'd say, 'Deal with him, Hemingway! Deal with him!' " Hemingway paused. "In the big league it is not the way it says in the books." Hemingway was not warm toward T. S. Eliot. He much preferred Ezra Pound, who at that time was still confined in St. Elizabeth's mental hospital in Washington in lieu of being tried for treason for his pro-Fascist broadcasts in Italy during the war.

The sea was undulating now with a motion that was getting to my stomach. Seeing the sudden greening of my complexion, **167**

Hemingway motioned me to lie down on the cushioned bench we were sitting on, took my notebook from my hand, and as I slowly recovered from the threat of seasickness, wrote out his comment on the mad, or presumed mad, poet:

"Ezra Pound is a great poet, and whatever he did, he has been punished greatly, and I believe should be freed to go and write poems in Italy, where he is loved and understood. He was the master of Eliot. I was a member of an organization which Pound founded with Natalia Barney in order to get Eliot out of his job in a bank so he could be free to write poetry. It was called Bel Esprit. Eliot, I believe, was able to get out of his job and edit a review and write poetry freely due to the backing of other people than this organization. But the organization was typical of Pound's generosity and interest in all forms of the arts regardless of any benefits to himself or of the possibilities that the people he encouraged would be his rivals.

"Eliot is a winner of the Nobel Prize. I believe it might well have gone to Pound, as a poet. Pound certainly deserved punishment, but I believe this would be a good year to release poets and allow them to continue to write poetry. . . . Ezra Pound, no matter what he may think, is not as great a poet as Dante, but he is a very great poet for all his errors."

Dusk was coming when *Pilar* turned toward Havana harbor, its skipper steering grandly from the flying bridge. What remained of the bottle of tequila and half of a lime rested in a holder bolted to the mahogany rail near the wheel. "To ward off sea serpents," Hemingway explained, passing the bottle for a ceremonial homecoming swig.

Hemingway's good spirits on his return helped to diminish his wife's concern about his overextending himself. She greeted us with chilled white wine and a hot oyster stew. Clutching an early nightcap, Hemingway sprawled with pleased fatigue in his big armchair and talked of books he had recently read. He had started Saul Bellow's *The Adventures of Augie March,* but didn't like it. "But when I'm working," he said, "and read to get away from it, I'm inclined to make bad judgments about other people's writing." He thought Bellow's very early book, *Dangling Man,* much better.

168   One of the postwar writers who had impressed him most was

John Horne Burns, who wrote a World War II novel, *The Gallery,* and two other novels and then, in 1953, died in circumstances that suggested suicide. "There was a fellow who wrote a fine book and then a stinking book about a prep school, and then he just blew himself up," Hemingway mused, adding a gesture that seemed to ask, how do you explain such a thing? He started at nothing, seeming tired and sad.

"You know," he said, "my father shot himself."

There was silence. It had frequently been said that Hemingway never cared to talk about his father's suicide.

"Do you think it took courage?" I asked.

Hemingway pursed his lips and shook his head. "No. It's everybody's right, but there's a certain amount of egotism in it and a certain disregard of others." He turned off that conversation by picking up a handful of books. "Here are a few things you might like to look at before you turn off the light." He held out *The Retreat,* by P. H. Newby; Max Perkins's selected letters; *The Jungle Is Neutral,* by Frederick S. Chapman; and Malcolm Cowley's *The Literary Situation.*

By seven the next morning a rabble of dogs yipped and yelped in the yard near the finca's small guesthouse. Hemingway, in a tattered robe and old slippers, was already half through the previous day's *Times.*

"Did you finish the Cowley book last night?" he asked. "Very good, I think. I never realized what a tough time writers have economically, if they have it as tough as Malcolm says they do."

He was reminded of his early days in Paris. "It never seemed like hardship to me. It was hard work, but it was fun. I was working, and I had a wife and kid to support. I remember, first I used to go to the market every morning and get the stuff for Bumby's [his first son, John] bottle. His mother had to have her sleep." Lest this should be taken as a criticism, he added, "That's characteristic, you know, of the very finest women. They need their sleep, and when they get it, they're wonderful."

Another part of the routine in the Paris days, to pick up eating money, was Hemingway's daily trip to a gymnasium to work as a sparring partner for fighters. The pay was $2 an hour. "That was very good money then, and I didn't get marked up **169** very much. I had one rule: never provoke a fighter. I tried not to get hit. They had plenty of guys they could knock around."

He reached for the mail, slit open one from a pile of fifteen letters. It was from a high school English teacher in Miami, Florida, who complained that her students rarely read good literature and relied for "knowledge" on the movies, television, and radio. To arouse their interest, she wrote, she told them about Hemingway's adventures and pressed them to read his writings. "Therefore, in a sense," she concluded, "you are the teacher in my tenth grade classroom. I thought you'd like to know it." Hemingway found the letter depressing: "Pretty bad if kids are spending all that time away from books."

The second day's fishing expedition was even better than the first—fewer fish, but two of them were small marlin, one about eighty pounds, the other eighty-five. They struck simultaneously and were boated, Hemingway's with dispatch, the second by me some twenty minutes later and at a cost of amateurish sweat and agony that was the subject of as much merriment as congratulations. This expedition was a sprightly occasion, too, because Mary Hemingway was able to come along. A bright and energetic woman with a strong streak of independence, Hemingway's fourth wife cared for him well and must have found that trying at times. She tried to anticipate his moods and his desires, played bountiful hostess to his friends, diplomatically turned aside some of the most taxing demands on his time and generosity. More than that, she shared the broad mixture of interests—books, good talk, traveling, fishing, shooting—that were central to Hemingway's life. His marriage to her was plainly the central and guiding personal relationship of his last years, though not always a serene one for Mary Walsh.

Hemingway gazed happily at the pair of marlin. "We're back in business," he said, and gave Mary a hug. "This calls for celebration," she said.

"Off to the Floridita," said Hemingway.

The Floridita was once one of those comfortably shoddy Havana saloons where the food was cheap and good and the drinking serious. By then, enjoying a prosperity that was due in 170 no small part to its reputation as the place you could see and maybe even drink with Papa Hemingway, it had taken on a red-plush grandeur and even had a velvet cord to block off the dining room entrance. "It looks crummy now," Hemingway said, "but the drinking's as good as ever."

The Floridita played a special role in Hemingway's life. "My not living in the United States," he explained, "does not mean any separation from the tongue or even the country. Any time I come to the Floridita I see Americans from all over. It can even be closer to America in many ways than being in New York. You go there for a drink or two, and see everybody from everyplace. I live in Cuba because I love Cuba—that does not mean a dislike for anyplace else. And because here I get privacy when I write. If I want to see anyone, I just go into town, or the Air Force guys come out to the place, naval characters and all— guys I knew in the war. I used to have privacy in Key West, but then I had less and less when I was trying to work, and there were too many people around, so I'd come over here and work in the Ambos Mundos Hotel."

The saloon's bar was crowded, but several customers obligingly slid away from one section that had been designated long before by the proprietor as "Papa's Corner." Smiles. "Hello, Papa." Handshakes all around. "Three Papa Dobles," said Hemingway, and the barkeep hastened to manufacture three immense daiquiris according to a Floridita recipe that relies more on grapefruit juice than on lemon or lime juice. The Papa Doble was a heavy seller in those days at $1.25, and a bargain at that.

Two sailors off a U.S. aircraft carrier worked up nerve to approach the author and ask for an autograph. "I read all your books," said one of them.

"What about you?" Hemingway said to the other.

"I don't read much," the young sailor said.

"Get started," Hemingway said.

The Floridita's owner appeared, with embraces for the Hemingways and the news that he was installing a modern men's room. Hemingway noted sadly that all the good things were passing. "A wonderful old john back there," he said. "Makes you want to shout: Water closets of the world unite; you have nothing to lose but your chains."

I returned home with a full notebook and a head crammed with impressions, enough material for a dozen cover stories—and with a crippling affliction. I had gotten too close to my subject. I could not stand back to compose a dispassionate appraisal. I had fantasized a trip into the past and into another's personality. I wanted to *be* that handsome young American back in the twenties doing what Archibald MacLeish had described, carving a walnut stick in that April city. As I worked my typewriter I would remember something like the opening lines of *A Farewell to Arms,* clean with discipline and pregnant with the sense of individual sensation, and that was enough to make me crumple the clumsy prose I was writing and try to start over again. I wondered how many would-be writers had been similarly discouraged by such perfection. Working painfully against a deadline, I lunched in the office—a stick of French bread, some cheese, and a half bottle of claret—while Edith Piaf tunes played in my head. I suppose if I'd had one I would even have worn a beret to work.

Without confessing my frustration I got in touch with Hemingway for some additional information. For example, I had listed with some precision the inventory of wounds he had suffered in his lifetime but was not certain of accuracy. He thought it would be "truthful and less blood curdling" to reduce the list to: He has been wounded in the head, the feet, both knees, both arms, both hands, and the scrotum. "Don't quote me on this and I would just as soon leave the scrotum out unless that constitutes indecent exposure. Hope not to run as a clay pigeon or the Legs Diamond of Letters."

The relentless approach of the deadline broke the spell and returned me to a reasonable degree of dispassion. The story I turned in was too long and I made myself unpleasant to Grunwald when he imposed the necessary editing which, though I hated to admit it, made the story more compact and professional. It was essentially the story I have related here plus ample biographical narrative, but delivered in the more aloof third person and adorned with some of the efforts at Olympian judgment that no *Time* cover story could be without. It portrayed a

172   man who in later life had made himself easy to parody, had

sometimes even seemed to parody himself, but who in his genre was impossible to equal. He sometimes did or said things that seemed almost perversely calculated to obscure his many gallantries and generosities and the enjoyments and inspiration he had generated for others. He could be fierce in his sensitivity to criticism and competitive in his craft to the point of vindictiveness, but he could laugh at himself too ("I'm Ernie Hemorrhoid, the poor man's Pyle," he announced when he put on his World War II correspondent's uniform) and surely was entitled to the pure pride of believing that he had accomplished much of what he set out to do forty-five years before in that Parisian loft. In the cover story I let Hemingway have the last word:

> You only have to do it once to get remembered by some people. But if you can do it year after year after year quite a lot of people remember and they tell their children and their children and their grandchildren and they remember, and if it's books they can read them. And if it's good enough it lasts forever.

Later I conceded to myself that, caught up as I was by the legend, I was perhaps too gentle, that I did not fully convey that even in the moment of Nobel Prize glory he was in only middle age a drained talent, a man who could brag that he'd scaled his particular Mount Everest but must have known in his troubled heart that he would never rise from the lowlands again, that his bright future was now behind him. Perhaps I should have been more alert and seen the look of that in his eyes and his behavior. I gave short shrift, too, to the fact that Hemingway's reputation was in decline at the time he won the Prize, that it had become fashionable among academicians and younger writers not just to denigrate Hemingway the posturer but to question the values of his best work, two very different things. They were entitled to their wrongheaded opinions, but I felt no obligation to respect them. I was satisfied that the profile I'd written was a damned good piece of work, a much deserved homage to a great artist, and worth all the agony it had caused me.

Hemingway had vowed that he would not read the piece, but of course he did and I was pleased to learn that he liked it, or at least most of it ("You were just as straight as you sounded on 173 the phone when I decided you were trustworthy"). He despised the cover painting, an Artzybasheff portrait showing Hemingway staring vacantly into space and a giant purple marlin curling around his bearded chin. And he caviled at a remark in the story that his work was not so great in the 1930s. That passage referred to his novel-writing but inadvertently neglected to allow for several magnificent short stories such as the *The Snows of Kilimanjaro* and *The Short Happy Life of Francis Macomber.* "I wrote them in '35 I think," he said sarcastically. "If you didn't read them I think you'd like them."

A year later he invited Maggie and me to visit Cuba for the celebration of his fifty-sixth "name day," the substitute for a birthday.

We had barely settled into the big living room, drinks in hand, when Hemingway gestured Maggie into a seat next to him and engaged her in animated conversation. I couldn't quite make out the subject but was astonished to hear my wife suddenly say to the great master of prose, "Please finish your sentence, Mr. Hemingway." He gave Maggie a startled look, laughed, then plunged again into what I later learned was a brief discourse on the mating habits of the whale shark.

That visit lasted for three uproarious days at the finca, aboard *Pilar,* and in assorted watering places. We spent a couple of evenings with them when they made brief visits to New York. We kept in touch by mail and telephone after they left Cuba for good in the summer of 1960. There were letters and postcards from Spain, where Hemingway spent weeks following the *mano a mano* bullfights of his friend Ordonez and his rival Dominguin and wrote disappointingly about them for *Life* magazine. A postcard from Peru showed him with a giant marlin he'd caught for the making of the movie of *The Old Man and the Sea:* "This was the Peruvian chiropodist that fixed up my back." When *Time* celebrated the novelist James Gould Cozzens on its cover he commented crankily: "He has lasted into a good time for him—when the synthetic is more popular than the real. He is very Fascist, too. . . ." The magazine ran a story about a divinity dean who had published an essay characterizing Hemingway as a dirty writer, as the man who had introduced "the mystique of merde" into American literature. Hemingway was irritated that *Time* had given attention to the essay and asked me to convey to the critic a brief history of the respectful use of the French word *merde* as the *mot de Cambronne,* a salute from one French soldier to another who is going into dangerous combat or in the theatrical world a wish of good luck to an actor about to go on stage. "I think my dear Dean that you should, as we say who respect another fine old word, not fuck around with subjects on which you have not been checked out."

The calls and letters came less frequently after the Hemingways moved to the new place he had bought in Ketchum, Idaho, close to the kind of shooting, fishing, walking that had beguiled him as a young man in upper Michigan. A letter dated January 18, 1961, was not in his usually rough typewriting or tight, slanting handwriting but had been neatly typed by someone else and came from St. Mary's Hospital in Rochester, Minnesota. It was ominously clinical:

> Everything is working out O.K. here. Have the blood pressure down from 250/125 to 130/80 yesterday and will be out of here shortly. Only problem is to hold my weight to 175 pounds which they say will control the whole blood pressure deal and to find someplace to work to finish the book that I am two months behind on now and has to be out this fall. . . . Best to you always from both of us and best love to Maggie. Tell her she moves me as deeply as always if that is in order.
>
> Yours always,
>
> *Papa*
>
> Ernest Hemingway

That was the last one. There was talk in the gossip columns that he had become paranoid, imagining that the FBI was out to get him, and another rumor that he had been restrained from throwing himself into a whirling airplane propeller. On the afternoon of July 2 that year Maggie and I were driving in the country when the radio announced that Ernest Hemingway, the famous writer and adventurer, had placed the barrels of a shotgun against his head and blown his life away. He was sixty-one.

I pulled aside and stopped the car. The memory of that night 175 in Cuba when he talked about his father's suicide darted like a twinge of pain to my mind. "Did it take courage?" I whispered to myself.

Maggie and I sat for a moment in silence. Then we drove home with tears in our eyes.

Chapter 12

Learning How to Pronounce *Banana*

L ondon lolled brazenly in the spring sunshine. The weather forecast of a rise toward seventy degrees had provoked scare headlines in the tabloids: HEAT WAVE THREATENED. Only in England.

I had come to that grand city only three days before to meet the men and women of the Time-Life bureau and to arrange for lodging for the family. After almost nine years of writing and editing in New York I had been offered a proposition too beguiling to be refused: chief of Time-Life's London bureau. Just after lunchtime on this mid-March afternoon I strolled along St. James Street toward the Time-Life Building with Raimund von Hoffmansthal, son of the Viennese poet and Strauss librettist, Hugo von Hoffmansthal. A charming, handsomely tailored man, Raimund was an American citizen with continental manners and an accent to match. He was a sort of minister without portfolio in the London office, resident boulevardier and guide to the higher echelons of British society and the Tory party. When Luce visited London he could count on Raimund to produce interesting and/or influential dinner guests in impeccable surroundings. He had married and been divorced from an Astor and now he was married to the beautiful Lady Elizabeth, one of the several socially prominent Paget sisters, whose **177** brother's inherited estate occupied a goodly portion of Wales including Mount Snowden. Raimund was attached to the business side of the Time-Life operation in London but preferred the company of the writers and correspondents.

"Allow me to introduce you to a special part of England," he had said that morning. "Join me for lunch at White's." Raimund was a rarity in that most exclusive and snobbish of London men's clubs, not just because he was one of the very few American members but because he was treated civilly by the other members of White's *in spite of* being an American. The lunch had been epicurean. Plovers' eggs and champagne in silver tankards at the bar, then lobster bisque, Dover sole that could not have been more than an hour out of the Channel, a bottle of excellent montrachet followed by a dessert soufflé that floated into the mouth, then a veritable beaker of hundred-year-old port to go with the Stilton. The eminent essayist and critic Cyril Connolly joined us for coffee. Evelyn Waugh swept up White's majestic staircase speaking to no one and carrying an immense ear trumpet in one hand. Von Hoffmansthal pointed out a brace of dukes, a government minister or two, and a man rumored to be the current bedmate of the Duchess of Argyle. Raimund was said to be privy to just about every illicit dalliance of import on either side of the Channel.

Sated, excited to be starting this new adventure, and caressed by the gleaming weather, I expressed my joy to my host. All my preconceptions are being destroyed, I said. First, I'd been warned to expect miserable weather, but it has been nothing short of sublime since I arrived.

Raimund smiled and nodded knowingly.

And the food! I exclaimed. I was ready for nothing but overcooked Brussels sprouts and tough mutton, but I've never eaten better meals in my life.

Again Raimund smiled and nodded knowingly.

And, ah, the women! I'd been braced for horsey types in dowdy tweeds or sharp-featured snobs in unstylish prints, I said, but I've never seen so many beautiful and well-groomed women in one place.

178   Raimund stopped and leaned toward me with a conspirator's

This photo and an equally stern accompanying mini-essay entitled "George the Surveyor" made up the author's first appearance in the *Binghamton Press,* as runner-up in a citywide writing contest for sixth-graders to celebrate the bicentennial of George Washington's birth in 1932.

Reading—with obvious approval—one of my first bylined stories in the *Press,* 1938. If memory serves, it was about the daily weather forecast.

My parents, Joseph and Agnes Brown Manning, at Fortress (now Fort) Monroe, Virginia, shortly after their marriage in June 1918.

City room of the *Binghamton Press,* with the city editor, later managing editor, Erwin Cronk, in charge (foreground). The fellow behind Cronk at the left of the copy desk is my friend Kimball Davis, who went on to become publisher of the paper. This was taken several years after my time, but it looks enough like old times to induce nostalgia. *Binghamton Press & Sun Bulletin*

Tom Cawley, the *Press*'s premier columnist (left) enjoys a morning stroll in Manhattan with former president Harry Truman (1961). *Binghamton Press & Sun Bulletin*

"Tracking the spring fever bug, 1943." One of the cartoons that accompanied my column in the Anti-Aircraft Replacement Training Center weekly, the *Skywatch,* at Fort Eustis, Virginia.

Leon Pearson of the International News Service and Manning of the United Press intrepidly spread the news while sharing tight quarters in the old State Department press room, 1944.

Hurdling over the opposition, a not untypical exit from the White House press secretary's office, August 14, 1945, as reporters rushed to their telephones to announce the non-news that Japan had not yet surrendered.

Edward Stettinius, a cheerful steel company executive, has just replaced stately old Cordell Hull as FDR's secretary of state. Joseph Fox of the *Washington Star,* Douglas Cornell of the Associated Press, and I wait in vain for a few words of wisdom. *Associated Press Photo*

FDR's faithful servant-of-many talents, Harry Hopkins, shows his grief—and his own failing health—in the White House lobby a few minutes after the president's funeral procession reaches the White House, April 14, 1945. *Associated Press Wirephoto*

The 1945–46 class of Nieman Fellows at Harvard are caught in a rare moment of mutual silence in the Nieman Foundation office. The four chaps at the rear left are (left to right) Arthur Hepner of the *St. Louis Post-Dispatch,* Leon Svirsky of *Time,* Richard Stockwell of station WCCO in Minneapolis (the first Nieman Fellow from broadcasting), and Frank Hewlett of the United Press. In the forefront, Ben Yablonky of the newspaper *PM,* Manning of the UP, Mary Ellen Leary of the *San Francisco News,* Cary Robertson of the Louisville *Courier-Journal,* James Batal of the *Cleghorn Courier,* Fitchburg, Massachusetts; Louis Lyons, curator of the Nieman Foundation, and Charlotte Fitz-Henry of the Associated Press. The gentleman sagely admonishing the Fellows is Professor Arthur Schlesinger, Sr., a sort of godfather to all Nieman Fellows of that time.

Harvard professor Theodore Spencer, who brought great poets back to life and enriched the Nieman year at Harvard. *John Brook*

A remarkable day at United Nations headquarters at Lake Success, when Andrei Gromyko (left) has just agreed with the Western powers to enforce the creation of the state of Israel. A look of skepticism was standard equipment when interviewing Gromyko. *Acme Photo*

A smile on the face of Andrei Vishinsky was a rare sight. He was Joseph Stalin's prosecutor for the infamous purge trials in the 1930s and now, in the 1940s, had become his deputy foreign minister. At a United Nations session in Paris in the fall of 1948 we reporters tried to discover whether Moscow was ready to declare an end to the Soviet blockade of Berlin. Not quite yet. *International News Photo*

How does one say, "Hello, honey. Give me rewrite!" in French?

The nonpareil *Time* writer Paul O'Neil and his son Mike as they prepare to fish Woodland Creek in the Catskills. *Jane W. O'Neil*

Talking about writers, poets, fishermen, and the mysteries of the sea, aboard *Pilar* off Havana, Cuba, shortly after Hemingway won the Nobel Prize in 1954.

Hemingway, his Basque freighter captain friend, Sinsky, alias Sinbad, and Maggie share an afternoon of laughs at a beachside restaurant near Cojimar, homeport of the Cuban fisherman hero of *The Old Man and the Sea*, 1955.

After making the dedication speech for the Ernest Hemingway memorial (rear) near Ketchum, Idaho, I pose for the ritual photo with Mary Hemingway, Hemingway's oldest son, Jack (right), and Don Anderson of Sun Valley Lodge.

caution in his eyes. "Shhhh," he whispered. "*That* one we are keeping secret."

The late 1950s was a wonderful time to be living in Britain and working as an American correspondent for a wealthy news organization. Britons were generally cheerful because at long last some of the good things of life were trickling downward. However grudgingly, the working classes had been permitted to engage in the pursuit of happiness. The postwar rise to power by the Labor Party and its lunging socialism had brought to the lower classes access to decent housing and medical and dental care, as well as the means to buy automobiles and pawky little motorscooters and to afford trips to the chilly beach resorts and Billy Butlin holiday camps or even travel in Germany, France, and Spain.

There were still deep moats between classes, still too many seats reserved only for those with the right titles, the right school ties and correct accent. Hard-working and heavily taxed members of the middle class bore far more of the burden of this redistribution of wealth than the indolent rich; we were to meet many a man who worked in respectable trades like publishing or banking who came close to impoverishing his wife and himself in order to send sons to Rugby or Winchester or whatever public school he'd been sent to by *his* father. Class bitterness still festered beneath the surface, of course, an abcess so deep it probably would never be healed. And the flood of black and Asian Commonwealth citizens from the West Indies, India, and Pakistan was just beginning to induce new tremors of social and racial tension as the newcomers competed for jobs and living space in the major cities. Only fragments of the crumbling Empire remained, and the responsibility of ruling them was costly and troublesome. The country was losing out to foreign competitors in the struggle to make goods and produce the wealth it was trying so energetically to redistribute. What is more, the country had not fully recovered from the orgy of frustration and recrimination provoked by its humiliating role in the Suez Canal fiasco of 1956, an event that dramatized Great Britain's unwilling retirement as a world power.

For all its woes, though, Britain at that moment seemed a happy, pack-up-your-troubles-in-an-old-kitbag sort of place, **187** suffused in an overall atmosphere of well-being that had never been before and was to be enjoyed before it melted away.

Luce considered the London bureau chief to be his Ambassador to the Court of St. James, so the bureau chief and his family lived accordingly—very well if not lavishly. We found a lovely Regency house with a huge back garden on the banks of the Regents Canal in a neighborhood called Little Venice. Time Inc. bought the leasehold as the bureau chief's residence, furnished it with antiques and fine rugs and draperies, and allowed us to move into a once rundown neighborhood that was fast becoming one of the most desirable in London. People from the world of theater had rediscovered it first. Our house had been owned by George S. Kaufman and the actress Leueen McGrath before they divorced, and Kaufman had adorned it with such desirable features as American-style central heating. Christopher Fry the playwright and Roger Livesey the actor lived down the street, Lady Diana Duff Cooper around one corner, and Winston Churchill's daughter Sarah a few doors in the other direction. A hundred yards west at the junction of the Regents Canal with the Grand Union Canal to Manchester was Browning Crescent, where the poets Robert and Elizabeth had lived and loved.

The three Manning boys, Rick, Brian, and Robbie, were enrolled—at Time Inc.'s expense, to be sure—in Arnold House, a boy's private (i.e., "prep") school that prepared youngsters to move on at the age of eight or nine to the better public (i.e., private) boarding schools. Somewhat dubious about taking in his first American boys, the no-nonsense headmaster put them into the school's gray flannel shorts and smashing scarlet jackets with green piping and beanies to match and quickly had them reading, writing, and speaking with the crisp accents so crucial to advancement in Britain. When one of them pronounced *banana* in the good old American nasal manner he was swatted with a sneaker.

About equal in size and suzerainty, London and Paris were the two largest bureaus after Washington. London's geographical responsibilities extended far beyond the British Isles to all the Scandinavian countries and the Mediterranean and African remnants of the Empire. We were situated in the Time-Life

Building, one of the first new buildings built in London after the war, a six-story structure on the corner of Bruton and New Bond Street amidst the expensive Mayfair shops. Time Inc. traveled first class. A huge bronze reclining figure by Henry Moore, one of his classics, dominated the handsome inner courtyard, a luxury in that space-starved part of Mayfair. Inside were a striking atrium-like reception hall convertible into a virtual ballroom for parties and on the top floor a cafeteria for employees and a grand entertaining suite where guests of the correspondents or advertising salesmen were treated to excellent lunches and fine wines served by the resident chef and butler. In case supply ran short (and it frequently did), reinforcements could be sped upstairs from the Justerini & Brooks spirits and wine shop on the ground floor.

I inherited a crackerjack staff of more than forty people, counting telegraphers, librarians, chauffeurs for the two bureau cars, a Jaguar and a Rover, and the technicians who manned perhaps the finest photographic darkroom on that side of the Atlantic. Most of the staffers were British, almost all of them very bright and cheerful. Among us emigrants from America was Joe David Brown, who had come back from a book-writing leave of absence to spend a couple of years in London as a correspondent. When he returned to the States to write more books, Michael Demarest, an ingratiating reporter and born bon vivant if ever I knew one, came to replace him as our correspondent for the lively arts. As my principal deputy I was lucky to get James L. Greenfield, an ex-poorboy from Cleveland who'd taken good advantage of a scholarship to Harvard. A man of infectious enthusiasms and an exceptionally sharp instinct for incipient news, Jimmy had served a tour under occasional enemy fire in the Korean war for the United States Information Agency before becoming Time-Life's correspondent in Japan and India. By the time he moved to London he was wise in the ways of foreign governments, of Americans abroad, and of the special problems inflicted on overseas correspondents by the Time-Life bureaucracy. As deputy on the *Life* side of the bureau, Richard Pollard, a man of calm authority, came from New York to deal with the sometimes peculiar and always demanding whims of the *Life* editors in New York and to humor **189** those most pampered of *Life* staffers, the photographers, who cruised through London and used the darkroom on the way to or from exotic assignments in faraway places. Many of the photographers were difficult prima donnas,* but by nice coincidence those home-based in London, the American Mark Kauffman and Englishman Larry Burrows, were two of the sweetest-natured and least demanding men who'd ever aimed a Leica; they were the most popular men in the bureau.

We Americans usually served for two or three years and then went on to other assignments. The London bureau got its stability and its continuity—and much of its best reporting—from the British staffers who had seen so many of us come and go. Veteran among those was Honor Balfour, who reported on party politics and the doings of Parliament with the confidence of an insider and the volubility of a modern-day Pepys. She'd once run unsuccessfully for a parliamentary seat herself with the slogan "A Lancashire lass for Lancashire," and had dozens of close contacts in all three parties, Conservative and especially Labor and Liberal. Honor was a perky, cheerful, and well-educated bachelor lady who seemed never to look on the dark side of life. "Nattering" was both her hobby and principal form of exercise and once she had finished each week's nattering with politicians of every shade her cable to New York would provide a writer with all he needed to know (and considerably more) about the state of politics in the United Kingdom as of that moment. Rarely was she wrong in an analysis or a prediction because Miss Balfour's material, as one admiring vulgarian once put it, "always came from so far down in the horse's mouth you could see daylight."

One of the encouraging aspects of reporting to Americans about Great Britain was Americans' fascination with British culture and customs, the manners and morals of those islands. Whether it be a piece of gossip about the Royal Family, a

---

*Example: Once on an elaborate swing through Africa, the photographer Eliot Eliofson was importuned by the *Life* reporter traveling with him. "Eliot, you've just got to stop telling everybody you're the world's greatest photographer. It's embarrassing." "I see what you mean," said Eliofson. "From now on, you tell them."

ruckus in the Church of England over the Archbishop of Canterbury's too-friendly letter to the Pope of Rome, an uproar in Yarmouth over the proper recipe for jellied eel, a controversy in the Letters column of the *Times* of London as to the true meaning of the term "Emily-colored hands" in an Edith Sitwell poem, readers in the States seemed never to have enough of such badinage. There was no one better than Monica Dehn (later Wilson) at writing about the quality of British life—education, religion, sociology, mores in general—and finding relevance in those quirks and rituals that made the Welsh Welsh, the English English, the Scots Scottish, the Irish Irish. Monica had distinguished herself as a correspondent for *Time* in the newly born state of Israel where her then-husband was also a news correspondent. After returning to England she applied her amused detachment and deft prose to the local scene and became one of the indispensables in the London bureau.

My first mission in London was more diplomatic than journalistic. Relations between the U.K. and the U.S. had been severely strained by the Suez crisis, when Washington rose up against the British, French, and Israel operations to wrest the canal from Egypt and colluded with the USSR to make them withdraw. Since it was American policy blunders in the first place that had brought about Nasser's seizure of the Suez Canal, it was not surprising that Secretary of State John Foster Dulles ranked only slightly below Adolf Hitler and about equal to Napoleon in the British unpopularity stakes. Among many who read *Time,* bitterness toward the magazine was also intense, for the magazine had equaled Dulles in its excoriation of poor Anthony Eden and its implied aspersions on British competence and morality. An inference that could be drawn from *Time*'s coverage was that the Suez expedition, coming at the same time as the Hungarian uprising against Russian domination, was a form of cold wartime treason by Britain, France, and Israel. In some American eyes, their attack on Egypt may have sabotaged the prospect of "the liberation of Eastern Europe" that Dulles had long blustered about without any commitment to making it happen. I had shared the widespread American indignation at the British-French-Israeli Suez adventure and a sense of righteousness at its deserved failure. But **191** now that I was situated as Luce's ambassador to a country he deeply admired, I felt some compulsion to mend relations between the two principalities, Time Inc. and Her Majesty's Government. Besides, if my colleagues and I were going to be effective reporters it made sense to persuade British officials that we were to be trusted as diligent and unprejudiced observers.

Early on I arranged to meet with deposed prime minister Anthony Eden at his country estate to pay respects and solicit thoughts on the state of East-West relations and that "special relationship" with America that was the center pivot of British foreign policy. In Eden's appearance and carriage there was still the reminder of the elegant foreign secretary in homburg and morning dress who some twenty years earlier had resigned in principal over Chamberlain's appeasement at Munich. But he was now wan and visibly suffering from the severe bile-duct affliction that was slowly killing him. He seemed remarkably philosophical for one who had waited for so long in the shadow of the Churchillian oak for the right to lead his government and then had the prize so rudely wrenched from him. In our meeting we barely touched on Suez, and then only when Eden said, as if pitying more than censuring Dulles, the man who more than any other had brought him down as prime minister, "I have no animus against Foster." He felt that Eisenhower and Harold Macmillan, his successor as PM, had already repaired much of the damage that Suez had done to the "special relationship." Eden was magnanimous, I thought, in view of what had happened to him, but later I concluded that he was simply too ill, too tired, and too resigned to cavil at fate. He probably had read Matthew Arnold, "Let the long contention cease, geese are swans and swans are geese."

Another mission took me for a day to Oxford to meet Sir William Hayter, who had been permanent undersecretary, the highest civil service position in the Foreign Office. After some groping questions about British attitudes toward the Middle East and Israel, the ethnic violence in Cyprus, the independence movements in a half dozen other colonies, I asked: "Is it possible to describe in a few words the goals of British foreign policy?"

192   "Why of course," said Sir William without any hesitation.

"Essentially it is one goal: To maintain insofar as possible the standard of living of these islands." It was a marvelously simple answer to a complex question. A far cry from (and far more realistic than) Winston Churchill's vow never to "preside over the disintegration of the British empire." Hayter's answer has served me ever since as the measuring stick with which to assess the underlying thrust or motivation of a given British policy, domestic or international.

I should not have worried so much about patching up *Time*-U.K. relations. Occasionally at a dinner or cocktail party a disgruntled Tory would poke a finger into the chest and grumble, sometimes very insultingly, about Washington's abandonment of its most loyal ally. But when it came to working the news beat, British pragmatism took care of the problem. England has no permanent allies or permanent enemies, only permanent interests, said the nineteenth-century foreign secretary Palmerston. This applied as well a century later in the case of a correspondent for a publication presumed to be influential, especially an American one. The Foreign Office, the Treasury, and other important government agencies were not going to let a past grudge interfere with the government's cultivation of the best possible pro-British understanding and sympathy in a new foreign correspondent.

I was welcomed into the exclusive Wednesday morning briefing that a polished and well-informed diplomat serving as head of the Foreign Office news department gave to correspondents for a select group of American news organizations. Our group enjoyed a similar Thursday afternoon conclave at Number 10 Downing Street with the prime minister's equally urbane and well-informed spokesman. The "background" information proffered at these meetings provided a substantial portion, though not by any means all, of the week's supply of high-level information gleaned by us reporters, among them Drew Middleton of the *New York Times* and Don Cook of the *Herald Tribune,* Bill Stoneman of the Chicago *Daily News,* Joe Fromm of *U.S. News & World Report,* Joseph Harsch of NBC and Charles Collingwood of CBS, and men from *Newsweek* and the *Chicago Tribune,* as well as myself or Jim Greenfield of *Time.*

Every three months or so the same group of us would assem- **193** ble in a drawing room at Number 10 for an informal background session with the prime minister himself. I cannot remember an instance where these sessions produced important news, but they were valuable for the sense they provided of Harold Macmillan's frame of mind and of some of his attitude toward internal and external affairs. Offering ample scotch, gin, or sherry to his guests, the PM would sit comfortably on a couch beneath one of Number 10's several Canneletto Venetian landscapes. One leg crossed over the other might betray a slightly frayed cuff to match the well-wornness of the rest of his attire, usually an outfit of Edwardian cast, soft unpressed flannel trousers, loose-fitting jacket, and unmatching vest, an ensemble that complemented the gray hair and bushy mustache and stopped just short of foppishness.

Very much a "special relationship" man, Macmillan in these sessions with American reporters made no effort to hide his belief (or was it merely hope?) that Britain, now declined in power but rich with experience, was playing Athens to America's powerful but clumsy Rome. His diffident manner and crisp yet soft speech, sometimes degenerating into a mumble, made it sound much less condescending than it was. He did little though to disguise his condescension toward his Labor Party opposition and in particular its leader, Hugh Gaitskell.

The movement toward well-being that grew out of Labor's postwar reorganization of British society had been nourished by the Conservatives after Churchill regained office. The Tories saw the political necessity of accommodating to the arrival of socialism; with a few minor changes they simply stole Labor's clothes. So when Macmillan called an election for October 1959, his campaign slogan, crassly materialistic as it was, had the ring of truth: "You've never had it so good." The country agreed, by a handsome electoral margin.

The day after Macmillan and the Tories roundly defeated Hugh Gaitskell and Labor, I invited Joe Harsch of NBC (and later the *Christian Science Monitor*) for lunch at Buck's, a veddy English men's club of which I had somehow become a member. We were seated at the small bar when another member drew up the stool next to us. "Congratulations, Prime Minister," said the always cheerful Irish bartender.

"Thank you, Patrick," said Harold Macmillan, "It did go rather well, didn't it?" His mood was as loose and comfortable as his attire. The dark striped suit had plenty of mileage on it and the rumpled sweater vest was powdered with cigar ash. "I'll have a glass of champagne."

Joe Harsch and I offered our own congratulations. "Yes, could have been worse," said he, surely knowing from the vernacular that he was speaking to two Americans but wondering what they were doing in Buck's, of all places. "When were you certain it was in the bag?" one of us asked.

"Really certain about four days before the end," he said. "They lost their guts, began promising everything. The pensions increase—that might have been enough. But then Gaitskell lost his nerve. The income tax promise, and then the purchase tax. It was all too much. When I was a lad at Oxford I remember you could bribe a policeman for half a crown. But if you gave him five pounds he'd arrest you. Well, Labor forgot that. People suspected, and with good reason."

Gaitskell was far from being a horny-handed son of toil and might have passed as a gentryman with his public school background, his dress, accent, and demeanor, a fact which made him suspect among the more militant union men and a fat target for a firebrand like the more charismatic Welshman Aneurin Bevan, but I thought he was the best his party had to offer. He was intelligent, decent, and possessed both the guts and the eloquence to save the Labor party from its left-wing unilateral nuclear disarmers and other extremists. His premature death in 1963 was a great loss to the Labor party and British politics. But Macmillan was aggressively disdainful of the man. With memories of his own hazardous combat service in World War I, he placed much value on military service. "Gaitskell's never led, never commanded. He's one of those people who's always talked to people, lectured them but never led them." He was contemptuous too of Gaitskell's principal form of relaxation, ballroom dancing. The prime minister sipped the last of his champagne. "Do you really think the British people would choose as prime minister a man who's never been in the trenches and dances all night?" Beckoning to Patrick. "I'll have another glass of that."

195

It became obvious as he talked candidly on about politics and personalities that he couldn't quite place our faces. Then suddenly a quiver of recognition crossed his own face: By Jove, these were two of those Americans who occasionally slurped down his booze and asked him impertinent or silly questions at Number 10 Downing Street. Journalists! And here he was chattering on like a Bloomsbury gossip. His composure unruffled, he drank a bit more of his champagne, climbed off the barstool, and said, "Remember, chaps. This is a club." With that magisterial reminder that what is said in a gentlemen's club never leaves the premises, he ambled out to rule Brittania for another several years.

If there had been any hard news in what the prime minister had confided in us, we might have gotten word quickly to our home offices. I reported the confrontation in a private letter to Luce because I thought it would amuse him. Otherwise, Joe and I stored up for future use the insights we'd gained into Harold Macmillan at his moment of gloating, and kept the pleasant interlude to ourselves. After all, we were gentlemen too, were we not?

Chapter 13

O 'Dem Golden Shackles

The Tories were ascendant and the Laborites rancorously divided among themselves, so domestic politics provided only mild entertainment. Even in periods of lassitude, however, political intercourse in the House of Commons is one of the most literate and entertaining of spectacles. I made periodic visits to the House to savor the superiority of British parliamentary discourse (though not always its substance) over that in the United States Congress. And I made a practice of covering the tribal rites known as Conservative and Labor party conferences, almost as noisy but tidier and more relevant than our own national nominating conventions. Covering domestic politics day to day was best left to the inimitable Honor Balfour.

Internationally, London was a nerve center even though the Empire was no more. Great Britain's long tenure as *pukka sahib* to a third or more of the world had stocked the foreign and Commonwealth offices with generalists as well as specialists who had knowledge both practical and esoteric of just about any region and were delighted to speak up. So hardly a week passed without requests from New York for background data and analysis of whatever palace coup, geological cataclysm, or other significant or not-so-significant development that occur- **197** red that particular week in Katmandu, Baghdad, Ulan Bator, or wherever else news was breaking.

The international scene was simmering, to use an oxymoronic word to describe the state of cold war politics, so the job took me on many trips to Paris, Brussels, Copenhagen for NATO alliance meetings, to Geneva for disarmament talks, to Berlin for a giant Communist propaganda extravaganza called the World Youth Festival, to Athens, Ankara, and Cyprus to examine London's tortuous efforts at solving the poisonous dispute between Greeks and Turks over the fate of the island. (Don't wear your Anderson and Shepherd suits in Nicosia, I was advised. The underground is shooting at Englishmen these days. Indeed, one visiting English banker was shot to death on a streetcorner during my visit. My disguise was an aged Brooks Brothers sack that could never be mistaken for Savile Row.)

Britain, of course, played an influential role in world politics, in the network of alliances that the Americans had fashioned to "contain" Soviet Communism and in the pervasive fields of international insurance and banking for which London was still a world capital. Macmillan with his "our Athens to their Rome" fixation fancied himself a potential broker between Washington and Moscow (somewhat to Washington's annoyance), so "summit diplomacy" was one of his preoccupations. When Macmillan scheduled a trip to Moscow in the winter of 1959 to conduct some one-on-one diplomacy with Nikita Khrushchev, many of the dozens of us who were going to cover the event trotted off to Moss Brothers, the venerable London outfitting shop where one could rent just about everything for exotic travel except cleft sticks for carrying messages through the jungle (Moss Bros would probably find even those on special order). We equipped ourselves with fur-lined greatcoats, hats made of various animal skins, and insulated boots to protect against the Russian cold. We arrived to the mildest Russian winter of the century. Since we had brought no light clothing with us we lumbered about the Moscow streets bathed in sweat while Muscovites licking ice cream cones stared at us as if we were refugees from some Siberian movie set. Appropriately to his role as leader, Macmillan looked the most incongruous of all, stepping off his plane in a gray hat about two feet tall that must have cost the lives of at least three Persian lambs.

Premier Khrushchev treated the British prime minister coolly, even taking over a reception at the British Embassy to stage a raucous impromptu meeting with the press while Macmillan retired upstairs with "a toothache." The Soviets had lifted all censorship for dispatches dealing with the meetings of the two leaders. Since the meetings themselves produced little news, we visitors wrote mostly of our impressions of Moscow, Kiev, and Leningrad and conversations with the few residents who dared to talk with us. Moscow-based correspondents used the temporary freedom for an orgy of dispatches detailing long pent-up material they had not been able to get past the censors.

The next confrontation with Khrushchev was even less productive, but that was not Macmillan's fault. In May of 1960 an army of us newsmen descended on Paris to cover the scheduled "summit conference" of Macmillan, Eisenhower, de Gaulle, and Khrushchev, but the game was rained out. Shortly before the leaders were to convene, a Soviet missile shot down a high-flying plane over Soviet territory and it proved to be an American U-2 spy plane. The shamefaced pilot, a hapless chap named Gary Powers, was intact, as was the suicide kit with which the CIA or Air Force had equipped him (as mine would have been under the same circumstance). Eisenhower made what the horrified traditionalists in all the big-power foreign offices and intelligence agencies considered to be the boobish mistake of actually telling the truth, that the U-2 plane had indeed been spying on the Soviet Union. That was all Nikita Khrushchev needed to disrupt a summit conference he may not have much wanted anyway. This was not the bumptious, amiable Khrushchev we'd joked with at the Moscow meeting. In a show of outrage as convincing as one of those familiar spittle-spraying Maurice Evans portrayals of a King Lear mad scene, Khrushchev held a table-pounding news conference to denounce the President of the United States for spying on Russia and having the effrontery to admit it; a summit conference was impossible in the light of such insolence, so he was going home.

So eager was Macmillan to serve as broker between Moscow and Washington that his press briefer had some of us almost convinced that he personally was winning Khrushchev's assent **199** to stay and save the summit. My *Time* colleagues Frank White of the Paris bureau and John Mecklin, who had flown in from Bonn, scoffed away my unfounded optimism: The rest of the leaders and their entourages were already packing their bags. The summit meeting was definitely off.

Khrushchev was a formidable force—and a walking puzzle. He bore a vague resemblance to a familiar face and suddenly it came to me whose it was; he was Wallace Beery in baggy pants but without the five-o'clock shadow. Mrs. Khrushchev could have made a passable Marie Dressler if she'd been a couple of feet taller. Though he reeked of peasant vulgarity and often behaved ominously, as he did in Paris or in his vow to "bury" the West, or clownishly, as when he removed a shoe and pounded it on his desk to interrupt a speech at the United Nations, he seemed to me to be the kind of crockery-breaker who might be dangerous but who on the other hand, if he could stay in power, might have the nerve to force real changes in the Soviet system and perhaps let some daylight into that forbidding, windowless monolith. My files to *Time* and to *Life* after the summit broke up reflected this, but others with far more knowledge than mine about the Soviet Union and the men who ran it were not so sanguine; they were more concerned by Khrushchev's reckless nature than aware of great potential for benevolence. The stories as finally published in both *Time* and *Life* shared the dour appraisal. I hoped they were wrong.

A more successful voyage was Macmillan's visit to British Africa in early 1960. One of the disagreeable chores that had been left to him by previous prime ministers was the dismantling of what remained of the Empire. Somewhat against his own inclinations he had resisted calls from some in his cabinet to oppose decolonization and instead encouraged an acceptance of nationalism as inevitable. I was the only American in the small crew of newsmen who accompanied Macmillan as he visited British Africa to examine the dismemberment in varying stages of process. Ghana had already won its independence and under the impetuous leadership of an American-educated rascal named Kwame Nkrumah was struggling, without many signs of success, to find the means of economic survival.

200   Nigeria got its formal independence before our eyes in Lagos.

The Nigerian capital was then suffering the odiferous effects of a strike by the city's night-soil collectors; that is, it smelled like a long-unflushed toilet. But into every life . . . etc., so Independence Day was not postponed. With a display of pomp and a cascade of speeches delivered mostly in Oxford-perfect English, in a house of parliament patterned somewhat after London's, the baton of nationhood passed from the British High Commissioner to the new prime minister of free Nigeria, an ornately costumed political leader from the Muslim northern region. From his seat of honor Harold Macmillan smiled benignly on the proceedings, perhaps pleased to see yet another white man's burden transferred to other shoulders. Nigeria had promise of becoming the largest and most powerful country in black Africa *if* its widely divergent north, east, and west regions could hold and work together. But the country had been arbitrarily tacked together as a patchwork "nation" by colonial masters a continent away who cared little about historic tribal differences, so leaders in all three regions were already sensing reasons why they might not live together happily ever after.

White-governed southern Africa was a quite different matter. Southern Rhodesia was the first country I'd visited whose immigration forms for arriving visitors demanded to know the sex of one's spouse. The white minority, most of them prospering in insurance, banking, or tobacco farming, pondered ways to have it both ways, full independence from the British on terms that allowed the whites to continue to segregate and dominate the black majority. In the capital, Salisbury, hypocrisy reigned. Whites talked of their increasing progress in broadening human rights while requiring blacks to live four or more miles from the capital and only grudgingly allowing the country's one black lawyer to rent an office in the capital. There was only one hotel where we could legally sit down to talk with black Rhodesians, and they were forbidden by law to drink alcoholic beverages unless they held a university degree (unlikely) or submitted to the indignity of applying for a special drinking license. A white politician pointed out proudly that the government had just repealed a regulation requiring blacks and whites to go to separate windows at post offices. Yes, a young black activist explained, the government did so only because Salisbury business- **201** men complained that their black messengers were having to spend hours waiting in line to pick up the office mail while the Whites Only windows were little used. Some white Rhodesians wanted federation with adjacent Northern Rhodesia and Nyasaland if only to avoid what some other whites preferred, union with South Africa and its imprisonment of its twelve million blacks in the segregation and inequities of apartheid.

South Africa, won for the Crown some sixty years before by the nasty war against the Boer settlers, was the least agreeable remnant of the Empire, now dominated by its unswervingly white supremacist Afrikaner population with the limp acquiescence of its prosperous Anglo community. It was here that Macmillan chose to perform perhaps the most statesmanlike act of his career. He was guest of South Africa's House of Parliament in Capetown, a gracious two-story high chamber paneled with burnished black stinkwood, a wood as beautiful as its name is ugly. A giant mace similar to that of London's House of Commons was in its appointed place, yet another memento of England's greatest export, the parliamentary system. On this summery January day Macmillan stood before the two hundred or so stony-faced men and two or three women who represented the three million or so whites who ruled a country of some sixteen million, most of them disenfranchised blacks and "coloreds." Even the legislators who "represented" the blacks and Asians were themselves white. Macmillan made no direct reference to the rigid system of apartheid which, enacted soon after World War II, had doomed the South African majority to pitiful wages, dismal education, and lives of general degradation. But he delivered a warning. "The most striking of all the impressions I have formed since I left London a month ago is of the strength of [the] African national consciousness," he said. "In different places it may take different forms but it is happening everywhere. The wind of change is blowing through the continent. Whether we like it or not, this growth of national consciousness is a political fact. We all must accept it as fact."

Hardly a body moved. Faces already stiffened and unsmiling grew even tighter as Macmillan read his lesson in his customary smooth, almost casual parliamentary manner. When he finished there was a scattering of applause, just enough to show politeness without enthusiasm. The South African prime minister, Henrik Verwoerd, looked for a moment as if he had been kicked in the groin, sputtered a few mumbled words of response, then dutifully shook Macmillan's hand and led him out the chamber. The guest of honor appeared quite satisfied with his day's work. News of the speech and especially the phrase "wind of change" quickly traveled to much of the world, enhancing the reputation of Harold Macmillan. As for Prime Minister Verwoerd and his government, they were unstirred by the breeze. Only a few days after Macmillan left the parliament voted to extend segregation along South Africa's bathing beaches from the high tide mark out to a three-mile limit—extra protection against pollution by those they looked upon as half-naked kaffirs and wogs from India.

A few months later the parliament voted to make South Africa a republic and end all allegiance to the British Crown. Severance of all ties to the Commonwealth would inevitably follow.

With all the traveling and the heavy load of other demands for international, political, and economic material, the London operation was a busy one. Still, with a staff so ample and versatile the bureau chief had time for some of the lighter pleasures of life, both professional and recreational. Occasionally I poached on Monica Dehn's or Mike Demarest's territory to take on an assignment that was literary or cultural, or even quaint little experiences of English eccentricity, the occasional event that was at least amusing. One day, for example, the local power authority in a rural corner of Yorkshire unveiled a new transformer to channel electricity to the area. With much fanfare the supervisor pulled a lever and pumped a few thousand volts out to the Yorkshire countryside. For miles around, TV sets, toasters, and other household appliances went up in puffs of smoke. Oops. Improper hookup. Shortly after that event a period of unseasonable cold caused the surface of England's first experiment with a superhighway, a much-vaunted stretch of roadway named the M-1, to crumble like the frosting on a stale wedding cake. "We hadn't counted on frost," the chief engineer explained.

These seemingly insignificant and seemingly unconnected **203** events struck a nerve. Somehow they symbolized, to me at least, the dilemma of postwar Britain, a country whose people and customs I had come to love. The Yorkshire fiasco reminded me of the crazy, slipshod electrical system in my own London house and the difficulty of getting standardized replacements for the five different shapes and sizes of wall plugs, some with removable fuses that blew at whim, some as big as avocados, no one type substitutable for another. This sort of electrical anarchy was commonplace in all but the most modern structures, but no one seemed to care about changing it. It was symptomatic of the "I'm all right, Jack" complacency with which too many Britons, the managerial as well as the working class, reacted to the spectacle of productivity diminishing and modernization lagging while other countries outcompeted them. Who was going to help meet Sir William Hayter's requirement, "to maintain insofar as possible the standard of living of these islands"? Not the plumber who'd arrive with a team of three or four helpers whose first act was to sit down for a tea break. Not the manufacturer of bicycles who was offered all the financing he needed to convert his old-style factory into a modern one that could produce thousands more cycles for much needed export but who preferred to do it his way because that's how his great-grandfather, his grandfather, and his father had done it. Not the arrogantly languid car salesman with the Oxford accent in Lagos who would not even rise up from his chair to greet a customer while the German salesman down the block was filling the streets of a British-run colony with Mercedes. Nor the assembly line supervisor who let go past him the Hillman Minx with a faulty gearbox or a Triumph with a carburetor that would shake loose at 50 mph.

Perhaps I was overreacting. It would have been stretching matters much too far if I used the seemingly insignificant examples of the blown transformer and the crumbled M-1 as the basis for a psychoanalysis of the British condition, the decline of its industry, the inability of labor and management alike to generate wealth as fast as its welfare state was spending it, the refusal to join in the movement toward a unified Europe in time to shape it to British interests. Instead, I blended the Yorkshire **204** and M-1 incidents into a brief lighthearted amusement that only inferentially dramatized how the nation that gave birth to the Industrial Revolution in the nineteenth century was having difficulty coming to grips with the technology of the twentieth. The story appeared in the next issue of the magazine.

When the phone rang several days later it became apparent that the little story had struck nerves other than mine. The caller was an amiable fellow named Dr. Charles Hill, who had become popular as "the radio doctor" for his cheerful, morale-building BBC broadcasts during the war. He now served as a sort of spokesman-at-large for the government. The story was not only insulting, he complained, but *Time* was unfairly and harmfully belittling British technology and British character. I demurred. "I should not need to remind you of Faraday," he remarked, "should I?" Of course not, I told him. The person who needed to be reminded of the discoveries of England's great electrical genius was that electrical supervisor up in Yorkshire who'd almost pan-fried an entire county. I invited Dr. Hill to lunch next day in the Time-Life dining room and though neither of us gave much ground we made peace over martinis, New York strip sirloins, a good claret, and imported fresh asparagus for dessert. Yes, in addition to using a crazy variety of wall plugs, driving on the left, stuffing sausages with what seemed to be sawdust, keeping their living rooms chilly and their beer warm, the English fancied asparagus for dessert.

When New York was persuaded to schedule a cover story on the sculptor Henry Moore, I pulled rank and took the assignment myself. I had no expertise in the field of sculpture but by going back to my first trip to Florence I could claim a sort of kinship-by-inspiration with the works of Michelangelo by way of his giant *Captives,* and I was more familiar with good sculpture than I had been with horseracing when I took on the Native Dancer assignment. So I went to visit Henry Moore at his Elizabethan cottage and cluster of studios on four tranquil farmland acres in Hertfordshire, about an hour northwest of London. I found him sitting in an old wicker chair in his main studio, crowded with workbenches littered with old bones, sticks, water-smoothed pebbles, shells picked up on English and Riviera beaches. Its walls were covered with curious drawings in pencil or sallow greens, yellows, and reds, disturbing, faceless **205** human forms composed of lines, curves, shadows, and holes, the most distinguishing mark of a work by Moore. This one of four studios on his land was the one Moore called his "generating room," the place where he developed his ideas.

Thinking of the many massive bronze Henry Moore figures that occupied places of honor in many cities of the world, like the pierced female that lay outside my office at the Time-Life Building, I had expected to meet a large man. Moore was sixty-one, small and compact, about five-foot seven and perhaps 155 pounds, with a high-domed face that looked both benign and craggy. He was warm and outgoing but businesslike as he talked of his work and demonstrated how he did it. He picked up a small blob of soft plaster in his left hand and with his right hand, thick-wristed and broad, he pressed with his thumb or flicked a small scalpel. The chunk of plaster began to take on form. But form of what? There was the vague outline of a female figure, one breast pushed forward from a gently twisted torso, but only a smooth crater where the other breast should be. The head didn't satisfy him so he reached for a smaller tool and pared the head into an elongated rectangular appendage, no larger than his thumbnail, perhaps one-twentieth the size of the body instead of nature's one-seventh. He studied the shape with a frown, then poked two small indentations for eyes. He put it aside to sit for a while, perhaps to germinate as the seed for another of the giant mother figures for which Henry Moore had become famous.

Without ever seeming immodest or self-centered, Moore was generous with his time and his commentary. He told how as early as age ten he became interested in sculpture, took trips to the London museums and galleries to gape at the works of early masters. He explained his several works in progress, including a massive elm tree trunk he was just beginning to carve into a giant figure, and walked me about the acre or more of carefully placed Moore works he was saving for his wife and daughter, including one large casting of his famous king and queen, two slender seated figures staring like hollow ghosts into the distance. Nearby was an equally haunting fallen warrior with shield. As we walked about he constantly rubbed and fondled one of the stones or pebbles he picked up along the way. "I am always feeling for texture and shape," he said. "In a way it goes back to my mother." She was an indefatigable mother of eight whose day began as early as 5:00 A.M. when Moore's father, a Yorkshire coal miner, was on the early shift and extended until late at night. On some days she suffered badly from rheumatism. " 'Oh Henry, lad,' she'd say, 'this shoulder is giving me gyp today,' and I'd rub the aching place with some oils." He pointed to a bronze figure standing in a grove of willows and said, "As I was making that figure I was rubbing my mother's shoulder again. She was constantly in my mind. Those moments all became a part of the sculpture." "There's no doubt," he said later with a smile, "I've had what Freud would call a mother complex."

After spending a considerable part of three days with Moore (and staying up nights to read about and compare Moore's work with that of other notable sculptors), I had absorbed enough to write about my subject with a reasonable amount of confidence. When the story appeared I was pleased to see how much of my file was used but disappointed that New York decided to dilute the Moore story with capsule profiles of half a dozen other living sculptors. That didn't seem to bother Henry Moore at all. He offered to come down to London and personally spruce up the patina on the reclining lady in the Time-Life courtyard.

The variety of work in London was one of the job's delights. Given the support of such a talented and versatile staff, there was also plenty of time to spend with Maggie and the boys in enjoying the many pleasures of Britain and the continent— summer vacations on the Riviera and in northern Wales, fishing trips to Ireland, skiing in Austria (a laughable sight), plenty of good theater (and cheap as well), many evenings with writers like C. P. Snow or William Sansom and an engaging mixture of actors, painters and sculptors, and journalists.

There were many pleasant evenings in the Chester Square house of T. S. Matthews, who'd chosen to live in London after his break with Luce. He was remarried, to Martha Gellhorn, the handsome foreign correspondent and novelist who had been Ernest Hemingway's third wife. Tom and Martha were both fiercely independent, in widely divergent ways; that did **207** not produce much stability in marriage (it lasted technically about ten years) but it sure made for a very lively ménage. Dinner party guests would be partly of Martha's friends, partly Tom's, and the twain did not always meet. Both Matthews and Gellhorn seemed to be comfortable with Maggie and me (Maggie had the kind of no-nonsense candor that was Gellhorn's trademark) so we often found ourselves seated at the Chester Square dinner table as quite willing and usually amused buffers between, say, an eccentric Anglican curate invited by Tom and an obstreperous tabloid editor who'd come as Martha's guest. It was near the end of one of those winey evenings that Tom Matthews gruffly volunteered that he'd been aloof toward me and many others when he was the top editor in New York not out of the arrogance or rudeness of rank but because he was afraid of newspapermen "because they all seem to know so much more than the rest of us." I laughed and told him that his fears were absolutely groundless in almost all cases and certainly so in my case. That evening sealed a warm friendship that lasted until Tom Matthews died in 1991, just days before his ninetieth birthday. A bishop's son, he was buried in a family churchyard in Princeton, New Jersey, after a grand Episcopalian funeral service that was planned in advance by the honoree and composed only partly by the hymnal and the Book of Common Prayer but mostly in the witty and discerning prose and poetry of T.S.M. himself.*

And there was our racehorse. The Native Dancer experience had introduced Maggie and me to the romance of the track in the States and we found it in abundance within easy range of London. We were pleased to discover that Mark Kauffman, the *Life* photographer, and his wife, Anita, were similarly addicted so we took to going to the races together. I am not certain who

---

*A sample of Matthews's advance instructions: "I should like to have the 19th Psalm read (not sung) at my funeral service. The text I want is in the Psalter of the Book of Common Prayer (1928/1662 edition—not the King James version, either Authorized or Revised). I'd like to have this great poem recited by a trained reader of verse—not in mincing chancel tones nor with oratorical vulgarity, but in a voice to match those majestic, heart-piercingly simple words. And I want this psalm read by a single voice, not in the dreary antiphonal between the precise priest and the slurred, shamefaced muttering of the congregation."

first suggested it—I have since alternated between taking credit for it and blaming Mark Kauffman for the idea—but after one languorous afternoon at the track in Windsor we decided it would be fun if we bought our own thoroughbred. The two wives didn't think much of this. "We already have three sons and three daughters between us," Anita said. "So who's going to clean up after a racehorse?"

But the dollar was strong and the flesh was weak. Owning a horse would have been far too expensive in the States, but in England we could keep a racer in full training for less than $30 a week, plus modest charges for insurance, racing silks, jockeys, and entry fees. All we needed were a couple of partners with whom to share the costs. We found them in in my deputy bureau chief, Jimmy Greenfield, and John Metcalf, a prospering English advertising man who liked to wager a nicker now and then and could afford to lose.

Mark and I made off to Newmarket on a pleasant spring day in 1959 for the annual auction of yearlings, promising our partners and our wives that we would not be impetuous but would bide our time until just the right creature came up for sale. We came across a bay colt out of the mare Dido, sired by a horse named Wilwyn. The sire was owned by the South African mining tycoon Harry Oppenheimer, who'd bought him for a reported $280,000. Kauffman gasped when he saw the name of the sire. "What a good luck omen!" he said. "I photographed Wilwyn when he won the first International at Laurel." We bought him with a bid of £325, or $910 in real money, the first bloody horse on the auction block.

We hired forthwith one of a pair of brothers named Smyth who were in the upper middle rank of English horse trainers, then we rushed back to London with the good news and a couple of photographs of our rather skinny and overlegged new possession. Since we were an Anglo-American partnership, we decided quickly on the colors of our silks—red, white, and blue for the color of both flags at the Battle of Yorktown. Agreement on a name was difficult, but Maggie resolved the problem. "None of the four of you has any business in the racing game," she said, "so why don't you name him Fourflusher?"

The horse was picked to run first by the newspaper touts on **209** the morning of his maiden outing but came in third. That was Fourflusher's all-time best race in England. In every outing thereafter our horse broke far out in front of the field but faded quickly. "I guess we can take some satisfaction," said Metcalf after several exhilarating failures. "We own the fastest two-furlong horse in the British isles." Greenfield and Metcalf never complained, but I don't think they got much satisfaction from our partnership except for the cocktail party glamour of being able to talk about "my horse." But the Kauffmans and the Mannings had a wonderful time with the animal, standing with him in the paddock before post time to give the jockey his instructions ("Win, any way you can!"), visiting him at his Epsom Downs stable every other week so the Kauffman girls and Manning boys could feed him sugar cubes, then repairing to a charming Swiss inn on the Brighton Road for a sumptuous Sunday dinner. After a year and some fourteen races, we sold the horse for almost what we'd paid for him (not counting, of course, what we'd lost betting on him) and retired the stable's colors. Last we heard, Fourflusher had been gelded and sent off to race in Malaysia. We hoped they specialized there in two-furlong sprints.

It was pleasant to be able to live this sort of life—and be paid for doing it. We had grown to love living in London, reveled in new adventures and friendships, enjoyed the marvelous theater, the antiques shops, the occasional opportunity to afford a painting at a Sotheby's auction, museums both great and obscure, the easy access to France and Italy, lazy Sundays at Kew Gardens or Battersea park with the children, or just loafing at home with the Sunday papers, the *Observer* and *Sunday Times,* which were then two of the best newspapers in the world, so packed with good prose that each would take longer to digest than all five pounds of the *New York Times.* Maggie was getting special satisfaction out of writing occasional Sunday articles for the *Chicago Tribune,* bright, amusing yet insightful pieces about life in Britain.

There were all those things and more to enrich us and engage us. There was something else, too. As we moved into our third year abroad we were getting homesick.

210   I began coming home at night with what Maggie described as

"that What next? look" in my eyes. Beyond our hankering to return to the familiarities of life in the States and to reintroduce the boys to their homeland before their British accents became permanent, there were professional reasons for bringing the overseas sojourn to an end. They divided into two categories. The first was simply the long-term career question: Did I want to stay with Time Inc. indefinitely? Wasn't it time to break out of Luce's golden shackles and before I grew too old and reliant on them to see what I could do on my own? Second was the question of what kind of workplace *Time* was going to become as time went on and what future it offered me if I did stay there. The tensions and compromises and conscience pangs inherent in "group journalism" were a considerable price to pay even in the best of circumstances. Under the wrong kind of group leader they could be intolerable.

Some change was inevitable. Luce had already begun preparing for his own retirement by annointing Hedley Donovan, the very able managing editor of *Fortune,* as his successor as editor in chief of the whole Time Inc. empire. That was good. Hedley was a topflight editor, a man who spoke softly but wielded stout principle. He was also a near neighbor and fellow commuter on the Long Island Railroad between Port Washington and Manhattan. We had become good if not intimate friends, and I greatly respected him. Now there were signs that Luce was going to bring tough old Roy Alexander's tenure as managing editor of *Time* to an end. The answer to the second question in my mind depended in great part on Luce's choice of the successor to Alexander. The likely choice was Otto Fuerbringer. This was not good. I hoped that Luce would have the wisdom to choose Tom Griffith instead. A poll would have shown a very large majority of *Time* writers, editors, researchers, and reporters to be sharing that hope.

Fuerbringer was an excellent technician, quick, conservative, forceful in his judgments, and Prussian in his exercise of command. He had a good instinct for timing of cover stories and for anticipating breaking news. He was sharp in matters of design and the use of illustrations. His talents, however, did not make up for his flaws. Not only was he tenacious in his grudges (a trait I must confess I could identify with) but he also was given   **211** to bullying behavior and hurtful vindictiveness. He was more a browbeater than a leader of men. I considered his politics to be more opportunistic and sychophantic than original. And I felt that if only by tolerating them he encouraged the liberties with fact, doctoring of quotes, and the other questionable practices which *Time* should long before have outgrown. He as deputy managing editor and I as a writer and then senior editor had gotten along passably well when I worked in New York, but relations between us gradually chilled, and they took a bad turn after I moved to London.

Joe David Brown had filed a long, meticulously researched profile for a cover story on the actor Alec Guinness. When the story appeared we in London could not recognize some of the material in it, found quotes that had been doctored and a lead that was mostly made up by the writer in New York.

Guinness was nonplussed and angry. So was Joe David Brown. At Guinness's insistence Joe David and I went to the bank of the Thames to visit the actor in a trailer he was using while playing the ramshackle artist Gulley Jimson in the making of the movie of Joyce Cary's *The Horse's Mouth*. The fright wig, unkempt look, and wild-eyed appearance of the zany painter who worked on a barge in the Thames made Guinness's tirade all the more convincing. I filed a protest to New York, including a lengthy list of "inaccuracies, distortions and figments that, in our opinion, make us look a laughing stock and, worse, irresponsible as an agency of journalism." The writer composed a response, admitting that his lead was indeed "partly fiction" and proudly detailing point by point how he had improved the cover story by making up certain details and putting words in Guinness's mouth. This was bad stuff. Emmet Hughes, who had come back from his stint in Eisenhower's White House to become chief of Time-Life's foreign correspondents and therefore my immediate superior, gave strong support to our protest. Later he could report only that the controversy had been brought to the attention of Luce, that Roy Alexander was bothered by it but did not seem inclined to take any action, that Otto Fuerbringer thought the writer's story and his defense of what he had done were perfectly acceptable.

212   When *Time* committed this sort of chicanery in pursuit of

political aims it could at least be understood if not excused on grounds of passionate ideological belief and the right of Henry Luce and his minions to push their biases and causes, no matter how wrongheaded, just as did the other press lords. After all, in A. J. Liebling's caustic construction, they owned freedom of the press because they owned the printing presses. However, when it came to everyday occurrences, matters that did not much matter to the course of human events, it was not only wrong but it was stupid for a prestigious journal to undermine its reputation by tampering with the facts, all the more so when the simple facts themselves were interesting, and were what readers were expecting to get.

Luce came to London for a brief stay just as he was moving toward his choice of the successor to Alexander. I invited a small group to dine with him at Claridges, among them the head of Reuters news agency, the editor of the *Times* of London, the chief of the BBC, and a couple of Macmillan's rising young ministers. As might be expected given the make-up of the gathering, there was much discussion of journalism. His guests were polite but there was an undertone of reserve about the role of *Time* magazine. As he and I sipped a nightcap after the dinner, Luce expressed concern that *Time* was, as he put it, "losing the common room vote." He wondered why. He said he was asking several of his editors to give their views on the question and urged me to express my thoughts if I cared to. I obliged a few days later, on the last day of 1959, with a screed that was heartfelt and because of that probably longer than it should have been.

It was pointless to tax Luce's humor by questioning his political biases and his right to proselytize them. "Your patience must have been worn thin by the kind of internal criticism that grows purely out of political differences between what you and your magazine say and what staffers might prefer to say," I wrote. "On the other hand, mine has been worn down by those of my colleagues who seem to try to turn aside all criticism of *Time*'s journalism by trying to maintain that it is really only disguised discontent with *Time*'s politics." There were many reasons other than politics why *Time*'s credibility was in jeopardy, I said, and in some detail faulted the magazine for an   **213** "unconscionable amount of errors of fact," for frequent imprecision of expression, for its absence of humor, for New York's frequent disregard or misuse of the magazine's own reporters' dispatches, as in the Alec Guinness affair.

And then the peroration:

> It is often said that where *Time* is unpopular . . . it is because of opinions or positions that go against those of its detractors . . . I just don't think that is how it is. It is very often the small things, the seemingly unimportant things, the avoidable sins of omission and the improper manipulations of fact or fancy to make a jazzier story. This isn't necessary. You pay enough for craftsmen who ought to be able to produce the best stories under the most exacting conditions. If they don't they can be replaced by those who can. I don't know how many times around the U.S. and Europe I have run into people who say something like this: "You know, *Time* is wonderful and I read it every week—but why is it always wrong about the stories I know about?" This is not political criticism, nor intellectual criticism. It is criticism that ought to hurt most because it is most avoidable. If the ethics of it are not at issue, as I think they are, it seems to me that *Time*'s own aims and ambitions are.

A short note from Luce thanked me for taking the trouble and said he was thinking about a lot of the comments that had been provoked by his concern over "the common room vote." His more emphatic response came in March of 1960 with the announcement that Otto Fuerbringer was the new managing editor of *Time*.

Since I was already contemplating a change, whatever Luce's choice, the timing of the Fuerbringer appointment was helpful. I was getting old, had recently turned forty, in fact. If I waited much longer I'd be too bound by Henry Luce's golden shackles, the good pay and handsome perks. If I delayed, it would become even more difficult to abandon "group journalism" for a career more independent even if less secure. Maggie's view was, as usual, clear and to the point. She had been loyal but never comfortable with *Time*'s kind of journalism and never would be; this was the time to try circumstances over which I
would have more control and there would be no one but myself

to blame for foul-ups. That was close to becoming my conviction too, so my mind was just about made up before Luce made his choice of the new editor. There was no denying, though, that it put a fat exclamation point to my decision, serving the function that Samuel Johnson ascribed to the approach of one's hanging—"it concentrates the mind wonderfully." I let my decision marinate for a few weeks and it only improved in flavor. So on one fine July vacation evening in Wales, while wading in a moonlit sea-trout pool in the Conway River, I mentally composed a courteous letter of resignation, offering to serve in London until a successor could come in the fall. It went off to Harry Luce next day. "This has a certain ring of inevitability about it. Please accept my resignation from Time Inc. I want to move to circumstances that offer what I can only call, for lack of a less pompous phrase, more self-fulfillment. . . . I intend to move back to Washington and from there to report and write."

Luce responded flatteringly, urged me to reconsider. "I would not be reconciled to your departure unless I felt that I had done everything I could to make it possible for you to do what would appeal to you here," he wrote.

I did what he asked, and pondered for a few days, then replied in part:

> The individualist has a place in group journalism but for all but the merest handful there is much inhibition. . . . Even though one may be shouting at the top of his lungs, or lecturing with Demosthenic eloquence, the sound does not pierce the walls that enclose the group. Or if it does it is as one voice mixed to the point of a modulated hum, a cappella. The end result, when the choir is in synchronization, can be marvelous. But the fellow who wants to regale the townsfolk with his own beery baritone rendition of Shortnin' Bread has got to leave the choir and find himself another music hall, or at least a spot on a busy streetcorner.

Luce next invited Maggie and me to join him for a weekend at the Ritz Carlton in Paris, wined and dined us at Maxim's with his wife, Ambassadress Clare, and Noël Coward for company, and tried to persuade me to stay in some capacity with Time Inc. Hedley Donovan, I learned later, had joined his boss **215** in composing a list of propositions that might keep me in the fold, various writing or editing arrangements on *Life, Fortune,* or *Sports Illustrated* or, since I was talking about working out of Washington and perhaps trying to develop a syndicated column of my own, why didn't I sign on as a sort of roving, jack-of-all-magazines writer for all the magazines? It was tempting, but I had seen some Time Inc.'s star performers, much more veteran than I, slide into similar arrangements, then find themselves cruising about the company searching in vain for an editor who might make good use of them, each a sort of human Flying Dutchman cruising about the gloomy seas with no port to dock in. I remember trying with some clumsiness to explain, and said something to the effect that I'd be better fitted for group journalism if the group were *my* group.

I left Paris with Luce's good wishes and the comforting feeling that he really had wanted to keep me. Later I was told that, when Hedley Donovan asked why all those several propositions failed to persuade, Luce said, "He wants *my* job."*

Soon thereafter, events in New York headquarters took an ironic turn. The Republicans selected Richard Milhous Nixon as their candidate to succeed Eisenhower as president. Managing Editor Fuerbringer was struck down by an aneurysm and forced to be away for a few months. The Democrats chose John F. Kennedy to run against Nixon. It fell to Tom Griffith to lead *Time* through the election campaign. What followed was a three-months' presentation of balanced, alert, and fair campaign coverage that showed what a superb magazine *Time* could be when it put the right kind of editor in charge and played the game straight.

Leaving that good life and good friends of those still wonderful islands was wrenching, but the regret at departing was softened by the cargo of happy memories we carried with us. The

---

*Several years later, in his book *The Powers That Be*, David Halberstam reported that after our meetings in Paris Luce told a *Life* photographer, Carl Mydans, "He wants to be me." I'll not quarrel with Halberstam's reporting, but the Donovan version sounds more like Luce and is the more likely one. Just to set the record straight—and with no offense intended—I could never have aspired to be a Yale man let alone a Presbyterian; also I preferred to keep my curly hair. As for Luce's job, that was already spoken for.

Queen Mary docked in New York with an excited band of homecomers aboard just as the polls were closing on Election Day, November 8, 1960. We went to bed and got up next morning in doubt, learning only many hours later that John F. Kennedy had been elected President of the United States. I was glad that we had decided to set up housekeeping again in Washington. It seemed that there was going to be plenty to watch and to write about there.

Chapter 14

War and Uneasy Peace
in Washington (2)

The first time I had breakfast with President Kennedy at the White House was April 11, 1962. Something that happened the day before had made the president so furious that he was still seething at 9:30 that morning when we sat down beneath a gleaming chandelier in the sumptuous second-floor dining room. The oval mahogany table gleamed too, with fresh flowers, white linen, and sterling. A handsome portrait of John Tyler, the tenth president, hung over the mantelpiece. A pair of waiters offered choices from silver trays—assorted juices, omelets, poached or scrambled eggs, bacon or sausage, coffee, tea, milk, or Sanka. A box of forbidden Havana cigars lay open on the sideboard. Neither the president nor the men he'd gathered together were much interested in food. Vice-President Lyndon Johnson, trying to quit smoking, solemnly dangled an unlit cigarette from his lips. Also present were Secretary of State Dean Rusk, Secretary of Labor Arthur Goldberg, White House aides McGeorge Bundy, Theodore Sorensen, and Meyer Feldman, the chief of the President's Council of Economic Advisers Walter Heller, and assistant presidential press secretary Andy Hatcher, substituting for Pierre Salinger, who was on a trip. Twice the president left the table to talk on a nearby phone with **218** Secretary of Defense Robert McNamara or Secretary of the

Treasury Douglas Dillon. The president and some of his key men were trying to put down a serious domestic insurgency.

Late on the preceding day Roger Blough, chairman of the board of United States Steel Corporation, had come to the White House to present the president with a bludgeoning piece of news: U.S. Steel, without any advance warning, was at that moment announcing a price rise of $6 a ton. This high-handed act infuriated the president, personally because he had been doublecrossed by the nation's biggest steel company just after persuading steelworkers to restrain their wage demands, but more importantly because this could provoke a price surge that threatened his administration's arduous efforts to achieve wage-and-price stabilization at home and protect the deteriorating American balance of payments and competitive position overseas. The president had coldly received Blough's *fait accompli,* then assembled a small council of war in the Oval Office, remarking bitterly as he did, "My father always told me that all businessmen were sons-of-bitches, but I never believed it till now."

By early next day, five other steel companies were following U.S. Steel's lead and some of the administration's counterinsurgency measures were already underway—efforts to persuade other steel companies to hold their price lines, moves to transfer huge Pentagon orders to steel companies that held the line, a study of how antitrust laws might be invoked against the companies that had raised prices. At the breakfast meeting conducted underneath the piercing glance of President Tyler, the principal item on the agenda was the drafting of a statement President Kennedy would read at his news conference that afternoon. He made clear that he wanted to mince no words. These bastards were jeopardizing the public good. The idea was to bring down not only presidential wrath but the force of public disapproval on the heads of Roger Blough and his board of directors. "Some time ago," the statement said in part, "I asked each American to consider what he would do for his country and I asked the steel companies. In the last twenty-four hours we had their answer."

The outcome of this confrontation was victory for the government: U.S. Steel, Bethlehem, and three other producers **219** tucked tails and rescinded their price increases before the week was out.

But wait a minute! What was Robert Manning doing there, having breakfast with the president on that April day, and how did he get there? The first question is easy: I was there because I was the president's new assistant secretary of state for public affairs. As for the other question, I got there by way of some stupid professional mistakes. This calls for a bit of backtracking.

We settled into Washington before JFK's Inauguration Day, in ample time to watch the capital change almost overnight from the languid putting-green and three-no-trump complacency of the Eisenhower years into a livelier, feistier Washington, a town with the kind of bustle and excitement, the modern-day version of clinking spurs and snorting steeds suggested by the words *New Frontier.* The men and women moving into the places of power were mostly young, aggressive, and confident like Kennedy himself. An easy and open relationship with the press was a hallmark of the new administration all the way through its top echelons. The excitement was infectious. Yes, there was plenty to write about.

My plan in 1961 was to produce some articles about the New Frontier while working toward the longer-term enterprise of a syndicated column. I got off to a good start (profiles of Attorney General Robert Kennedy for the (Sunday) *New York Times Magazine* and Secretary of the Interior Stewart Udall for *The Saturday Evening Post*). For press credentials, an absolute necessity in official Washington, I inherited an arrangement Teddy White had engineered with *Saturday Review* while doing the reporting for the project that was to become his landmark book, *The Making of the President 1960.* Teddy, now headed for best-sellerdom and financial independence, no longer needed the credentials. I discovered in a few weeks, though, that I had seriously miscalculated. First, after all the years of working with pressing deadlines, a water-cooler or coffee pot down the hall to gather around, other people to talk to and exchange jokes with, I had great difficulty working alone; a metabolic condition, no doubt, which could be cured in time. But also I was pained to discover that free-lancing was a most precarious

220

way of making a living, even a sparse one. The token fees for the occasional columns I wrote for the *Review* barely paid the telephone bill with change left over for paperclips, and the fees for the more demanding and time-consuming articles were good for a few months' rent at best. It was imperative that I execute ahead of schedule Phase Two of my Independence Plan: Sign up for a syndicated column and its more predictable source of income.

Again I had grievously miscalculated. I approached the major news syndicates only to discover that none was interested in signing on yet another Washington columnist. The head of one of the biggest and best of the syndicates happened to be a close friend of Maggie's father, who was a prominent Chicago attorney, and the syndicate chief leveled with me. He wished he could help, but the market was saturated with liberal columnists, he said. If I were a conservative, even a right-wing kook, he could probably get me started with twenty, even thirty newspapers on a trial basis. "But I assume you have no desire to become a conservative or a kook of whatever persuasion." He was right, though his message did cause me to wonder whether being a right-wing kook could be a much worse fate than onrushing insolvency.

There is often a moment in a drawing room comedy when the telephone rings and signals a dramatic twist in the plot, something disastrous or providential. The voice on the other end of this call was that of John Hay Whitney and his words were providential. He asked if I might meet with him in New York to talk about the Sunday edition of his newspaper, the New York *Herald Tribune.* I thought I knew what was on his mind.

During my period in London, Jock Whitney was the American ambassador to Britain. He had the usual qualifications for that job, immense wealth and generous contributions to the American political party in power, but he brought other qualifications to the job as well. He had succeeded another very rich man whose term there was noteworthy for little more than his avid pursuit of good-looking women. ("You have sent us an ambassador with a closed mind and an open fly," a British diplomat said of him to an American counterpart.) Whitney was a most popular successor, a big cut above many of his 221 predecessors, intelligent, personable, with wide interests that ranged far beyond husbanding his wealth, from thoroughbred racing and Impressionist paintings to theater and movies (he was one of the investors in *Gone With the Wind*). He had a good sense of international affairs and an instinctive diplomatic touch, as well as the sense to assemble some good career diplomats for his London staff. All in all, a classy fellow. Like several of the American correspondents, I made a point of calling on Jock now and then for a drink and some talk about current affairs. Usually the talk turned to his latest acquisition, the foundering *Herald Trib,* and his efforts to save it from extinction. We shared admiration for London's *Observer* and *Sunday Times.* They compressed in fewer pages more good prose and useful information than did any American Sunday paper, including the Sunday *Herald Tribune* and excluding only occasional gems buried within the fat of Sunday's *New York Times.* Though it was a better-looking paper and offered more good writing than the Sunday *Times,* the Sunday *Trib* was never going to beat the big heavyweight in a pound-for-pound competition. Instead, it had to use karate techniques, use trimness, quickness, and sophistication to outwit the much bigger antagonist. Jock and I had talked more than once about the possibility of converting the *Herald Trib*'s anemic, hemorrhaging imitation of the Sunday *New York Times* into a compact East Coast emulator of the London *Observer,* a new kind of American newspaper that, given modern speed of delivery, could attract a readership stretching from Richmond and Washington north to Boston and beyond. It would require some suspenseful risk-taking and a lot of heavy breathing to build, but it could well mold a new body of loyal readers and advertisers and grow into a publication of both profit and influence. It appeared that he had not forgotten those discussions.

In New York, Jock introduced me to his publisher, Walter Thayer, and the man he'd hired to be overall editor of the *Herald Tribune,* John Denson. At the end of dinner I had signed on as editor of the Sunday New York *Herald Tribune.* We all shook hands firmly to seal the deal. Maggie and the boys were not as dismayed as I'd expected them to be when I told them we were moving to New York, but I nevertheless felt pangs of guilt

222

for uprooting the family again after only a few months in a new home, and some regret as well at leaving Washington at such an exciting time. We rented for a song a cavernous white elephant of a townhouse on upper Park Avenue and with the clout of one of Jock Whitney's business associates got the boys into a private school nearby that was patterned after the kind they had attended in England. Now I had again what I'd been missing: pressing deadlines, a water-cooler down the hall, and colleagues to trade yarns with, plus a real mark of achievement in the news trade, my own tab at the Artists and Writers Club, a West Side saloon better known as Bleeck's (pronounced Blakes). Located only doors away, it was a sort of *Trib* clubhouse, where the likes of Stanley Walker, Lucius Beebe, John Lardner, Red Smith, and other newspaper luminaries used to irrigate their minds and play the match game well into morning, and where a promising young journalist named Joseph Alsop once saved the *Trib*'s owner, Ogden Reid, from drowning when drink had caused him to fall asleep in his soup.

It might have been a job made in heaven or thereabouts except for one crucial fact: John Denson had not so much as hinted it when he welcomed me to the team with a solid handshake, but he did not want anybody but himself shaping the Sunday newspaper. Denson was a hill-country Louisianan whose red-neck prejudices (against blacks, Catholics, and most foreigners, for starters) had resisted the civilizing influences of service on some twenty newspapers as well as short stints at *Fortune* and in *Time*'s Washington bureau, then a longer stretch as editor of *Newsweek*. He was not much of a thinker, but he had undeniable talent for packaging other peoples' ideas and for making a front-page or a newsmagazine story seductive. His approach to the reader was similar to that of a Missouri mule trainer to his beast—first hit him over the head with a two-by-four to get his attention. He was a relentless, almost maniacal worker who had licked a bottle problem some years before and now consumed coffee by the hogshead while, with bugging eyes and much grinding of dentures, spending hours on the makeup of pages and the cropping of pictures to make the paper attention-getting no matter how thin its content. It wasn't the handsome *Herald Tribune* anymore, the paper that had won the love 223 of journalists from all over as well as prizes for its content and its typography, but Denson's cosmetics had admittedly generated much-needed excitement and beefed up daily circulation. He had neglected the Sunday paper, a forlorn package, but when I was taken on by Jock Whitney it became suddenly the object of his passionate attention. He subjected it to an overnight redesign (without any improvement in content) even before I'd settled into my office, killed stories I had commissioned, refused to meet or take my phone calls, and dealt with me only through a pair of KGB-like dolts he'd brought in from outside. A fine romance!

I protested, asked for at least a chance to lay out the blueprint for a slimmer but better newspaper of the kind Jock Whitney and I had talked about. Then came a real stroke of bad luck. Just as the confrontation came to a head, a heart attack took Jock out of the action. I tried for a while to do battle with the man I came to call Mad Dog Denson and to persuade Publisher Thayer and his efficiency experts at least to examine the rudiments of the "East Coast Sunday paper." It admittedly would require throwing away most of what little advertising there was and starting almost from scratch; it would cost more money at first but arguably could earn it back and more in time. The "bottom line" boys were afraid to risk the plunge—or the wrath of Denson. With my mentor in a sickbed, there was nothing to do but surrender. (My love for the *Herald Trib* allowed me no comfort when Denson's tyrannical behavior got him sacked several months later—too late to save the paper from eventual expiration.)

Now I knew how humiliated that hapless English road builder must have felt, the man who "hadn't counted on frost." What a fool I was for having walked into a bloody ambush without first scouting the terrain and sizing up the players. The realization of my naiveté (a French word I now employ in order to avoid admitting to outright stupidity) almost obscured a concern that was more pressing, the embarrassment of sudden unemployment.

Whoever it was who said "God takes care of fools and the United States" could have had my case in mind. Before I had

224   finished my last few days at the *Trib* and cleaned out my desk,

an associate from United Press days called to congratulate me on being considered for a position with the United States government. I told him he was mistaken. No, said my friend, he'd been visited by an FBI agent who was conducting a security check and wanted to know whether Robert Manning was a Communist agent, a pinko fellow traveler, an admirer of the anti-Franco side in the Spanish civil war, or a reader of dirty books. My friend said he told the man I was clean of all such sins except perhaps for the last one. He had refrained from saying how much we both despised Francisco Franco for fear of incriminating me.*

The mystery was solved a few days later when a telephone caller identified himself as Ralph Dungan of the White House. He was one of the president's principal talent scouts and wanted to interview me for a possible job in the New Frontier. Dungan was a pleasant, relaxed man who seemed as unpretentious as his big corner office in the White House West Wing was impressive. I'd hardly taken a chair when he said the president was looking for someone to take over the State Department's Public Affairs operation and my name had been mentioned. Dungan struck me as tough-minded in the way that invites tough-mindedness in return. And by now I was as wary as a springbok in lion country edging toward a waterhole at dusk. No ambush this time!

What about the fellow who'd been filling the job for the past year? I asked. Well, Dungan said, he just hasn't worked out and is being moved to a comfortable ambassadorial post in Europe. What does that mean, he didn't work out? I asked. Well, said

---

*I don't know how reliable or useful or even necessary they are today but the security checks conducted by J. Edgar Hoover's FBI were a cause not just of fear but also a considerable amount of ridicule among persons being scouted for government employment during the cold war days. When many years later under the Freedom of Information act I obtained censored copies from government files concerning me I found the material dealing with the FBI's "security clearance" inquiries to be straightforward and accurate. I was startled though to read in material from CIA files that I had been graduated from Harvard (from which I never graduated) in 1935, when I was age fifteen, and had lived at one period in a street I had never heard of in a distant part of New York City I had never even visited. The remainder of the contents described a subject whose life was so commonplace and uneventful I was glad he wasn't I.

Dungan, he just didn't seem able to do the job in a way that pleased either the secretary of state or the president. Who's he supposed to be working for? He's a presidential appointee, Dungan said, so I guess that means while he works for the secretary of state he'd be wise to please the president as well, since Mr. Kennedy has a very special interest in how the State Department deals with the public. Does Mr. Kennedy even know who I am? Yes, said Dungan, he'd heard from some people that I might be a good prospect for the job. Dungan didn't say who they were, but I thought it possible they included some of the Stevenson campaign advisers whom Mr. Kennedy had summoned in large numbers to high places in his administration. Arthur Schlesinger was in the East Wing as the president's in-house intellectual, Bill Wirtz was secretary of labor, Dave Bell was running the foreign aid program, Ken Galbraith was ambassador to India, George Ball was an undersecretary of state. After about an hour of cross- and cross-cross examination, which Dungan had the knack for making relaxing and reassuring, he said he'd looked me over and was satisfied, so if I was interested in proceeding further I ought to travel to Foggy Bottom and be looked over by the secretary of state.

This was a very different, far less comfortable meeting. Dean Rusk and I had already looked each other over, several years before. He was prominent on the American team at the United Nations that had tried the last-minute maneuver that almost untracked the Palestine partition decision in 1947 and dissembled about it, threatening my job in the bargain. While he was not the man with whom I had the unpleasant exchange over the State Department's deception, Dean Rusk had been a part of the murky goings-on and that seemed to say something emphatic about his attitude toward relations with press and public. The memory of that incident hung in the air between us as surely as his cigarette smoke (Chesterfields) when we sat together in the huge, dark-brown secretary's office on the seventh floor of the Department of State and mentally circled each other before deciding whether to pee on a tree stump, growl, or wag tails.

We exchanged pleasantries and inquired of each other's doings in the years since those early UN days. I had already been told the rudiments of the job—stewardship over a large bureau of some 150 people, a too-small budget of about $2.5 million, and responsibilities that included publishing the several volumes each year of U.S. diplomatic history, the hand-holding of well-intentioned members of World Affairs Councils and other citizens groups around the country with an interest in foreign policy, running a nationwide speakers' bureau, editing a stream of Department publications, providing Department "policy guidance" to the United States Information Agency, and, most importantly, serving as one of the government's main conduits of information to the public and a very hungry press corps. It was the secretary of state's and the president's attitude toward that last function that would determine whether a man should consider serving as assistant secretary for public affairs, especially if the man contemplating the job was by now so snakebit he'd not trust even Mother Teresa to cut the cards unless she wore sheepskin gloves. Jack Kennedy's first year as president indicated that he had a healthy attitude toward the information process, and Dungan's stress on that point made that doubly clear. But what about his secretary of state?

After the small talk, Dean Rusk looked at me gravely. With the remnant of a Georgia accent that still tinged his speech after years of living in Yankee country he asked, "Are you willing to lie for your country?"

That's it, I thought, and moved as if to end this conversation quickly, but as he saw my reaction Rusk intervened with the tiniest flicker of what might have been a smile and indicated that he was just asking a question, not making a proposal.

"No," I said. "And anybody would be a fool to think he could lie to the press even once and still be an effective spokesman. Anyway, it is not necessary to lie." I went on to say that, while it might not always be easy, a government official ought to be able at the worst to say nothing instead of dissembling (a polite choice of word) when national security demanded it or premature babbling would upset a delicate negotiation.

The matter of our unpleasant experience at the United Nations did not come up directly but implicitly I had just alluded to it. Rusk said he was satisfied with my response to his blunt question. That emboldened me to press some other matters   227 before deciding whether this was the right step for me. I told the secretary nobody in the job could serve him or the president well unless he had the full confidence of his superiors AND (I spoke the word in capital letters) unless he was granted full access to the major deliberations and major decisions and was granted clearance to see top-secret and other classified documents and cable traffic. This would require sitting in some of the sudden, impromptu meetings in which many big decisions are made as well as formal gatherings like the secretary's morning staff meetings and many of the exchanges with foreign officials both in Washington and abroad. This would mean also traveling with the secretary to important international gatherings, like the meetings of NATO and the other Western alliances and East-West arms control negotiations.

A spokesman known by the State Department press corps to be out of touch with intimate affairs (today it seems to be called "out of the loop," the way George Bush says he was during his vice-presidency) would simply be bypassed, I pointed out, and reporters would get their information from a scattering of sources, including some with special axes to grind and others who didn't know all the facts. If I could trust him to give me sufficient access to information, then he could trust me to do the right thing and thereby, in Mark Twain's phrase, "gratify some people and astonish the rest." The secretary seemed to think I should take the job. I promised to let him know quickly.

The passage of time tends to rewire a man's recollection, usually to the benefit of his own reputation, but though I made no notes to look back on I believe I have accurately recollected here the substance of that important meeting. I left Dean Rusk's office with the feeling that we held seriously differing notions of the extent of "the people's right to know" and how government should honor that obligation and that I would need to be a persistent persuader. But I felt also that we understood each other and that in a crunch—and I sensed that there might be many of them—he would play fair with me. Just for extra assurance, though, I walked a few yards across the seventh floor to the office of George Ball to take out what the insurance industry calls an "umbrella policy." George had just

228   become, or was about to become, the principal undersecretary of state, number two man in the department. We had seen little of each other since the day of Adlai Stevenson's jolting defeat in 1952, but he greeted me as the kind of friend you make by having hunkered down in a shellhole together during an enemy barrage without whimpering or wetting your pants. I told him of my concerns about access to important information and decisions. Don't worry about it, he said in effect. As long as I'm here you have it whenever you need it.

The assurance that I had the number two man strongly behind me convinced me I should take the job, that I'd find a new excitement and a sense of purpose in working with the shapers of events, no matter how peripherally, rather than being a mere commentator. I signed on with the New Frontier, with the stipulation that I'd return to journalism in two years. So it was back to Washington again.

"Why don't we buy a horse and one of those gaily painted gypsy wagons, with our pots and pans banging on the sides and our wash flapping off the roof?" Maggie suggested. Good scout as always, sarcasm notwithstanding.

So that explains how I found myself having breakfast at the White House on April 11, 1962. By coincidence, that was the day I was to be sworn in by Dean Rusk at the department. I had already been on the job for six weeks, learning my way about the characterless brindle-brick building with corridors so reminiscent of a hospital that you expected gurneys and wheelchairs to roll around each corner and a public address system for "Calling Dr. Kildare." I perused my first classified position papers and cables, sat in on policy meetings, conferred with officials at the Pentagon and other branches of government, began reorganizing the Public Affairs bureau staff. All this before I was "cleared" for security. I could not be formally sworn in until investigators had completed the slow-moving security check process. So I'd already had weeks of access to "secrets" and other forbidden data long before the FBI decided whether I was a security risk. If I'd been found to be a threat to the republic I presumably would have been forced by means of castor oil and stomach pump to disgorge all I'd learned lest it be passed to the Soviet Embassy on 16th Street NW.

This was a decidedly image-conscious administration with a **229** heavy macho overlay. Hardly a week passed without gossip column items or newspaper photographs portraying Attorney General Bobby Kennedy scaling Mount McKinley or Secretary of Defense McNamara plunging downstream in a white-water raft, or the president himself catching a touch football pass at Hyannis Port.

Shortly before I took the job, several newspapers ran a picture showing the secretary of state bowling, about as non–New Frontier an image as one could imagine. Soon after I began working at State the morning papers ran another picture, this one showing Dean Rusk shoveling snow off his sidewalk. A friend telephoned that afternoon to say wryly: "You're doing a great image-building job, Bob. Keep up the good work." Fortunately, Dean Rusk was little interested in personal image. He once described himself as looking "like a bartender." He was the one truly self-effacing high-ranking official in the publicity-conscious administration, a man of unobtrusive modesty and deep loyalty to the president. He zealously guarded the privacy of his family and his own feelings. Though we were to have our differences about what one had to do to achieve it, he encouraged the understanding that my job was not to enhance personalities, his surely among them, but to build an information operation that served the public without harming the conduct of foreign policy.

One of my first and wisest moves was to get in touch with Jimmy Greenfield, who'd been my right-hand man in London. He too had responded to an invitation to experience government from the inside and was serving at the Pentagon as an aide to Deputy Secretary of Defense Roswell Gilpatric. Jim was finding his work at Defense less interesting than he had expected, boring in fact, and was happy to cross the Potomac and work with me again, as principal deputy assistant secretary of state. Already on hand as a deputy assistant secretary was Carl Rowan, a smart, brave, and outspoken Tennessean who had risen from poverty to a distinguished career, one of the pioneers who broke through the barriers against blacks in journalism. I probably would not have superimposed Jim Greenfield on Carl

Rowan were it not apparent that Carl, who was certainly qualified to fill my post himself but had been passed over, would prefer a more challenging assignment. (In fact, after we worked well together for several months Carl moved with his family to Helsinki, where he served with distinction as American ambassador to Finland.)

Another deputy already in place was Katie Louchheim, an attractive and gutsy lady who was equally at home in Georgetown society, a Democratic party imbroglio, or a conclave of fellow poets.

For most of the bureau's operations a core staff of experienced administrators, writers, historians, and assorted specialists was in place; there was a handful of tired time-servers among them, but most were dedicated and hard-working civil servants who seemed eager to please and to guide the new boss—yet another one!—through the maze of bureaucracy. The big sector, the one that I was given to understand the president felt needed much improvement, was the operation of the news bureau and the day-to-day channeling of information to a never satisfied diplomatic press corps.

Gone were the days when a half-dozen or so correspondents would cluster around taciturn old Cordell Hull for tidbits of non-news. A band of some two hundred correspondents, American and foreign, were now accredited to the department. They were men and women who mostly did their homework, who could not only smell a half-truth from a block away but knew how to root out the other half somewhere else. Some of the more experienced correspondents, American and foreign as well, knew as much of the background and possible consequences of matters they were covering as the officials who were supposedly experts in them, sometimes more. I knew many of the correspondents. Some, like John Hightower of the AP and Stu Hensley of the UP, I knew from as far back as my own days as a UP correspondent in the forties, others from the more recent days of covering NATO meetings and other international conferences when I worked overseas. With the alert help of Jim Greenfield, who quickly established himself as a cheerful, knowledgeable, and forthcoming source for newsmen, I built early rapport with the State Department press corps. I came to **231** call them, with more affection than chastisement, "the Hounds of Gutenberg," and they in turn chided me as "a poacher turned gamekeeper."

There were times when we quarreled, times when we frustrated each other, times when I couldn't give them as much information as they wanted (and sometimes deserved). There were some among them who were merely headline-hunters, others more interested in writing about what was *going* to happen, who was going to be appointed to or sacked from what job, than in giving the reading public some insight into what *had* happened.

All in all, though, the State Department correspondents were the smartest and least easily satisfied segment of the huge Washington press corps. I respected them and they seemed to return the compliment. I of course had been one of them, and even though I had now crossed the road that earlier kinship certainly helped to make working with the reporters of the news the easier part of a difficult job.

Dealing inside the government with the makers, the protectors, the leakers, and the would-be suppressors of the news was a decidedly different matter. A major part of the problem was, purely and simply, official ignorance. I discovered to my astonishment that from the very top on down, most government officials had only the most elementary knowledge of how journalism works, of its motivations or its limitations, of the myriad ways information gets circulated in an open, democratic society, and of the hopelessness of wishing that the press would just go away. The career Foreign Service in particular seemed to inculcate in its officers at an early stage a hostility to the press that ranged from simple mistrust to outright contempt. The civil servants in the department (as distinguished from the more elite Foreign Service corps) were no less uncomfortable with the information function, and this was startlingly true also of many of the political appointees, presumably sophisticated men who came from "the outside world"—industry, business, law offices, and university faculties—to serve this particular administration. Persuading people with such a mind-set to deal constructively with press and public was close to impossible, so we bent our efforts to persuading them to let us in the information field

232

do it for them. Then there were more forthcoming officials, of two different kinds. The troublesome ones were those appointees in State, Defense, and the White House who liked to deal directly with the press themselves, sometimes in order to push a particular policy initiative or sabotage someone else's, in other cases to polish their own images or tarnish others', or simply to enjoy the sensation of being "in" with certain reporters and columnists. They were a considerable source of embarrassment or irritation to those of us responsible for the flow of information because we were first to be blamed for their frequently inaccurate effusions and then obliged to try to correct them. The helpful kind were those who, even if some did not see it as an obligation, understood the virtue of building a forthcoming information process as one of the principal ways of building understanding and enlisting the support of Congress and of public opinion in general.

Fortunately, this enlightened group included the President of the United States (in spirit if not 100 percent of the time in practice) as well as some importantly placed people on his White House staff, chief among them Pierre Salinger, the press secretary, McGeorge Bundy, chief of the National Security staff, and Kenneth O'Donnell, one of JFK's so-called Irish mafia who was the president's shrewd and sometimes underrated appointments secretary. There was a small handful of similarly enlightened officials at State, most notably George Ball and Averell Harriman, and those famous exceptions to the Foreign Service norm, Ambassadors Chip Bohlen and Tommy Thompson.

By the time I moved onto the scene, in late February of 1962, the Kennedy administration had undergone a year of severe cold war testing. The East-West confrontation in Berlin had deteriorated. Castroism seemed to be threatening much of Latin America. The Soviet Union was infiltrating the heretofore Western preserve of Africa. The president had been hit by the Bay of Pigs disaster in April, a near-crisis in Laos in May, the jolting truculence of Nikita Khrushchev at the Vienna summit meeting in June, the shock of the Berlin Wall in August, the resumption of Soviet nuclear testing in the atmosphere in September. Some of the response was to call up 150,000 reservists, initiate a national program of nuclear fall-out shelters, orches- **233** trate a new arms build-up to close what the president in his election campaign had described (inaccurately, as it turned out) as a dangerous "missile gap," and to resume our own nuclear testing above ground.

It was in this superheated atmosphere that the administration also contemplated one of the most perplexing inheritances from the Eisenhower administration, a belief in "the domino theory" that posited the Communist takeover of all Southeast Asia if the divided country of Vietnam was lost to Communist forces, and the commitment of U.S. arms and military advisors to keep that from happening. At that time, though, in the spring of that second Kennedy year, the president's concern over Vietnam was secondary to his preoccupation with the U.S.-USSR confrontation, Castro and Cuba, and the bloody civil strife in the Congo.

This was equally true of the State Department, where Dean Rusk and his high command concentrated on Europe and sudden flare-ups in places like the Congo while across the river Secretary of Defense McNamara and the military engineered a gradual escalation of the American military "advisory" presence in Vietnam, while the CIA, without bothering to tell State much about it, experimented with clandestine programs designed to infiltrate the Communist network and win the loyalty of Vietnamese in the countryside. There were about six hundred U.S. military operating in South Vietnam when Kennedy became president. That number was now rising by the thousands (to reach sixteen thousand by 1963), and many of these troops were participating in a growing number of armed confrontations and taking casualties.

Official information about Vietnam, whether it was that circulated within the government or that offered to the public, was coming almost entirely in terms of enemy "body counts" and "captured enemy weapons" from General Paul Harkins and his persistently optimistic military briefers in Saigon or in Washington itself from a swaggering Marine General named Victor Krulak, whose intragovernmental briefings presented us with color slide shows of dead bodies, statistical graphs, and pitiful piles of crude weapons captured from the Vietcong to prove that the enemy was being defeated in Vietnam. Krulak wasn't

234

much bigger than a duffle bag, but he made up for that with a fierce demeanor, like the fellow at the end of the bar who says, "I can lick anybody in the place," and doesn't tempt anyone to dispute him. I wasn't surprised to discover that he was known in the Corps as "Brute."

The main preoccupations of the Bureau of Public Affairs were of course the same as the administration's, particularly the ongoing Berlin tension. There were day-to-day questions pertaining to negotiations at Geneva for East-West arms control agreements, the glacial movement toward European unity, dealings with West Germany's Konrad Adenauer, who was suspicious of any American move that smacked of conciliation with Moscow at Bonn's expense, and with Charles de Gaulle who resented American influence in West European affairs and especially the Anglo-American "special relationship," which he felt demeaned France.

Jim Greenfield and I spruced up the operations of the News Office, which provided each day's noontime briefing to the press, and we found that by pressing hard we could extract more forthcoming material for those briefings than had habitually been provided by the operational bureaus—those dealing with European, Middle Eastern, Far Eastern, African, Legal, and United Nations affairs. We opened a rich new source of background material and guidance for State Department correspondents with the enthusiastic cooperation of Roger Hilsman, who with his deputy Thomas Hughes was then running the State Department's division of Intelligence and Research. INR's staff included experts on just about every country and every corner of the world and was also plugged into the CIA, Defense Intelligence Agency, and the other intelligence-collecting operations of the government. Career people higher up in the department's hierarchy blanched at this heretical mating of newsmen and the governmental intelligence network, but we had Dean Rusk's and George Ball's approval, and Mac Bundy's as well, so they could only grumble and swallow their misgivings.

Dean Rusk's uneasiness with the information function persistently manifested itself. More than once when I traveled with him to Geneva arms negotiations or a NATO ministers' conference he wondered out loud why I wasn't back in Washington **235** "doing your assistant secretary's work." I tried diplomatically to remind him that being on hand to explain and perhaps even understand what he was doing *was* a major part of my work. We traveled in relative splendor on the big plane that was Air Force One when the president traveled in it, or in one of the equally endowed backup planes, Air Force Two or Three. These planes were equipped with instanteous communications with the White House and the Pentagon and also carried a UPI news ticker. From this I could keep track of anything of importance that may have happened during our flight.

Just before landing on our first trip together, for Geneva arms negotiations, I apprised Dean Rusk of a news item and advised him that correspondents might ask him about it at the airport. "Correspondents?" he said. "Why not just tell them to stay away? I won't have anything to say." I told him that was not the way things worked. On our next overseas flight together, the same thing would happen. "Why do they bother to come out?" Rusk asked. In exasperation I said, "Because, Mr. Secretary, you are the representative of the President of the United States and the newspapermen want to be there in case the plane crashes and we all go up in flames." At the terminal, the secretary would respond affably and knowledgeably to newsmen's questions. I was sure, though, the same thing would happen again, that this was only the beginning of a long and difficult educational process.

More than anything else, it was the president's interest that made the work exciting and, more to the point, made doing the job possible. Usually that interest was conveyed through Pierre Salinger and our frequent meetings in his office, other times by way of a call from Mac Bundy or one of his assistants, but sometimes the president himself was on the other end of the telephone line. One night at suppertime he called to ask about an unpleasant development in Berlin and instructed me that he wanted it handled in "a quiet tone of voice."

Like presidents before him and since, Kennedy often was infuriated by news leaks, even when the object of the leak was of limited significance. One morning at seven o'clock one of the ingenious White House switchboard operators tracked me

down at the pay phone alongside the St. Albans tennis courts and the president came on the line. "I suppose you're out there loafing with the likes of Bundy, Rostow, and others [he was right] when you all should be at work," he said sarcastically, and then complained angrily about a story about a forthcoming U.S. position in the United Nations that had leaked into that morning's *New York Times.* He wanted to know before the day was out who had leaked it. The leaker could have been any one of a couple of hundred people or even more who were familiar with that particular—and not very weighty—matter. When I called him at midday to confess that I could find no clue as to who the culprit could be, Kennedy interrupted to say with a laugh, "Never mind. I found the son-of-a-bitch right here in my own nest." As in most such cases, the matter had already ceased to be important.

At one point Salinger passed the word that the president thought I should myself deliver the daily State Department briefings; he was increasingly bothered by the "cold war rhetoric and confrontational tone" that he ascribed to Lincoln White, who had been handling the briefings for more years than most could remember. His tenure in the news office stretched back to Cordell Hull's time. I argued that the several hours required each morning to prepare for the briefings would keep me out of the high-level meetings at which important decisions were being made or discussed and thereby undermine my general credibility.* The president ordered instead that I replace the much-admired Linc White with a new face. This task I approached with deep reluctance and a sense of guilt, but Linc gracefully accepted a diplomatic assignment in Australia and the opportunity to get onto a superb golf course almost every afternoon. This created the opportunity to bring a respected Foreign Service officer, Richard Phillips, into the role of the News Office's daily briefer and to promote as his assistant and eventual successor an equally intelligent, equally unflappable

---

*In 1977, when fellow journalist Hodding Carter became President Jimmy Carter's assistant secretary for public affairs, I strongly advised him to avoid the daily briefing task for the reasons cited above. Hodding refused my sage advice and soon thereafter, with his handling of the Iranian hostage crisis, became a national celebrity.

News Office supernumerary named Robert McCloskey as the back-up briefer. Both earned the respect and confidence of newsmen and government officials alike, accolades rarely granted by both sides to those who labor in that no-man's land between them.

An occasional breakfast at the White House was yet another part of the job. Preparations for the presidential press conferences began late on the day before, when Arthur Sylvester and Dix Donnelly, my opposite numbers at the Defense and Treasury departments, and the information chiefs of most departments gathered in Pierre Salinger's White House office. Each of us brought a briefing book listing questions we thought might be thrown at the president next day, together with factual material and suggestions as to what the president might usefully say—or should avoid saying—about each subject. We discussed those for an hour or so, then Salinger delivered the briefing books to the Oval Office for the president's bedtime reading. Breakfast next morning was the occasion for an intimate and often entertaining drill session. The regular participants were usually Vice-President Johnson, Dean Rusk or George Ball, sometimes both, Mac Bundy, Ted Sorensen and his deputy counsel, Meyer Feldman, Pierre Salinger, and myself. Sometimes Robert McNamara would attend, as would other cabinet secretaries now and then, when a matter of concern to them was afoot, as was the case for Secretary of Labor Goldberg on the morning of the steel price confrontation.

We would gather at about 8:30 or a bit later, begin talking while the food was being served. The president usually had digested what he felt he needed from the briefing books, sometimes asked for an update, perhaps the state of a complicated labor problem or precise figures on aid to some Third World country. Salinger and Sorensen took the lead in throwing up questions that were most likely to be asked plus others that might be sleepers. Others of us chimed in when a comment or suggestion seemed pertinent, or responded to Kennedy's questions. At most of these breakfasts the president was more relaxed than he was at that first, tense meeting I attended in April. Often he would dismiss a suggestion with a quip, other **238** times propose with a straight face an answer that brought laughter from his breakfast guests but would not be appropriate for export. The president's relaxed manner discouraged inhibition, invited easy-going suggestions or responses to his questions. The vice-president was not a man for masquerading his discomfort at being second fiddle, but the president always treated him deferentially and made a point of easing him out of his studied silence by soliciting his views on the important matters. After about an hour, it was all over. Salinger and I, and sometimes Sorensen, would reassemble in the afternoon just before the news conference to acquaint the president with the latest from the newswires.

Pierre would sometimes plead: Mr. President, this time *please* don't call on Sarah or May. Then Kennedy would stride out before the press corps and TV cameras in the State Department auditorium, pluck at his suitcoat while straightening his shoulders, read a statement or two, and invite questions. On the several occasions in which I participated in that singularly American ritual I don't remember a single question of great import for which the president had not prepared himself. There were, though, some lesser questions that no one had anticipated; almost all of them were asked either in the brassy voice of Sarah MacLendon of Texas or from beneath the turn-of-century Ma Kettle–style hat of May Craig of Maine. John Kennedy simply could not keep himself from calling on those two women whenever they stood up, and more times than not they confounded him with inquiries from the far outfield, questions about obscure happenings in the Texas Panhandle or the coast of Maine. JFK was a polished and frequently entertaining performer in his news conferences, more deft and effective than any president since FDR, and under much more difficult conditions. His success was only partially due to careful preparation; the task was made easier by the Washington press corps's habitual failure to organize its questioning and take constructive advantage of the rare opportunities to grill the President of the United States.

My contacts with the president were not merely good for the morale and the ego or for the excitement of witnessing up close how the leader of the Western world looked, acted, and confronted big decisions. It was more important that the presiden- **239** tial connection, even one so limited, dramatized for State Department officials that the information function was supposed to be taken seriously. Not everyone took the hint, but it surely helped. Among the Washington correspondents it provided the extra measure of assurance that they were dealing with a source who spoke from some inside knowledge.

The hours were long: leave home by 7:00 A.M., if lucky get back for supper by 8:00 or 8:30. The daily routine was less tiring than it seemed because the pace of events and the profusion of new experiences and sudden demands kept the adrenaline pumping in a way that put off fatigue. Compared to the first Kennedy year, the second was proceeding with relative calm. Problems with de Gaulle, as usual. Another thousand military advisers to Vietnam. Some small signs of Moscow's willingness to consider a nuclear test ban treaty. The first tentative discussions of an odd administration proposal for something called the Multilateral Nuclear Force, a plan whereby all the NATO allies would get fingers on the trigger of Anglo-American nuclear weapons by fitting out nuclear-armed submarines with multinational crews. Some of the many of us who thought it a silly idea suggested it would collapse because the French, British, and Germans could never agree on the nationality of the chef. The proposal never got that far.

Since the Bay of Pigs and the building of the Berlin Wall, nothing had happened that deserved the label "crisis." As autumn came and politicians began jockeying for the 1962 congressional elections, some Republicans, notably Senators Kenneth Keating of New York and Homer Capehart of Indiana, were indulging in scare talk that the Soviet Union was installing missiles in Cuba, only a short leap from American shores. Where they were getting their information, or inspiration, we did not know. Arthur Sylvester at the Pentagon and I at State sought—and got—assurance from higher authorities that the senators were talking through their hats. As recently as mid-September the combined U.S. Intelligence Board had looked into such rumors and concluded that the USSR would not consider making Cuba a military base. The scare talk persisted but the department was so calm in mid-October that

240   Maggie and I traveled to Maryland's Eastern Shore for a rare long weekend, a reunion with old friends. We'd hardly gotten there when Jim Greenfield telephoned to say, "Something's going on and you'd better hurry back." I asked him for details and he said ominously that he could not say anything more on the telephone.

We rushed back to town. I learned that the president and the highest officers of his government, only twelve men in all, were in urgent conference at the White House. The CIA had irrefutable photographic evidence to show that the Russians had indeed begun building missile launching sites in Cuba and seemed also to be building a submarine base and stocking airfields with IL-28 bombers.

The crisis meetings had been going on for four days and the major decisions about the U.S. response had been hammered out by that Saturday, October 19, when Pierre called Sylvester and me to a meeting at his Virginia home and said that we were expected to sit in on the remaining deliberations. We had missed some very high drama, but there was plenty of tension and suspense remaining as the emergency group called "the Excomm" (for executive committee of the National Security Council) pondered how to execute the president's final plan. The debate had ranged from a proposal to do nothing, on the valid assumption that the number of missiles installed in Cuba would do little to alter the balance of power, to proposals to bomb the missile sites out of existence, to invade Cuba and replace Castro's dictatorship with a new government. The relatively peaceful decision was to blockade the Soviet ships bringing the missiles to Cuba and wait for Nikita Khrushchev to make the next move. The more drastic steps, and steps even more drastic than those already discussed, still had to be contemplated if Khrushchev dared to challenge what we discreetly called our "quarantine" but which was in fact to be a naval blockade.

Secrecy was essential over that weekend, lest Moscow be alerted in time to prepare countermoves, perhaps in Berlin, perhaps in Western Europe, who could be sure where? By Monday, Washington was thrumming with the sense that something serious was happening. The *New York Times* and the *Washington Post* had fairly well established that the Soviets were installing missile sites in Cuba, but Kennedy himself (Salinger and I **241** learned later) prevailed on their publishers and/or editors to suppress their stories. Scotty Reston and Walter Lippmann got some special treatment from George Ball, a confidential briefing on Monday afternoon. They kept the confidence and the line was held until the president made his speech that evening revealing the crisis to the world. Leaders of all our NATO allies had been notified in advance, but we were fairly certain that no hint of the nature of the American response had leaked to the Soviet Union.

I was ordered to arrange a mass press briefing at State for all accredited White House, State Department, and Defense correspondents, to coincide with the president's speech. George Ball told the crowd of perhaps three hundred correspondents what was going on; Roswell Gilpatric from the Pentagon showed slides of the CIA's U-2 photographs of missile sites being cleared and launchers installed. I had orders to keep the doors closed until the briefing was finished so that no one could scoop his and her colleagues. This dismayed the European correspondents. A Frenchman braced me at the door, on the verge of tears. It was already deadline time in Paris. A British correspondent, two from Germany, one from Italy piled up behind him, bathing me in looks of supplication. "Don't give me away," I said, unlocking the door, then quickly closing it behind them. What the hell, we had already told our allies' governments what was happening; why shouldn't their people know as well?

Now the entire world knew that a superpower confrontation was on the way. The next days were even more suspenseful than those that preceded the blockade decision. The U.S. government had to prepare for the worst. As I sat in on those preparations—silently and at the far side of the packed Cabinet Room—and observed the exchange of doom-shaded messages between the Premier of the USSR and the President of the U.S., I experienced a strange sensation. Perhaps I was badly out of focus, but I just could not believe that we were on the verge of war, nuclear or otherwise. Several of the participants in the debate, including Robert McNamara, were of the opinion that Soviet missiles emplaced in Cuba would not make any real change in the East-West military balance. Yet here were brave

242

and intelligent men, the verymost leaders of the most powerful nation in the world, gloomily contemplating the possibility that one man with little but a psychological gambit, a propaganda flourish, to gain would spark a nuclear holocaust.

The one man, of course, was Nikita Khrushchev. He was leader of a country that possessed, according to reliable intelligence at that time, three hundred strategic missile warheads to America's five thousand. Here the Talmudic intricacy of the nuclear confrontation came into play: Many if not most nuclear "experts" viewed the ratio of three hundred Soviet missiles to five thousand American missiles as "parity" of sorts because of the destructive power of even one missile. But even if this debatable deduction was accepted in Washington, how could we assume it would be so accepted in Moscow, even without the Soviet paranoia factor? There, it almost certainly had to be looked upon as a sign of massive American superiority. True, Khrushchev's weapons if launched were sufficient to kill tens of thousands of Americans and perhaps cripple many more. But at that same moment ours would be wiping all his people from the face of the earth. When Khrushchev chose to insert Soviet nuclear capability only ninety miles off our shoreline he surely risked the possibility of conflict. How great was that risk? However great—or small—the threat all but dissolved, it seemed to me, when the president eschewed a violent response and made instead the admirable choice of a blockade. That had left the choice squarely and solely up to Khrushchev and his military chiefs.

Khrushchev's most important message during the increasingly emotional Kremlin–White House exchanges of that week was a passionately personal one that came by back channel and could only have been written by himself. It made obvious what his choice was. "Only lunatics or suicides, who themselves want to perish and to destroy the whole world before they die, could do this," he told President Kennedy. The president and the men who sat with him in those White House deliberations were surely not so lunatic as to start nuclear war over an enemy maneuver that would not seriously affect the military balance. Khrushchev was an impetuous, even reckless man, but was he a lunatic, a would-be suicide? That emotional, earthy back-chan- 243

nel letter from Khrushchev was the work of a very sane man
who knew he had gone too far. Ergo, the missile crisis, while
certainly dangerous, had not really brought us to the brink of
nuclear Armageddon.

I felt that the world had probably come as close, perhaps a lot
closer, to war several years before, during Russia's blockade of
Berlin in 1948 and 1949 and the threatened one in 1959. There
was at least as great a chance then of a misstep or accident that
could have exploded into conflict that would have made inevitable a Western nuclear response to attack by overwhelming Soviet conventional forces. I was certainly not inclined to intrude
these counterconclusions into the ritual of self-congratulation
that followed the peaceful passing of the missile crisis. Such
reflections were little short of heresy if not blasphemy in euphoric New Frontier circles, but wrongheaded as it might have
been that is how I felt. Nothing in the mythology that was
subsequently generated by both American and Soviet participants in the crisis,* nothing in the torrent of commentary, anal-

---

*The mythologizing process was formalized in a series of meetings beginning in
1987 at which American, Soviet, and some Cuban officials who had participated in
the 1962 missiles confrontation exchanged information, traded theories, and
praised each other for having avoided war. During the latest of those conclaves in
Havana, a Soviet general named Anatoly Gribkov maintained that the Soviets had
actually sneaked not just the rockets but short- and medium-range missiles complete with nuclear warheads into Cuba without detection by U.S. reconaissance
and that Soviet officers in Cuba had been given authority to launch the short-range
missiles if the Americans invaded Cuba. This was the same Soviet bureaucracy
that earlier sent to its new "ally" in the equatorial country of Guinea tanks that
were winterized for service in frigid Siberia. But logic suggests that if the Soviets
were going to all the trouble of sending missiles to Cuba they would have sent their
warheads as well. There was in fact some post-crisis evidence that a few nuclear
warheads were in place and ready to be "mated," or in some instances already
"mated," to rockets.

Still American intelligence during the crisis period detected no sure sign of
missile warheads on the ground or on Soviet ships leaving Cuba after the Russians
bowed to the blockade. We have little more than the boast of a Soviet general
thirty years later that deadly warheads in profusion as well as rockets were sneaked
into Cuba, and his far more questionable claim that Soviet commanders on the
scene had authority to shower them at will on the U.S. mainland if there was even
a hint of an American effort to invade Cuba—an effort, incidentally, the United
States had no intention of mounting.

244   John Newhouse, the most authoritative American journalist writing today

ysis, and postoperative psychoanalysis by pundits, politicians, and academicians that followed in later years caused me to change my mind.

---

about the armaments and the geopolitics of the nuclear age, was present at that Havana conference and when he sized up General Gribkov's performance and measured his claims against earlier, more believable information from Moscow, Newhouse implied in an impressively detailed report for *The New Yorker* that Gribkov was something of a show-off and blowhard who left Newhouse and some others "feeling suspicious and very skeptical." That was not the case, however, for Robert McNamara and some of the other former American officials present. News reports portrayed them as startled and impressed by the general's boast and accepting it at face value. We had come "even closer" to nuclear Armageddon than he had believed at the time, McNamara was widely quoted as saying. Another who attended the conference, the estimable historian Arthur Schlesinger, Jr., wrote in the *New York Review of Books* that, while they did not square with the earlier testimony of a far higher-positioned Soviet official, Gribkov's unsupported claims should be presumed to be "right" because Gribkov had been on the scene and the rest of us had not been.

Manning's maxim, for what it's worth: When participants in a dangerous confrontation tend to see it as more threatening than it was this makes the defusing of it—and the defusers—seem more heroic than they were.

Chapter 15

City of the Wagging Jawbones

There is a hilarious moment in Brendan Behan's *The Hostage* when an Irishman in a trenchcoat bursts into the Dublin whorehouse in which the play takes place. He swaggers about the stage and shouts, "I'm in the Irish Secret Service and I don't care who knows it!" I was reminded of this scene frequently as I experienced from inside that peculiarly American dilemma, the problem of conducting foreign policy and political-military affairs in an open society. The CIA offered an interesting case in point: The more I learned about its operations, the more "the Agency" struck me as a sort of multi-WASP composite of Behan's swaggering Irishman. It was the only espionage and intelligence agency in the world with its own full-scale public relations office; in some world capitals, even in a combat situation like Vietnam, its ostensibly secret agents wore only the flimsiest of camouflage, if any; they were spooks without sheets who seemed even to revel in being well-known for what they were. Men like Duane R. (Dewey) Clarridge, alias Daks LeBaron or Dewey Maroni, who frequented the best places in Europe and elsewhere wearing flamboyant white suits, expensive shoes, flashy pocket handkerchiefs, and a cloud of expensive cigar smoke. This compulsion to show off while oper-

ating as a presumably secret agent was no doubt an outgrowth of the Agency's home-base culture. Washington was not only the nation's governmental capital but also the nation's publicity factory. The rule seemed to be, the higher the official, the more publicity-conscious. That is why it is said that the American "ship of state is the only vessel afloat that leaks from the top."

Every department of government and every major committee of the Congress and many of its individual members had a full complement of in-house ghost writers and information dispensers (usually called public affairs officers and other times disguised as special assistants). Any number of officials in the Congress and in the executive branch dabbled at being their own image-polishers and gossip dispensers.

In addition to my extensive Bureau of Public Affairs operation, each of the State Department's nine other bureaus had its own set of information officers doing the bidding of their superiors, sometimes without coordination with my own office, which was supposed to supervise what the department was telling the world. My opposite number at the Pentagon, Arthur Sylvester, had a budget fifteen or twenty times that of State's public affairs budget and a battalion or two of civilian and military personnel plus other platoons in each of the military services to help him—and the intraservice jealousies and public relations rivalries to bedevil his efforts. He had even more trouble than I in attempting the impossible, a big government department that spoke with one voice. Pierre Salinger's staff in the White House press office was at least quadruple that of FDR's day.

All in all, this was probably by far the most outspoken, most forthcoming administration in American history. Measuring the outpouring of information by quantity rather than pertinence, a cynic might be excused for likening one day's output of press releases, information pamphlets, speech texts, and other wordage dispensed to the public to what a detractor once called the complete works of Carlyle, "the history of silence in thirty volumes by Mr. Wordy." A person of more charitable judgment might construe this devotion to feeding information to the citizenry as a passionate interest by government in what some people, mostly we journalists, liked to call "the people's right to know."

There was an opposite side to this passion for garrulity. In the more sensitive areas of government, namely the Departments of Defense and State and the White House's national security staff plus the assorted (and competing) intelligence agencies—that is, among the people dealing with foreign affairs, diplomatic negotiations, relations with allies, involvement with the Third World, international military activities, and, of course, all matters concerning the cold war—there was an equally intense passion for "classifying" official information. These people were seized with a seemingly irresistible compulsion to stamp "confidential" or "secret" or "top secret" or "eyes only" or some even more ominous warning words on official documents in the name of national security. Dean Rusk, not by any means a man to discourage confidentiality, remarked more than once that the work of government was at the very most 10 percent secret. Why then did it seem that about 90 percent of State, Defense, and NSC documents dealing with the public's business were restricted by classification? This was an inheritance from previous administrations, a reflex conditioned by years of cold war nervousness and bureaucratic practice.

The original purpose of the security classification procedure was to keep the small proportion of necessary government secrets secret, to conceal new weaponry or research discoveries and hide military movements, for example, or to allow delicate negotiations to proceed in private or to protect the sanctity of the government codes in which overseas cables were transmitted. By the 1950s the procedure had spread like some kind of bureaucratic algae through the state and defense departments and the White House. I was astonished to discover during my initiation into the rites of bureaucracy that there were operatives at the Pentagon and now and then one or two at State who imposed "confidential" warnings even on newspaper clippings, texts of statements or lectures that had already appeared in print or been broadcast. A classification could be imprinted at the whim of almost any official of middle or up, by his secretary, even by a very junior assistant. Once that stamp was imprinted it automatically proscribed a document from being shown or its contents revealed to an "outsider" lest the discloser be himself classified—as a lawbreaker subject to punishment. Classification was easily corrupted into a tool by any official who preferred to control and ration what Americans were to be told about their own government's activities.

Obviously, if a government information man took the classification process literally he could not function. It was necessary, then, to apply distinctions, to protect the few facts or activities that deserved to be kept private (often only momentarily) and discreetly curve around the classification process when responsibility or simple common sense dictated disclosure, because if a news reporter doesn't get the facts straight and clear from a person in authority he or she will get them elsewhere, and frequently in only partial or twisted form.

The saving grace was that the publicity-conscious side of Washington usually prevailed over the secretive. The town teemed with talkative snoops and chronic blowhards and show-offs as well as savvy operatives in government offices and on Capitol Hill who knew that information is the golden currency of democracy and enjoyed spending it. The poet Carl Sandburg, who called Chicago "city of the big shoulders," would have had to call Washington, D.C., the city of the wagging jawbones. So when the passion for secrecy collided with the passion for disclosure in that town, disclosure almost always won, though often with ragged results.

There are, of course, the exceptions that make the rule. The Cuban missile confrontation was one of those exceptions. The news media penetrated but did not violate the secrecy imposed by the White House in the few days between the government's verification of the Russians' Cuban missiles gambit on October 16 and President Kennedy's disclosure of the blockade response on the night of October 22. Some reporters, as has been related, learned approximately what was about to happen but in what they correctly believed to be the national interest refrained from printing or broadcasting what they knew. In the tense days that followed, with the world waiting for Moscow's response, the media clamored for more information than they were getting. For example, they wanted to put reporters and cameramen at the U.S. base in Guantanamo and aboard ships sailing out to **249** the blockade, and they sought forbidden information about air and ground deployments that were the prudent preparations for an unfavorable Soviet reaction.

All commentary about the crisis was being carefully orchestrated by the president and the Excomm, with Arthur Sylvester handling military matters at Defense and I dealing with the diplomatic at State. We were not exactly verbose in our briefings, in part because though we knew what was happening at our end we knew no more than outsiders what the Russians were planning to do. Denied the fuller access they desired, the media people were in a grumbly mood when Pierre Salinger, on the president's orders, asked them to heed voluntarily a twelve-point set of guidelines that put a variety of mostly military matters off-limits for the duration of the crisis.

The mood of the press darkened when a New York City congressman, a beneficiary of a risky White House program to brief members of the Congress on the progress of the crisis in the naive expectation that they would all keep their mouths shut, immediately called a press conference to announce what he had been told—that the U.S. Navy blockaders had halted their first Soviet ship. The tanker *Bucharest,* carrying no suspicious cargo, was allowed to proceed. Correspondents were understandably infuriated to be scooped by a publicity-seeking congressman.

Matters got even worse when Arthur Sylvester in an unfortunate fit of candor said in response to newsmen's complaints, ". . . In the kind of world we live in, the generation of news by the government becomes one weapon in a strained situation. The results, in my opinion, justify the means." Then a short time later he said, or caused himself to be quoted as saying, ". . . It is inherent in our government's right, if necessary, to lie to save itself when it is going up in nuclear war. This seems to me basic." Art Sylvester was a seasoned newsman with a bluff, open manner and a kind of spunk and forthrightness that made him an effective spokesman for Robert McNamara and the Pentagon. He also had a lot of common sense but must have left it home at that sensitive time; his choice of words was about as

helpful as was Marie Antoinette's when she said, "Let them eat cake" or the commander of the Light Brigade on that fateful day in the Crimea when he shouted "Charge!"

Sylvester's statements really got the Hounds of Gutenberg to baying and snarling. "Weigh those words," the Washington *Star* said. "Their meaning is truly sinister. . . . The result is that Mr. Sylvester and his superiors, from this time on, are suspect. . . ." Matters did not stop there. Now it was the president's turn to poke a stick at the aroused hounds. Kennedy had been alarmed by stories emanating from unnamed officials at State and Defense that he felt violated the crisis guidelines. "How can we expect the press to cooperate with us," he told Salinger, "when people at Defense and State put out information we are asking the press not to publish?" The President was provoked into an unwise move.

Through Salinger, Kennedy ordered Arthur Sylvester to require all Pentagon officials, military and civilian, to report in detail the substance of their intercourse with members of the press or to have an information officer sit in on every press interview. Secretary of Defense McNamara endorsed this procedure with inordinate enthusiasm. The president ordered the same procedure to be applied at the State Department. I protested that this was unnecessary, that it would not stop news leaks, that it would bring down more condemnation on the administration and on the president personally.

Salinger, while endorsing the imposition of the procedure at Defense, supported my argument that it was both unwise and unnecessary for State. We were on the verge of winning it, I believe, until the substance and some of the precise wording of a classified cable from UN Ambassador Adlai Stevenson to Secretary of State Rusk that had arrived at the State Department early one morning were carried on the AP wires even before Rusk had had time to read the cable. This was too much for the secretary and the president. It gave them the extra resolve they needed to impose at the State Department a modified but still restrictive news procedure.

On White House orders all too readily endorsed by the secretary, I circulated throughout the department a memorandum stating that officials who granted press interviews, in person or **251** by telephone, should file a simple notice of that contact with their respective bureau information officers. The memo pointedly omitted the Pentagon requirement for reports of the substance of the meetings and the requirement that third parties sit in on interviews. I used the occasion to emphasize to my State Department colleagues, thinking especially of those who, given their hostility to journalists, would welcome this memorandum, that it was their duty to meet with and to deal forthrightly with the press as the public's representatives. There was no way of disguising, however, that this procedure would be interpreted by the press as an effort to inhibit exchange between State Department officials and journalists, and that it might be seized on by some officials to do precisely that. I was against the procedure but not entirely without sympathy for a central justification for it. Under the pressure to devise the least objectionable practice, I became convinced, and so stated, that

> a point of important principle is involved. In the conduct of the public business for which he is responsible, the Secretary [of State] of course has the right to know what his policy officers are doing in this regard; whether, for example, they are paying sufficient attention to this important aspect of foreign affairs. It is equally necessary that the Assistant Secretary of State for Public Affairs, who is charged by the Secretary of State with responsibility for informing the public, has the right to know and to examine the flow and pattern of relations between the department and the communications media.

In nongobbledygook this meant: Who's the Spokesman around here, anyway?

Jimmy Greenfield and I knew that of course the memo would be leaked to the press, and even agreed as to which office was most likely to curry press favor by leaking it. We traded guesses about how long it would take to happen. "No more than a day," I said. "It won't take that long," Jimmy said. He won. In little more than an hour from the moment the memo was distributed I received a call from a State Department correspondent to whom it had been handed asking me to explain "this new effort by the administration to gag the press and manage

the news."

"It's not that at all," I responded. "The memo clearly encourages officials to keep the press well informed." "Bullshit!" he explained, and went off to write the first of a deluge of stories charging the government with managing the news.

Thus, out of the overly candid words of Art Sylvester and the president's effort to interfere with the normal information process was born John Kennedy's "news management" flap. Serious as it seemed to those of us caught up in it, the event was really no more than a nuisance, a short-term embarrassment, but an unpleasant one all the same. I had no doubts about the government's right, its obligation, in fact, to invoke the secrecy it invoked during the ticklish missile business. I had no doubts either about the media's right to press for all the information it could get, and to cry out at the slightest evidence of governmental distortion or suppression, though there were several in the pressroom who greatly overdid the whining. I wished Arthur Sylvester had chosen silence and that President Kennedy had let matters run their normal course. As time passed, the much-maligned memorandum induced not a single complaint from regulars among the State Department correspondents of being denied proper access. In little more than a month I was allowed to wipe it off the books. Relations between the press and my office returned to their cheerful but appropriately wary state; the Hounds and the Gamekeeper were still on good terms with each other. At a hearing on "news management" called by a House committee that concerned itself with government information and First Amendment matters, I explained our information policies and felt able to claim without dispute that "the State Department is as wide-open as Yankee Stadium." The hearing offered an excellent opportunity to put the "news management" onus right where it belonged. There was indeed a serious news management problem, I testified, and it belonged to the media: The profusion of events and the acceleration of modern communications confronted the press, radio, and television every day, every hour, every minute with far more information than they knew how to manage. Perhaps in time to come they would discover how to serve us better.

If it did nothing else, all that furor may have had one long-term effect, to help fix the missile crisis even more firmly in **253** legend as an eyeball-to-eyeball flirtation with nuclear war. Other than that, the news controversy was simply a noisier-than-usual episode in the ongoing process by which a democracy tries to conduct its international business in a basically undemocratic world. Wrestling with that pesky privacy versus disclosure conundrum was what I was hired to do. The best way of dealing with it, I found, was to apply a simple rule of thumb:

> Once an American policy has been clearly enunciated by the government to the Congress and to press and public the government is entitled to interludes of privacy in which to achieve or further that policy. On the other hand, the government has no right to use privacy—secrecy—in order to alter or retreat from a publicly enunciated policy or sneak in a new one. The long-stated, widely accepted Monroe Doctrine, for example, would be more than sufficient justification for developing in secret a plan to keep Soviet missiles out of Cuba. Escalation of the American military advisory role in Vietnam might qualify as a borderline example of abuse of privacy, since the government was not altogether owning up to its true nature. (To carry my point, I move forward in time to a much more clear-cut instance of the abuse of secrecy to alter policy that came many years later: the devious Reagan Administration efforts to trade weapons to Iran for the release of American hostages in contradiction of righteously declared Reagan policy, and to provide arms to Nicaraguan Contras in direct violation of congressional legislation.)

That rule-of-thumb served very well for most circumstances. For a variety of reasons growing out of the delicacy of negotiations or the secrecy practices of other governments with whom we were dealing, public on-the-record briefings and press conferences frequently limited an official in how much he could say and how he could say it. So the bulk of the information we imparted about the workings and complexities of foreign affairs was delivered through one-on-one, not-for-attribution meetings between various officials, frequently the secretary and undersecretary themselves, and a correspondent, or in so-called "background" sessions with groups of correspondents. At international meetings like NATO ministers' sessions or Geneva

254 disarmament talks, or at times of sudden events like violence in the Congo or a coup in Argentina, I or one of my associates normally would give public on-the-record briefings confined generally to the basics and then provide considerably more detail on a not-for-quotation "background" basis in private meetings with American correspondents and selected representatives of the foreign press. This "background" process served both government and public, but sometimes it was (and still is) sanctimoniously assailed at editors' conventions or by academic inquests into the evils of government as a form of manipulation and the source of too many unattributed quotes from officials who do not want to be held accountable. Every once in a while some editor would announce that his correspondent was henceforth forbidden to participate in such meetings, but usually within a few weeks the correspondent was back and eagerly filling his or her notebook.

Now and then some official might abuse the process to float a trial balloon or sabotage a rival's undertaking. Occasionally a newsman would violate the semiconfidentiality of it. But the background briefing had long been and would continue to form the very blood bank of the Washington news process. More times than I can count in more places than I can remember—in a crowded hotel room in Geneva, the backroom of a taverna in Athens, a commodious suite in the Crillon in Paris or the Excelsior in Rome, a discreet corner of a saloon in Saigon, in a chartered press plane following the president and secretary of state overseas, a multimillionaire's villa in Palm Springs, at private luncheons with correspondents in Washington hotels or in my own brown-and-brindle, government-issue office at Foggy Bottom—I confided to correspondents much if not all of what they needed to know in order to write about the event at hand. For closed conference sessions or private meetings between American and foreign officials in which I participated, I drew mostly on my own notes. At these international gatherings spokesmen for other governments were doing the same thing, so most of the group at my briefing had already heard, or would hear shortly, what other delegations wished to convey and could compare it with what I had told them.

For the day-to-day process at home, dealing with a variety of developments in many places, I drew on information provided **255** by my superiors or from the cable traffic and the pertinent position papers and memoranda, some of which I had to worm out of reluctant officials. Much of this material was, of course, classified ("Next they'll be classifying the signs on the restroom doors," an associate said one day), but I'd learned from old pros like Chip Bohlen and Tommy Thompson when I was on the other side of the street that there were discreet ways of disregarding this when it was obvious that the material deserved to be in the public domain. Common prudence dictated (how the late Bobby Baker would laugh to see me use that phrase for which we at *Time* chided him several years before) certain precautions in discussing classified information with reporters or editors:

> Never show to another the actual document itself, especially a cable whose only reason for classification might be that its wording could provide clues to the government code from which it was deciphered. Always paraphrase, usually for the same reason or in order to improve on clumsy prose. Always take account of the source of the material; some American diplomats were superb reporters (reporting, after all, was supposed to be one of their prime functions) and at the other extreme were some who rarely put matters into reliable context. Don't trust anything emanating solely from the CIA.

The procedures here described were widely practiced, and long had been, at State, Defense, and the White House, amply supplemented by news sources on Capitol Hill and in many other parts of the government. For some odd reason, such otherwise sophisticated people as the President of the United States, the secretaries of state and defense, and some of their most trusted aides could not absorb this reality. Long after the Cuban missile flap they still fancied that with only a bit more discipline from government officials and more "loyalty and patriotism" on the part of journalists the flow of news could be made sublimely amenable to the people in power. Every time a leak bothered the president or some other higher-up, the finger of blame pointed first to the Bureau of Public Affairs, the last agency with reason for leaking. In some cases even the FBI would be called in to track down the scoundrel. I recall no case in which the G-men found their man. Overreaction to leaks was a waste of time and emotion that could be better directed at more serious matters so, with a great deal of help from Jim Greenfield, I composed a ten-page primer called "Mechanics of News Reporting." We sent it to George Ball on the understanding that his endorsement when he passed it on would encourage his high-ranking colleagues—perhaps even the president—to read it. The covering note said:

1. We "flap" too much about individual news stories and exaggerate their potential impact on the conduct of our work.

2. We must avoid restrictive practices or attempts at "control" that would not solve the problem of leaks and would almost certainly produce consequences harmful to the Administration, and the President in particular.

3. We have simply got to grow up and learn to live with the practices of free journalism in a free society.

The primer went on to describe in detail how intelligent reporters comb not only the State Department but foreign embassies and privy legislators and aides on Capitol Hill for the tips and fragments that fall into place as legitimate news stories. It described how, for example, a reporter might on one day learn the name of the next ambassador to India from Chairman William Fulbright of the Senate Foreign Relations committee, range over an array of important negotiations at lunch with the committee's extremely well-informed staff chief, discuss Laos with a CIA officer across the river at Langley, learn over cocktails from the nervous German ambassador about what happened in the latest four-power ambassadorial meeting dealing with Berlin. Before the day was out he might even get a chatty call from a White House staffer with a bit of news to peddle.

Besides foreign embassies and the Congress, the memo went on, people at the Pentagon and CIA received most of the pertinent cables, position papers, and other documents dealing with State Department business and they participated in much of the policy-making and policy-executing activities. No fewer than 105 copies of that troublesome (but relatively unimportant) **257** leaked cable from UN Ambassador Stevenson to Secretary Rusk, for example, were distributed to individuals in various parts of the government before it was conveyed on the same morning to an Associated Press correspondent.

> If the Congress is the Comstock Lode, the White House is the Federal Reserve Bank for Washington newsmen, especially those with the biggest reputations and most important news outlets. If I have too many volunteer Assistant Secretaries of State for Public Affairs to help me, Pierre Salinger suffers the ailment a hundredfold by comparison. . . . There is a most intelligent understanding there of the importance and value of the communications media and . . . this awareness translates itself very broadly through the White House staff into an active practical application of this understanding. In a few words, there is very steady traffic between reporters and White House officials during, after, and before office hours. The White House cachet enhances the importance of a source in a newsman's eyes; even a lower echelon member of the relatively small group around the president speaks with more seeming authority than some relatively high-ranking officers in other parts of town. When a White House staff man talks, even casually, about what is (or might be) on the president's mind, he may think he talks only as a man, but to the reporter he often sounds like the Delphic oracle.

The memo was intended to be educational, but admittedly it was self-serving, too. We hoped it would protect from naive restrictions and even help enhance the program that Greenfield and I were constantly pushing to make the most knowledgeable State Department officials more comfortable with the press and more forthcoming. "A Department officer who is good enough to deal tactfully with foreign diplomats ought to be able to deal equally tactfully with an inquiring newsman." I could not be sure how many in the intended audience would bother to read the primer or whether it would have any long-term effect, but for a while there was some dimunition of fulminations about leaks. In the stubborn nature of things, that would not last. I suspect that with only some changes of the names of the players the primer and its good advice would be as applicable in today's

Washington as it was then—and as readily ignored by high officials.

We were in testing times, but into the somber conduct of international affairs a little frivolity must fall. We were graced with a president who had a sense of humor and that encouraged occasional lapses into light relief in even so strait-laced a place as the State Department's seventh floor. One day when Walter Lippmann published a column saying that what was needed at the Department of State was "an infusion of fresh and unfrightened minds, not to replace the men who are there but to refresh them," I recalled an amusing paper that my former *Time* colleague Paul O'Neil had concocted several years before about imagined goings-on at the magazine. Cribbing shamelessly from O'Neil's small opus, I delivered to the undersecretary of state a formal memorandum describing how the Bureau of Public Affairs was exploring means to provide such "infusion":

It is too early to arrive at definitive deductions and recommendations but I hasten to write this memorandum to report that we have come across a phenomenon that is delicate if not downright embarrassing. We must begin from the beginning:

On orders from the Assistant Secretary, a special assistant set out to survey various key officials on the subject of brain fatigue and cerebral-refresher techniques. His first call was at the office of Assistant Secretary for International Organization Affairs Harlan Cleveland. There he discovered that Mr. Cleveland had left the country on a mission to the Congo. While poking about in Mr. Cleveland's desk to see if the Assistant Secretary had perchance left behind some secret documents, a few Lifesavers or a bit of change the special assistant made an astonishing discovery. He opened a lower drawer and discovered a human brain. It was but the work of a second to discover that it was, worst luck, Assistant Secretary Cleveland's brain. It was slightly larger than a nectarine and reposed in a chipped teacup celebrating the 50th birthday of His Royal Highness Prince Albert, which also contained three quill toothpicks and a Grant & Nixon campaign button.

The discovery was, of course, disconcerting. Especially since Mr. Cleveland had been traveling and negotiating in the Congo

259

for five days and had already filed . . . some 12,500 words of memoranda and cables dealing with the complex Congo situation. What is more, the documents were even better than Mr. Cleveland's usual work.

When my deputy Assistant Secretary, two security men. . . . plus Dr. Woodward of State Department Medical undertook a further investigation, we soon arrived at an even more disquieting conclusion. Deputy Assistant Secretary for International Organization Affairs Woodruff Wallner reported the loss of a souvenir cricket ball which he had quietly pocketed during the 1936 Test Match at Lords. It was the more valuable because Mr. Wollner, an old scrimshaw man, had spent a good many hours of his spare time engraving its exterior with passages from the published works of Joe Louis.

It was evident that Mr. Cleveland had in haste taken Mr. Wallner's cricket ball and left his brain behind and there was evidence, too, that the rather highflown style of his dispatches was being influenced by the literary style of none other than Mr. Louis (e.g., the reference to Mr. Moshe Tshombe and Mr. Cleveland's conclusion, 'He can run but he cain't hide.')

The fact that the exchange had, in Mr. Cleveland's case, caused no particular harm certainly cannot be regarded as a comforting fact. A rigorous scrutiny of other . . . offices of the Department has since ensued and it was discovered that there is a *widespread practice* in the Department of State, on the part of high officials, of leaving their brains at the office when going home late Saturday or Sunday nights. The notion is that such anatomical divorce, if we may call it that, provides for weekend infusions of freshness and fearlessness of the quality sought by Mr. Lippmann. . . .

After citing several other examples the memo concluded: It is too early to conclude that this widespread practice is sufficiently worthwhile to provide the quality of fresh and unafraid minds thought so desirable by Mr. Lippmann. What is more, I gather from Assistant Secretary for Congressional Relations Frederick Dutton (he sets *his* on the TV set during Senator Keating's Sunday TV show) is somewhat concerned at the probable outcry on the Hill were it to be discovered that the topmost United States conductors of foreign policy make a habit of removing and variously experimenting with their, ah, mental processes. . . .

My investigators are greatly perplexed about one aspect of this odd affair: They cannot find out how they get them out of their heads.

Undersecretary Ball responded to the disclosures with less emotion than I'd expected (perhaps because he was deeply preoccupied with a complexity concerning American airline rights overseas but more likely, I suspected, because he must have neglected to remove and refresh his own brain during the preceding weekend). He suggested withholding the report at this time. The study could not be complete until the investigation was extended to the White House and we ascertained the cranial recharging habits of such important policy-shapers as McGeorge Bundy, Theodore Sorensen, Carl Kaysen, Arthur Schlesinger, Jr., and Pierre Salinger. This was a sensible proposal, but unfortunately the press of other business kept me from completing that admittedly bizarre inquiry.

The most stirring event in mid-1963 was President Kennedy's trip to Europe. It was envisaged not chiefly as a means of conferring with European leaders but as an opportunity for the president to speak directly to the people of Europe, to give them a personal sense of America and, yes, an opportunity to see and hear the handsome, forceful young leader of the country that, by virtue of its military presence, was in a sense the most powerful country in Western Europe—but not one determined to dictate how Europeans should shape their future. Stodgy, cautious State Department prose was not right for this mission, so Ted Sorensen turned his talents as he had so often before to shaping texts tuned to John Kennedy's style and personality. The speeches dealt with major issues and concerns of the day, of course, but they were tailored to the main intent of the visit, which was not to press issues but to demonstrate on this journey that Europe's ally across the sea had a reliable grasp of the pressing problems and of their meaning to Europeans as well as to his own people.

Inevitably there were private meetings along the way, with Chancellor Konrad Adenauer in Bonn, Prime Minister Macmillan in Britain, a clutch of Italy's revolving door leaders in Rome, plus a call on the new pope, Paul VI, who as Cardinal **261**

Montini had been a Kennedy family friend. The only one I was privileged to sit in on was the meeting of the young president and the stern Der Alte.

At eighty-seven, Adenauer was almost twice the age of John Kennedy, had led his country for seven times as long as Kennedy had been president, had guided West Germany from the ashes of defeat into healthy democracy and a position of growing power in the Western alliance. They sat across from each other at a long table, flanked on each side by their under-lings. Moving slowly, talking little, listening with the attentive patience that had carried him effectively through two postwar occupations of his country, Adenauer reminded me of one of those wrinkled, leathery Galapagos turtles from the pages of the *National Geographic* or frames of a PBS nature film, ageless as the sand, stubborn and sinewy with accumulated wisdom. Through half-closed eyes the old man was studying the young leader of the Western alliance. The president treated the chan-cellor with deference but was not at all bashful about reciting some of his concerns of the moment, among them his determi-nation to seek an American-Soviet nuclear test ban treaty and his desire that such negotiations between the two great powers would not intrude on the solidity of the Western alliance and West Germany's increasing role in it.

The suspicion that the one or more of the four conquering powers might make deals at the expense of West Germany was a matter of great sensitivity to Adenauer. As the dialogue con-tinued, what seemed at first to be aloofness on Adenauer's part gave way to a more relaxed demeanor. This often happened with Adenauer, Dean Acheson had once written about him, when "after due deliberation, he gives his confidence and friendship." The Kennedy entourage left Bonn in the confident belief that relations between Der Alte and Der Junge were in decent shape.

The greater import of the Kennedy voyage was its outdoor spectacle; it was a person-to-people journey, much like a full-fledged American campaign swing. The people obliged by the hundreds of thousands, applauding, shouting, laughing, filling **262** streets, and crowding rooftops wherever the president appeared. Downtown Frankfurt was jammed for the Kennedy motorcade and his speech at the Paulskirche. That was but a pallid rehearsal for what happened in Berlin. The long auto caravan to the city hall produced the largest, most joyful crowds I had ever seen, bigger than the V-J Day crowds in Washington and just as exuberant. People shouted, waved, cheered every vehicle and each of its passengers along every yard of the trip until all of us, members of the press and officials alike, felt obliged to wave and bow in response, every one of us a momentary hero.

Even this was not preparation for the sea of Germans that poured into the huge plaza before the city hall to hear John Kennedy's moving *"Ich bin ein Berliner"* speech. Sounds like the roar of one unbelievably immense animal or perhaps a multitude of Godzillas must have carried well past the hated Berlin Wall well into the gray streets and glum houses of East Berlin as the crowd responded to his every remark. Here and there a person fainted within the impenetrable swarm of the crowd. When that happened, onlookers lifted the prone bodies and passed them overhead, hand-by-hand, to ambulance crews waiting on the fringes—German efficiency even amid hysteria. I don't think any of us visitors including the president himself had experienced anything like it. I certainly hadn't. The flickering images and guttural shouts followed by thunderous approval shown in 1930s newsreels of Hitler rallies came perversely to mind. The demonstration was enough to make the heart beat with pride at being an American at this moment and in this place, but there was something about it also that made the skin crawl.*

The rest of the journey, to Britain, Italy, and a sentimental detour to Ireland, went equally well, and the president returned to Washington in triumph. How all of us who made the journey

*The president was obviously exhilarated by this demonstration of mass affection but, it became apparent later, he was also disturbed by it. Arthur Schlesinger, Jr., wrote in his history of the Kennedy presidency, *A Thousand Days,* that ". . . he . . . remarked on his return, that if he had said, 'March to the wall—tear it down,' his listeners would have marched. He always regarded crowds as irrational; perhaps a German one compounded the irrationality."

felt was best described by Schlesinger when he later wrote, "In the summer of 1963, John F. Kennedy could have carried every country in Europe."

The glow from that experience grew even warmer when in August the treaty with the Soviet Union banning underground nuclear tests was completed. To the politicians, diplomats, scientists, and other technicians who had fashioned the agreement it was exciting yet only a small step in the effort to put the nuclear genie back in the lamp. To the men and women around the country, it had a far more compelling significance that could be put quite simply: It would keep fallout poison out of their children's milk. When the president went out of Washington into the countryside, he discovered with pleasant surprise this popular appreciation of what had been achieved. On a Western tour for which he had prepared chiefly political speeches dealing with various regional interests, he found that a mere glancing reference to the test ban treaty set off a reaction akin to adulation. He scrapped much of his prepared speech material to make room for talk of the test ban treaty during the rest of his Western swing.

So 1963 was shaping up as a very good year for the Kennedy presidency—the calmly achieved victory in the showdown over Cuban missiles, the triumphant tour to Europe, and now the breakthrough toward control of the nuclear danger. Domestically, the economy was expanding, with the GNP rising more than the 5 percent a year Candidate Kennedy had promised; the dollar was in good shape and the highly vulnerable senator from Arizona, Barry Goldwater, loomed as the most likely Republican to oppose John Kennedy in the 1964 election. It would have been shaping up as an even better year were it not for one swelling concern, the increasingly sullen turn of events in Vietnam.

Like just about all the government officials whose opinions and judgment I respected, I was a believer in both the practicality and the morality of the Vietnam policy instituted by the Eisenhower administration and bolstered by the increasing involvement by the Kennedy government. To attempt to influence events in Vietnam, to provide guidance and military and
264 other aid so that South Vietnam could save itself from absorp-

tion by the Communist North, seemed both prudent and achievable. The goal of containing Communist expansion established fifteen years before in the Truman administration was still the keystone of American foreign policy in 1963.

The extension of containment from Europe to Asia was posited on a strong American belief in the monolithic nature of Sino-Soviet alliance; even though by 1963 a few were timidly suggesting that it was not all that monolithic, the readiness of the Chinese to intervene against the U.S.-U.N. forces in Korea had contributed to the seriousness with which the Kennedy administration viewed the the possibility of a Sino-Soviet, or perhaps a solely Chinese effort, to absorb Indochina and then all Southeast Asia—Dwight Eisenhower's "dominoes"—into the Communist orbit.

There were several long-standing National Security and Joint Chiefs of Staff documents stressing the strategic importance of Indochina. The Joint Chiefs in particular had long maintained that the area was a vital source of food and raw materials, as well as a gateway to the conquest of all Southeast Asia. They argued that American security and the security and economic health of our ally Japan depended on preventing the Soviet Union or China from denying the West and Japan access to the area. The Pentagon had even developed contingency plans plans calling for general American war including naval blockade, interdiction of communications lines, and extensive air operations against Chinese targets should the Chinese directly intervene in Indochina.*

So it would seem there was a solid base for believing that our intrusion into Vietnam served the national interest. As for the efficacy of that intrusion, hardly a day passed in the early months of 1963 without optimistic progress reports of South Vietnam's military activities against the Communist Vietcong and political and social programs for winning the loyalty of the

*See *The History of the Joint Chiefs of Staff: The Joint Chiefs and the War in Indochina: The History of the Indochina Incident, 1945–54* (Historical Division, Joint Secretariat, August 20, 1971) chapter 7. For discussion of the war contingency plans see a paper prepared by Robert E. Osgood, Johns Hopkins School of Advanced International Relations, for Woodrow Wilson Center for International Scholars, January 1963.

South Vietnamese population. General Paul Harkins predicted from his military command post, MAC/V in Saigon, that the government of Ngo Dinh Diem could win the war "within a year." Secretary of Defense McNamara, the man with the megabyte mind, after another of his innumerable trips to the area proclaimed that "we have turned the corner in Vietnam." "Brute" Krulak's upbeat assurances continued apace and reports from Americans on the scene supported them with reports of some thirty thousand casualties inflicted on the Vietcong in the year 1962 alone, more than we'd been told earlier constituted the entire enemy force at that time. From Ambassador Frederick Nolting's embassy in Saigon came confident reports of the success of Diem's strategic hamlets program for bringing the people to the support of his government.

Problem: There was a mounting number of signs that this optimism was unfounded. Newspaper reports suggested that Diem's army was doing little to combat the growing Vietcong forces and his government was losing, not winning, the support of the countryside. Our military and diplomatic officials on the scene discounted these reports and depicted the correspondents who sent them as little more than immature malcontents determined to topple the Diem government.

The tenacity with which we in Washington accepted the good reports and dismissed or rationalized the bad spoke strongly, I believe, for the sincerity and the missionary conviction with which Washington pursued its Vietnam policy. It was unthinkable that the South Vietnamese, equipped with the modern weaponry and the guidance of the world's most powerful nation, could not overcome ragged bands of little men in black pajamas and sandals cut from old automobile tires with only their spindly legs or bicycles to transport them and their pathetic weapons. It was also unthinkable that the Vietnamese people, given the choice between democracy and communism, could not be led to choose democracy, even if it was flawed by ineptitude or inhibited by ancient Asian autocratism.

As 1963 moved on, it became more difficult to sublimate the bad. Increasingly the news reports flew in the face of the official version: Diem's army was reluctant to fight; his government was stumbling badly and becoming more repressive as it did so.

Relations between the American correspondents and American officials on the scene had deteriorated into mutual bitterness and mistrust. Relations between the American press and the Diem government were even worse. When Diem's troops brutally attacked Buddhists who demonstrated to protest a Diem decree prohibiting them from even showing Buddhist flags, several were killed and many more wounded. It was as if a lid had been blown off some giant, seething cauldron. A shiver of anti-Diem revulsion crossed South Vietnam.

The shudder reached all the way across the Pacific: Americans winced at pictures in their newspapers and on TV screens of a Buddhist bonze burning himself to death in a city square. Some American correspondents covering the increasingly tempestuous protests, chiefly the young reporters whose dispatches to the States had so angered both Vietnamese and American officials in Saigon, were roughed up by police under the command of Diem's devious brother Ngo Dinh Nhu. Two of them were taken into custody for hours of questioning. This was taken by newsmen as an omen of more violence to be directed at them. They were outraged. Some of them were scared. The correspondents expected little sympathy at the American embassy or American military headquarters, so they sent a joint telegram of protest directly to President Kennedy.

That is why, on the night of July 15, I found myself scrunched into a narrow seat on a Pan Am troop transport, the only civilian among perhaps two hundred soldiers, wondering what I would find when we landed in Vietnam.

Chapter 16

The Death of Lancer

W hat I found in Vietnam was a public relations mess.

I was the president's response to the Vietnam correspondents' telegram. My instructions were to examine the situation and do what I could to mend relations between the American press and the American establishment. Just as I was leaving, the mission was expanded. I was ordered to try to meet with President Diem to explain in the most diplomatic way possible that his government's mistreatment of American correspondents and the bad press his government was engendering in the United States could undermine American public support for him and, worse, for South Vietnam's struggle.

The growing American community in Saigon seethed with the antagonism between the American press corps on the one hand and American and South Vietnamese officials on the other. The principal targets of official wrath were a few smart, aggressive, and young correspondents, David Halberstam of the *New York Times,* Malcolm Browne of the Associated Press, Peter Arnett also of the AP, and Neil Sheehan of the United Press. They were all brash and strongly opinionated, especially Halberstam, whose voice and self-confidence were both as big as his imposing frame, but to their credit they were putting their brashness where their mouths were; they ventured out into the

268

field to get their information by directly observing some military operations and talking with the American officers who, though described as "advisers," were increasingly involved in the fighting.* Their reports usually collided head-on with those of the formal military briefers at General Harkins's MAC/V headquarters. By this time, their skeptical views of the progress of the war and of the competence of Diem's regime had become widely shared by the bulk though not all of the more experienced American correspondents covering Vietnam. Many of them were not permanently stationed in the country, but most were experienced Asia hands who traveled in and out frequently and kept in good touch with the situation.

The newsmen were fearful for their personal safety from Nhu's troopers and harassed by the ever-present threat of expulsion by the Diem government. Correspondents for *Newsweek* and NBC had already been kicked out for dispatches reflecting poorly on Diem and his relatives. When I arrived, two others, Browne and Arnett, were being threatened with arrest for having "attacked" the police. The newsmen were emphatically, no, stridently, unanimous in their belief that the Diem regime had to go if South Vietnam's freedom was to be preserved. They were contemptuous of General Harkins's and MAC/V's assessment of the war's progress and felt they were being deliberately lied to on a daily basis. Their opinion of the American embassy staff was not much more flattering. The American diplomats, they felt, had been blinded by their commitment to "winning with Diem" and could not be relied on for objectivity or candor.

A surprising discovery was that the correspondents did not oppose the war or the American involvement, only the way it was being managed. For all their anger and hostility, they seemed to agree to a man that our participation was honorable and in the national interest. The programs underway in Vietnam, military and political, were basically necessary and feasible. They did not appear to question at all their government's

---

*The most prolific of these reporters' sources was John Paul Vann, the maverick army colonel whose turbulent role as a deeply flawed hero was portrayed in Neil Sheehan's biography, *A Bright Shining Lie* (New York: Random House, 1988). **269**

belief in the morality or the wisdom of the American commitment, only its implementation and Washington's reliance on
Diem and his brother Nhu as the implementers.

Most of the American embassy people I talked to did not
credit the newsmen with such supportive sentiments. They
viewed most of them at best as rude, insulting, and insufferable
(all adjectives which I am sure were sometimes deserved) and at
worst, deliberate opponents of their own government. A few at
the embassy questioned aloud the correspondents' patriotism,
but most of the few diplomats and higher military officers who
had the patience to discuss the subject with me appeared to see
the press corps chiefly as inexperienced, mostly immature
young men who did not remotely understand what they were
witnessing. They were a nuisance, an inconvenience to be endured rather than treated with intelligent candor and cultivated
as potential allies. "The Embassy's instincts," I wrote in my
notebook, "are to keep from the press all but the most transparently desirable stories. . . . Faced with a passionately hostile
press corps, the Embassy is entitled to sympathy for its wariness. . . . But the result of its efforts has been the complete
destruction of the Embassy's credibility."

One important exception to this sweeping generalization was
John Mecklin, chief of the United States Information Service
mission in Vietnam. Like myself, Mecklin had worked for *Time*
and crossed over to serve in government. We had worked together on many stories. Mecklin brought a real professionalism
to the USIS operation and had achieved the almost impossible:
He was on good working terms with the embassy staff, the
MAC/V high command, the press corps, *and* many South Vietnamese officials. He seemed to me to be the one American official on the scene who had a clear view of the situation, but he
was not in a high enough part of the pecking order to change
the practices of his peers and superiors. It was Mecklin who
accompanied me to my separate appointments with President
Diem and his brother, the Minister-Counselor Nhu.

Our appointment with the President of South Vietnam was
for fifteen minutes. As we walked into the presidential palace,
270   its beige facade scarred by the signs of a succession of military

coup attempts against Diem, Mecklin said, in effect, Count on at least an hour and politely seize on any slight chance to get some words in edgewise.

Diem was stocky, somewhat dumpy looking for a mandarin autocrat. Wearing a summery tan suit, he sat in a fat armchair, his feet barely reaching the floor. He seemed at first a forlorn figure, but his dignified demeanor and direct, if somewhat sleepy gaze, communicated the indomitableness and Catholic fatalism that had sustained him through years of danger and adversity as the man chosen by the United States to save South Vietnam. He asked me why I was in Vietnam. Because, I said, Washington was disturbed about his government's efforts to intimidate the American press corps and feared that this would have an unfortunate effect on public opinion in the States. Politely, in softly spoken French, with an interpreter at his side, Diem delivered at great length an easily condensed response: The American correspondents' main aim in life was to see him ousted from power, whatever the consequences for South Vietnam and for the American national interest. They had been given every opportunity to see the truth but persisted in ignoring it and in giving aid and comfort to the enemy.

Following Mecklin's advice, I did not try to argue but said that America presence in Vietnam was becoming a controversial issue among Americans and that efforts to prevent scrutiny of the situation by American reporters would only make more difficult President Kennedy's efforts to maintain public support for South Vietnam. Again at great length Diem delivered a short message: American help is welcome, but he and his fellow Vietnamese, not Americans, will decide how to govern Vietnam and how to deal with their enemies, including hostile newspaperman. I asked him to drop police charges against Browne and Arnett and to readmit the expelled correspondents. He said he would think about it. I told him it might be fruitful if he were to swallow his distaste and attempt to persuade some of the correspondents by meeting with them. He seemed to find this a most undiplomatic suggestion but would not be so undiplomatic as to tell me so. He would think about it.

The fifteen-minute appointment had stretched into an hour **271** and a half and I left with the thin comfort that I could say that Diem had at least been willing to listen to my modest requests before rejecting them.

The meeting with Diem's "evil brother" Nhu lasted even longer and made the somber meeting with Diem seem an amiable chat by comparison. I found little resemblance between the two brothers. Nhu was slim and trim, ascetic in appearance yet fierce in his gestures and speech. If he were to grin I was certain the adjective to fit it would have been "satanic," but no hint of a smile visited his face during his long and saturnine lecture, also delivered in French and requiring an interpreter. He seconded his brother's indictment of American correspondents ("These young reporters want nothing less than to make a new government") and then startled me by saying he suspected that the U.S. government might also be hankering for a new leadership in Saigon. In a manner that was defiant, not at all resigned, he said: "All conditions are favorable for a complete U.S. change of policy in Vietnam. It is a great opportunity and it would be a tremendous sacrifice for those hostile to the [Diem] government to give up this opportunity." I could only murmur that the U.S. government was firmly committed to President Diem.

Nhu had good sensory perception, though. He was half correct. As best I knew at that time, Washington still intended, as the critics' chant went, to "sink or swim with Ngo Dinh Diem," but not necessarily with Nhu; some Americans suspected that he, in addition to being the symbol of oppression, was maneuvering for some sort of deal with the Communists, so it would be helpful if Diem were to send into exile both Nhu and his wife, the ferocious Dragon Lady who wished to see American correspondents "barbecued" in public as was that unfortunate Buddhist bonze who several weeks before had doused himself with gasoline and burned to death in a city square. Those who professed to know Diem and his reliance on Nhu's implacable deviousness thought this was mere wishful thinking.

I left the presidential palace with the distinct impression that I had failed in my first and no doubt last assignment in diplomacy, but was pleased to learn just before my departure for Washington that the Diem government was dropping charges against Browne and Arnett and that James Robinson of NBC was being readmitted to Vietnam. The correspondents welcome that news and seemed in general to have been calmed by my visit, but when I told of having urged Diem and Nhu to meet occasionally with them and to be more forthcoming several merely snorted and said they wouldn't go if invited.

During the long flight home as I brooded about the sullen state of affairs I had encountered and wondered what if anything might be done about it, one of those old comic-strip light bulbs flashed above my head: The basic cause of our trouble lay not in Saigon but in Washington. The report I quickly prepared for the secretary of state and the president pointed the finger first at the home office:

> The press problem in Vietnam is singular because of the singular nature of United States involvement in that country. Our involvement is so extensive as to require public, i.e. press, scrutiny and yet so hemmed by limitations as to make it difficult for the United States government to promote and assure that scrutiny. *The problem is complicated by the longstanding desire of the United States government to see the American involvement in Vietnam minimized, even represented as something less than in reality it is.* The early history of the handling of the situation is marked by attitudes, directives and actions in Washington and in the field that reflect this United States desire.

The administration had succeeded in obscuring abroad and at home the escalation of American involvement at the price of a long-term credibility problem for American military and political authorities in Vietnam and also here at home, the report said.

> ... The public attitude in the United States has been mature and unexcitable—so much so that earlier fears of reaction to American casualties and other aspects of the program may be said to have been exaggerated. This last point argues strongly for relaxation of some—but not all—of the strictures still imposed on American press coverage of the situation, and it argues for a more relaxed attitude on the part of U.S. officials to the reports and assessments of the U.S. press. This would do much to reduce the somewhat [sic] sullen Alice in Wonderland miasma that sur-

rounds the Vietnamese press situation and it would help to build a degree of mutual confidence and mutual credibility between American authorities and American correspondents covering Vietnam.

The report, whose prose and length I now concede were stolidly bureaucratic, detailed the substance of my several meetings and interviews and included full-dress memos of the conversations with Diem and Nhu. Beyond recommending an end to the administration's make-believe approach to the facts about Vietnam, I urged that the president himself require his military and civilian representatives to work more strenuously and honestly to cooperate with the press. Just before my excursion to Saigon, President Kennedy had decided to send a new ambassador to replace Frederick Nolting, no friend of the press. The new man, to the surprise of many of us, was Henry Cabot Lodge, the man Kennedy had beaten for the U.S. Senate seat in 1951 and who had run on the Republican ticket for vice-president in 1960. I suggested that this offered an excellent opportunity for mending relations with correspondents.

There was no way, though, that the report could avoid a cheerless observation: "The basic problem will be removed as a critical factor . . . only by time *and* decisive GVN victory over the Viet-Cong."

"Decisive victory over the Viet-Cong"—that was seeming more and more to be but a wish and a promise. In other words, the problem had become far, far deeper than just public relations.

By the time my report reached the secretary's office and the president's staff, the matters it dealt with were fast becoming subordinate to broader concern over the very viability of the American strategy in Vietnam. While he had done little to construct the policies that had been generally etched by McNamara's Pentagon, Secretary Rusk opted strongly for the Pentagon's optimistic, militarily oriented view. Meanwhile, however, a few of the president's other appointees at State, foremost among them Averell Harriman, who was then assistant secretary for the Far East, and some junior aides in the National Security Council, were beginning to assert their concern that present U.S. policy wasn't working, no matter the claims being made for it.

So that irritating sideshow, that pesky problem posed by little men in black pajamas and rubber sandals in a patch of mountains, jungles, and rice paddies thousands of miles across the Pacific had pushed and nudged its way up the agenda to a point where it demanded increasing attention from the president himself. He assigned General "Brute" Krulak and Joseph Mendenhall of the State Department, one of the very few persons in the U.S. government who knew anything at all of Vietnam, its people, and its customs, to go there as a team and make an objective survey.

After hearing Krulak's report that the war was going swimmingly and Diem was the rock on which we should base our policy, and Mendenhall's report that matters were in a dreadful state and the Diem regime was on the edge of collapse, the president looked at them and said, "You two did visit the same country, didn't you?"

Frustrated, the president authorized yet another "fact-finding" mission by Secretary of Defense McNamara with his built-in computer and General Maxwell Taylor, chairman of the Joint Chiefs of Staff, with his hearty soldier's "can-do" approach. For those of us who were trying to clarify policy for the public the upshot of this mission was a paradox. McNamara came back a reluctant convert to the belief that Diem government was failing, yet he publicly announced that as many as a thousand American soldiers could soon be brought home. It was a pleasure to have some ostensibly good news to report, a planned *reduction* of U.S. forces, but the odd combination of positive and negative brought to mind the old Viennese saying, "The situation is hopeless but not serious."

During all these comings-and-goings, everyone I knew to be involved in the Vietnam deliberations, myself certainly included, still shared the confident assumption that the most powerful nation in the world surely could bring this matter to a satisfactory conclusion. During the summer and well into the fall, argument over how best to do it intensified. More and more it centered on Diem and family. In Ambassador Lodge they no longer had a believer running the U.S. Embassy. He had virtu- **275** ally given up trying to reason with Diem and added his strong voice to those in Washington urging increasing pressure on his government, including withholding of American aid. That was a loud signal to anti-Diem elements in Saigon. More than once before a band of army generals had plotted coups against Diem and Nhu but held back for fear of failing. Now they dusted off their old plans.

At this point, communication between Lodge and Washington went far underground or, in government parlance, into "back channels." Even General Harkins and his Saigon HQ were not informed of what was happening. As in the early stages of the Cuban missile crisis, my office knew something important was going on but did not know what until I was brought into the White House meetings at a later stage. I was startled to discover later that there had been two meetings, on October 26 and October 28, at which White House Defense and CIA officials discussed details of an impending attack on Diem by the dissident generals. No one from the State Department was included in the discussion.

As pieced together later, the evidence showed that while the secretary of state and his aides were discussing whether a coup should be encouraged or postponed ("It's a case of wound the tiger, kill the tiger," Rusk warned), Ambassador Lodge and other U.S. officials were giving what amounted to the go-ahead. A CIA agent, Lieutenant Colonel Lucien Conein, was in steady contact with the conspirators and reporting regularly to Lodge. At one point Conein even provided the plotting generals with money to pay damages to families of soldiers killed in the coup attempt. The Department of State got four hours' notice that a coup was truly in the works. This time the dissident generals did not falter. As Saigon dozed in the midday heat on November 1, 1963, they went ahead with their plans. In a few hours they captured the presidential palace, only to find that Diem and Nhu had fled to a nearby Catholic church. There was a rumor that the two had escaped, perhaps to mount a countercoup, but later reports indicated they were dead.

The confused reports were still coming in next morning, Washington time, when the president met in the big cabinet room with Secretaries Rusk and McNamara and the usual band

276

of civilians and soldiers who made up the Vietnam advisory group. The discussion centered on the generals who had engineered the coup and speculation as to which of them might have the talent to run the South Vietnamese government. It was now important to start the AID pipeline flowing again, because the new government's main problems, the Excomm group agreed, would be economic. "We haven't got any alibis anymore," Dean Rusk remarked, "so we had better get on with the job."

The president was concerned about the fate of Diem. One of three different versions of their deaths suggested that Diem and Nhu had committed suicide. The president said he doubted this. After all, they were Catholics. An aide entered the room with the latest cable from Saigon to the White House Situation Room. It said that the insurgent generals had captured Diem and Nhu, piled them into an armored personnel carrier, and summarily executed them, shooting Diem in the back of the head, then shooting Nhu and stabbing him repeatedly. Kennedy winced as if in pain as he read the message. He glanced briefly about the long table and said something. I couldn't quite hear the words but the movement of his lips suggested he had said, "Why did they do *that?*" He was plainly upset. I had never seen the president that way before.

By now there were slightly more than sixteen thousand American military and political advisers in Vietnam, and the flow of military and civilian aid was mounting. President Kennedy had wanted to limit American involvement ("It is their war to win"). But self-delusion on the part of American officials and an overoptimism based in part on extreme falsification of military statistics by the Diem government had hastened the very trend the president had wanted to avoid, a trend toward overmilitarization and over-Americanization of Vietnam's struggle.

The legacy left by Diem, worse when inventoried than had been feared, and the fragility and inexperience of the new leadership called for a high-level conference. A group of us led by Secretaries Rusk and McNamara went to CINCPAC (Commander in Chief, Pacific) headquarters in Pearl Harbor on November 20 to confer with Ambassador Lodge and General Harkins. Depending upon whose assessment one chose, the 277 situation was grim or hopeful. Apparently the plan to withdraw a thousand American military would be held in abeyance.

Rusk and the rest of our small party were joined two days later by other American officials who were to proceed from there to Tokyo for a meeting with Japanese officials. Warmed by the bright Hawaiian sun on that November morning, we mounted the steps into the cabin of a VC 137, one of the Air Force's presidential jets, tail number 86972. Along its white and blue flanks were the words *United States of America.* This was appropriate, for among the passengers were most of President Kennedy's cabinet, more than had ever traveled together on an overseas mission, plus enough other administration members to feed the illusion that if this plane went down, the process of government would falter for at least an instant. But we had no such gloomy thoughts as we took off from Honolulu's Hickam Field for the three-day meeting in Tokyo with our opposite numbers in the Japanese government.

There were thirty-three of us, including Secretaries Rusk of State, Douglas Dillon of Treasury, Stewart Udall of Interior, Willard Wirtz of Labor, Luther Hodges of Commerce, and Orville Freeman of Agriculture. Also aboard were White House advisers Walter W. Heller and Meyer Feldman, and the White House press secretary, Pierre Salinger, who had chosen to take this trip instead of accompanying the president on his political fence-mending trip to Texas.

Dean Rusk occupied a small compartment forward of the main cabin where he could confer in private with the other cabinet secretaries. Further forward, just behind the plane's big flight deck, was a communications shack with all the sophisticated devices that connected our flying cabinet meeting with the White House and almost any corner of the globe. It also contained a chattering United Press International newsticker.

I could hear the noise of the ticker as I walked toward the secretary's compartment. A quick sounding of bells came from the teletype. I knew what that meant: a news "flash," news of extraordinary importance. The plane's communications sergeant leaned over to read the ticker, then recoiled. It was 8:34 A.M. Honolulu time. We knew that because the newsticker said so. We were eight hundred miles west of Honolulu.

"The secretary will want to read this," said the sergeant. He tore the paper from the printer and we stared together at the message. First, a flash bulletin from Dallas, garbled but all too decipherable:

THREE SHOTS WERE FIRED AT PRESIDENT KENNEDY'S MOTORCADE TODAY IN DALLAS.

Then, at 8:38 A.M. (12:38 P.M. Dallas time), an irregular tumble of words:

FLASH . . . KENNEDY SERIOUSLY WOUNDED . . . MAKE THAT PERHAPS SERIOUSLY WOUNDED . . . KENNEDY WOUNDED PERHAPS FATALLY BY ASSASSIN'S BULLET.

Events that happened in a matter of seconds at that time now clamber through memory in slow motion. I handed that dreadful piece of paper to Dean Rusk, who was the senior official, the man in charge. At his request I signaled the cabinet secretaries, who had gone to the main cabin, and Mike Feldman and Walter Heller to join the secretary of state.

At 8:50 A.M. the communications shack had Pierre Salinger on the phone with the White House Situation Room. Using his code name "Wayside," he inquired about "Lancer," the code name for the president, and was told that Kennedy had indeed been shot and rushed to a hospital. At that confirmation, Dean Rusk ordered the pilot to return to Hickam Field. The big plane roared into a stomach-sinking turn. Number 86972 was homebound.

Not knowing then the condition of President Kennedy, we established by radio contact with the State Department that the main party would return to Washington and that Rusk, Salinger, and I would transfer in Honolulu to a smaller aircraft bound for Dallas.

Dean Rusk spoke over the plane's public address system to convey what we knew of the bad news. Then came the voice of the pilot, stating that refueling at Hickam would take only twenty minutes. Orville Freeman tried to soften the suspense, telling us that a man could be shot in the head and survive. That had happened to him in World War II.

Just as pain frequently is not felt until some time after the bone is broken or the bullet tears into the gut, we all seemed at first anesthetized by the news, or perhaps by the tension of waiting for more. Then at 9:32 A.M. Pierre Salinger reached the White House again. A voice said, "Wayside, Lancer is dead." Pierre sobbed. The pilot gently took the phone from Salinger's hand, acknowledged that the message had been understood, then signed off. Pierre returned to the assembled cabinet members. "He's dead," he said. "The president is dead!"

Dean Rusk, a most imperturbable man, had difficulty composing himself as he made his way forward to speak again on the intercom. "Ladies and gentlemen . . . We have received official confirmation that President Kennedy is dead. I am saddened to have to tell you this grievous news. We have a new president. May God bless our new president and our nation." A few sobs sounded softly, then a wave of anguished cries, "No! No!", then a long stretch of no sound save for the straining of the jet engines. We composed a joint public statement by the cabinet to be delivered at Hickam Field. Rusk also composed a message of condolence to Jacqueline Kennedy and another expressing encouragement and support for the new president, Lyndon Baines Johnson.

It took us only one hour and fifty-five minutes to return to Hickam Field. While Rusk and Salinger pushed through the crush of reporters and photographers to talk by phones to the State Department and White House, I read to the press the short cabinet statement of grief and condolence. Word came from the White House Situation Room that the new president expected all to return straightaway to Washington. He would convene a cabinet meeting on our arrival, or early next morning.

The flight from Hickam to Washington seemed endless. The luxurious VIP plane, one that had carried President Kennedy on some of his trips, had turned into a prison, an immense cell in the shape of a metal tube in which men holding some of the most powerful positions in the world sat in impotence. They made some efforts, of course, to think about next steps and how to serve the new president. The talk turned to puzzlement—what kind of person would kill a president? Surely it was some right-wing extremist. The place was Dallas, after all. Then came the shock of another UPI bulletin saying that the assassin was a man named Lee Oswald, who had spent time in the Soviet Union and had pro-Castro connections. If there were some tie to Moscow, said Rusk worriedly, there would be dangerous repercussions at home and abroad.

No one cared to talk for long. For the rest of the journey most just sat, locked in numbness and helplessness. A few had the good fortune to have the company of their wives. I watched Pierre Salinger and his wife, Nancy, her eyes streaming tears, console each other. God, how I wished Maggie was with me. The couples held hands or rested head against head. Those of us who were alone tried for a while to read or only stared into the atmosphere. A few scratched out notes of what was happening. At one point a few of us plunged into a reckless poker game, little caring who won or lost. It was not blasphemy, only desperation. "You want to shout," said Mike Feldman, "but what good would it do?"

Eight hours and thirty minutes after taking off from Honolulu we approached for a landing at Andrews Air Force Base at 12:30 the morning of November 23, 1963. Perhaps we would feel better as soon as Air Force 86972 touched wheels and we were free of that dreadful prison. Perhaps. Perhaps.

But no. It was not to be.

Chapter 17

Running Again with the Hounds

igh on a hill stands a great pantheon, much larger than the one in Rome, made of pure white marble except for its dome of gleaming crystal. This is the place where dreams and promises are stored. The crystal dome glitters and dances with the reflections of them. Standing in the center of the vast space is the Promise-Keeper. He is a handsome, commanding figure, the youngest man ever elevated to the job of Promise-Keeper. He selects the dreams that are to be nurtured and the promises that are to be kept and designates those who are to help keep them. The dreams thrive and multiply without much attention; there are more of them than can be counted. It is the promises that need much care and thought. No promise is easy to handle and some are much more difficult to keep than others, but it is an honor to be one of those chosen to seek ways to keep them, even if it means working on the impossible ones. Scanning the crowd of volunteers I am surprised to see myself, standing in the distance and suddenly singled out by the Promise-Keeper. I am pleased, excited when he beckons me to join the small band at his side and says, in a thought borrowed from one of his favorite poets, "Join me because we have many promises to keep and miles to go before we sleep." I move eagerly forward to grasp his hand and be welcomed into the small group of chosen warriors, but as I do a thunderclap shakes the mighty pantheon. The gleaming dome shatters. I am blinded, then stunned by a rain of crystal shards. When I awaken the crowd has vanished, the Promise-Keeper is gone. I am alone in the vast and sunless ruin, amid fragments of the shattered dome and the still shimmering remnants of broken dreams and promises. In the center is a pool of blood that glistens even in the dark.

To each his or her nightmare in the aftermath of John Kennedy's death. That was mine.

For those days of trauma and numbness, Washington was not a city so much as a huge hospital ambulatory ward, everyone back to work but spiritually limping. Recurrently, my mind wandered to that April day eighteen years before when I rushed into the White House lobby to learn that Franklin Roosevelt had died. That had been an unforgettable moment of shock and incredulity. This time was worse. FDR had been able to live to the full his rendezvous with greatness. John Kennedy had shown that he could charm and inspire multitudes and, I firmly believed, had greatness in his stars, only to be cruelly cut down before his promise could be fulfilled. "Life is unfair," he had once said. So too was death.

Work was the best therapy, and work was what the new president demanded from us all. "Let us continue," was the first command of Lyndon Johnson. "Continuity" became his watchword as he asked all of John Kennedy's appointees to stay in their jobs and help him complete the JFK program and move on from there. He had lusted for the highest office and as vice-president had suffered silently but visibly in the oh-so-close shadow of it. Yet one had to be moved when he stood before the Congress four days after his swearing-in and said, "All I have I would have given gladly not to be standing here today."

It could not have been easy for a man of LBJ's vanity and his hunger for allegiance to reach out to the people who had owed their jobs and their loyalty (often fervently demonstrated) to his predecessor. Many in the White House and in other parts of JFK's government had not treated the vice-president with the deference Kennedy himself had shown him. Beyond the natural ambivalence anyone would feel about that, Johnson betrayed a feeling that was part inferiority complex—he felt with some **283** justice that many of these people looked down on him as a shit-kicking Texas vulgarian—and part a mistrust verging on contempt for their highfalutin university backgrounds, polished manners, and what he correctly fancied in many instances to be their social and/or intellectual snobberies. Still, in a time of need that was as great for the nation as for himself he reached out with his irresistible gift for persuasion and gave us JFK appointees the LBJ power handshake, the grip that had wrestled the U.S. Senate into awed compliance for so many years. Almost to a man and woman we responded by staying at our jobs.

The challenge was still there. But the romance was gone.

No one could be surprised that working in the government would be different under Lyndon Johnson. Those of us in the information offices found that out little more than a week after the assassination. Late one afternoon the new president ordered Pierre Salinger to assemble the information chiefs from Defense, State, Justice, and the other cabinet departments in a side office of the White House that got to be called the Fish Room after Franklin Roosevelt installed a personal aquarium there. Johnson kept us waiting for about half an hour. He hurried in and after only the barest greeting explained that he was about to give a pre-Christmas reception for "the important people in the government" so he didn't have time to deliver more than a quick message to us. It was approximately this: You people are supposed to be generating news that is good for the government and, especially, good for the president. When you have good news to release in your department, you send it over here to the White House so Pierre Salinger can release it; if you've got bad news, take care of it in your own departments. He had been studying the federal budget and discovered that the government was spending almost a billion dollars on us information people. We'd better start earning it.

Aside from elating us with the news that he didn't count us among "the important people" in government, the new president's message was not exactly startling. The privilege of dispensing the good news and fending off the bad was as much a part of all the presidencies I had known as were listening to
284 "Hail to the Chief," greeting each year's MS Poster Child, en-

tertaining foreign potentates at dinner, and lighting the White House Christmas tree. LBJ was, to put it mildly, just more blatant about it.

To him, subtlety was some effete Eastern word for timidity, like calling fish eggs "caviar" or saying "pee-pee" when you mean "piss." Those of us who had opportunity to observe him became the richer in figures of speech, though many had to be classified "lim dis," for Limited Distribution. "That fellow is noisy as a cow pissin' on a flat rock" was one of the more presentable ones. For a clumsy chap like Gerald Ford: "He cain't fart and chew gum at the same time." For a new recruit to the Great Society: "I want that fellow to think he can charge hell with a bucket of water and put it out." For a senator who had just been promised a dam or some new convert to a Johnson cause: "Now I've got his balls right here in my pocket." On why he refused the remove the dark and devious J. Edgar Hoover as director of the FBI: "I'd rather have him inside my tent pissin' out than outside pissin' in."

He also was a great believer in the use of visual images to influence or, if you will, manipulate public opinion. A USIS photographer was at his call night and day to record the Johnson presidency for posterity (left profile, please) and to produce a torrent of autographed photographs as gifts or inducements for members of the Congress, corporate visitors, government servants, and others whom the president had reason to caress.

In January 1964 a comical-looking Vietnamese general with a goatee named Nguyen Khan staged a successful coup against the military junta that had deposed Diem. Johnson ordered Secretary McNamara and General Taylor (the two of them were making yet *another* "inspection" visit to Vietnam) to travel around the countryside and be photographed at every stop holding the hands-above-the-head victory grip with General Khan in order to demonstrate that he was "America's boy." The president got the photographs he wanted. Whether because of them or in spite of them, Khan lasted as leader of the Saigon government for no more than ten months before being ousted by a junta of younger generals.

In that same month, trouble erupted in Panama when Panamanian students and Americans in the Canal Zone clashed in a **285** dispute over display of the American and Panamanian flags. The clash exploded into rioting and shooting; U.S. Army troops were called in to support the Canal Zone police and before the rioting was over eighteen Panamanians and six or seven American soldiers were dead. I was one of a special team the president sent to Panama to investigate what had happened. Led by Secretary of the Army Cyrus Vance, our group included one of Vance's deputies, Harry McPherson, a smart and charming Texan who was to become one of LBJ's most influential White House aides; Thomas Mann, assistant secretary of state for Inter-American Affairs, and his predecessor in that post, Edward Martin; Ralph Dungan, the Kennedy man who had recruited me and who was still working in the LBJ White House; and a monosyllabic man in a black suit who was presented to the rest of us as Colonel King, the CIA's deep-dish expert on "Red subversion" in Panama.

We spent three days dodging Panamanian snipers' bullets and conferring with American military and civilian and some Panamanian officials. The snipers were poor shots, so the closest I came to physical harm was an encounter with a *Washington Post* reporter who had written a graphic but highly imaginary tale of Americans assaulting defenseless Panamanians with tanks and machine guns. I accosted the reporter, a fellow named Kurzman who was younger and a great deal bigger than I, and angrily pointed out that not a single machine gun had been unlimbered and the American forces did not have a single tank in Panama. What in hell did he think he was doing? According to Harry McPherson's subsequent report, "Kurzman pleaded lack of time to weigh the army's evidence. He would write a factual piece later. Manning thumped him on the chest and said he would wait to see it." Kurzman did not thump back, but I don't recall that the second story ever appeared.

We fact-finders returned to Washington unscathed and only moderately enlightened about a very confused set of events. At a meeting in the cabinet room we reported to the president and a group of White House, Defense, and State Department officials. Our report, while not by any means unanimous—Tom Mann being a hard-liner when it came to dealing with Latin Americans and Colonel King suggesting with a conspiratorial rolling of eyeballs that we hadn't even begun to comprehend the Communist influence in Panama—tended to suggest that the American authorities, both civilian and military, had over-reacted and probably made an already unpleasant situation far worse. There was seething discontent among the Panamanians and deep feelings of grievance against the conduct of the American "Zonians" and Americans in general, some of us pointed out. Perhaps it was time for the United States to be magnanimous and begin the lengthy process of turning over the Panama Canal to the Panamanians. The president snorted in disgust. That would have every American Legion post in America kicking his ass.

Instead, said Johnson, we should dig out those old plans for building a sea-level canal in neighboring Costa Rica. George Ball started to intervene, Mr. President, he said, That idea has been put aside long ago as impractical and. . . .

George, the president interrupted, I don't give a damn whether it's practical or not. Here's what I want you to do. I want a team of those army engineers to go down there to Costa Rica or whatever place it is, with all their surveying equipment, and I want an AP photographer down there to take pictures of them surveying the place for a new canal, and I want that picture to appear on every front page in Panama and all South America.

Johnson tapped the table a couple of times as if to say, That ought to shut up those Panamanian protesters for a while. The order wasn't carried out (I wondered whether he really expected it to be), but I believe that was the last time anyone dared to suggest to Lyndon Baines Johnson that he should even *think* about handing over the Panama Canal to the people of Panama.

Working for Lyndon was, among many things, entertaining. He was two different men squeezed into one big, rangy body, the outcome of some transcentury gene-cross of the Roman emperor Commodus, who replaced the head of every statue in Rome with his own likeness, with the Oklahoma cowboy impersonator Will Rogers. Though I was offended by Johnson's methods and what I considered to be his demeaning of the information process, I was not sorry that I had agreed to stay on **287** for a while after Kennedy's death. Otherwise I would have missed the experience of working for one of the most remarkable figures ever visited upon the American public. But it was time to go. Lyndon Johnson didn't want information officers on his payroll. He wanted press agents.

April, my original deadline for returning to private life, had come and passed. I yearned to resume my real trade, to shuck off the governmental straitjacket, pull on my old soft-soled boots and bramble-proof jacket and be a poacher again, run with the hounds. A change was only a matter of time, anyway; life as a president's political appointee was transitory at best, subject to the whim of either a president or the electorate or both. What is more, it was financially draining. My pay was $20,000 a year, not much for a family of five in expensive Washington and considerably less than what I had already been earning even in the relatively low-paying news trade. The entertainment allowance for the assistant secretary of state for public affairs was a lavish $200 a year, enough to finance perhaps one superb dinner for my French and British counterparts, considerably less than I'd spent weekly for the care and feeding of news sources in my *Time* days. Some two-and-a-half years in public service had eaten up all the profit-sharing booty I had taken with me from Time Inc.

There were a few options worth considering. I supposed I could return to Time Inc. in some capacity, but I'd already traveled that route. Phillip Graham, the brilliant, mercurial boss of the *Washington Post* and its new acquisition, *Newsweek* magazine, had talked to me earnestly of coming to work for the *Post,* but the troubled publisher had subsequently committed suicide. Phil's widow, Katharine, who had bravely stepped in and was just beginning what proved to be a masterful job of taking over and building the Washington Post Company empire, picked up on his initial suggestion, but, even if she were at all interested in my services, she had what no doubt were sound reasons for not imposing an outsider on the *Post* hierarchy at that sensitive time.

I was even beginning to think again about trying to establish a syndicated column when I got inquiries on two successive **288** days from two old friends. One was Evan Thomas, then an editor at Harper and Row, the book publishers, wondering if I would be interested in coming to work for *Harper's Magazine* in New York. The second came from Charles Morton, urging me to travel to Boston to talk about joining *The Atlantic Monthly*. What an astonishing coincidence. From as far back as Binghamton *Press* days, these were the two publications that many of us news hands admired most and dreamed of writing for. They were the country's two quality magazines of ideas, respected and influential beyond the circumference of their small circulations and modest incomes. As far as journalistic quality (though not, I hasten to add, wages) was concerned, this was like being asked to choose between Tiffany and Cartier, between Rolls-Royce and Bentley.

A choice was difficult, but it did not take much time to make it. Both magazines were looking for a number two man as eventual replacement for their present editors, Jack Fischer at *Harper's,* whom I had come to admire during the Stevenson campaign, and the venerable Edward Weeks, who had been editing *The Atlantic Monthly* for more than twenty-five years. Both those editors were willing participants in the search. Both people who had the power of decision, Cass Canfield of Harper and Row, and Marion Danielson Campbell, who had inherited ownership of *The Atlantic* from her late father, were enthusiastic in their offers. *Harper's* had for me the appeal of being somewhat more politically oriented than *The Atlantic* and for Maggie the attribute of being in New York. We both sensed, though, that Ted Weeks was willing to be more specific about handing over the editorship in a couple of years than was the younger Jack Fischer. In addition, in Boston I would inherit not only the editorship of the magazine but also its book publishing arm, the Atlantic Monthly Press. The clinching fact was that Marion Campbell, while she enjoyed rare visits to a small tucked-away office and sitting in once in a great while (silently) at a story conference, had no desire to participate in or otherwise try to shape editorial decisions. Unless the editor started to drive the company off a high cliff or committed sodomy in the Boston Public Garden, *The Atlantic* was his to make of it what he could. Remembering my 1960 conversation with Harry Luce, I resisted an urge to write and tell him that I would now be run- **289** ning my own "group." So I made the choice, and the correct one it was, for I discovered later that Canfield and his associates were about to sell *Harper's Magazine* to Canfield's son-in-law, John Cowles, Jr., and his Minneapolis Star-Tribune Company. That did not bode well for *Harper's.*

I had waited longer than some to stray off LBJ's ranch. By now the Kennedy people in the White House—Schlesinger, Sorensen, O'Donnell—had gone, replaced by close Johnsonites like Jack Valenti, Walter Johnson, and Bill Moyers, all strangers to me. Pierre Salinger, with whom I had such a comfortable working relationship, had gone West on a doughty but doomed quest to win one of California's seats in the U.S. Senate. (He lost to the Republican George Murphy, a Hollywood song-and-dance man. An omen of worse things to come?)

Mac Bundy was still running the NSC and with Kennedy's principal cabinet secretaries had made the switch to Johnson, certainly not without some discomfort but with no discernible difference in the advice and confident assurances they gave to their president.

Vietnam was still Bob McNamara's and the Pentagon's province, and more than ever their emphasis was on military measures—more of the same—rather than the political and psychological effort to win over the people of that increasingly torn country. Now that he was devoting more of his time to Vietnam, Dean Rusk shared the McNamara–Joint Chiefs of Staff view, though he tolerated and was privy to growing discussion by George Ball, Averell Harriman, and others of the minority at State who were speaking their view that the overly militarized course of action was ill-conceived and dangerous. Such discussion contradicted administration policy and was of course conducted in private. I had come to share the belief that while military help was indispensable, overemphasis on it was allowing aid programs and efforts to extend leadership and benevolence to the Vietnamese people by the Saigon regime to disintegrate into mere token gestures. We needed to rebuild our aid and citizen-protection programs and force the South Vietnamese government into more rapport with the people in the cities and countryside. I still stoutly believed that we were right to be in Vietnam, that we still had the power and the will to do good there.

For a man who looked on any resignation as a case of desertion under fire the president accepted mine graciously, with a letter of a sort he'd already written to several others and whose sentiments he repeated in person on my last visit to the White House. He extended the LBJ power grip with his right hand, gently massaged my right shoulder with his other hand, gave me his mournful basset hound gaze, and said in his ingratiating Will Rogers mode, "I want to thank you for what you've done for your country." I was grateful for a few kind words.

Jim Greenfield was a natural successor to my job and I was pleased to see the secretary of state heartily agree and the president send his nomination to the Congress. Until I began counting I hadn't realized how many new friends I had made and how many people I had come to respect and admire, to all of whom I now had to say good-bye. They were at all levels of government, the lower and middle of the civil service and foreign service, and upper reaches as well. High on my list was Dean Rusk.

Ours was a peculiar relationship. We had traveled at least three times the distance around the world together, bummed each other's cigarettes, dozed off together (along with Mrs. Rusk and the rest of our travel-weary group) during an interminable feast given in Rusk's honor by Generalissimo and Madame Chiang Kai-shek in Taipei. We had sweltered together perilously close to the funeral burning ghat as they ceremoniously split Jawaharlal Nehru's skull and set him afire outside New Delhi. We had been benumbed together by the dreary oratory of unnumbered meetings of NATO, CENTO, SEATO, and assorted other councils of ministers, endured together all over the globe the insipid questions of unprepared journalists and the all-too piercing inquiries of the knowledgeable. We had shared together the difficulty of remembering which of the several possibilities would be the next president of South Vietnam. On long flights together he had beaten me at bridge or I had licked him at poker. We had been together at that especially terrible moment when I handed him and he read the news that President Kennedy had been shot. Through all that and more. **291**

Yet I didn't feel I had gotten really to understand Dean Rusk. I knew, though, that I had been working for an extraordinarily dedicated man.

He was the least glamorous of Jack Kennedy's principal cabinet members, the undistinguished-looking fellow with the bald head who never surfed off Malibu or slalomed with fading European countesses at Aspen. Rusk's hero was General George C. Marshall, whom he had served both in wartime and during Marshall's stint as secretary of state. He patterned himself after Marshall's stoic privateness and unstinting loyalty to the commander in chief. He could put complicated matters into clear prose and he was at times an eloquent speaker, but he was definitely neither a showoff nor a showman. Partly because of that, I think, and for other reasons that never become altogether clear to me, he was intensely disliked by some of the Kennedy administration intellectuals whom I particularly respected, like Arthur Schlesinger and Ken Galbraith. After Kennedy's assassination, an article in *Life* drawn from the book Arthur Schlesinger was writing about JFK's thousand days in office said that Kennedy had intended to replace Rusk in his second term. It caused a furor, and that passage was absent when the book was published. Before he died several years later in Boston of grief and self-neglect, as much a victim of Lee Oswald's bullet as was Kennedy himself, JFK's close and faithful servant Kenneth O'Donnell praised Rusk's service to the president and angrily denied that Kennedy had planned to dump Rusk; he was just the kind of self-effacing secretary of state the president wanted, Kenny told me. Vice-President Johnson, after months of cannily measuring the Kennedy cabinet colleagues through squinting eyes, once remarked to Carl Rowan, "This guy Rusk is a great man. They're shitting all over him in high places and low places and he goes on doing his job. That's the mark of a great man."

Great man in the historical sense? Not in this era when it is the events and the issues that are great and the men who try to deal with them small, but I never before had met a man who gave more in service to his country and asked so little in return. Once in a while, usually at the end of a fifth or sixth eighteen-hour day in a row, his patience would give way to irritation.

Late one day after a series of frustrating events he pointed to a newspaper story about the latest Supreme Court decision. The court had just ruled in *New York Times v. Sullivan* that libel could not be found in a case brought by a public figure unless he or she could prove deliberate malice on the part of the alleged libeler. "See that, Bob," Rusk said, more in rue than in anger. "They work us to death, pay us too little, and now they can libel us with impunity." As one whose advice and whose deeds were supposed to protect or further the U.S. national interest, he sometimes took hard stances. When the administration was under some pressure to send food to prevent a predicted famine in China he remarked, "Why should I put food into the bellies of Chinese soldiers who might someday be shooting American boys?"

I suspect but do not know for certain that, like others of us, he felt that President Kennedy's gaudily promoted Alliance for Progress was essentially a triumph of inflated prose over limited substance. At any rate, late one day after fatiguing hours of listening to endless oratory at a meeting of the Pan American Union, he took a sip of his scotch-on-the-rocks and asked rhetorically, "Why should we knock ourselves out like this and send money down there so the comfortable Latin American leaders can live the good life and take their siestas every day?" Were it delivered in public this was not the kind of talk that would please liberals or provoke charity-minded church groups to standing ovations, but it was a kind of toughness a president could use.

We had never been truly comfortable with each other. Hard as he may have tried to feel otherwise, my presence was an ever-present threat to the diplomatic privacy he instinctively and justifiably protected. That protectiveness made me uncomfortable in turn; I now philosophize that it was something like the extra lead weights a handicapper tucks into the saddle to really test a horse's mettle. Dean Rusk didn't make it easy for me to do the job, but he played square with me and I think he appreciated my efforts. He deserved that old-fashioned encomium, a true American patriot. It would have embarrassed him to have it said to his face. So when it came time to say good-bye to Dean Rusk, I said simply I had been honored to **293** know him and to work for him. And I meant it truly.

The British correspondents in Washington threw a special farewell party and gave me not one but two engraved pewter mugs; they knew I didn't like to drink alone. At a farewell luncheon the State Department Correspondents' Association handed over a beautiful silver box engraved with my readmission ticket:

With Deepest Appreciation
THE HOUNDS OF GUTENBERG
July 28, 1964

So here I was, running with the hounds again, and a good thing it was. I was not at all regretful that I had left the pack for a while to experience what I had experienced, though one stint in government would be enough to serve me for a lifetime. I departed for Boston and a new life with several thoughts mingling in my mind. First, I felt I had learned much about how government works—and does not work—and knew that I could use that knowledge to good effect as an editor. Second, now that I had experienced from both sides the natural, prickly, suspicion-clouded, occasionally angry antagonism between press and government, I had become more convinced than ever of its indispensibility.

The case of Secrecy v. Disclosure is on perpetual trial in a democracy. The reflexes of government are conditioned toward secrecy. The duty of the press is to disclose. Even if the American people sometimes behave as if they do not want it, they need the protection of a free, vigorous, even a sometimes reckless press. In that conflict between secrecy and disclosure, government's power to conceal, distort, or obfuscate far outweighs the ability of the press to penetrate and disclose. Though I had witnessed no major abuse in my few years in government, the tools for abuse for political and other far more questionable purposes are always at hand and the temptation to use them is ever present. Government of course has the duty to invoke secrecy in the national interest and to enjoy a certain privacy in its execution of stated policies, but even there the lines are not always clear. For example, it could be argued (as it is by some) that by withholding what they knew some in the press honored

294

the secrecy that allowed the government's Cuban missile strategy to succeed; that restraint certainly could be said to have served the public good. Yet the same kind of press restraint a year earlier may have achieved the opposite. Kennedy himself lamented that if the *New York Times* had disregarded his administration's plea to withhold and had instead printed what it had learned about preparations for the the Bay of Pigs operation, that humiliating fiasco probably would not have happened.

After some two and a half years in government, I had no doubt where I stood in the matter of Secrecy v. Disclosure. I reserved a hallowed place in my rulebook for a proposition best put by Alan Barth, a much respected editorial writer for the *Washington Post.* "A press which enjoys such independence of government is almost bound to be, by definition, in some degree irresponsible," he said. ". . . Our country right or wrong is a dangerous sort of sentimentality for individuals; for newspapers it represents a total abdication of responsibility. For the responsibility of a newspaper is not to governments; it is to values, to ideas, to human beings."

My last departing thought took the form of a resolution. I decided to stop asking myself, What if John Kennedy had lived? There was nothing to be gained by such wishful thinking, nor time for it.

Chapter 18

Boston Sketches

If Charles Walton Morton had stayed with his father's hard-
ware business in Omaha, Nebraska, he probably would have
made much more money and my life would have worked out
differently. Charlie didn't. He tried it for a while, after studying
at Williams College and working briefly on a ranch at Pitch-
fork, Wyoming. During an afternoon lull in the nuts-and-bolts
trade he bought one of those three-decker Corona typewriters
from a shop down the street and soon discovered that he was a
writer. One day in 1928 he said good-bye forever to two-penny
nails, weed killer, and ironing board covers, and packed his
wife, Mildred, an eight-year-old daughter, a cook, an Irish
wolfhound, and a Kerry blue terrier into a big used Cadillac
given to him by his father. In cheerful defiance of Horace Gree-
ley the entourage drove East. For the next several years Charlie
brought smiles to the faces of readers of the *Boston Herald* and
then the *Boston Transcript,* a newspaper that was as eccentric as
Charlie himself but in a less entertaining fashion.

Maggie and I got to know the Mortons during our Nieman
year at Harvard. They had been friends of her mother and father in pre-Depression Omaha. To Charlie this friendship implied an automatic obligation to shepherd two innocents
through the ways and peculiarities (Charlie was a connoisseur

of peculiarities) of Cambridge. This he did with generous hospitality and much vivacity. By then he had left the daily newspaper grind to become associate editor of *The Atlantic Monthly,* a job in which he served as creative lieutenant to the editor, Edward Weeks, while carefully cultivating his own garden, a special section in the back of the magazine. It was called "Accent on Living" and featured brief essays and reviews that dealt with the pleasures (and hazards) of living, eating, drinking, reading, talking, traveling, listening to music. Charlie's own engaging commentary always led the section. He was essentially one of God's angry men, graced with a courteous demeanor and a soft voice that masqueraded his life's true mission, to take churlish monthly inventory of the absurdities and some of the attributes of contemporary life. He was the proud owner of more warm friendships than he could count and a breathtaking array of grudges. Charlie was still cultivating that same garden when we returned to Cambridge almost twenty years later. Our return was in great part due to the fact that for several years Charlie Morton had been pressing Marion Campbell to bring me into *The Atlantic* as its prospective next editor. He harbored no such ambition for himself or if he once did, had abandoned it long before.

By now Morton was sixty-five and suffering the inroads of emphysema, but aging had not diminished in the least his enthusiasms or his animosities. His good eye for writers and subject matter plus his built-in skepticism—the kind of shit detector advocated by Hemingway—did much to keep *The Atlantic*'s banality quotient low and its quality high. He was one of that perpetually endangered species, a nonconformist. In the days when he was a smoker, Charlie usually flaunted some obscure brand with a peculiar name like Wings or Spud, with odor to match. Every year or so he would press on guests his latest discovery of a bourbon that was dirt cheap but "believe me, better than Wild Turkey or Jack Daniels." This year's brand— 1964 vintage—was a Pennsylvania product that was labeled Old Solace or something like that. His search for wine bargains sometimes though not always led him to equally lamentable results. He still traveled every year to England, his favorite country after his own, and came back with at least one new suit   **297** or sport jacket that would announce his presence from some distance; Charlie did not stint on money for suiting, always choosing expensive fabrics notable for their wearability and delicate weave but most of all for their high decibel count.

He was also a pioneer environmentalist, as demonstrated whenever he discovered a lingering speck of egg yolk on a spoon or any other slight omen of pollution in one of the many restaurants he favored, then abandoned for one cranky reason or another. The one that kept his loyalty was the Café at Boston's Ritz-Carlton, which was then a tastefully run hotel and a sort of luncheon clubhouse for *Atlantic* hands. Even at the Ritz, before accepting a table he would run his hand underneath to ascertain whether some polluter had parked a piece of unbiodegradable chewing gum. One day when he was lunching with his good friend Edwin O'Connor, the novelist, Charlie spotted a housefly sunning itself on a window near his table. He summoned the waiter, an attractively cocky young fellow who also happened to be called Charlie, and in typical Morton fashion pursed his lips, said nothing but pointed accusingly at the offending insect. Charlie the waiter moved close to study the fly, then said with genuine admiration, "Gee, Mr. Morton, they're making them bigger this year, aren't they?" The older Charlie didn't relax his angry grimace, but he doubled the usual tip.

So thanks in great part to Charlie Morton here I was, back in New England, living again in Cambridge and traveling each day to the Boston side of the Charles River to work in the attached pair of lovely old brownstones that housed the offices of *The Atlantic* and the Atlantic Monthly Press. The magazine was approaching its 107th birthday anniversary. I was approaching my forty-fifth, not exactly a kid anymore but young and eager enough for at least one more adventure.

Greater Boston was a nourishing place for a magazine like *The Atlantic*. It was also an engaging place in which to live and work, more suggestive of London than any other American community, though of course much smaller and less sophisticated. Because we had a comfortable familiarity with Cambridge from our several months of living there twenty years before, we chose to move there first, into a Victorian ark of a house just off Brattle Street. This was Harvard or "gown" Cam-

A bit of spoofery at Oxford, 1958.
Brian Seed

Here is evidence for the *Time* and *Life* editors in New York that the London bureau chief was covering all sides of the cold war news.

Ready for his first eight-furlong race in a brief career as perhaps the fastest two-furlong thoroughbred in England, Fourflusher gets the skeptical appraisal of his trainer, Ron Smyth, at Epsom Downs.

The Manning boys, Robert, Brian, and Richard, properly togged in their London school uniforms, 1958.

Henry R. Luce, founder of *Time, Life,* and *Fortune* magazines and proclamator of the American Century, helps to lay the cornerstone of his new headquarters, the 48-story, $70 million Time-Life Building at Rockefeller Center, 1959. *UPI Bettmann*

As an engineer of the Suez Canal debacle in 1956 a brooding Anthony Eden is forced to resign after little more than a year as Britain's prime minister, the job for which he had so long prepared in the shadow of Winston Churchill. *UPI Bettmann*

Eden's successor, Harold Macmillan, liked to think of Britain as playing Athens to America's Rome. He enjoyed several years as prime minister and struck up a comfortable, easygoing relationship with President Kennedy. *UPI Bettmann*

While Maggie and Secretary of State Dean Rusk look on with what appears to be apprehension, I am sworn in as Assistant Secretary of State for Public Affairs in the administration of President John F. Kennedy.

Why, then, are these people laughing?

On the porch of our comfortable, shaggy old house in Washington's Cleveland Park section in 1962 the master and mistress relax with (from left) Rick, Rob, and Brian Manning.

One of several high-level reconnaissance photographs shows, at San Cristobal, Cuba, one of the missile sites being constructed by Soviet forces in October of 1962. Several such photographs were made public on the night of October 22, when President Kennedy announced the naval blockade of Soviet ships bound for Cuba.

In the Oval Office, October 22, 1962. President Kennedy has just signed the proclamation putting into effect the U.S. embargo of arms to Cuba. *UPI Bettmann*

Anti-American violence in Panama City and the Canal Zone during January of 1964 caused LBJ to send an investigating team to the scene. Aboard the Air Force jet (counterclockwise from left) are the then Deputy Secretary of the Army (and later key LBJ aide) Harry McPherson, White House Latin America specialist Ralph Dungan, Secretary of the Army Cyrus Vance, Assistant Secretary of State for Public Affairs Manning, and Assistant Secretary of State for Inter-American Affairs Thomas Mann. The CIA spook aboard did not wish to pose for the camera.

Rusk, on a visit to South Vietnam in 1964, and Henry Cabot Lodge, U.S. ambassador to South Vietnam, are not quite sure what to make of a briefing by South Vietnamese military officers, nor am I. After President Diem was killed in a coup matters grew steadily more dangerous.

Japan's deputy vice foreign minister Takio Oda (second from left) and I brief the press after the third annual U.S.-Japan economic conference in January 1964, the meeting that had been postponed by the assassination of President Kennedy two months before. *Osamu Énomoto*

Open-air conference at the LBJ Ranch with the secretary of state and Benjamin Read, chief of the department's secretariat, during President Johnson's meeting with West German Chancellor Erhard in spring of 1964.

The novelist Edwin O'Connor in a serious moment after savoring the success of *The Last Hurrah* and a Pulitzer Prize for *The Edge of Sadness*.
Charles Dixon

Atlantic Monthly editor Charles W. Morton. Benevolence and wit resided beneath that curmudgeonly mien.

During his political heyday as a member of Boston's City Council, Clement Norton addresses a crowd in the Boston Common.

Brahmin though he was, U.S. Senator Leverett ("Salty") Saltonstall was a veritable pied piper when it came to gathering the votes of Boston's Irish—as well as other Massachusetts voters.

Professor John Kenneth Galbraith presides benignly over his annual Harvard Commencement Day lawn party.

Joseph Stalin's only daughter, Svetlana, was four years old when photographed in 1920 with her mother, Nadezhda. Nadezhda was repelled by the bloody deeds of Communist leaders, including her husband, and following a quarrel with Stalin one day in 1932 she killed herself. *UPI Bettmann*

Svetlana, married and divorced from a Russian named Alleluyeva, could not stand Soviet society either. In 1967 she defected to the United States and soon thereafter published in *The Atlantic* her farewell to her native land. Three years later, while living in Princeton, New Jersey, she reacts to the news that the Kremlin had just stripped her of Soviet citizenship. *UPI Bettmann*

The *Atlantic*'s editorial staff met in my office frequently, usually animatedly and some-times almost successfully in our ongoing effort to outpace chaos and anticipate events. The group here includes among others Charlie Morton, Emily Flint, Louise Desaulniers, Anne Murphy, Michael Janeway, Phoebe Lou Adams, and C. Michael Curtis. *JET Commercial Photographers*

'Jimmy! There's an article heah callin' y'all arrogant, ignorant, spiteful, complacent and insecu. . . . Funny – he'all was here jes' a minute ago!'

When in 1979 *The Atlantic* published an article by Jimmy Carter's former speech writer James Fallows that was critical of Carter's presidential style, the cartoonist Oliphant enshrined the White House reaction in pen and ink.

Established as a media mogul after his acquisition of *The Atlantic* and *U.S. News & World Report* magazines, Mortimer Zuckerman ornaments the Manhattan social scene in the company of his now former friend and flame, Gloria Steinem. *Marina Garnier*

Theresa Manning and her husband, Bob, find much to smile about as, strolling a strip of Cape Cod beach, they contemplate the future.

bridge as distinguished from working-class or "town" Cambridge, so we found ourselves again wrapped in the atmosphere of academia. Over teacups or glasses of sherry, academia's favored lubricant, alas, the cultivated faculty ladies were as insistent as ever in their opinions and as consistent in their habits; some in fact seemed even to be wearing the dresses we'd seen two decades before. Several of the most inspiring professors of the Nieman year had passed on, but some of the once young and budding faculty stars we'd gotten to know then, like Archibald Cox at the Law School, Harry Levin in the English Department, John Dunlop in Economics, Wendell Fury in Physics, and Oscar Handlin in History, were still much in evidence, by now fixed for life in the Harvard firmament, thanks to tenure. They were a bit gray, more than a bit paunchy, and looking over their shoulders to see which young ones might be gaining on them. Harvard itself also seemed grayer and paunchier, still a great university but neither as yeasty nor as confident of its superiority under the unadventurous presidency of Nathan Pusey as it had seemed in James Conant's day. Universities like Stanford, Michigan, Duke, and Berkeley were catching up. Many of the faculty were as self-satisfied as before, even more so, it seemed, though with less reason, but the place surely was less placid. The rude intrusion of "the counterculture" was gradually provoking professors and students into unseemly disputes and nasty divisions.

Twenty years before, the Nieman program and the intense studying it required had kept Maggie and me within this relatively tight Harvard community of teachers, students, and fellow Niemans. Now our circle widened to bring us into contact with a far broader range of what in some communities would be described as "society" but in Greater Boston was better thought of as clans and tribes—the Irish, the Italian, the WASP (incorporating the shrinking remnant of what had once been the mighty Brahmin tribe), the Jewish, the Black (now spilling over into Irish turf from the Roxbury ghetto that had once been the home of impecunious Jews). Smaller bands of other ethnic groups added their special spices to the stew, including a fast growing influx of Chinese, Koreans, Vietnamese, and assorted Hispanics. There had been of course some mixing and as-   **311** similating over the years. For example, in the profusion of twenty-five hospitals and three medical schools, the tight Anglo-Saxon monopoly had eroded and Boston now boasted the world's largest mixed tribe of Shamans, an illustrious collection of medicine men (and a grudgingly accepted few women) in which, for the most part, Jewishness, Irishness, Waspishness stopped, or so it was claimed, at the admissions offices of the medical schools and the doorways of the operating rooms and hospital wards. General assimilation was a long way off, though, if indeed it had any chance at all. Life in greater Boston was much affected, made more interesting but also more worrisome by the persistence of those tribal rites, superstitions, religious and ethnic prejudices that time seemed unable to wash away.

The academic tribal reservation centered in Cambridge around Harvard and MIT but reached in all directions, to Tufts and Boston universities, Boston College, the University of Massachusetts, and out to the more than 160 other universities, colleges, and junior colleges situated within a short auto or streetcar ride from the center of Boston. The area was awash in teachers, tutors, professors of widely varying skills as well as a ragged army of writers, poets, and painters most of whom could pay their rent only by teaching though they would rather just pursue their art. Like medicine, education was one of Massachusetts's major industries.

Of the many imposing figures in Cambridge, one was a particularly helpful guide to academia's charms and its pomposities. Through our adventures together in the Adlai Stevenson campaign and the Kennedy government John Kenneth Galbraith, the economist, author, and former Kennedy ambassador to India, and I had become friends. At 6 feet 8½ inches in height, he towered over his environment like some giant gray heron surviving from prehistoric times, a man of prolific talent, strong and usually solid opinions, and bullet-proof certitude; a keeper of the liberal flame even as it sputtered in increasingly unfavorable weather. His and his wife Kitty's ongoing salon in Francis Avenue was a steady source of amusement and enlightenment. When the dinner guest was not Jacqueline Kennedy Onassis it might be a fiery young Radcliffe graduate named

Benazir "Pinky" Bhutto, who was on the way out of political exile to become, for a brief, turbulent time, the first woman prime minister of Pakistan. Or perhaps a British ambassador, a Soviet economist, or Tom Lehrer singing "The Vatican Rag" and others of his zany song spoofs. A pair of Nobel Prize–winners, a stray senator or two from Washington, or a sitar player from New Delhi. Or a couple of British MPs who hadn't been speaking to each other since Suez. Between shuttling to Washington to testify before congressional committees, traveling the world as a lecturer or consultant, and pouring out new books to build on the success of his early best-sellers, *The Great Crash, 1929* and the particularly influential *The Affluent Society,* Galbraith presided over one of the most popular courses at Harvard.

As classes in economics go, Galbraith's was decidedly unstructured. He had in addition to high intelligence and wide experience the necessary tinge of charlatanism that distinguishes a good teacher from a workaday one. He brightened "the dismal science" with a blend of droll skepticism, wit, and anecdotal entertainment that caused some of his envious peers to grumble that the Harvard course catalog should list it as "Galbraith on Galbraith." Having decided years before that "modesty is a much overrated virtue" and having forthrightly demonstrated at every turn his belief in that maxim, Galbraith accepted his colleagues' envy as simply another deserved compliment. Over the years he was to be a most congenial and helpful ally to me and *The Atlantic,* providing innumerable articles and essays as well as a steady stream of suggestions and critical comments, not all of them kind but most of them constructive.

It was typical of Galbraith and his joy at seeing his work in print that he also kept on friendly terms with Jack Fischer and Jack's successor editor at *Harper's,* Willie Morris. Galbraith took great pleasure once from having sold separate articles to each of us without the other editor's knowing it, then listening with merriment to Willie's and my angry complaints that he had tricked us into listing on the covers of both magazines in the same month contributions by John Kenneth Galbraith. Galbraith feigned surprise at our protests—after all, he said, the 313 articles dealt with different subjects. Willie and I agreed to count our blessings and file the experience under H for Chutzpah.

In our earlier time Maggie and I had barely become acquainted with Boston itself, but now we found its special charm. The more we savored it the more determined we were to live in its midst. This we did when the boys got off to college. We bought a spacious condominium only five blocks from the *Atlantic* offices, on Commonwealth Avenue, a beautiful Parisian-style boulevard. Our apartment house was the first one built after acres of odiferous muckland were filled-in during the 1850s and 1860s to create Boston's Back Bay neighborhood. We settled happily into the very center of a city that was steeped in history and was more entertainingly eccentric than any other in America. The Back Bay, being a recent creation, was laid out in logical city blocks and squares; the rest of the town was a monument to three centuries of city unplanning. A new resident was well advised to seek instruction in Boston's geography.

My guide was a friend of our apartment house superintendent, a long-time City Hall hanger-on who knew the best point from which to survey the entire city in one sweep. "You can see right into every precinct from here," he assured me as we sped one sunny afternoon to the top of the Prudential Center, then the city's tallest building. In the foreground was the Boston Common, substantially the same open green space that was staked out during the city's founding in 1630; it is where cows once freely grazed, witches were hanged, and an elephant once bathed in its Frog Pond. Well beyond it stood Bunker Hill Monument, marking but one of the area's many history-making moments. To its right, visible through a giant picket fence of new high-rise office buildings, was the steeple of Old North Church from which Paul Revere received his signal to ride and spread the word. I could see nearly twenty miles away to Concord and Lexington where Revere's warning was heeded.

Caressing Boston on this side and Cambridge on the other was the Charles, a noble if not mighty river that in good weather and sometimes even in bad was speckled with the shining shells of rowers and white flecks of sail. Beneath that golden Bulfinch dome straight ahead sat the General Court of the

Commonwealth of Massachusetts, source both of some of America's most progressive legislation like the first child labor laws, and some of its most blatant rascality. Slightly to the right of our vantage point was the South End, which the newcomer must learn was not the same as Irish South Boston, which stood not exactly south by compass reading, just as the Italian North End lay not truly north, nor East Boston truly East, nor the West End truly west. Save for a few who had lingered on Beacon Hill or in Back Bay townhouses, pure Yankees could be observed only at Boston Symphony concerts or during working hours when they traveled in from the lusher suburbs to count their money, adjust their investments, and ascertain that the politicians in power had not sold City Hall and shipped it, furnishings and all, to Dubuque. Within easy eyesight were the many xenophobic Boston neighborhoods—Charlestown with its decaying U.S. Navy Yard and the USS *Constitution* afloat at its dock; Mattapan, Dorchester, Roslindale, Roxbury, Jamaica Plain, as well as lace-curtain West Roxbury. Nuzzling up close to Boston neighborhoods were the separate, independent cities and towns of Brookline, Cambridge, and Somerville, whose residents sucked on Boston's resources and enjoyed its pleasures while denying the central city the tax revenues it needed. If they had been blended into Boston itself the city might have become what it was not, truly governable.

By squinting hard from the top of the Prudential I could even dimly make out the statue of William Lloyd Garrison with his gleaming bald head, seated imperiously in a giant chair of bronze only a few yards from my front door on Commonwealth Avenue. Every day as I walked to or from my office I saw on its granite pedestal some of the combative abolitionist's fighting prose: "My country is the world. My countrymen all mankind" on one side and on the other, "I am in earnest. I will not equivocate. I will not excuse. I will not retreat a single inch. And I will be heard." A bit on the pompous side, yet useful sentiments for an editor to keep in mind.

Boston was far less abrasive, less nervewracking, and less expensive than New York. Also, it mercifully lacked the singlemindedness that in Washington made politics and government the only preoccupations during daylight hours and the **315** only subjects of conversation at night—the kind of place in which then Senator Hubert Humphrey, the honored guest at a Georgetown dinner party I once attended, would say quite naturally to his hostess on departing, "Thank you for the lovely meeting."

It was a relief to move to a place where politics was simply one of the popular sports in a thoroughly sports-addled city, a community in which elderly matrons collected old baseball scorecards and unshaven, bleary-eyed fathers arose at 3:30 A.M. to drive their young sons to practice on the municipal hockey rinks. How could a citizenry *not* be addled when so many gave their hearts and entrusted their sanity to the maddening ups and downs of the Bruins, Celtics, and Red Sox, the baseball team that had peddled Babe Ruth to the hated New York Yankees? In Boston, politics was right up there with the other favored bemusements and governing seemed to the uninitiated outsider to be a sort of neighborhood pick-up game among the Irish, the Italians, a goodly splash of yeoman WASPS (particularly in the west of the state), and a scattering of Greeks, Armenians, and other ethnics. Occasionally some remnant of the old Yankee governing class would be allowed to play if he would provide money for uniforms, new balls and bats, and a growler or two of beer.

In fact, a couple of them held high office at the time. Endicott Peabody, who had attended exclusive Groton School and made All-American as a Harvard football lineman, was Massachusetts's Democratic governor in the mid-sixties and by his performance had already earned as his accolade from the practicing pols the legend that three Massachusetts cities were named after him—Peabody, Marblehead, and Athol. Another Yankee, a Republican, was then the state's senior U.S. senator. Lean and leathery, with a hatchet jaw and the grin of a leprechaun, Leverett Saltonstall was warmly admired all over the state, and particularly by the Irish Bostonians whom his forebears had so roundly abused in not-so-distant times. Saltonstall reveled in the fact that his facial features always caused him to be taken for Irish when he marched in South Boston's annual St. Patrick's Day parade. "If there's any Irish in you at all, Lev," a

316 Southie Irishman named Patrick J. (Sonny) McDonough once

scoffed, "it's from the family chauffeur's side." Lev just smiled and kept on taking the applause—and the Southies' votes—year after year. Scratch Lev Saltonstall, though, and you found a true-blue, penny-saved-is-a-penny-earned, never-dip-into-principal Brahmin. He would carry fresh eggs from his farm in the western suburbs when he traveled to Washington early in the week and bring the empty cartons home on Friday. One day, the story is still told, he was lunching in the Tavern Club when an ash from the cigarette of a smoker seated next to him burned a tiny hole in the senator's trousers. The smoker apologized abjectly while slapping Saltonstall's thigh to extinguish the smoking ember. "Senator, I am terribly sorry. I am mortified." "You should be," Lev snapped. "These pants were my grandfather's."

There could be no better tutor in the ways and foibles of Boston than Edwin O'Connor, son of a Rhode Island doctor and a graduate of Notre Dame. Well before the success of his endearing novel, *The Last Hurrah,* and its Pulitzer Prize–winning successor *The Edge of Sadness,* both published by the Atlantic Monthly Press, Ed O'Connor had become a beloved member of the *Atlantic* family. Charlie Morton had nourished his faith as a writer by buying several of Ed's short pieces and encouraging him to give up his work as a radio announcer and concentrate on writing fiction. During nine years of free-lancing, barely supporting himself as a newspaper critic of radio, counting every penny, he lived in a furnished room on Marlborough Street, a few steps from the magazine's offices. He formed the habit of dropping by the *Atlantic* offices after breakfast and again before or after lunch. He had, as a friend once remarked, "a musician's ear" for speech and would deliver a funny story with a mimicry that was devastating without being unkind. He might shift his large frame into a brief soft-shoe to the humming of "Keep working, keep singing America!" Or examine a stack of books awaiting review, complaining about the low caliber of a much ballyhooed new novel or urging attention to some new but yet unrewarded young talent. Esteem, success, prizes eventually came in abundance, but he never lost his modesty. One day after *The Last Hurrah* had become a hit and was selected by the Book-of-the-Month Club, bringing his **317** days of penny-pinching to an end, Ed sauntered into the office of Louise Desaulniers, one of the magazine's editors, with a penny in his hand. "See this, Louise," he said, "this is what I care for money!" and he tossed it out a window. Louise retrieved it and kept it in her desk from then on. A brief visit from Ed for a shot of enspiriting badinage or a longer interlude with him for lunch at the Ritz or Locke-Ober instantly became an important part of my working routine and my enjoyment of my new hometown. The pleasure of the company of this charming, witty, wise, and gentle prose poet, with reddish curly hair and a face that was as handsome and Irish as a Bantry Bay sunset was in itself enough to make me glad that I had become, like him, a naturalized Bostonian.

Though he guarded his privacy, refused invitations to join exclusive clubs, and stringently avoided the speechmaking, talk shows, and TV appearances that go with bestsellerdom, his fame as a writer had made O'Connor a widely recognized Boston character. And though he hated it, the movie version of *The Last Hurrah* with Spencer Tracy as Mayor Frank Skeffington made Ed even more so. Politicians, newspapermen, policemen, ordinary citizens would stop him in the street or cross over to his restaurant table to exchange pleasantries. Through Ed I got to meet real-life characters who were as entertaining as those soiled saints and haloed sinners and assorted scalawags he had enshrined in *The Last Hurrah*.

Clement A. Norton, for one. He was the real-life prototype for the maddeningly comic Charlie Hennessey in Ed's novel. Clem had made a precocious entry into Boston politics when young, as a city councilman and then school board chairman. He had run more times than most could remember for mayor, but Clem suffered from an extreme case of logorrhea—couldn't stop talking except for the few hours he slept each night. So when he sought higher office he invariably prattled his electoral chances to death. "Talking to Clem Norton," said one opponent, "is like trying to take a drink from a fire hose." By the time I met him Clem had become a sort of street entertainer, a short, dumpy man who wore long underwear in summer as well as winter and spent some of each day roaming about in search of someone familiar to whom he could relate some scandalous doing or improbable situation he had just uncovered. He would prepare for each day's ramble in the Boston Public Library reading room, poring over newspapers, magazines, and esoteric journals, all the while dictating long memoranda to himself into an early model of the vest-pocket tape recorder, "God's gift to the peripatetic scholar," as Clem described the machine—and himself.

O'Connor introduced me to Clem Norton one day when he hailed us across the street from the Public Garden. I saw Charlie Hennessey himself just as Ed had described him—"a short stout man with oddly protuberant eyes . . . dressed in a rumpled gray suit. . . . There was something about him which suggested perpetual and hectic movement; one felt thus to see him at a standstill was like seeing a hummingbird forcibly immobilized. It was somehow unfair." As we were chatting or, rather, Clem was chattering, Paul Dudley White, the heart specialist, approached on foot, pushing his by now familiar bicycle at his side. White had achieved worldwide fame as the doctor called in to treat President Eisenhower after his heart attack. He had turned his fame to good purpose by persuading thousands of Americans to take up bicycling or other energetic exercise as a preventative of heart disease. "I want to thank you for what you're doin' for humanity, Dr. White, getting people off their duffs and onto bicycles. You're a saint, that's what you are," said Clem. Dr. White smiled in appreciation and moved on.

"What a disaster!" Clem muttered when the good doctor was out of earshot. "All over the country he's got people pumping away and they're droppin' like flies from over-strained hearts or exploding arteries. A catastrophe, my good man. A catastrophe!"

On another occasion Clem stopped me as I was walking past the skeleton of the sixty-story John Hancock skyscraper then going up in the Back Bay. He pointed to the structure and sighed mournfully. "See that? There's nothing but swamp underneath. Mark my words. We'll live to see it sink softly into the mud, every bit of it gurgling right out of sight." He clucked at the ignorance of the architects and engineers. Where was Bru- **319** nelleschi when we needed him?* As his tongue danced along from one subject to another, I tried to interrupt to ask a question. He didn't pause. "Be patient, my good man. Be patient and you'll learn that the best part of conversation is in the digressions."

Another tutor in the ways of my new hometown was Thomas Winship, who was just taking on one of journalism's major restoration challenges as the new editor of the *Boston Globe.* At that time the city still had seven daily newspapers, more than most American cities including New York and Washington. Trouble was that all of them were deplorable except for the *Christian Science Monitor,* and that publication of "the Mother Church," while it sometimes offered some good coverage of goings-on in the State House, was really aimed at an audience sprinkled far beyond Boston. Winship was a Harvard man and the grandson of a Congregationalist minister, but he took pains to describe himself as a "swamp Yankee," a subspecies which, one of Tom's irreverent admirers instructed me, "suffers from the same genetic defects but has less money than the Brahmins." His shirtsleeves-and-suspenders informality and Aw shucks! manner made for easy personal relations while disguising a fierce competitor's heart and plenty of ambition. After a couple of years of working on Capitol Hill as Senator Saltonstall's press secretary, ten years of grooming on the *Washington Post,* and then a few years of working upward on the *Globe* staff, he had succeeded his father, Laurence Winship. The older editor was beloved inside the shop. He was personally much admired in the wider community as well, but the same could not be said of the two newspapers he edited, the morning and the evening *Globe.* They were not even the best of a sad lot of dailies. The new editor's challenge was to rescue them from

---

*The building defied Clem's dire prediction and is now the tallest tower in the Boston skyline, gleaming and changing reflections with the rising and falling of the sun. It did suffer an embarrassing period when many of its windows mysteriously fell out and had to be boarded over with plywood, causing much wariness on the part of passersby and much chagrin for the insurance company as well as the famed architectural firm of I. M. Pei and a variety of builders, contractors, and glass and window frame makers, none of whom cared to accept blame. The public has never been told what went wrong.

deep torpor and growing irrelevance. On his first day as new editor the younger Winship breathed hard and replaced in one sweep eight of Larry Winship's key news executives. The older editor didn't even blink. Instead of thinning out the predominantly Irish-American staff he'd inherited, Tom Winship coopted them and from then on he was off and running.

Though our publications and our audiences were far different, Winship and I found that as newly launched editors we had much in common. For one thing, each had been given command of his ship with full authority to sail it where and as he pleased. Appreciating the rarity of this privilege, we took to sighting icebergs and menacing shoals for each other. Few were the editors (in fact we knew no others) who could do as they pleased with their printing presses without having the wherewithal to own them. At lunch every two or three weeks we exchanged notes, second-guessed and critiqued each other's work.

Early in this process he worried that I was too tolerant of the Vietnam policy of the administration I had so recently served; drawing on the observations of his area-wide staff of reporters he provided me with instance after instance to stiffen my suspicion that the magazine should show how the Vietnam involvement was building toward a national trauma. Winship also was generous with his own wide array of friendships and acquaintances, taking pains to introduce me to many of the movers and shakers as well as some of the less influential but more amusing characters in town. For my part, I pestered him for allowing almost all top editors—including Winship himself—to live outside the increasingly tense and divided city whose inner workings they were supposed to scrutinize and understand. This was a subject of much sarcasm among Boston politicans and neighborhood activists, many of whom already looked on the newspaper that had once served the working class as one that had now become flabby and aloof. The president of the state senate, a powerful and autocratic Southie with a cutting tongue named Billy Bulger, could always count on a laugh when he remarked to his fellow senators that to reach any top editor of the *Globe* you needed to dial an area code first. Winship was particularly sensitive to this, living as he did in the elite village of Lincoln, a western suburb. He could boast, though, that he was making the *Globe* far more relevant than it had been and turning its magnifying glass both on the city's corrupt politics and the problems, tensions, and aspirations of the inner city minorities. Under him the *Globe* was to play a leading role in moving the city toward the federally enforced busing program that provoked sniper's rifle fire at the newspaper's offices and spasms of racial violence in the city (but which, alas, seems not to have improved Boston's educational system or its race relations). Winship felt with good reason that he could be considered as Bostonian as anyone in town.

One day, he and I were enjoying lunch with Kevin White, another of the Boston Irish types who had parlayed charm, savvy, a quick wit, and the nerve of a bandit into political power and was now Boston's mayor. We were three men happy in their work; White was in his second term as mayor and savoring every minute of it as much as Winship was enjoying putting out his newspaper and I my magazine.

Winship asked the mayor if he had seen a startling story that had appeared the day before on the front pages—the editor of a leading Atlanta newspaper had been kidnapped and ultimately rescued, but only after many hours of fears for his life. "Does it make you worry, Tom?" asked White with a laugh. Well, said Winship, who knows? It might put bad ideas into the head of some nutcake in Boston; God knew, the newspaper had plenty of enemies. "How about a little police protection, Kevin?" Winship said. The mayor grinned at me and I at him as we savored this irresistible opening. White said, "Tom, you've come to the wrong goddamn mayor. Ask the mayor of Lincoln."

Personnel problems were frequently on Winship's mind. Something in the air, perhaps the salty breezes from nearby Dorchester Bay, seemed to induce an inordinate amount of extramarital activity within his large news staff and Tom took a fatherly interest in trying to prevent, or at least keep to a minimum, the break-up of marriages, out-of-wedlock pregnancies, and dissolution of families. He had done a remarkable job of coopting the Irish mafia that dominated the staff and, to the discomfort of many of those old-timers, was now bringing in **322** fresh young talent from such WASP strongholds as Harvard and Yale. He hated to lose any of his star performers to free-spending fellow editors like Abe Rosenthal of the *New York Times* or, especially, Ben Bradlee, whose Scaramouche-style invigoration of the *Washington Post* Winship observed with admiration and not a little envy. In order to insulate a good but restless reporter from outside blandishments Winship would offer some of his own. In some cases a fancy title would suffice. I was particularly qualified to help Winship fashion impressive new titles on the *Globe*'s masthead for executives who were in fact being demoted, having learned the fine art of masthead manipulation at *Time,* where if it was not invented it was brought close to perfection. Another maneuver favored by Winship was to offer a prized reporter the prestige and exposure of a feature column of his or her own. I chided him for this, suggesting that he was converting a lot of good reporters into poor or mediocre columnists. It wasn't long before the paper was top-heavy with columnists, many of whom had been good reporters of other people's thoughts and deeds but whose own thoughts in too many instances were boring, fatuous, or both.

Winship responded to my chiding by appointing yet another columnist. One of his professional embarrassments was the low character of the *Globe*'s treatment of books. A community of such cultural interests and a newspaper of expanding cultural pretensions surely deserved better. His proposed solution was to hire my wife as the newspaper's principal book reviewer. The work was a belated fulfillment for Maggie, a challenge worthy of her literary discernment and wide range of interests. Soon she was poring over as many as a dozen books a week and producing bright, opinionated reviews of the two or three that piqued her interest. It was not long before Winship asked her in addition to reviewing to take over editorship of the Sunday Books section, or what passed for one. This was even more of a challenge, for on most Sundays it was difficult even to find the Books section in the pulp jungle, and when discovered tucked into the Help Wanted or Automotive sections it might offer two or three reviews sharing one page with the Hobbies features. Maggie wangled more space, reached beyond the *Globe* staff into the broader world for reviewers. She ultimately cajoled the editors into anchoring the section in a more fixed and promi- **323** nent location in the more respectable company of the rest of the fine and the lively arts—but not before waking up one Sunday morning to find her week's work stuffed among the used car ads. Next morning Winship and each of his top lieutenants found smoke coming from his mailbox in the form of a Maggie Manning memo.

New England was the home of proportionately more book buyers than any other part of the United States, but Maggie never succeeded in her effort to win for literature all the space and respect it deserved, not even as much as the *Globe* editors lavished on rock music or movies, presumably in the belief that these were more popular pursuits (could they possibly have considered them more important?). Management, of course, supported this imbalance because the pop stuff brought in more advertising dollars. The blame fell too on the book publishing industry itself. The publishing houses constantly pressed to have their books reviewed. Yet never did they buy more than occasional small, token advertisements for books in most newspapers and many magazines, choosing instead to throw almost all their promotion budgets, as much as 90 percent, into ads in the *New York Times Book Review.* Most of the rest went to the costs of shipping authors around the country to appear on television talk shows. The fewer the ads in regional newspapers, the less space for book reviews.

For all the frustrations, Maggie found much satisfaction in this work and brought to book reviewing her own special chemistry of flair, candor, cogency, damnation for the bogus, and love for good prose that won her an admiring following and two near-miss contentions for the Pulitzer Prize for criticism. And on overtime, she still served as my own most penetrating and valuable critic.

During Winship's editorship the *Globe*'s several competitors dwindled to only one and he brought the newspaper into deep engagement with the community it served, occasionally wrongheadedly but often to the community's benefit. It worked its way to recognition as one of the ten best papers in the country and took in a dozen Pulitzer Prizes. Not by any means did he rid the *Globe* of all its bush-league ways, but that was perhaps **324** understandable since its community could not shake them either. After all, what old Clem Norton believed about conversation was true of greater Boston itself—its digressions were what made it so interesting, a flawed place that was easy to fall deeply in love with—with the intimacies its smallness made possible, with its odd characters and dusty customs, with the raucous crowds at Fenway Park and the Boston Garden, the equally raucous and frequently comic meetings of the city council and the school board, even with Boston drivers who would not have beaten out the close contenders in New Jersey or Lagos or Rome for the "worst in the world" title were it not for that extra edge of malice they bore toward their fellow motorists and anyone so unfortunate as to be on foot.

Superb libraries, the Boston Public and the private Atheneum, and the great Boston Symphony Orchestra symbolized but were only particles of the musical and literary richness that pervaded the area. Above all, there was the tidal flow of bright, eager young people, shimmering schools of them arriving each autumn to seek education, flowing out each spring to discover whether the real world bore much resemblance to the one they'd presumably been preparing for. This last pleasure diminished for a while, I must confess, during the ugliness of the late sixties when defiance and protest, drugs and disorder wracked the peace, but that affliction soon passed. The vibrancy and idealism of youth was indelibly as much a part of Boston as its very bricks and mortar; one of every six of the city's 650,000 residents was a student. Mingling with them, vicariously experiencing their vivacity and playfulness, somehow made an elder feel younger. Nobody called Boston "the Athens of America" any longer, except sardonically, but neither had any other place earned any claim to that mantle and every year Boston ranked high up on someone's list of "most livable American cities."

In addition to its amusing divertissement and amiable surroundings Boston provided an environment that was close to ideal for the serious business at hand, the making of a magazine that explored the world of ideas and sought fresh, provocative material about the arts, the sciences, and public affairs as well as bright new fiction and poetry. The universities and colleges, the world-famous medical schools and hospitals, and the burgeoning high-tech industry offered us editors at *The Atlantic* a trea- **325** sure-house of authorities and experts, of authors and critics, of new ideas and momentous discoveries-in-the-making. If the expertise or inspiration we needed was not swimming about in the great intellectual ferment close at hand, there was inevitably someone here who could point us elsewhere to find it. Of course, we needed to beware the trap of academic mind-set or New England parochialism. This required constant vigilance. There were times when I rejected an article or an article suggestion that had merit simply *because* it was so New Englandy or smelled too much of the college library stacks. It was unfair to the authors, perhaps, but we did not want *The Atlantic* to be thought of as a provincial magazine.

There was always that danger. Almost a century had passed since New York had replaced Boston as America's cultural capital. The big city was unarguably the heart and nerve center of the publishing trade and the gathering place of the powerful and incestuous American literary *mano negra.* Washington was the global political capital, the place where so much of the workings of America and the rest of the world were dictated. For several months I worried about that, about working too far from the two big cities, out of handshake range with the movers and shakers, out of touch with the capital's Georgetown gossip and deprived of the lit-chat at Elaine's saloon in Manhattan. In the early part of my editorship I felt a not-quite-accountable compulsion to visit both of the capitals in order to take my own temperature reading and to keep up longtime acquaintances and make new ones, as if by living so far from those scenes I might be missing something important. On one of those early visits to New York, I was lunching at the sumptuous La Caravelle restaurant with Mary Hemingway to discuss some Hemingway poems I was hoping to publish. We were spotted by one of Ernest and Mary Hemingway's old friends, Leonard Lyons, a tiny, gregaricus fellow who looked and acted like a hungry sparrow as he made his living by hopping about Manhattan watering spots each day and evening to collect crumbs and second-hand oatseed for his gossip column in the *New York Post.* Noting the delight with which I was forking in the excellent Caravelle cuisine, Lyons asked, "Where do you go for a good **326** meal in Boston, Bob?" "I take the Eastern shuttle to New

York," I said. Smart-ass Manning. I'd forgotten that the Leonard Lyons column appeared regularly in the *Boston Herald*. Two days later, my phone at *The Atlantic* barely stopped ringing with calls from Boston friends, each with the same question: Bob, what name are you planning to use from now on when you ask for a dinner reservation in Boston?

I survived the chagrin of that, but, trivial though it was, the experience sharply reminded me that Boston was now my hometown. And it helped to remind me too of what Boston did offer that New York and Washington with their bigness and self-absorption did not—a connection with the rest of America that granted a clearer sense of the country at large. My colleagues and I had no excuses: If we could not make a magazine of pertinence and wide appeal with this better visibility and the rich material so compellingly at hand, the fault would lie only with us. Since I was at last about to be in charge of my own operation, I should put that more precisely: The fault would lie only with me.

I could think of no pleasanter place in which to try, even if the Red Sox were going to break all our hearts again and I might at any minute be run over by a truck, a sightseeing bus, or a police car casually running a red light.

Chapter 19

"The ... Old ... True Magical Light"

he Atlantic carried the luster—and the burden—of four generations of distinction. It was born at two successive dinner parties on May 5 and 6, 1857, in Boston's Parker House Hotel. The diners assembled at three each afternoon, an odd time for dinner by today's reckoning, and stayed until eight in the evening. By the time the wine had run out and the brandy supply was dwindling on the second day the guests, among them Ralph Waldo Emerson, Henry Wadsworth Longfellow, James Russell Lowell, and Oliver Wendell Holmes, reached a judgment: America needed a new magazine devoted to literature, art, and politics. Holmes volunteered the new publication's name. Lowell, the poet-scholar of Cambridge, consented to be its first editor.

Charles Eliot Norton, a distinguished Harvard professor who was to write many articles for the new magazine and to influence several of its editors, heard about plans for it while visiting Paris. ". . . Such things are never permanent in our country," he wrote to Lowell. "They burn brightly for a while, and then burn out—and some other light takes their place. It would be a great thing for us if any undertaking of this kind could live long enough to get affections and associations connected with it, whose steady glow should take the place of, and

328

more than supply, the shine of novelty, and the dazzle of the first go-off. . . . I would give a thousand of our new lamps for the one old, battered, but true magical light."

Lowell's "first go-off" had plenty of shine. He could reach out from his office and almost touch most of the best-known American writers, so clustered were they around Boston. Early issues presented work of most of them, Emerson and his cranky neighbor Henry Thoreau, Holmes, Hawthorne, Whittier, Prescott, Harriet Beecher Stowe, and Thomas Wentworth Higginson to mention only a few. Longfellow's *Paul Revere's Ride,* Edward Everett Hale's *The Man Without a Country,* and some of Whitman's *Leaves of Grass* first reached readers in early editions of *The Atlantic.* The founders were abolition-minded so the magazine focused early on the issues and emotions that provoked the American Civil War. In the October 1860 issue, Lowell wrote a spirited endorsement of Abraham Lincoln for president, an act of political partisanship the magazine was not to repeat for more than a century. For a fee of $4 Lowell bought a poem by Julia Ward Howe entitled "The Battle Hymn of the Republic" which when put to music quickly became the North's mighty anthem in the war to save the Union. The work of Harriet Beecher Stowe, Bret Harte, Mark Twain, Sarah Orne Jewett, Jack London, entire novels of Henry James *(Portrait of a Lady* and *Daisy Miller)* all appeared in its pages. *Atlantic* readers were first to see some of the writings of historians like George Bancroft and Francis Parkman; naturalists like John Muir and John Burroughs, Lafcadio Hearn on Japan and A. T. Mahan on American sea power. They heard from public figures like James Garfield, Grover Cleveland, and later Theodore Roosevelt, Woodrow Wilson, and Alfred E. Smith, who in 1927 was given the opportunity to state in this Waspish magazine why a Roman Catholic could be a good president.

After a few years of Lowell the editorship passed on to others at intervals averaging about ten years each. When the literary vein began to thin out in New England, subsequent editors reached further out into America and across the sea to Britain for material. Through the decades the magazine varied in content and quality depending upon the talents and whims of successive editors. It never paid much money to its authors or **329** editors nor made much profit for its owners, but it paid well in other coin—in prestige, as a bully pulpit, as a launching pad for literary careers, as a most favored showcase for major and minor poets, essayists, and others who sought the attention of a small but elite audience. From its beginning *The Atlantic* was an obviously if not avowedly elitist periodical. "To inoculate the few who influence the many," was the way one of its admirers described the magazine's mission.

Ellery Sedgwick, a short, self-assured man with a generous mustache whom I never met except in a photograph which made him look both impish and debonair at the same time, bought the magazine in 1909 from Houghton Mifflin, the Boston book publishing house, and carried it into the twentieth century. He introduced his readers to, among many others, the work of Robert Frost, Henry Mencken, Charles Nordhoff, and James Hall of *Mutiny on the Bounty* fame and, at last, Emily Dickinson, whose important poems had been methodically rejected by previous editors. Ernest Hemingway's *Fifty Grand* was the first of his startling short stories to appear in a major American periodical. Sedgwick founded the Atlantic Monthly Press in order to exploit, in the good sense of that word, the many talents he uncovered with the magazine by putting their writings between hard covers and bringing extra revenue to the company. In 1928, after trying him out for a few years on his staff, Sedgwick put a jaunty young man named Edward Weeks in charge of the press, where he helped to build an impressive list onto a platform of several Nordhoff and Hall best-sellers and James Hilton's *Goodbye Mr. Chips,* and adding in later years books by Walter Lippmann, Samuel Eliot Morison, George F. Kennan, Agnes De Mille, and Catherine Drinker Bowen. To quote one accurate admirer, Weeks "cut a figure of gaiety and grace." His first notable feat in publishing came when as a young salesman for Horace Liveright in the 1920s he made a big sale of books to the usually resistant buyer for Macy's while dressed in white flannels and cradling a tennis racket under one arm. Weeks had dropped out of Cornell during World War I to drive an American Field Service ambulance in France. He brought home a *croix de guerre,* and then graduated from Harvard. By the time I met him he had lost all vestige of his New Jersey beginnings and become a Boston fixture and a crowd-pleasing rider of the genteel American women's club lecture circuit, a weekly radio performer, an inveterate clubman and, in addition to being a successful editor of his prestigious magazine, a deft editor of books.

Weeks learned the magazine trade from Sedgwick, and when in 1938 the older editor tired of the game he handed over his chair to him. Two years later, Weeks and Donald Snyder, an enthusiastic, innovative young man who had been working for Sedgwick on the publishing side, persuaded Sedgwick to sell the company. Snyder and Weeks lacked the resources to buy it themselves but found a willing angel in Richard Danielson, a polished devotee of the arts and the sporting life. Danielson had some money of his own and much more at his disposal by way of his marriage to Barbara Deering, an heiress to the great International Harvester fortune. He had dabbled in magazine publishing before, producing with Christian Herter (who was to become governor of Massachusetts and a U.S. secretary of state) a lavish sporting magazine aimed at a millionaire clientele; unfortunately, they had chosen to launch it just as the Great Depression put even some millionaires to rout.

Dick Danielson preferred writing and other pursuits to the arithmetical routine of business and was happy to entrust his new enterprise to Don Snyder and Ted Weeks. The two had a major reclamation job on their hands because in his waning years as editor, Sedgwick had become a passionate Francophile; the object of this passion, sadly, was not La Belle France but the Spanish dictator, Generalissimo Francisco Franco. Sedgwick's admiration-in-print for the fierce ally of Adolf Hitler and Benito Mussolini had seriously diminished *The Atlantic*'s once loyal following. Snyder and Weeks reestablished the magazine's democratic credentials and substituted for Sedgwick's by now lackadaisical formula a thorough redesign of the magazine and a vigorous search for less languorous, more timely material. The new editor-publisher team shepherded *The Atlantic* through World War II, a time of severe paper rationing and inhibited advertising, and brought it into full flower, its most prosperous era, in the years after the war. When Richard Danielson died in 1957, his and Barbara Deering Danielson's **331** daughter Marion inherited the company. Like her father she assumed the presidency but entrusted the day-to-day running to Don Snyder and Ted Weeks.

When I came aboard in the fall of 1964, Don Snyder's flair for circulation-building ideas and Ted Weeks's talent for implementing and improving upon them had increased the magazine's circulation threefold, to 265,000, by far its highest up to then, and its balance sheet into steady if modest profitability. Marion Danielson Campbell took none of the profit for herself but channeled it back to Weeks's editorial budget and into an employees' pension plan that was modest yet generous by the prevailing standards for such a small company.

I inferred that I might not have been Ted Weeks's first choice as his successor, that it was Charlie Morton's importuning with some seconding from Don Snyder that had settled Marion Campbell's mind, with Weeks then joining in. Once the decision was made and particularly after he discovered that I was almost as nutty as he about trout fishing, Weeks welcomed me with a warmth and graciousness that I felt certain could not have been feigned. He promptly got me admitted to his exclusive small fishing club in the cranberry bogs near Cape Cod and to his favorite Boston men's club. More importantly, he brought me—as promised—instantly and fully into the planning of future issues, the choice of subjects, and the commissioning of writers to write them. The issue for October 1964 was then being prepared for the presses, but there were time and room for one more article. When we talked about the forthcoming presidential election Weeks and I found ourselves in agreement that the election of Senator Barry Goldwater would be a national disaster. Why shouldn't the editor do in 1964 what the first *Atlantic* editor did in 1860, something no editor of the magazine had done since? we said to each other. In a ringing editorial lamenting Goldwater's right-wing "factionalism" and reckless judgment, Weeks endorsed Lyndon Johnson for president.

I couldn't imagine that the country would choose a feckless, impetuous man like Goldwater over the experienced and, I felt, far more cautious Lyndon Johnson. Neither could most of the

332

American electorate. Yet LBJ's landslide victory belied a growing undercurrent of public concern over the steadily growing American involvement in Vietnam. There was something in the New England air, a feeling of disquiet and concern unlike anything I had felt while working in Washington. It became obvious that the same disquiet was growing all over America—except in the nation's capital. The "Inside the Beltway mentality," as it came to be called, had severely dulled Washington's connection with the rest of America.

The dogged, antiseptic concentration on the Pentagon's computer printouts, body counts, weapons shipments, and wishful field reports that shaped the government's approach to the Vietnam war had in a way desensitized the men who were running the nation. I could attest to this because I had once been caught up in the self-anesthetizing process; otherwise I would not have been so startled by what I was now seeing and hearing. The administration's single-mindedness was caused not so much by arrogance but an almost manic determination to fit the facts to Washington's conviction that the enemy, especially one so motivated by "evil" dogma, simply could not indefinitely resist the world's superpower, dedicated as it was to democracy and a higher morality.

Ordinarily a president and his men would be receiving impulses of the public discontent from the daily press and the Congress. But in those early days of the war the newspapers and newsmagazines were not offering much coherent coverage of the public's growing disaffection, while Congress was giving a "wartime" president almost anything he wanted in order to "nail the coonskin to the wall" in Vietnam, including the war powers he sought through the Tonkin Gulf resolution.

I had left Washington a bobtailed hawk, a believer in the rightness if not the efficacy of the government's policy. Now I was being reeducated, in part by a growing restlessness among the young that was becoming evident almost outside my windows. Not only in the Boston area with its abundance of colleges and universities, but in similar university complexes around the country, young people were raising questions about both the morality and the wisdom of the involvement in Viet- **333** nam. Maggie's sensitive antennae had caught the murmuring early, presciently, almost as soon as we had left Washington. One evening early in 1965, before President Johnson's major American escalation into combat had gotten underway, we were seated around the supper table discussing some mundane family concern with our three sons when Maggie abruptly changed the subject. "This war," she said, "is *wrong!*" I was startled; I had not yet come to feel that strongly about it; but a rumbling surely was rising. The catalyst for the campus protests was the impact of the selective service system. That was ironic in a way—the protest rising first from among those who benefitted most from the inequities of the military draft, young men (and their women sympathizers) who could avoid military service simply by staying in school. Some were moved by a sense of guilt, but more no doubt sensed that as the war went on their immunity was threatened; the draft notices might soon yank them away from their sanctuaries.

Weeks was easily persuaded that we should publish a special section on the draft, how it favored the middle and upper classes while drawing manpower from the lower. I returned to Washington to talk with Secretary of Defense McNamara about it and to solicit what plans the Pentagon had to improve the system now that being drafted more and more introduced the draftee to the possibility of being shot at or being torn to pieces by a Vietcong land mine. McNamara was friendly and wanted to be cooperative, but he expressed surprise at my inquiries. What problem was I talking about? We've got no problem with the draft, Bob, he said. We've already got enough problems here, as you well know, without someone finding another problem where there isn't any. All I could say was, Wait and see.

We went ahead with the special section for the February 1966 issue of the magazine. A young twenty-one-year-old Harvard senior and *Crimson* editor, Donald Graham, wrote a conscience-pricking report on the confusion and guilt being felt by young men who stayed in school not out of desire for more learning but to avoid being drafted. Mr. Graham subsequently

lived out the title of his article by "Taking a McNamara Fellowship" and serving a volunteer enlistment in Vietnam.* Another twenty-one-year-old, a radical protest leader at the University of Michigan named Jeffrey Goodman, highlighted tellingly the inequities of the draft ("The poor get children and the children get shot at") and outlined a possible extension of the draft to all young men with a choice of some form of "national service." Keith Johnson, an experienced reporter for the *Herald Tribune* and *Time,* spelled out in careful detail how the draft worked, the various options open to men who volunteered, and various proposals for improving on the system—should the government decide to do anything about it.

The three articles added up to a quietly thoughtful appraisal, but more to the point, they were a biopsy of what was becoming a national malignancy. Low-key as they were, the articles had to be disturbing to those who read and thought about them. They were the cure for my "Inside the Beltway" myopia.

The Atlantic could not afford to send a correspondent of its own to Vietnam; there were already more than enough journalists there anyway and one more voice would not make much difference. What we could better do was document how the Vietnam involvement was affecting Americans at home. The 1960s were becoming an ugly decade profaned by assassinations and riots at home and senseless slaughter abroad. Rudeness and crudeness were crowding politeness and civility out of the national dialogue. Customs, manners, religion, family relationships, the concept of law and order, even the norms of music, poetry, and other literature were all suddenly under severe, sometimes violent attack. Of course, not all the questioning and arguing was unjustified, yet, surprisingly, the press and television were failing to bring the phenomenon and its causes into useful focus. This national paroxysm, for it was nothing less than that, was to become a central preoccupation of my editorship of *The Atlantic.*

---

*Subsequently, young Graham, son of Phillip and Katharine Graham, signed on as a cop in Washington, D.C., to learn more about the city in which he was by inheritance to become a dominant force as publisher and a principal owner of the *Washington Post* empire.

My apprenticeship to Ted Weeks ended on January 1, 1966, shortly after that special issue on the draft had gone to press. Weeks had run *The Atlantic* for twenty-eight years. Except for Sedgwick's, his was the longest editorship in the magazine's history. He now agreed to stay with the company indefinitely as an in-house resource and an active senior editor of the book division. Weeks graciously handed over the editor's chair as well as the large and stately second-floor office with its crystal chandelier, an oriental rug, and wood-burning fireplace. There was also a white marble bust of a man with a slender face, thinning neatly combed hair, opulent sideburns, a large and dapper mustache. "The bust goes with the job," Weeks said. It was the likeness of Charles Eliot Norton, the same who had prayed at its inception that *The Atlantic Monthly* would live on to become "the one old, battered, but true magical light."

I had become the tenth in the magazine's long line of editors. As I sat there in my new grandeur, overlooking Boston's lovely Public Garden, I thought I saw the old boy throw a skeptical glance at me from the corners of his marble eyes. Hey, give me a chance, I muttered. I'll do the very best I can. Professor Norton stared straight ahead. He was, after all, a college man. I wished William Dean Howells, the unschooled outlander from Ohio, was there instead. He had been the third *Atlantic* editor in line, and I reckoned he would have been more understanding.

In my first issue of *The Atlantic,* that of April 1966, I promised readers I would seek to uphold Weeks's high standard and to "survey the world with an optimist's eye and a skeptic's squint, trying to abjure trifles, to look beyond the awkward incidents of the hour, and to illuminate the long sweep of events—and find excitement in doing so." So, there were promises to keep.

The staff I inherited was small but seasoned and solid. There was first the inimitable Charlie Morton. A young Cornellian named C. Michael Curtis had a sharp ear and clear eye for promising new short story writers as well as a good grip on the many social issues with which the magazine concerned itself. Mike was a shy and complicated fellow whom the vicissitudes of childhood had afflicted with a stutter that magically disap-

peared when he taught creative writing at nearby colleges to pad out his small *Atlantic* paycheck or when he held a good hand at the poker table. Phoebe Lou Adams, a handsome and emphatically opinionated lady, had brought to the magazine her superb Vassar background in the classics, a high taste for travel articles and literary essays, and that rare and much-valued talent, the ability to write capsule book reviews that were witty and telling. (After Ted Weeks's first wife died in 1971, he and Phoebe Lou married.)

Emily Flint, an invaluable woman of formidable tenacity, totally lacking in fear of higher authority, was the managing editor and Grand Protector. Her assistant was a gentle, cheerful, and equally resolute bachelor lady named Louise Desaulniers. Both were gutsy, literate, and tasteful; the two of them knew every small nut and bolt of the production process, but more than that were fierce as a pair of Dobermans when it came to protecting the quality of the prose, sniffing out the bogus, forcing editors and authors to meet deadlines—and nipping at the editor in chief when his usually good manners deserted him. The only case I can remember of a writer who challenged either Emily's or Louise's editing and beat her into quiet submission happened before my time. The West Coast nonpareil Raymond Chandler, irritated by a change that someone had made in the galley proofs of an article by him, wrote:

> Would you convey my compliments to the purist who reads your proofs and tell him or her that I write in a sort of broken-down patois which is something like the way a Swiss waiter talks, and that when I split an infinitive, God damn it, I split it so it will stay split, and when I interrupt the velvety smoothness of my more or less literate syntax with a few sudden words of barroom vernacular, this is done with the eyes wide open and the mind relaxed but attentive. The method may not be perfect, but it is all I have. I think your proofreader is kindly attempting to steady me on my feet, but much as I appreciate the solicitude, I am really able to steer a fairly clear course, provided I get both sidewalks and the street between.

To strengthen this crew I brought in Michael Janeway from the weekly opinion journal *New Leader,* where he worked after 337 stints with Long Island's daily *Newsday* and *Newsweek* maga-zine. In his Harvard undergraduate days he also had the eye-opening experience of working as an intern on the Majority Leader's staff on Capitol Hill when Lyndon Johnson was run-ning the U.S. Senate. Mike was a political animal with a wide-ranging mind and strong opinions in other matters as well. His tact in personal relationships needed some cultivation, but he partly made up for lack of subtlety with a persistence that could wear down an alp.

This good crew and I were still getting accustomed to each others' ways when a bad blow struck 8 Arlington Street. On the night of September 23, 1967, during his annual visit to London, Charlie Morton's heart gave out—it could no longer keep his damaged lungs working. Though he had avoided religious asso-ciations the best place for the memorial service was the beauti-fully austere First Parish church in Cambridge. There, Harvard professors, writers, leading figures in publishing mingled with friends like Joe Vitale, the maître d' and a clutch of his waiters from the Ritz Café, and dozens of others who had gathered to shed a tear and share much laughter as Ed O'Connor and some of Charlie's other associates illustrated in a multitude of anec-dotes Morton's "majestic capacity" for limning life's absurdi-ties.

The final Morton essay appeared in the November 1967 issue, a nifty little piece about a visit to see Admiral Nelson's flagship HMS *Victory* with the implied lament that they don't make admirals or navies that way anymore. Tacked above it was our brief good-bye which concluded: "Wherever he is—somewhere in Thurber Country with Mencken, Mr. Dooley, DeVoto, and the other rare ivory-billed woodpeckers of Ameri-can letters—he is certain to be appalled by the food, outraged by the service, and unavoidably generous to the fellow at the door."

Bad news came in threes. The year 1968 was already shaping up as an ugly one for America and that was especially true at 8 Arlington Street. Only six months after Morton's death, Ed O'Connor collapsed with a brain hemorrhage and never re-gained consciousness. He was only forty-nine. He left behind **338** the beginnings of two more ambitious novels and for me an unfillable emptiness; I could not have felt more grief if I had lost a beloved older brother. A great deal of the pleasure of living in Boston disappeared on that day. Not much later the man who had been groomed to become the new publisher of *The Atlantic* and work in close partnership with me as Donald Snyder had with Ted Weeks was struck down by cancer. Frank Herbert had spent years preparing for the job, learning the arcana of a nineteenth-century operation striving to survive in the twentieth; we had quickly reached a kind of mutual respect and working rapport. Don Snider came back into the publisher's chair from retirement while we searched for a successor to Frank.

The search ended happily in only a few months, when in October of 1968 we persuaded Garth Hite to leave Washington and his job as publisher of *The New Republic.* Garth was a neatly dressed, neatly composed Midwesterner with a sense of humor and abundant sophistication. He had attended the University of Iowa and graduated from the University of Colorado, earning his way by playing the clarinet in his own popular dance band, lived and worked in San Francisco and New York as well as Washington. My expectations jumped a few extra notches when I learned that he also had served in the marines during World War II.

He brought to *The Atlantic* more publishing experience than had ever graced its front office. At *The New Republic* he learned how to cope with and overcome most of the difficulties of publishing a weekly journal that needed an angel with deep pockets to survive. Before that he had been first advertising director and then publisher of the prosperous monthly *Holiday,* owned by the Curtis Publishing Company. It had been the country's leading travel magazine until the turmoil that brought down *Holiday*'s big brother, the *Saturday Evening Post.*

Garth had developed the kind of respect for editorial freedom and initiative that attracted respect in return. He was direct and outspoken, often resorting to hyperbole to drive home a point, whether in conversation or in a written memorandum. We became equal partners in running the Atlantic Monthly Company, each inviting the other's comments and intrusions, each sensing when to stop short of meddling with the other fellow's business. We lived in the same apartment building, one 339 a floor above the other, walked our dogs together, drank and listened to jazz together, fussed and labored together over the fate of our enterprise. He sat in on editorial meetings when he pleased, as I sat in on advertising and circulation planning meetings.

Frequently I would seek Garth's opinion on a manuscript or a story proposal dealing with music, the environment, politics, or any of his many other areas of interest. He felt free to call on me for a pep talk to the advertising staff or a speech to some potential advertising clients. We worked closely together in our overseeing of our book publishing operation, a clanking Rube Goldbergian contraption fashioned by lawyers many years before which subjected our books—and any profit or loss from them—to the mercy of the venerable Boston house of Little, Brown and Company. Garth's and my working relationship was the exact opposite of the separation of church and state that was so crucial at Time Inc. and a rare few other publishing operations. It was not by any means free of tensions, arguments, even occasional angry explosions, but it was the best kind of relationship for a company so small and self-contained that every rise or dip in one area could seriously affect the overall enterprise.

For the other losses that death had inflicted on us in a brief span of time there was no relief. Nothing could fill the hole that Ed O'Connor's death left in my atmosphere. And the particular psyche that was Charlie Morton's was not duplicable, nor was his "Accent on Living" section, which was so dependent on his whims and foibles.

It was some time before I could find the person to bring the magazine staff back to a semblance of balance. Richard Todd had once applied for a job at *The Atlantic* when none was available and had then signed on as a young book editor at Houghton Mifflin. (His boss at Houghton Mifflin was miffed by my recruitment of Todd and protested stuffily: "We don't do that sort of thing here in Boston.") Todd's natural gifts of style, dry wit, and perception, nicely honed at Amherst, meshed smoothly with the differing personalities of Janeway and Curtis. When these three did not agree on the merits of a manuscript, an

340   author, or a concept, their disagreements, usually expressed in exchanges of entertainingly satirical memos (and Lord knows how many private expressions of dismay or discontent at their editor's judgments), sometimes produced better ideas than the ones they were arguing about.

The staff was much too small for a magazine of our ambitions, but fortunately we could also draw on an auxiliary set of sensibilities, "the people upstairs" who staffed the Atlantic Monthly Press, one of the prize-winningest small publishing houses in America. Its director, Peter Davison, a poet himself, was a demanding judge of poetry and agreed to take on the added duties of magazine poetry editor.

Though its wages were minimal and its premises Dickensian underneath their Back Bay charm, *The Atlantic* attracted a steady stream of bright young college graduates who saw it as a springboard into the combined worlds of literature and journalism. This brought a constant supply of bright and ambitious young interns and apprentice editors for whom a year or even a few months of poorly paid work provided useful hands-on experience and an impressive entry on their résumés. Many of them went on to bigger and better-paying work in the same trade. Shortly before my arrival young Whitney Ellsworth became publisher of the newly launched *New York Review of Books*. Joseph Kanon, whom I brought into the shop out of Harvard as a junior reader of unsolicited manuscripts, rocketed through a series of high executive jobs in book publishing, eventually returning to Boston as director of Houghton Mifflin's prestigious trade division. Another was a handsome young man named John L'Heureux, who had just left the Jesuit priesthood and aspired to be a poet and novelist. L'Heureux joined the staff under an arrangement that kept intact his vow of poverty. He evolved from that apprenticeship into a prolific writer of fiction and a teacher of writing at Stanford University.

I found that there was much to be learned—and it needed to be learned quickly—about the eugenics of producing a monthly magazine. After years of working at a wire service pace with "a deadline every minute," I had thought the routine at a weekly newsmagazine would be more leisurely but had discovered differently; the pressure was still there but it was packed intensely into the last part of each week. Now I anticipated that a **341** monthly deadline would be comparatively luxurious. Wrong again. There was still just as much pressure, but it was eccentrically distributed through the month. There was no interval for resting between issues of the magazine. While putting one issue into final shape we needed to be working on the next two or three or even four issues, commissioning articles for the most distant, deciding on the cover that would grace the next one or two, and at the same time to be thinking of next season and the ones beyond. If planning a spring issue featuring travel to the Far East, say, or the rape of the Brazilian rain forest, it was necessary to plan a whole year ahead for it would not do to have photographs that were out of joint with the season.

More difficult were the commitments that had to be made months in advance—first the commitment to a story idea, then the commitment to a writer who could be counted on to deliver it on time and in publishable condition, and then, frequently before the manuscript was in hand, the commitment to feature the story on the cover and the commitment to a design for the cover. By the nature of things, and particularly because there was no money in the budget to be wasted, these decisions were usually irreversible once made.

We experienced more than one close shave. In late March we were about to send the May 1968 issue to press with an article by Tom Wicker examining how the Vietnam war was contorting LBJ's presidency and destroying his dream of the Great Society. A cover featuring LBJ AND THE WAR in large type was ready to be printed when Johnson startled the world by announcing that he would not seek another term as president. We held the presses overnight. The Wicker assessment was so inadvertently prophetic that all we had to do was change the title to THE WRONG RUBICON and insert a few words into our introduction to note that, as the inside story amply documented, LBJ had become a self-pronounced casualty of a war he had not started but had made into his own.

In a sensational Boston trial in June of that same year the United States government succeeded in getting Benjamin Spock, the famous "baby doctor," the Reverend William Sloan Coffin, who was chaplain of Yale University, and two other

men convicted of conspiracy to provoke and abet violations of the military draft. Several months later we published a segment of Jessica Mitford's angry book about the trial and the way it was conducted by overzealous government prosecutors and an elderly judge who was overtly hostile to the defendants. Our title was quite appropriate and we displayed it boldly across the cover: GUILTY AS CHARGED BY THE JUDGE next to the image of a judge's gavel. The presses had just started to run when a U.S. appeals court threw out the verdict and the accused were all freed. We ordered the printers to stop the presses and sent an engraver to the printing plant. He superimposed on the illustration the rubber-stamped word: REVERSED! It made the 112-year-old monthly appear to be right on top of the news—which it was.

There were, of course, many articles of a less perishable nature. They could be stored to be published when needed. These might be stylish essays on books, music, and other subjects; profiles of interesting writers, painters, and other characters; articles on medicine, psychiatry, religion, the environment, physics, biology, and the other sciences, all of them manuscripts whose contents had a long shelf-life. These were *Atlantic* staples, vital to its franchise. *Atlantic* readers expected to find them presented with a perception and depth not provided by newspapers and newsmagazines and as reliable in their content but far more decipherable than the material in professional and academic journals. We tried to maintain a decent inventory of such material, as well as a stock of good short stories (not all that easy to find) and poems for use at random. But a magazine made up of that material alone was likely to have an overly tranquil tone, the look and feel of something genteely preserved in amber.

Ellery Sedgwick once described his approach to the magazine in this way: "I always treated *The Atlantic* as a dinner party to which guests with differing opinions were invited. I insisted their manners must be reasonably good and I tried, as host, to lead arguments in the direction of my own opinions and, at times, to summarize them." This was a gentle and charming approach that served in its day, but it was too subdued for me.

Even the approach Ted Weeks had established to good effect, a heavy (though not exclusive) reliance on contributors like the 343

CEO of a steel company, say, or a university president, who stood back and surveyed issues and phenomena from a comfortable elevation and distance, seemed to me somewhat too leisurely, too stand-offish when events were moving so quickly and unpredictably and many of the basic tenets of personal and political and literary behavior were under such noisy—and sometimes noisome—reexamination. I respected the slow and magisterial approach in others, but I was not built for it; I felt it necessary to reduce the time it took to get the magazine to press and thereby cut closer to the current of events. To accomplish this it was necessary to rely on top-notch reporter-writers. There was still need for the long-view and ivory-tower thinkers, and we continued to publish them. But the flow of events called more and more for articles by writers who were fast on their feet, to whom "Thou shalt meet thy deadline" was as sacred as any commandment Moses brought down from the Mount. Their prose had to be readable and thoughtful and they had to be able to run the distances and not, like my old racehorse Fourflusher, only a furlong or two. Most newspapermen or newsmagazine writers cannot do that, so such writers were few. To produce this ambitious kind of journalism on a monthly schedule called, first, for accurate anticipation of events and trends and, second, the knack of marrying the right writer to the right idea at the right time.

The first required taking chances and gambling some of our meager editorial budget on assignments that might not pan out. (It was helpful, too, to experience the kind of good luck we encountered with the LBJ resignation or the court's timing of its reversal of the Spock verdict.) The second, since our fees were small next to what writers could earn from other publications, required much cajoling of writers and difficult negotiations with their agents. We could not compete with the prices paid or the generous contractual arrangements offered by magazines like *The New Yorker* or *Life,* or with the fancy money paid by the skin magazines, *Playboy* or *Penthouse,* which feigned respectability by placing name writers between crotch shots and condom ads. An *idea,* the challenge of the invitation, had to be sufficiently beguiling to persuade a writer

344   that he or she would be happier to appear in *The Atlantic* with

all its prestige than somewhere else that paid better. That is how we persuaded professional writers, both generalists and specialists, to take on assignments that were extremely demanding of their time, energy, and thought.

Even this was not enough. The search for new talent was essential to *The Atlantic,* and the occasional discovery of it was one of the most delicious rewards of editing the magazine. For fiction, Weeks had established and I continued the custom of seeking out previously unpublished short story writers by offering special *Atlantic First* prizes and encouraging new poets by presenting their works in annual or semi-annual supplements devoted to Young Poets. In nonfiction, we relied not only on our own contacts and relations with literary agents but also on word-of-mouth among established contributors to the magazine and friends on campuses or in newspaper and magazine editorial rooms to call promising writers to our attention.

As another source of talent we encouraged the submission of unsolicited manuscripts of all sorts—fiction, poetry, essays, brief reports, travel shorts, or lengthy articles—and promised relatively prompt responses to those who submitted them. This brought an average of seven hundred to eight hundred manuscripts into 8 Arlington Street each week, a steady stream which we panned with the diligence of stubborn grubstakers certain that the next shake of the sieve, just one more, will produce a nugget's gleam or (to muck about with the metaphor) a seed pearl or two. Sifting these required the full-time work of one, sometimes two junior editors and then considerable time of one or more senior editors to examine manuscripts that the juniors felt deserving of a second opinion. More than once I threatened to abolish what we called "the slush pile" and get rid of its bother and expense only to be deterred in each case by the timely discovery of a string of poems, a moving short story, or, less frequently, a publishable nonfiction article or the potential for an Atlantic Monthly Press book. The first two novels by a former Los Angeles policeman named Joseph Wambaugh, *The New Centurions* and *The Blue Knight,* grew into Press best-sellers from a seed manuscript he'd sent in to the slush pile. A sheaf of manuscripts in a fine italic script brought the nature poems and touching short stories of the Welsh poet Leslie Norris into

345

the magazine. The first published short stories of many now-popular writers such as Joyce Carol Oates, Ann Beattie, and Bobbie Ann Mason appeared among the unsoliciteds, as did those of the remarkable black writer James Alan McPherson, who went on to provide us with a series of stories which won him the Pulitzer Prize and later a MacArthur Foundation "genius grant"; he also became a valued contributing editor of the magazine. An unsolicited story by another unknown named John Sayles was too long for our available space but Mike Curtis sent it upstairs to the press and it became *The Pride of the Bimbos,* a rollicking baseball novel that launched Sayles on his brilliant career as writer and moviemaker. As the years passed I came to wonder how I could have been so obtuse as to even think of discontinuing that weekly influx of tattered manila envelopes, lovingly typed, coffee-stained manuscripts, each with a stamped self-addressed return envelope enclosed along with the author's silent prayer that it would not be returned. If our attention to the slush pile produced only one or two small nuggets a year—and there were years when it produced not even that—our pleasure of discovery rivaled that of the discovered and made the process worthwhile. Many other magazine editors and book publishers benefitted from our "slush pile" as well, for in many instances once *The Atlantic* found and published a new writer, some editor at *The New Yorker* or other higher-paying magazine would recognize a new talent and woo him or her to its pages. We would smile a rueful smile and turn back to panning the slush for the next nugget.

Our constant process of search and discovery was made even more necessary after a few alert book publishers saw that a change in reading habits after World War II made it possible to make handsome profits from the shortcomings of day-to-day and week-to-week journalism. The American appetite for reading about politics and public affairs grew sharply. Readers were eager for more than the transitory fare of newspapers, news-magazines, and television. A book publisher who had the wit to abandon the industry's archaic methods and bring out a book in a matter of weeks or at least a few instead of several months could reap heretofore unimagined profits. Atheneum did just

346   that with Theodore White's *The Making of the President 1960,*

published only a few months after Jack Kennedy's election. It was the archetype for publishing's rush into book journalism, speedily produced books about major events rushed into bookstores on accelerated schedules. Not long after the White book rocketed onto the best-seller lists, many reporters who had the stamina and a good book-length idea found they could abandon daily deadlines and build their professional lives around the juicy advances and potential royalties that more and more publishers were willing to offer. This made life trying for a magazine editor. It became difficult if not impossible to persuade a Teddy White, Gay Talese, Robert Donovan, David Halberstam, J. Anthony Lukas, or any of a number of other stars of this newly born stable of "book journalism" authors to take on for a relative pittance an assignment conceived by a magazine. Once in a while we would succeed. In other cases an editor had to look elsewhere for a less sought-after writer to bring his idea to life, or be content instead with carving an excerpt from whatever book the star writer was working on once it was written.

Over my years *The Atlantic* published many pieces of excellent political or sociological reporting that were carved out of soon-to-be-published book manuscripts, as did *The New Yorker* in much greater volume, *Harper's,* and many other magazines. Most of those articles were worth printing, yet I viewed each of the instances as a kind of defeat, a reliance on material conceived and shaped by others rather than original material conceived and controlled in our own shop. To deserve its franchise the magazine, I felt, was obliged each year to explore where others did not, to break some ground of its own. This was not easy, for the days were past when a magazine like *The Atlantic* could use prestige alone as the substitute for cool green cash.

Chapter 20

Close Encounters

ccording to independent research that was widely accepted
in the publishing and advertising communities, each copy of
The Atlantic was passed around and read by at least four,
probably five or six persons. On that basis our readership grew
modestly from something more than 1,250,000 in the mid-1960s
to at least 2,000,000 by the end of the 1970s. How many of these
readers really read the magazine's contents? It was a safe bet
that no more than three persons—Emily Flint, Louise Desaulniers, and myself—literally read everything printed in it. There
were many who read a substantial amount, but probably a majority read only one or two pieces. This I am sure was, and still
is, true of almost any general magazine, newsmagazines included. Anyway, our minimum goal was to provide in every
issue a mixture in which a discerning reader would find at least
one rewarding article, would feel encouraged to try others as
well, and finally would be satisfied enough to try the magazine
again next month. Variety, therefore, was not just the spice of
life but an essential to survival.

Traditionally, each issue of *The Atlantic* offered a good sam-
pling of contemporary poetry and preferably two short stories
or now and then a novella or excerpt from a major novel. Poetry, for all Ted Spencer's inspirational teaching, was not one of

my strong points, but I was not inclined to imitate Harold Ross, who was said to have vowed as editor of *The New Yorker* never to print a poem he couldn't understand. If I had taken the same stance, many poets of the newer generation would not have seen their work in our pages, but I trusted the judgment of Peter Davison and Phoebe Lou Adams, reserving only the infrequently exercised right to veto a choice I felt was too esoteric and/or too long. Our readers were the richer for that. I needed no coaxing, though perhaps an explication here and there, when it came to the works of Robert Penn Warren, Elizabeth Bishop, Robert Lowell, James Dickey, W. S. Merwin, Richard Wilbur, Maxine Kumin, W. H. Auden, May Swenson, Stanley Kunitz, James Merrill, Peter Davison himself, or even (for me) the more elusive John Berryman. I took extra special pleasure from publishing the works of two poets who became long-time contributors of both prose and fiction to the magazine and good friends in the bargain.

Except for their gentle manners and soft speech, no two men could have been less alike than Leslie Norris and L. E. Sissman. Norris's poems at first came by mail from England, handwritten in flowing italic script. I had published several before Maggie and I, during a visit to London, journeyed down to Chichester where he was teaching to meet the poet. We found a short chap with tousled hair and round and merry face standing before a small suburban cottage, doting over a pair of prancing dogs while he fed migrating wild ducks in his small garden pool and dreamed, he told us, of the sewin (sea trout) he might be catching or the songs he might be singing if he were home in his beloved Wales. In addition to a fresh sheaf of his beautiful poems of nature and country life, I carried home the beginnings of a friendship and the first of the many of his short stories *The Atlantic* was to print. The stories were poignant invocations of life in Wales; in the words of one critic, they spoke of "the lazy joys and quick terrors of boyhood, the unpleasant surprises of middle age, and the aches of lives fallen into inconsequence. . . ." Leslie talked as warmly and entertainingly as he wrote. So did his wife, Kitty. When he went to Brigham Young University in Utah for what was intended to be a brief visit as poet in residence, he and Kitty were immediately recognized as natural **349** teachers and became beloved members of the faculty community. "We feel like dwarfs out here, with kinks in our necks from looking up all the time. All these Mormons are giants," he reported later. Of his first, disappointing experience with what was described as New England clam chowder he said, "Bob, it was so thick a mouse could trot across it." We had become such instant friends that I was not at all resentful but proud instead when William Shawn and his poachers from *The New Yorker* began publishing his work. There was enough of it for both magazines.

Ed Sissman was a tall man who walked with a slight list to starboard, well over six feet even when bent over in contemplation, as he usually was. His curious eyes peered through big round eyeglasses past tendrils of smoke from one of his collection of briar pipes. He had been a teen-age prodigy in Detroit, winning a national spelling championship and performing as one of the precocious "Quiz Kids" of radio fame. A slight Midwestern twang and a Detroiter's avid interest in cars, old and new, had survived Harvard and years of living in the East. Ed wrote poetry as an avocation and made his living as one of Boston's most creative advertising men. He had been a passable poet at Harvard and for several years after. In 1965 he was struck with Hodgkin's disease. In the crucible of that "routinely fatal" scourge Sissman was transformed into a singularly good poet, able to write "like one possessed of a knowledge remote from most of us, the knowledge of real time," as his fellow poet friend Peter Davison put it. By submitting to the ordeal of chemotherapy and radiology Ed won almost ten years of remission. "Instead of a curtain falling, a curtain rose," Ed wrote after resigning to the nature of his ailment. "And stayed up, revealing a stage decked in defining light." He turned to prose as well as poetry, and over five of those reclaimed years, working always in the shadow of death but never for a moment giving in to gloom, he provided *The Atlantic* with one of its most looked-for features. His column, aptly praised by John Updike as "a monthly report on nothing in particular" was called "Innocent Bystander." There was no telling what next month's column would bring—a memory of being "hypnotized" at a Revere Beach carnival, an appreciation of Evelyn

Waugh, auto racing at Watkins Glen, the humiliations of air travel, an array of "middle-aged curmudgeonations." Whatever the subject, Sissman scanned it with a gentleness that belied his sharpness. We could tell by the letters that arrived after the curtain finally came down for Ed Sissman in 1976 that thousands missed him as much as did those of us at *The Atlantic.* He left behind three books of vibrant, touching poems and a collection of the columns, *Innocent Bystander: The Scene from the 70's.*

Though basically a nonfiction man, I was somewhat surer of myself with prose fiction than with poetry. Admittedly I had to struggle to suspend my skepticism when I was pressed by Mike Curtis to give platform to some of the new voices in fiction, like Grace Paley or Ann Beattie, whose excursions into human relationships struck me at first as all-too-somber explorations into the insignificant. (I, of course, did not confess this when *The Atlantic* was praised and won prizes for bringing such new talents as these to the fore.) The magazine had always presented the works of major writers and we made extra efforts to keep that good reputation burnished. A partial inventory over those years between 1966 and 1980 would have to include John Gardner, John Barth, John Updike, Thomas McGuane, Jorge Luis Borges, Key Boyle, Richard Yates, Herbert Gold, Donald Barthelme, Tobias Wolff, Philip Roth. I fell in love with the bluesy, boozy stories of the San Francisco–based writer Alice Adams and could not get enough of them.

I was startled to realize that two of the most brilliant American writers, Saul Bellow and Bernard Malamud, had never appeared in *The Atlantic* so I moved to correct those glaring omissions. Bellow came in the form of a substantial, self-standing excerpt from his *Mr. Sammler's Planet,* the novel that cut tellingly to the darkening sensibilities of urban America in the sixties, one of the several works that later brought him the Nobel Prize. Bernard Malamud, some of whose short stories, *The Magic Barrel* for one, certainly deserved to be in any anthology of All-American Best, required some avid pursuit on my part. He was, he guessed, pleased to be invited into *The Atlantic.* He did not add, "at last," but his tone of voice implied that. Still, he wanted to know more about me, why I was pressing him to submit his work, how many of his stories and novels had I read, what did I think of them, what were my views on the state of fiction in general. He was a small, intense man with disappearing hair and plain round eyeglasses, conservative in his habits and manners and intolerant of small talk, but always courteous, generous in his advice and his humor when a conversation pleased him. He did not laugh a great deal and usually did so more with his eyes than his mouth. He was a painfully slow writer, the most meticulous workman I had ever met. As we were arranging to publish the first of his stories to appear in the magazine, one about an American visiting a writer in Moscow called *Man in the Drawer,* Malamud called time after time to make changes of nuance and adjustments of atmosphere that, while almost imperceptible, heightened the tension of his tale. This first encounter led to many opportunities to socialize with him (socializing usually meant talking about writing) and observe his slow, scalpeling work on new novels and stories. After I had told him about the talent and artistic intensity of young James Alan McPherson, Malamud insisted that I arrange for them to meet. He was then working on an odd and complex novel called *The Tenants* involving confrontation in an almost abandoned city apartment house between a white and a black man, so he spent much time in conversation and correspondence with McPherson for help in achieving the exact idiom and rhythm of speech of the novel's black protagonist. The novel did not achieve the great success of such other Malamud novels as *The Natural, The Fixer,* or *A New Life,* but a year or so after it appeared I overheard two black writers expressing astonishment that a white man could so effectively capture a black man's speech, especially a crazy one like that man in *The Tenants.*

When James Dickey came to town it was best to lock up the pretty women and anchor any valuable object that might get knocked down in the turbulence. In person he was very much like his poetry, unbridled and fierce with the gusts and yearnings of living. He might show up with a thirst just as fierce and with a guitar in his hand, prepared to play mountain music into the night. He (and readers as well) had greatly enjoyed seeing "Looking for the Buckhead Boys," a rollicking recollection of his old neighborhood in Atlanta, and several others of his extraordinary poems in *The Atlantic,* so when he came to town to hand over his first completed novel to Houghton Mifflin he said he thought we'd find a lively excerpt in it for the magazine. I read a copy of the manuscript between five and seven one morning after Dickey had drunk all my scotch, lunged at two woman guests without injury to any party, and woke up more than one neighbor with a series of guitar solos rendered outdoors while he awaited a taxi. I am willing to boast that the magazine printed a lot of top-rate fiction in my time; none of it competed for narrative force and suspense with the central episode from Dickey's wild river-country thriller *Deliverance,* a cliff-hanging (literally) manhunt between a hillbilly rifleman and a city boy armed only with a bow and arrow.

Jim invited Maggie and me to New York for the film premier of *Deliverance.* A line of moviegoers stretched for almost two blocks along Third Avenue. We found Dickey in leather boots, a crumpled ten-gallon hat, and lumberjack's shirt, striding back and forth and telling the people in line with a melon-ripe southern accent what to look for in the movie. The author had a small part in the movie, that of a beefy red-neck southern sheriff, a perfect piece of casting. When Dickey's round, joyous pan flashed onto the screen he rose in his seat in the crowded movie house and whooped, "That's me, folks. That's me!," drowning out his few lines of dialogue on the screen. When the film ended, Dickey rushed to the exit to poll the departing crowd. "How'd you like it? How'd you like the sheriff?" We told Jim we liked him jes' fine, but Burt Reynolds as the deflated macho man and Jon Voigt as the hero-by-default were a helluva lot better looking. Then we went home to rest up for the pleasure and exhaustion of the next Dickey sweep into Boston.

John Cheever: I think I'd read every novel and every short story he'd written. I would have performed contortions to be able to publish a Cheever story, but for years all his work had gone automatically to *The New Yorker* under contract. So I settled for a chance to meet him when he moved to Boston for a few months in the fall of 1974. Maggie and I got a call from John Updike one day saying that Cheever was lonely and needed company. Updike was rallying a few friends to offer the   353 writer some relief from his monkish isolation in quarters provided by Boston University, where he had come to teach "creative writing" for a semester or two. After several efforts to reach him we invited Cheever to dinner one autumn night. We had heard that after an initial bout of shyness he could be a charming conversationalist, so we looked forward to a relaxed evening over drinks and supper. When at last he knocked at our door, he looked much as I'd expected John Cheever to look, like one of his well-born New Englanders from *The Wapshot Chronicle,* or one of his bewildered Westchester County commuters in weekend gray flannels and tweed sport jacket with frayed elbows. But I hadn't expected him to look so small and vulnerable. The weather had turned blustery and he seemed to be shivering as he moved unsteadily into the room. He was rather drunk. Unfortunately, he said, he had lost his hat during the dozen or so city blocks from his apartment to ours. "It was one of those good old Locke hats," he said mournfully.

The evening was not a success. Cheever was dispirited, even despondent. He wasn't enjoying his teaching work at BU and wasn't writing much either. His marriage, he said, was on the rocks. On top of that, he feared that the people at *The New Yorker* were no longer interested in his work. I said I found that difficult to believe, but if he had some good stories that needed a home, be *The Atlantic*'s guest. Maggie offered some supper, but Cheever said he wasn't hungry. Perhaps another martini instead. One more martini led to another. Feeling guilty at having added to his unsteadiness, I walked the author partway home, searching in vain for his lost hat along the way.

Cheever telephoned two days later to thank us for our hospitality and hoped we could get together soon again. We tried again about three weeks later, with somewhat but not much better results, though he seemed pleased to have been reinvited. What a disturbed and unhappy man he was. There was never a third time because Cheever abruptly cut short his stay at the university. Later we heard that he had signed into a drying-out sanitarium in an effort to give up the booze. Months later, word came that John had shaken the habit, was at home again and writing some of his best work, novels and stories suffused with an uncharacteristic lightness and joy of life. Direct evi-

354

dence of that arrived one day in the mail, a new Cheever short story. It was not up there with the very best Cheever stories but an excellent piece of prose, ruefully warm and very funny. It was called *The President of the Argentine.* Its narrator finds himself walking along the Commonwealth Avenue mall, musing on the eccentricities and perversities of his Boston Brahmin relatives. He is wearing a Locke hat and a rare vicuna topcoat "left to me by my fourth father-in-law, a Des Moines haberdasher." He was carrying it over his arm "because my father taught me never to wear a coat unless it was absolutely necessary. If I wore a coat I might be mistaken for an Irishman."

Passing several of the statues on the mall he comes to one of the president of the Argentine, a "bulky and vulgar" bronze figure, and wonders (as do most who venture upon it in real life) what in the world it was doing in the middle of Boston. The narrator decides to deposit his hat on the head of the president, only to be deterred on the first try by a passing policeman and on the second by the distraction of a young girl with "marvelous legs and breasts," who is studying "how to beautify death" at an embalming academy. Accompanying the story was a note saying that it had been written especially for *The Atlantic,* a sort of thank-you card for our offering him some solace during a most unhappy and disordered time. I printed the story with pleasure. And with relief that I now knew how John Cheever had lost his treasured Locke hat one fall night while tipsily making his way to supper with a pair of would-be Samaritans.

We had only brief opportunities to see Cheever again, once at the wedding of one of John Updike's daughters in Ipswich, later at a party his publishers gave for him in New York when he won the Pulitzer Prize for his collected short stories. He was back with his wife, had licked his drinking problems, and was writing well—but with who knows how much pain and anguish? for he was now confronting the ugly fact that, after pulling himself upward from deep down in despair he had been dealt a premature sentence of death by cancer.

There was not a great deal to laugh about in those not very humorous years; or perhaps the problem was that there was much going on that was laughable but there was less willingness to enjoy it. In any event, humorous short stories were hard to

come by, as was humor of any kind unless the bitter satire of
Mort Sahl or the black monologues of Lenny Bruce and their
emulators qualified as humor. No one had come along to replace Thurber, Perelman, Benchley, or Russell Maloney and
the rest of those humorists bequeathed to us by the 1920s and
1930s. Imports from the *Punch* writers in London had fallen in
quality as well. I found the man I believed could reverse the
trend in a long-time friend from my days of living in the Long
Island suburbs named John Slate. John was a top-flight Manhattan lawyer whose specialty was international aviation. His
work took John on long trips abroad, providing him with
lengthy intervals in which to stay up too late drinking with
associates, or worse, by himself, and to fiddle with one of the
zaniest senses of humor I'd ever encountered. He was much like
Robert Benchley in appearance and in his quiet, deadpan delivery. He composed song lyrics: "When your hat's on fire, smoke
gets in your eyes," or "There'll *never* be an England." For one
song, "If You Loved Me Half as Much as I Love You," he
worked out an elaborate equation to explain the title's mathe-
matics. He contemplated iconoclastic historical tomes: "The
Day They Built Rome" and its sequel, "Rome Wasn't Burned
in a Day." He invented amazing new medical procedures like
the *audialnasalornithectomy,* the surgical removal through the
ear of a bird that has flown into the head through the nose. For
a friend's birthday he had a pair of tattered sneakers, size
twelve, bronzed like baby shoes.

To fight the emptiness of overseas airports and the loneliness
of faraway hotel rooms he took to telephoning friends at all
hours or sending mysterious cables. He and I invented a Colonel Blimp character named Durston Chop, ret., who lived in
Upper Bageshot and rode to hounds on a camel. We amused
ourselves by writing to each other accounts of Chop's bizarre
adventures. When I was at work in the Department of State
there would arrive an occasional cable signed Colonel Durston
Chop, ret., or simply Chop. One of them said, "Please advise
Secretary of State of following ultimatum: If United States does
not change its foreign policy immediately I shall seize it." Another said, "Please advise all Embassies: Am negotiating for a
new international television quiz show called 'Stump the Ex-

perts' in which some experts are hit with some stumps." Since these cables filtered through the State Department's message center, one of the most security-sensitive (and most humorless) cubicles of the U.S. government, they were a cause of some consternation. I learned this when a director of the center, no less, came to my office personally with a look of deep concern on his face and holding out as if offering a burning ember with tongs a cable from Istanbul which said, "Have left hospital in fine fettle. Ready for immediate espionage assignment. Urgently yours, Chop." I tried to explain the source and to assure the man there was no threat to the national security, but he went away looking even more worried than when he'd entered.

Were he to turn just to writing, John Slate, I was certain, could have established himself as a topflight humor writer, somewhat in the vein of the Canadian nonsense master Stephen Leacock. Through *The Atlantic* I presented samples of his antic imagination to a wider public. He obliged with several short pieces that brightened the back-of-the-book, among them an analysis of hospital food entitled "No Soup *du Jour* Today," a detailed instruction for "Frontal Lobotomy Self-Taught," and a brief do-it-yourself manual, accompanied by appropriately lunatic illustrations, called "So You Want to Build Your Own Ocean Liner." The ocean liner piece was reprinted in more than 150 publications around the world, including several national naval publications, shipbuilding, yachting, and architectural journals.

Slate was a spendthrift of his talents and of his health as well. He worked too hard and drank too much and like all the best clowns he no doubt endured more than his share of those three o'clocks in the morning in the dark night of the soul. One night in September of 1967 his heart gave out and he never awoke. He was only fifty-two. His name is still part of the title of his old law firm, Skadden, Arps, Slate, Meagher and Flom, now famous or notorious, depending on whether one was a client or an antagonist, for its prodigious feats in the mergers and takeover game. Among the Slate papers were the beginnings of two plays inspired by his earlier japes, one featuring two real estate developers named Joe Romulus and Harvey Remus in "The Day They Built Rome," the other casting someone like Slim

Summerville or Andy Devine as Nero in "Rome Wasn't Burned in a Day." Of course, he was the absent star of his own memorial service. We all were reminded of a trove of joyful absurdities, like the time John picked up a telephone one morning at Brown's Hotel in London and said solemnly, "Hello room service. This is Mr. Slate. Will you please serve me a room?" So laughter softened our sadness.

The relationship of *Harper's* and *The Atlantic* was one of the peculiarities of the magazine world. Each sought its readership from the same national pool of generally sophisticated, high-IQ readers. Each drew on substantially the same kinds of (and sometimes the very same) writers. At cocktail parties, in college seminars, and elsewhere one of the magazines would frequently be confused with the other. The two were friendly but intense competitors for readership, for advertisers' dollars, for prestige—yet they were partners in an important way; they shared the same advertising sales organization. That seeming paradox came about in the 1950s, when proprietors of the two monthlies saw Madison Avenue becoming more and more enthralled with magazines' circulation numbers irrespective of the quality of content. An advertising sales organization that represented both *The Atlantic* and *Harper's* could offer advertisers a total circulation package of more than 500,000 (meaning a likely readership of 2,000,000 or more) with little duplication in that readership; no more than 10 percent of subscribers to one magazine subscribed also to the other.

The combined audience was still small potatoes next to the mass circulation magazines, but for many years it enabled Harper-Atlantic Sales to bring to each of the two magazines a degree of advertising income and stability that neither could have achieved by itself, particularly with the advertising community sinking ever deeper into its preference for numbers over quality, so much so that they let such major American institutions as *Collier's,* the *Saturday Evening Post,* and *Life* go belly-up by switching their loyalty and largesse to the even bigger numbers of television.

The joint sales operation also had the virtue of bringing editors of the two magazines into frequent contact because both sat on the Harper-Atlantic Sales board of directors (a healthy infusion of editorial considerations and caveats into the crass business of soliciting ads). We editors frequently spoke to groups in behalf of H-A Sales and participated in annual conferences at which our assembled editorial staffs, on separate days, would give the advertising salesmen previews of issues to come and, we hoped, equip them with inspirational thoughts and words for their sales pitches. These activities brought me back in touch with the bright, no-nonsense, and by now veteran editor of *Harper's,* Jack Fischer, whom I had admired since meeting him in the Stevenson campaign's Elks Club word shop. When Jack retired, his job went to a young man from Yazoo, Mississippi, named Willie Morris.

I have not met anyone who didn't like Willie Morris. Perhaps learning to smile tolerantly as people laugh when you tell them you come from a place called Yazoo engendered his pleasant temperament and politeness even toward boors. From Yazoo, Willie went to the University of Texas, where he broke into journalism on the university paper. From college he went to *The Texas Observer,* the irreverent weekly that made a name for itself by cocking a snoot at the Texas establishment and nurturing a batch of young writers like Ronnie Dugger, Mollie Ivins, and Willie, whose work attracted attention far beyond Austin. Willie was only twenty-five and fresh from a Rhodes scholarship at Oxford when he found himself gawking at the tall buildings while wandering about Manhattan in search of a job in journalism or book publishing. Jack Fischer had the wit to bring him into *Harper's* as a junior editor and groom him to take over as editor in chief, which he did in 1967 at the age of thirty-three.

Willie's youth and country-boy fascination with the sophisticated big city made people want to help him. Small inquisitive eyes set like raisins in his plump boyish face, his soft Mississippi accent and courteous manner made him seem even younger and more vulnerable. This eased his entry into the Manhattan literary scene. Jack Fischer, stern in manner and somewhat conservative in style, had been a formidable competitor, and so in a more unbuttoned and experimental way was Willie. He was intelligent and had a good eye and ear for fresh subject matter and a willingness to gamble with untested contributors. Soon **359** after moving to New York he wrote a prize-winning book about falling in love with the city. It was called *North Toward Home*. In his six years of being groomed for the job he had established good relations with many top writers and their agents, among them such high-visibility performers as Tom Wolfe and Norman Mailer. He made the guest list at most soirees with any vestige of journalitic or literary merit, whether it be a seance of intellectuals at the apartment of Norman Podhoretz of *Commentary* magazine and Podhoretz's wife Midge Decter or a birthday bash for someone like Barbara Walters. He rated a preferred table at Elaine's, the dark and dingy saloon at which writers and show business celebrities mingled in ostensible enjoyment of blatant snobbery, execrable food, and heavy drinking. The only time the outlander editor of *The Atlantic* got a table among the favored clientele at Elaine's was when he went there, usually to his regret next morning, with Willie.

As Jack Fischer was with Ted Weeks and then me, Willie and I were friendly competitors who enjoyed keeping in touch with each other. We didn't exchange company secrets (what few we had from one another) any more than did *Newsweek* and *Time* or Macy's and Gimbel's, but we liked each other's company. We lunched or took drinks together on some of my frequent trips to New York, exchanging reminiscences growing out of our vastly different backgrounds and ruminations on the trials and tribulations of our very similar responsibilities—for example, how to make coherence out of the sometimes impenetrable bramblebush of certain famous writers' prose and thereby keep alive for them reputations for cogency they did not deserve. Of course, we also shared with each other the occasional literary successes and happy surprises that made our work worthwhile.

Willie made one major move as editor that produced some strikingly good short-term results but was to induce unfortunate long-term consequences, and probably contributed to his downfall. He gambled a major part of his editorial resources on contracts with a half-dozen talented New York–based writers, among them the hard-driving and by then famous David Halberstam and the entertaining émigré, Texan Larry King. This special coterie brought some very good, attention-getting pieces to *Harper's* and turned the magazine for a brief time into what Madison Avenue liked to call a "hot book." (Madison Avenue is always calling one periodical or other a "hot book," but its editor is wise to keep his cool because the compliment quickly melts away.) I envied Willie his success but was not about to copy his formula. The amounts of money the arrangement cost *Harper's* were not by any means immense, but both magazines had perilously thin budgets for editorial material; mine was a relative pittance of about $12,000 for each month's bundle of articles, essays, poems, short stories, and other features—little more than *Life,* for example, would pay for just one article. The fees and travel expenses of the *Harper's* in-house writers consumed the bulk of Morris's editorial budget. That heavy expenditure meant that he had to use the material he'd paid for not only when the writers produced compelling material, but also on the not infrequent occasions when they did not. By mortgaging much of the available space to his contract writers whether they were on or off their feed, the arrangement severely limited the amount of magazine pages available for other material.

I had scheduled one of our New York lunch dates with Willie in New York one day in 1971 and awoke to the news that he had been fired after only four productive years as *Harper's* editor in chief. The ostensible reason was the furor that followed Willie's publication of a long piece by Norman Mailer called *The Prisoner of Sex,* a piece so studded with graphic sexual and anatomical detail it might have confounded even Krafft-Ebing. Far worse, it brought down on *Harper's* the wrath of those who found it to be blatantly "sexist."* The magazine's principal owner, John Cowles, Jr., of the Minneapolis Star-Tribune Company, was said to be one of those offended by Mailer's Anglo-Saxon explicitnesses, only a few of which he apparently had heard or seen in print before, and decided Willie must go.

---

*Mailer's response to the accusation that he was antiwoman appeared in print several years later: "If anything I had always believed that women were marvelous, and it took women's liberation [movement] to make me realize that women can be just as rotten and lousy as men." (*New York Times Magazine,* September 22, 1991.)

Apparently, though, the cause was somewhat less immediate than that, a deepening rift between church (Willie Morris and his editorial staff) and state (the owner Cowles and his publisher, William Blair). The rift was caused in great part by the mounting costs in money and magazine space of Willie's traveling in-house hit team. As happens all too frequently in journalism, the state won.

I telephoned Willie to give my condolences and to say that I supposed that under the circumstances he would prefer to cancel our luncheon date. Not at all, Willie said. He needed a sympathetic ear. We drank a most nourishing lunch at the Four Seasons restaurant, one of the world's prime places for eating well and showing off at the same time, but Willie was in a state of shock, not quite certain what had hit him or why. It was as if he was one of his favorite Civil War characters, Jeb Stuart; his horse—his whole world—had just been shot from under him. What now? I tried to reassure him that with the reputation he'd made at *Harper's,* his talents as both writer and editor, and the many friends he'd made in New York, he would find plenty of opportunities for rewarding work. It didn't seem to cheer him much, but we toasted that sentiment with another drink and then adjourned to, of all places, Madison Square Garden. It was Willie's turn for some custodial time with his young son, David. To make this a very special occasion Willie had arranged a date for the boy to shoot baskets with the New York Knickerbocker's great player Bill Bradley.

What an unlikely place to sit upon the ground and talk about the death of dreams. For nearly an hour we hunched heads together in that cavernous arena, the only occupants of the Garden's thousands of seats, watching the proud and excited little tyke get lessons in hook shots and layups from the giant Knick, our mournful conversation punctuated by the echoing muffled crack of leather against polished wood. Willie kept shaking his head in disbelief at what had happened, just as I would have done if it had happened to me. I clumsily offered what must have been very cold solace, wishing I could be a more comforting, a wiser elder to a most disconsolate son, and truly disconsolate myself at the loss of a sweet and worthy competitor.

362

In a show of loyalty to Willie (and no doubt recognizing that their arrangement with *Harper's* was now about to end), most of Willie's writing stars dramatically left with him. Willie himself did not make another connection in Manhattan, perhaps because his love affair with New York had been forever ended, an interlude marred by his divorce from his wife Celia and then dealt the death blow by John Cowles, Jr. He moved for a while way out to what is referred to as "the fashionable southern fork" of Long Island, mingling with the writing and painting crowd in the Hamptons. He wrote a touching book about integration in his hometown of Yazoo, also a book for children called *Good Old Boy* and a not very good novel called *The Last of the Southern Girls,* whose flamboyant and earthy protaganist could be taken to be the real-life Washington demisocialite with whom Willie had enjoyed a passing relationship. He also wrote a loving memoir of his friend the writer James Jones. We never got together again. Next thing I knew, Willie had moved back to Mississippi, south toward home.

My relations with Willie's successors at *Harper's* were cordial and enjoyable but not as warmed by the affection I felt for him. Robert Shnayerson was wooed away from *Time,* where he was one of the most highly regarded senior editors. Shnay, as quiet and introverted as Willie was outgoing and communicative, was an effective editor with an inventive flair. He was teamed with a new publisher who apparently had persuaded owner Cowles that *Harper's* should pay more attention to the "counterculture." Between them the new editor and publisher experimented unsuccessfully with a flurry of special inserts and pull-out features that seemed to be aimed at the young people who were already being served more effectively by such new publications as *Rolling Stone* and *The Whole Earth Catalogue.* Next into the editor's chair came Lewis Lapham, bright, debonair, and well-born, a grandson of a former mayor of San Francisco. Lew was highly opinionated, disdainful of many if not all aspects of American life, and especially contemptuous of contemporary politics and most of its practitioners. A cogent writer, he brought a kind of rich man's nihilism to *Harper's* pages. He and I now and then found reasons to talk about mutual concerns and ambitions, but as the character of the two journals diverged **363** and, more to the point, Lapham and I each found ourselves increasingly preoccupied with our magazine's economic problems, the occasions dwindled. The special joint advertising sales arrangement continued for a while to link the two friendly enemies. Just as before, it did not diminish in any way the competitive urge, the drive to be each month the better, more pertinent magazine. Whenever I was asked to define the difference between the two, I twisted to my own purpose something Mark Twain once said about himself and Rudyard Kipling: "Between us we share all human knowledge. *The Atlantic* knows all there is to be known and *Harper's* knows all the rest."

Chapter 21

Facing the Future

I did not carry heavy ideological baggage or insidious prejudices into *The Atlantic*. The self-suspended state of my Catholic indoctrination made me tolerant and at the same time
wary of attitudes toward God, including disbelief in Him or
Her. I had grown up in a place where there was no racism
because there were virtually no victims on whom to impose it,
thinking that racism was a sin mostly of the South; I had come
long since to know better, and shared in what I believed was, or
should be, a nationwide sense of guilt and of desire to see it
expunged by the extension of true equality to blacks and all
minorities—though not certain how great were the personal
sacrifices I might offer to help it happen. I had seen enough of
Communism and state socialism in operation to recognize that
they did not work, were indeed failed gods, though anyone familiar with Great Britain before World War II had to see that
Labor Party socialism surely improved the lot of the British
working class before it trailed off into its contemporary vapid-
ity. As for capitalism, I viewed it with something like Winston
Churchill's attitude toward democracy. It was the worst system
except for all the others—imperfect, too often cruel and com-
passionless, and it worked only with reliance in many sectors on
government help, that is—heaven forfend!—substantial infu-

sions of socialism called by other names. Surrounded as I was by women like Maggie who had made careers for themselves without benefit of the feminist movement I nonetheless sympathized with it, though not with its more strident disciples and sometimes comic extremes.

My own political perspective, which I would describe as updated New Deal liberalism and mostly though not exclusively Democratic in the voting booth, naturally influenced my judgments, but I felt my journalistic mission obliged me to give voice to others' as well. While I found Ellery Sedgwick's monthly dinner party analogy too genteel for our times, I certainly shared its major intent: *The Atlantic* should be a place of many and differing voices. With one caveat: The editor would not just control the flow but stringently influence the conclusions.

As for content, my attitude in composing each month's issue was that readers should be told not whatever it might be they wanted to hear but what the editor felt they should know. Far bigger and wealthier magazines were slowly moving toward impotence or extinction by bowing to grandiose reader surveys and public opinion studies that drained away their juices and set them to competing to give people only what they wanted to read. My chief measuring stick was my own mixture of curiosity and ignorance: If something struck me as new and interesting, illuminating, or therapeutically nonsensical, it would do the same for the reader. Proposals for remedying social and political ills were always welcome in our pages, but I shared with Mencken the belief that a man need not have his own cure for cancer in order to attack a quack one. All this surely made for a presumptuous posture, perhaps even arrogant. It was also risky, given the range of my ignorance. But it was the only reliable gauge I had.

Another objective was to put together a magazine that offered one kind of predictability, call it expectability, while avoiding the other kind, the predictability that induces monotony. A section called "Atlantic Reports" that Snyder and Weeks had inaugurated up front in the magazine I greatly broadened into each month's Reports & Comment section.

366 Readers could anticipate every time a solid, thoughtful report from Washington written by one of a varied group of well-established correspondents like Douglas Kiker, Sanford Ungar, and in my final years as editor, James Fallows, who turned from being one of President Jimmy Carter's White House speech writers into one of the most impressive magazine journalists of this era. The section also carried two or three reports from foreign countries, written either by experienced correspondents on the scene or in many cases nonjournalists—business people, diplomats, academicians with long experience in those countries. We also dealt with such areas of public concern as the environment, public health, urban planning. Walter Lippmann once confided to me that he counted on those Atlantic Reports to apprise him of situations that would otherwise elude him. If they were valuable to Lippmann, I reasoned, they were certainly useful for the rest of the magazine's audience.

Toward the end of the book, readers could count on some excursions into the lighter side of everyday life, as well as sets of intelligent book reviews from Ted Weeks and Phoebe Lou Adams or the likes of Alfred Kazin, Oscar Handlin, and a string of other distinguished critics. Then there were our regular columns, Ed Sissman's Innocent Bystander, Tom Griffith's Party of One, Ward Just's media critique Newspaper Days, and Caskie Stinnett's Wary Traveler. I tried but never succeeded in finding a movie critic worthy of the job.

With fixed features in place, I then sought the unpredictable in articles that would be consistently well-written, stimulating or provocative, or, now and then, creatively wrong-headed. A special section dealing more with the tribulations than the blessings of married life; Richard Poirier on the cultural meaning of the Beatles; Wilfred Sheed's disrespectful examination of American labor union leaders; Allen Ginsberg in praise of marijuana; caricaturist Edward Sorel's irreverent blueprint for the Richard M. Nixon Library. Elizabeth Drew's first ventures into national reporting included a meticulously researched exposé of the tobacco industry's success in toning down government efforts to curb cigarette smoking and another telling how a small lobby financed by the wealthy widow of a cancer victim succeeded in channeling the lion's share of National Institutes of Health research money to cancer at the expense of other disease research. **367**

They were textbook-solid lessons in how government can be manipulated by special interests.

When a young Harvard scholar named Bruce Jackson presented us with a dramatic firsthand portrayal of big-city police drug patrols, he also confronted us with a dilemma that never confronted James Russell Lowell or most of his successors as editor: Dare *The Atlantic* say "fuck" in print? We did. The incident in Jackson's story in which a ghetto urchin no more than seven or eight years old felt free to stick his head in a prowl car window and with Anglo-Saxon brevity tell a pair of cops what he thought of them, to wit "Fuck you, Cops!" would have lost its strength and pertinence if bowdlerized. We made this decision knowing that several thousand issues of each month's *Atlantic* went into high school and college English classrooms. A Massachusetts high school teacher was sacked for using the Jackson story in his class, but a U.S. appeals court judge found the dismissal untenable and required the school board to reinstate the teacher on the sensible ground that the teacher was probably the only person in the classroom who didn't regularly utter the word in public.

Book publishers had already broken through that language barrier (though not without trouble from the would-be guardians of public morals and the courts), but up to then only such sex-oriented magazines as *Playboy* or *Penthouse* regularly used the everyday vernacular as she was truly spoken. With the coming of "the cultural revolution" of the sixties, this acceptance of the way people really talk became inescapable for publications that prided themselves on dealing with real-life situations. Still, it was several years before *The New Yorker* would even allow a man and woman to bed together. As inevitable as the new permissiveness was, I was never altogether comfortable with it and used our freedom discreetly.

In the spring of 1967 the world learned that Joseph Stalin's daughter, Svetlana Alleluyeva, had fled from the Soviet Union and was going to seek political asylum in the United States. Next I heard that Svetlana was planning to write a book and that George F. Kennan, the diplomat and foremost American student of the USSR, would join her in Switzerland. Shortly thereafter, I got a call from George Kennan. *The Atlantic* had a tie to Kennan; we had published some of his articles and his books. He was visiting Harvard and suggested in an almost conspiratorial voice that I come meet with him. He was helping the flustered daughter of Stalin negotiate a three-way deal with Harper and Row, the *New York Times,* and *Life* magazine for what was sure to be a best-selling memoir. So I could not hope to get the book for the Atlantic Monthly Press. But, said Kennan, Svetlana had already written a short, passionate essay, a sort of farewell to her homeland, and wanted it to appear in an American magazine of "high literary quality." That to Kennan spelled *The Atlantic.* If I moved fast, I might score a coup. Kennan gave me the name of one of his Princeton neighbors, a high-powered Manhattan lawyer. It took three days of intensive negotiations with this barracuda-lawyer, and a telephone conversation in my pidgin Russian with Svetlana herself in her temporary Long Island hideaway to get the piece. An emotional good-bye letter to Svetlana's son and daughter in Moscow, it was not great literature but it was a touching document, and, of course, a matter of great curiosity interest. I got it just as the magazine was going to press. We had to scrap one cover and hastily design a new one that promised in bold type the first published words of Joseph Stalin's daughter, and then add eight pages to the rear of the magazine to print it. We doubled the usual newsstand distribution and took out a full-page ad in the *New York Times* that cost more than I had paid for the article so that we could boast (mostly to Madison Avenue) of our feat. That issue was a near-sellout.

Not until later, in Princeton, did I finally meet my author. Svetlana was plainly a troubled lady, not by any means settled or happy in a new land. A brief marriage to an American architect ended in divorce and she moved to England, an unhappy émigré from both superpowers. What were her feelings, I wondered years later, when she saw pictures of her father's toppled statues and his defaced photos on placards?

One important area closed to American journalism in those days was what our government, in deference to Generalissimo Chiang Kai-shek, called mainland China. One of our contributors was a young Far East scholar at Harvard, an Australian named Ross Terrill. Since he was not an American citizen, I **369** suggested that he get a visa from the Chinese consulate in Ottawa, then wander and write about China for the magazine. Ross was in China when Kissinger made the secret visit that led to Richard Nixon's dramatic China "breakthrough." This made even more timely Terrill's two lengthy articles, the first full-fledged, on-the-scene reporting from mainland China to appear in any American publication in thirty years. Soon thereafter, we published them as a book, *The 800,000,000,* that was critically acclaimed. Not much later I had the pleasure of standing as a sponsor for Ross when he appeared before the Immigration and Naturalization Service to acquire his American citizenship. I was grateful that he had waited until we'd gotten him into—and out of—China.

One of the most inflammable subjects of public discourse is human intelligence, the debate over nature versus nurture. I learned how inflammable firsthand in 1969 when Michael Curtis and I commissioned Professor Richard Herrnstein of Harvard, a behavioral scientist, to write an article on theories about the shaping of human IQ. Extremists like William Schockley were attributing IQ entirely to inheritance and seemed to suggest that blacks were by nature inferior in intellect to whites and others. At the other extreme were social scientists who said that environment was everything, that a person's IQ could be expended or stunted solely by upbringing, economic circumstance, and schooling. Herrnstein saw some merit in both positions, though he gave somewhat greater weight to nature than to nurture. He did not go so far as Arthur Jensen of Berkeley, who started a controversy by arguing that educational programs like Head Start would not produce any improvement in IQ.

We knew that Herrnstein's view would provoke argument, as did almost any theory in this volatile field, but were not prepared for the ferocity of the response. Extreme nurturists in the Boston area were lying in wait for Dick Herrnstein. Led by a radical Harvard philosophy instructor the demonstrators gathered loudly before Herrnstein's Harvard office, waving placards and shouting that he was a racist whose teachings should be suppressed. Then they traveled across the river to gather before the *Atlantic* offices. There were no more than thirty-five or forty of them, but their bullhorns made the sound of a good-sized mob as they spat that same ugly word, "racist," at our windows. I knew we didn't deserve the insult, nor did Herrnstein. The faces in the small crowd were contorted with hatred and the demonstration passed from simple dissent to intolerance. It hurt to be so accused, but it also infuriated, especially when one demonstrator announced in a whiny European accent that he had fled Germany to escape Nazi thinking and Nazi oppression. "We do not want that here," he shouted. "Every copy of this magazine containing this article should be burned." So much for freedom of speech and opinion. That nasty little man hadn't escaped Nazi thinking after all.

I had been forced to grapple with the subject of heredity earlier. In the practice of journalism one quickly learns a bit about many things but hardly much more. That was true for me, particularly in the sciences. In late 1967 I had to learn more than a little bit, and very quickly, about revolutionary developments in biology. Word got out that Harvard University Press had decided not to publish a book by one of the two scientists who had won the Nobel Prize for discovering the structure of DNA, that fundamental chemical substance of which genes are composed. Not only did the manuscript not meet a university press's requirements for ponderousness and the full quota of footnotes, it was irreverent and mischievous as well.

When we discovered that there would be time to serialize it in *The Atlantic* before its formal publication by the New York firm of Atheneum, we seized on *The Double Helix* by Dr. James D. Watson. My crash course in the rudiments of biology equipped me to compose a lengthy introduction that confidently explained the meaning of the DNA discovery. We ran the entire book in two successive issues. It was a grand success.

The heart of Watson's story was a fascinating and easy-to-understand explanation of how the youthful Watson and the somewhat older English scientist Francis Crick, working together at Cambridge University, became first to solve the mystery of deoxyribonucleic acid (DNA) and work up a simple, well-defined, three-dimensional model that showed its structure—a feat that opened up the possibility of understanding and manipulating the chemical basis of heredity. The door was 371 open now to genetic engineering. The impact on biology was rivaled only by Darwin's and Wallace's ideas on evolution and by Mendel's discovery of the basic laws of heredity. What made the yarn not just informative but entertaining as well (and scared Harvard off) was the disingenuousness, the little boy's zeal with which Watson told how he and Crick beat out various rivals in the race for discovery and how those in the laboratories of high science were as prone to jealousy, back-biting, and internecine competition as the rest of us.

The fun began with Watson's opening line, "I have never seen Francis Crick in a modest mood." It went cheerfully on from there, telling how Crick and Watson raced against time, knowing that scientists in labs next door to them were working in the same directions while thousands of miles away in California the brilliant and ambitious Linus Pauling, already the recipient of one Nobel Prize for chemistry and now in his nineties, was on the verge of plucking another for DNA until Watson and Crick barely beat him to the breakthrough.

Through many of the years that such articles passed under my pencil, Vietnam throbbed like a migraine in the national consciousness. In fact the war that was never officially called a war had been going on for almost five years before I became editor of *The Atlantic.* I still had sympathies toward both sides of the battle being waged by those reporting the war and those directing it. But the public was beginning to discover the impossibility of winning or even getting out with honor. The brutal truth was that America was undergoing a divisive national trauma worse than any since the Civil War.

For several years after 1966 an issue of the magazine rarely went to press without at least one article and sometimes more dealing with Vietnam and its consequences at home or abroad. We drew from a multitude of sources, war correspondents and domestic reporters, foreign observers, men who had served in the White House, State Department, and the Pentagon, novelists and even poets who had things to say about this deepening national dilemma. There was not much to laugh about, but we did find some in "Minutes of a White House Meeting," a hilarious parody by James C. Thomson, Jr., who had served on the National Security Council staff. When President Lyndon Johnson heard about it he grumped that it sounded like something his former protégé, "that kid Moyers, would write." And we offered a smile or two in some piercing Edward Sorel caricatures illustrating some pertinent Unfamiliar Quotations: the dandified Vietnamese Air Marshal Ky—"My only regret is that I have only one country to give for my life"; a grinning LBJ trailing a World War I–style aviator's scarf from his seat in the cockpit—"It is better to have bombed and lost then never to have bombed at all."

By the end of 1969 we had published enough material dealing with Vietnam and its ramifications to fill a book. At Mike Janeway's urging, we did. He and I took our title, "Who We Are," from a dark poem by W. S. Merwin that had appeared in the April 1969 issue:

> When the war is over
>> We will be proud of course the air will be
>> Good for breathing at last
>> The water will have been improved the
>>> salmon
>> And the silence of heaven will migrate more
>>> perfectly
>> The dead will think the living are worth it
>>> we will know
>> Who we are
>> And we will all enlist again

The book, like the war strategies of Presidents Johnson and Nixon, bombed. At that stage of the Vietnam involvement, people were willing to take the facts about Vietnam in smaller servings in a magazine but apparently did not want set before them a huge helping of somber and mostly depressing information. We soldiered on, convinced that there was much that still needed to be said about the Vietnam experience.

To deal with that trauma I had set aside an alarming amount of the company's resources in order to sign up two of the finest reporter-writers I knew. Early in 1967 I sent Dan Wakefield, a young, Indiana-born journalist, on a picaresque tour of the country. Months later I gave over almost all the pages of the March 1968 *Atlantic* to "Supernation at Peace and War," **373**

Dan's searching, engagingly intimate chronicle of Vietnam's growing impact on everyday life in America.

Later, as America's impatience with the unending war soured into a search for scapegoats, I turned to Ward Just. Like Wakefield, he combined the sensitive touch of a novelist with the careful energy of a good reporter. Ward had seen combat and been wounded by shrapnel in the Vietnam jungles and had studied the military mind in covering Vietnam for the *Washington Post*. I sent him off on an assignment more narrow than Wakefield's but no less demanding. At West Point, in visits to army bases, and at the Pentagon he was to interview officers and enlisted men alike to report how Vietnam had affected them, their morale, their thinking about strategy and tactics. He was also to examine how the Vietnam experience might shape the armed forces of the future. This also was to fill almost an entire issue of the magazine.

Through trial and error I had learned that the most important part of an editor's job takes place before the writer has even begun to set words to paper. In commissioning an article an editor must make clear what he is looking for and not looking for without handcuffing the writer with crippling preconceptions. Otherwise, both writer and editor may find themselves in head-to-head combat when the manuscript comes in. This was particularly true at *The Atlantic,* which, though the editor set the overall tone and focus, was fundamentally a writers' magazine. Our operating rule, so sacrosanct that it should have been engraved in the sandstone over *The Atlantic*'s portal, was that nothing in a manuscript could be altered without the writer's approval. This sometimes led to floor-stompings and angry exchanges, but we prided ourselves on a respect for an author's work that was by no means standard in the trade.

Since Wakefield lived nearby in Cambridge we were able to get together often to map the journey and discuss its objectives. On his departure I composed a farewell message that in retrospect too much resembled the sort of overblown pep talk a football coach delivers to the team before kickoff:

No man can cover everything, but travel and capture as much as you can of America, its people, its moods, its troubles and disil-

lusionments, its still bright and valid dreams, its many ways of
life . . . ; portray what you can of the entire great, ingenious, rich
and poverty-stinking, beautiful and beer-can glittery, generous
and selfish, mixed-up and marching on to what? (a bigger and
better destiny or the primeval asphalt swamp?), powerful yet
impotent, clear-the-slums and kill-the-goddam-grizzlies, pick
your-1968-choice and take-your-chances kind of country this is.

What I was seeking, I told Wakefield, was a prose poem on the
condition of a nation "at war halfway around the world, at war
with itself, and about to choose its leaders for the next four
years." Dan forgave my hyperbole and came back eight months
later with all that I had hoped for and more.

One of the interludes in Wakefield's "Supernation at Peace
and War" told of a rally in a theater in Washington, D.C.,
before thousands of antiwar protesters began their dramatic
October march on the Pentagon. Norman Mailer, "the nation's
most prominent example of the writer as performer," as Wakefield called him, had taken over the microphone as self-ap-
pointed emcee. "He was wearing a dark suit with vest and holding a cup that apparently contained something stronger than
coffee. . . . He told the audience that 'on Saturday we all goin' in
and do something none of us done before.'

"He let out a deep, hoarse, braying sound, and then said,
'The reason I have no respect for LBJ is he talks just like me.'
He sipped from his cup, and said, 'Reason I'm late is because I
had to take a leak and there weren't any lights in the men's
room up on the balcony here.' " Anticipating that the newspaper reporters in the crowd would write unfavorably next day
about his performance, Mailer challenged them all to come to
the stage and fight him. No one accepted the challenge. "He
stood there proudly, his stomach pushed out and his tousled
head thrown back and one hand thrust jauntily in his pocket
and one hand holding the mug. Fearless."

Mailer was to write his own account of that turbulent antiwar weekend in Washington, including in splash-by-splash detail his own version of his inability to hit the urinal in the Ambassador Theater. It was an entertaining and in some places
powerful piece of personalized journalism called "Armies of the   375

Night." By accident or design, it took up most of the March 1968 issue of *Harper's Magazine* (and like Wakefield's opus, later came out as a book). Going head-on against the famous novelist and showman Norman Mailer was not a confrontation I would have invited, but I was more than pleased by the result. Both accounts were well worth reading, but ours, I thought, offered more nourishment. The March issue of *The Atlantic* with Wakefield's "Supernation" outsold the Mailer issue of *Harper's* on the newsstands by several thousand copies.

The coincidence of the two monthly magazines side-by-side lengthily dealing with the same subject produced stories heavy with irony in *Time, Newsweek,* and the *New York Times.* But I thought the real irony lay in the fact that both magazines had labored so heavily to chronicle the war's effect on America because the rest of the press had reported it so poorly.

Ward Just's "Soldiers" was a more difficult story for me to formulate as an assignment. As a World War II private who had been no closer to combat than a fight between soldiers and Seabees outside a Newport News, Virginia, saloon, I left it to Ward to set the boundaries. He had seen the war in Vietnam close-up and had come to know some of the army's most interesting planners and theoreticians. We agreed in advance that it would be best to confine the scrutiny to the army and not decide on the final focus until Ward had finished his travels and written a draft. That draft was an impressive piece of reporting and writing, but we both agreed that it needed work.

It is relatively easy to say where a manuscript should be cut or rearranged; it is harder to tell a writer what is missing, especially when he knows more about the subject than you do. I sent Ward five single-spaced pages suggesting what needed to be added and what needed more or less emphasis. Ward is a real pro. He took the critique as the encouragement it was meant to be and a few weeks later turned in a finished manuscript that filled much of the October and November 1970 issues with an invaluable examination of the U.S. military in transition, stricken by a defeat—"an absence of victory"—that was not of its own making and now striving to regroup for the future. "I'll be damned if I'll let the great institution of the U.S. Army be torn and tattered to pieces by that goddamned little war," said one of Ward's colonels.

Told you so, I was able to say to Ward Just after his "Soldiers" won that year's coveted National Magazine Award for Reporting Excellence, the magazine trade's equivalent of the Pulitzer Prize.

One of the most startling pieces of our Vietnam coverage was a government document: the full text of a long "top-secret" memorandum by then-Undersecretary of State George W. Ball dated October 5, 1964, in which Ball pleaded for a halt in the administration's escalation policy and, insofar as it was possible, an exit from the war. It was a powerfully reasoned brief that portrayed the Joint Chiefs of Staff assessments as the ever-optimistic misreadings they proved to be and it warned President Johnson and his top advisers that their policies were leading to military humiliation and political disaster. "Once on the tiger's back," Ball warned, "we cannot be sure of picking the place to dismount."

Though it was still classified top secret, I published the document in the July 1972 issue not only because it was important in itself but because it pointed up a serious flaw in the Pentagon Papers, that highly touted but seriously incomplete collection of secret documents assembled on orders of Secretary of Defense Robert McNamara. The papers and the analytical comments of the assemblers gave the impression that debate had raged only between hawks and superhawks, omitting the small but important body of documents showing the internal government opposition to the war. Ball's was by far the most eloquent example, for it confronted policymakers with a sensible if painful alternative—something that readers of the Pentagon Papers alone would not learn.

When the time came much later to look back at those years I felt that dealing with Vietnam and its consequences stood out as the most rewarding act of my many years as editor in chief of *The Atlantic*. From the Civil War onward the magazine had always been at its best in times of national adversity. I believed that we had upheld that record in a period of national trauma, providing a body of work on which future historians might   **377** profitably draw. We did so, I also believed, without neglecting the other nourishment our readers had come to expect.

After Vietnam, the next big spectacle to capture public attention was Watergate. This was a drama made for daily newspapers and television, so swiftly moving that the newsweeklies were often out of date. It was a particularly frustrating time for a monthly publication. Groping for a way to share in the journalistic excitement I invited George V. Higgins, the lawyer-turned-author of *The Friends of Eddie Coyle* and other tough-guy novels, to take his notebook, his sharp eyes and ears to Washington. Who could have anticipated that Higgins would get a crush on J. Gordon Liddy, one of the creepiest villains of the drama, and would pillory Judge John Sirica, one of its heroes? Higgins's "The Friends of Richard Nixon" made for entertaining reading, but it was so perversely contradictory of the common perception—surely mine—of the Watergate case that it more than met my criterion of unpredictability. And it had the virtue of letting J. Gordon Liddy know that he had at least one friend left in this world.

As a footnote to Watergate's revelations I later wrote on the Editor's Page a brief note of appreciation to Mr. Nixon and his staff for having included me in the elite company of the three hundred or so citizens on the Nixon "enemies list," an honor that may have explained why my federal income tax returns had been audited three times during the Nixon regime. (Got a clean bill of health each time.)

After Vietnam and Watergate a natural tendency of Americans was to look inward. LBJ's Great Society was first undercut by his guns-*and*-butter economics, then gutted by the indifference of a succession of Republican administrations. The high aspirations of the 1960s civil rights struggle was mocked by the continuing complacency of the public and the growing poverty and homelessness in the inner cities. We attempted to take readers inside the lives of urban blacks when the writer James Alan McPherson turned to nonfiction. In one probing article he wrote about a Jekyll-and-Hyde sort of black street gang in Chicago and efforts to turn its energies to community betterment. In another he documented an important legal battle that
378 opened decently priced housing to blacks on Chicago's South

Side. Not crowd-rousing subjects, I knew, but they were subjects that deserved to be laid before the more comfortable citizenry.

An excerpt from an impressive philippic by Arthur Schlesinger, Jr., spelled out the dangers posed by "the Imperial Presidency" of the kind attempted by Richard Nixon. Then, as if to heed Schlesinger's warning, came the somnolent presidency of Gerald Ford and the puzzling reign of Jimmy Carter. I lost my right-hand man, Michael Janeway, to the Carter administration, which he joined as an aide to Secretary of State Cyrus Vance (a post he kept until he tired of writing speeches for an official whom he felt wasn't sure what he wanted to say), but I gained a new Washington editor.

James Fallows, not long out of Harvard, was another frustrated speech writer. He joined President Carter's staff. After a few weeks inside the White House circle he was startled by the president's passion for petty details. When Fallows left the presidential staff to resume his journalistic career I persuaded him to write for *The Atlantic.* In his memorable first article he told how the president of the greatest superpower, engulfed by the cares of a turbulent world, personally oversaw each day's list of those privileged to use the White House tennis court. His unique insight into the president's character, sympathetic but critical, was widely reported in the press.

The post-Vietnam impulse to look more closely at our own country led me also to publish special supplements on regions of the United States. A special issue on Texas brought together a dozen writers, most of them Texans and some of them damned proud of it, who produced a frolicsome issue, heavily inclined toward bizarre politics and official chicanery. I drew three lessons from that special issue. First, never offer in print a recipe for chicken-fried steak; I doubt there are two Texans who agree on exactly what it is and how to cook it. Second, don't eat one. Third, future supplements might be more effective if fewer hands did the cooking.

I next commissioned my friend and former editor at *Time,* Tom Griffith, to go back and portray the land he came from, the Pacific Northwest. Far removed from the usual travel article gushes about golden sunsets and happy cookouts in bosky **379** dells, Griffith's "God's Country: Please Keep Out" let you hear the giant trees falling in the forests and worry with the people around Hanford who lived day by day with the threat of nuclear pollution, but also made engagingly clear why nonetheless the Northwest was a beguiling place in which to live. In the following year we presented an equally substantial portrait of "Rocky Mountain Country" by a father-and-son team, the historian and novelist Wallace Stegner and his son Page. The writing shone with the father's deep knowledge of the mountain country and his son's shared love for it.

Projects like these were necessary to sustain our franchise as a magazine of depth, of ideas and imagination in a new climate of magazines aimed at very specific audiences—automobile buffs, orchid growers, muscle builders, rock fans—and hostile to general magazines. When our small group sat around the large, littered table in my office every week or so to plan for the months ahead we always had plenty of notions about what we needed to do but we lacked the resources to execute them.

Embarrassingly low staff salaries needed to be raised. Whenever I negotiated fees and expenses with writers and artists (or their agents) I felt as if I were wearing dark glasses, walking with an incurable limp, and holding out a tin cupful of pencils. The ludicrously insufficient monthly budget of only $10,000 to $12,000 for articles had to be at least doubled, preferably tripled. The magazine was in severe need of a design face-lift and, after years of stubbornly avoiding the tyranny of an art director, I now realized that it was time not only for a redesign but for the hiring of a top-flight, full-time designer with a handsome budget.

Circulation was growing (it had passed 300,000) but too slowly, not enough to bring in the necessary cash, nor when combined with the circulation numbers of our weakening partner-rival *Harper's,* was it enough to bring in enough advertising income. We were running in the red. In order to make money we needed to put in more money, at least a few tens of thousands a year for editorial ventures and more also for promotion, even though the only true way to sustain a larger loyal audience is to improve a magazine's content. We could be proud of our National Magazine Awards, a total of four by

380

1978, more than any magazine up to that time except *The New Yorker,* which put out fifty-two issues a year against our twelve. But past achievements were exactly that—past. We needed more resources to make what I considered to be a good magazine into a great one. Where was the money to come from?

In more than forty years in journalism I had never met an employer more thoughtful or more generous than the company's owner and president, Marion Danielson Campbell. Her respect for editorial freedom and her willingness to let Garth Hite run the business free of interference and second-guessing made our jobs as publisher and editor among the most enviable in the trade (though admittedly not in terms of pay). She had taken no profits, had reached into her own pocket to flesh out the company's meager pension fund, and assumed the burden of a substantial loan to carry us through a temporary cash shortage. She allowed a dozen of us key employees to buy shares in the company at a low price to induce us to stay on. She had substantial wealth of her own, but the bulk of it was in the stern control of trust managers in Chicago. She had recently undergone difficult but successful cancer surgery; neither of her two sons had any interest in the company. The trust managers looked at the *The Atlantic* and the Atlantic Monthly Press with a disinterest amounting to contempt. They were not going to invest more in the company.

In this condition the company might have survived for a long time to come, but life at 8 Arlington Street would have become increasingly frustrating and unsatisfying. By early 1979 it had become apparent that we must look outside for a healthy infusion of cash if we wanted to live happily ever after. Marion Campbell and the board of directors, including two outside holders of small blocks of stock, gave Garth Hite and me the mission of finding an outside investor who would become part owner. If we found no such enlightened citizen, Marion Campbell was willing, though reluctantly, to sell the business outright to a company or, preferably, an individual, provided the buyer would promise to keep the enterprise in Boston and would guarantee to provide additional cash injections of $500,000 or so a year for three to five years to carry us into a growth pattern and a bright future. As a first step we commissioned Bankers **381**

Trust Company to undertake a complete examination of the company and prepare an analysis of it and an estimate of its worth. The Bankers Trust agents surveyed our past and present and came up with what they termed an approving report they said was conservative. They thought the company, with its real estate, its great goodwill, and its future prospects, worth six to seven million dollars.

Garth Hite and I tucked the Bankers Trust study into our pockets, equipped ourselves with tents, mosquito netting, machetes, a corkscrew, a few gallons of insect repellant, and a supply of cleft sticks for sending back messages. Then we set forth into the forbidding jungle of entrepreneurial America.

Chapter 22

Snakebit

To put the Hite-Manning jungle-trek into context I must take a somewhat eccentric detour, by way of the work of the charming artist, Saul Steinberg. In addition to being a great cartoonist and an imaginative painter, Steinberg established himself as probably the country's best-known cartographer with his memorable *New Yorker* map of the United States. A large land mass called Manhattan sits in the foreground, bounded on the west by a mighty river called the Hudson, then the irrelevant rest of America except for Hollywood recedes into the background in ever-diminishing strips of color.

With grateful credit to Steinberg's salute to geographical subjectivity, I now present Manning's Exceedingly Selective List of Major World Disasters and Catastrophes:

A.D. 410 The Visigoths sack Rome under leadership of Alaric, a very thorough workman
   1066 October 14, William the Conqueror and one of his Norman archers defeat King Harold and his English defenders at Hastings
   1348 Bubonic plague, the Black Death, sweeps Britain and Europe
   1769 First great Indian famine strikes Hindustan

1840 Cholera epidemic encircles the world

1863 A young American printer, John W. Hyatt, makes first synthetic billiard ball from nitrocellulose. This has merit of conserving precious ivory but foreordains by several decades the coming of the age of plastics

1871 October 8, Patrick O'Leary's cow kicks over flaming lantern in Chicago; smell of burned bacon permeates Midwest

1906 April 19, Earthquake destroys San Francisco, except for veteran columnist Herb Caen

1912 April 15, SS *Titanic* hits iceberg; 1,595 drown as band plays on

1914 June 28, Gavrilo Princip assassinates Archduke Francis Ferdinand at Sarajevo, precipitating World War I, which lays groundwork for World War II

1917 April 16, Vladimir Lenin returns from exile at Finland Station in St. Petersburg, later to be called Leningrad, and later yet to be called St. Petersburg

1929 October 29, New York stock market crashes; Great Depression follows, starring Henry Fonda and immense supporting cast

1939 September 1, Adolf Hitler's armies invade Poland, with lamentable results

1954 Bill Haley's recording of song called "Shake, Rattle and Roll" rises to list of Top Ten Records; rock and roll era has arrived

1977 March 27, KLM and Pan Am planes collide *on runway* (!) at Tenerife, Canary Islands, killing 582 in history's worst aviation disaster

1979 June 17, Robert Manning lunches with real estate developer Mortimer B. Zuckerman at Boston's Downtown Harvard Club

The sixties were a great time to be in Boston if you were quick with the abacus, aching to get rich, and knew how to turn empty lots, rusting railyards, condemned buildings, and one of the world's renowned burlesque theaters into big money. For the previous thirty years there had been such deep mistrust between the Yankees who held the pursestrings and James Michael Curley and the other Irish pols who held city hall that the city had fallen into deep stagnation. Rather than subject themselves to what they feared would be systematized grand larceny (or, if you looked at it from the other side, benevolent Robinhoodery) the Yankee leadership of Boston's insurance, investment, banking, and law firms, a powerful group that came to be

384

known as The Vault, had withheld investment and thereby imposed a moratorium on the development and growth of their
city. The appalling total of one private building of significance
had been built between 1925 and 1960. After Curley was succeeded by a succession of mayors they thought they could trust,
the Yankees opened wide the door of The Vault. The real estate
developers poured in, salivating and holding wide-mouthed
satchels in their hands. The youngest and probably brightest of
them all was Mortimer B. Zuckerman.

The building boom that created "the new Boston" was already underway when Zuckerman joined the feeding frenzy. He
was born on June 4, 1937, into a well-to-do family in Montreal,
Canada, "a small country to the north of the United States,
generally unknown in this country," as he came to describe his
native land after he became an American citizen. He graduated
from Montreal's McGill University with a degree in political
philosophy and then took a law degree from the McGill Law
School, a master's degree in business administration from the
Wharton School, and a master's in law from Harvard Law
School. At twenty-five he became the *wunderkind* of a real estate
development firm with one of the most properly Bostonian
names imaginable, Cabot, Cabot and Forbes. Zuckerman rose
quickly at CC&F in rank, responsibility, and personal wealth.
Then something unpleasant happened, culminating in a firing
or a resignation depending on whom one believes; at any rate,
Zuckerman and the firm parted company. They met again in
court where, after considerable wrangling, Zuckerman won a
judgment of five million dollars, give or take a couple of million. By then Zuckerman had formed Boston Properties, a development firm which he owned 50-50 with a partner who was
content to stay behind the potted palms and concede all the
limelight to Zuckerman. Mort, as he was called by some, or
Mortie, as he was called by others, got somewhat more of the
limelight than he wanted when Boston Properties proposed to
rehabilitate a schlock-ridden four-block area of the city with an
elaborate high-rise complex of office and apartment buildings
called Park Plaza. When they discovered that the proposed
high-rise structures would forever block the sunlight from Bos-   **385**

ton's Public Garden, one of the loveliest urban beauty spots in the world, a large cross-section of citizens united in outrage to block it.

The handsome tax loss he must have taken on the Park Plaza project did not entirely assuage Zuckerman's hurt at this rebuke by his adopted city, but by the time I met him in the mid-seventies in a routine "Nice to meet you" exchange at some otherwise forgotten Cambridge cocktail party Zuckerman seemed to be displaying little bitterness. His design for one of those expensively cheap Marriott hotels to be built on Boston's waterfront came in dead last out of eight entries in the design competition, but Zuckerman had a friend at city hall. With the energetic backing of Mayor Kevin White he was about to clinch the deal to build it. He had many other deals cooking, in the Boston and Washington, D.C., areas, in California and elsewhere, and he had reached, or was just edging onto, *Forbes Magazine*'s list of the 400 Richest Americans (estimated fortune then: $150 million).

After that first brief meeting Maggie and I found ourselves on Zuckerman's occasional guest list for his usually populous parties. Zuckerman entertained a lot at his residence in Spruce Street, a house large enough in Beacon Hill terms to be called a mansion. He was expensively installed there, served by a Chinese chef named Ah Shu, who had a talent for carving turnips, carrots, and other root vegetables into the likenesses of rabbits, squirrels, and other rodents, and Au Shu's wife, who cleaned and served (and was called Gezundheit by some irreverent guests). Zuckerman was a genial host, circulating to see that all were properly watered and nourished, stopping now and then to insert a joke or an amiable banality into one of the conversations. He was a small, trim man who dressed expensively, eschewed his own booze, and obviously took good physical care of himself in other ways as well. He displayed the nervous movements and darting eyes of one who is never comfortable standing in one place, always itching to move on to the conversation in the next room or in business life to the next deal. He was not at all bashful about his wealth or his desire to make more. His way of showing it off did not quite qualify as flaunting, though. Rather, I remember thinking, he displayed it as if it

386

were a grand tool, somewhat in the manner of a violinist showing off his newly acquired Guarnerius or perhaps a sculptor displaying his expensive new set of chisels. All in all, I found him an interesting character, obviously very smart, with an apparent sense of humor, much amiability, and smooth power of persuasion. Even though he seemed always to be smiling, a somewhat disconcerting characteristic, there was plainly an interesting and complex personality beneath the veneer. What really lay—or did not—beneath the confident-seeming, cheery surface I did not know, but what I saw of him I found charming, even likeable.

At one of those parties Zuckerman remarked that he was fascinated with journalism. He pointed to a dozen or more magazines sprayed across his huge coffee table and said he was "a real magazine maven"; he had in fact explored the possibility of buying or investing in several publications. These, I learned later, were *Esquire* and *Washingtonian* magazines and also the once-yeasty New York weekly, *The Village Voice.* I had no way of knowing how serious those overtures were. Later, though, sometime in 1977 or 1978, he told me he was wondering whether to buy *Boston Magazine,* a booster-type monthly that the Chamber of Commerce had sold to an absentee publisher in Philadelphia. By coincidence, Garth Hite and I had explored the possibility of *The Atlantic*'s buying *Boston* a few years earlier, when the Chamber first put it up for sale. I invited Zuckerman to our offices to meet with Garth. We told him about our earlier, aborted plan for bringing *Boston* under *The Atlantic* roof and making it a better, even profitable publication by taking advantage of the advertising, circulation, and accounting mechanisms as well as editorial talent we already had in place. Zuckerman seemed intrigued by that idea, but nothing came of his approach to *Boston*'s owners. We heard no more from him about it.

It was about two years later when those brief conversations with Zuckerman floated back into my mind. Our search had produced no angel willing to become an investor. It had aroused some serious but temporary interest from some big players. One approach came from Richard Snyder, who was in the process of transforming Simon and Schuster from an al-   387

ready large octopus into the Great Giant Squid of book publishers. He invited Garth and me to lunch with him and the
president of Gulf & Western (now Paramount Corp.), the conglomerate that owned S&S. The food and wine were delicious
and the view of Central Park superb, but the conversation
deteriorated when the president indicated that he had never
seen *The Atlantic,* let alone read it, but had been told that it was
some kind of "intellectual" magazine. He spoke the word "intellectual" in the tone of voice of one who had just stepped in
dog shit with his new custom-made Peal shoes. When he learned
that it might cost S&S six or seven million dollars to acquire the
company and that it almost certainly would never reach a profit
margin of more than a few percentage points, the meeting was
for all practical purposes over. We went home with the comforting knowledge that we were not going to become just another tentacle of the Great Giant Squid.

The reputation of *The Atlantic* meant something to Kay Graham and her son Donald, and when they learned that it might
be for sale they dispatched to Boston a high-powered team of
seven or eight executives, including the president of the Washington Post company and the publisher of *Newsweek,* to examine the company. For two days they thumped and prodded the
torso, took CPA blood samples, examined the books, pored
over years of certified audits, pondered the long-term bottom-
line potential. Their conclusion was what we had already told
them: *The Atlantic* could be a possession to be proud of, but it
could never be counted on to make anyone rich or make stockholders in a big corporation happy.

There were several other knocks on the door, mostly from
big, profit-driven companies like Hearst, Canada's Thomson
Group, and the giant Bertelsmann empire in West Germany. In
contrast, there came an approach by a smart young Boston-
based attorney who was interested in buying the company if he
could assemble a few investing partners. At this I reminded
Garth Hite of our original meeting with Mortimer Zuckerman
and suggested that I inquire whether Zuckerman, dynamic,
young, rich, socially ambitious, and a self-proclaimed "magazine maven," might care to be one of those investors in our

388

prestigious enterprise. Why not? Garth shrugged. So I made a date for lunch. Be my guest, said Mort Zuckerman. Harvard Club Downtown, June 17 at 12:15.

Mort and I had hardly begun sipping the Harvard Club's vintage V-8 juice, or whatever it was, when he asked how *The Atlantic* was doing. It was just the opening I had expected, and wanted. I told him in some detail of our frustrations, of the desire to raise the magazine and book publishing operation off their plateau, of our interest in finding an investor. Zuckerman seemed most interested in what he was hearing. He quickly made clear he was not of a mind to become just an investor, nor was he willing to hook up with any group of would-be buyers. If he were interested at all, he said, he would want to be sole owner of the enterprise. I reported to Garth Hite that we had a flicker of interest from a man of means.

That flicker of interest grew quickly into lustful pursuit. He would be interested in buying the company outright, he told us, but only if Hite and I would stay with the enterprise and run it for him since he knew absolutely nothing about magazine or book publishing. Over the next few months, he flung a dizzying succession of offers at Hite, Marion Campbell, and the Chicago lawyer whom Mrs. Campbell's financial managers had chosen to represent the company. Each offer had a deadline attached, but frequently a new one would come in before the previous one could be studied. That was the way real estate developers make their deals, someone who had worked with Zuckerman explained. On one occasion he delivered an offer to Garth Hite, discussed it with him for a while, then a few minutes after leaving he picked up the car phone in his Mercedes to deliver an extensively revised proposal. While Zuckerman was fiddling with figures and playing with complicated pay-out schemes a small group of well-to-do Bostonians entered the scene with a proposal offering a somewhat higher purchase price than Zuckerman's. Hite, Mrs. Campbell, and I liked the look of the people and their offer, but the Boston group didn't really have its proposition in solid shape and as far as the Chicago managers were concerned, it was now late in the game. While the "the North Shore group," as we called it, asked for more time, its **389** intervention worked like a shot of adrenaline on Zuckerman. He stopped his mating dance and moved toward a more businesslike proposal.

By early 1980, after Zuckerman and his minions had consulted with many outside experts and people in publishing, he assembled the essentials of a deal: Zuckerman would pay in four yearly installments $3.6 million for *The Atlantic Monthly,* the Atlantic Monthly Press, and the primely placed real estate. I thought the figure too small considering the value calculated by Bankers Trust and considering the rich package Zuckerman would be getting. But Hite and I felt that far more important than the money we stockholders would receive was Zuckerman's agreement in writing to plow at least another $1.5 million above the purchase price into the company's editorial and promotion budgets over the next three years—the means we felt could put the company on a growth course. And then there were his solemn promise to keep the company in Boston and his equally solemn promise, sealed with contracts, to keep Hite as publisher and Manning as editor in chief. Not only would he insist on our staying in our jobs, said Zuckerman, but he would be too busy with his burgeoning real estate operations to have time for playing a major role in the company even if he wanted to, which (said he with a look of sincerity as beatific as a Botticelli smile) he did not.

These were welcome words, since before giving over to a younger successor I was eager to see *The Atlantic* invigorated and to enjoy at least a brief fling, no more than year or so, at running the magazine and presiding over the book publishing operation when there was enough money to spend. A purchase and sale agreement was duly signed by Zuckerman and Marion Campbell, and his pursuit of all crumbs of information—the process called due diligence—went on apace. Zuckerman had a school of sharp-toothed lawyers working out the most advantageous tax arrangements and a daunting list of warranties he expected from the sellers. He conferred with our Bankers Trust advisers. He sought the advice of a variety of financial, newspaper, and magazine people. He or his lawyers and accountants examined every detail of the company's condition, including more than twenty years of certified audits, showing that as it moved into the 1980s the company was losing money.

Over the next several weeks he and I conferred several times about editorial matters and I presented him with a detailed outline of what I felt we could accomplish with additional resources. He met far more frequently with Hite to learn the financial realities and to be made aware among other things of many intangibles, like the persistent rise in the costs of paper, printing, postage, and the other unpredictables in publishing a magazine. In his enthusiasm he even expressed interest in also buying ailing *Harper's Magazine,* which was suffering more than *The Atlantic* from our mutual problems. He persuaded Hite to compose for him a hypothetical scenario, a set of figures that Hite carefully explained were "back of an envelope" speculations and "guesstimates," suggesting what might happen if the two venerable journals were brought under our roof. This was a prospect I found especially exciting.

The thought occurred, of course, that Zuckerman could be offering his fervent assurances only because he sensed (correctly) that without Hite's and Manning's enthusiastic endorsement, he would not succeed in buying the company whatever his offer. Yet I found him altogether persuasive, especially when he offered both Hite and me those contracts binding us to our jobs for up to five years. Unlike most contracts, ours offered no severance pay or other extra compensation, but I saw in them the additional virtue of putting us in a position to protect the rest of the company's thirty-two employees. Now that I had become more familiar with Zuckerman and his ideas I sensed shortcomings—a tendency toward banality, an addiction to clichés—that, odd as it might seem, were reassuring. These deficiencies helped me to find it entirely believable that, while he was perhaps one of the smartest money men in the country, and while in his earlier explorations he had accumulated a considerable body of knowledge about magazine finances, Zuckerman intuited that he had neither the intellectual touch nor the political and social sagacity to put out a magazine without an experienced publisher and an experienced editor in charge. That is how I reasoned. So I supported the sale, blithely confident that I would enjoy for the first time the pleasure of having the financial resources to make the promise of continued editorial free- **391** dom more meaningful. Then I would happily slide away from the heavy pressures and demands of a job that had consumed more than a quarter of my lifetime. I even had the well-qualified successor in mind.

The deal was consummated on April 30, 1980. In a high-rent law firm office overlooking gleaming Boston harbor the schools of lawyers for both parties with their time clocks running at full speed shuffled papers, Zuckerman handed over a bundle of checks as first installment payments to the dozen or more *Atlantic* stockholders as well as duly signed contracts to Publisher Hite and Editor in Chief Manning, and we handed over to him title to "the . . . old . . . true magical light." It was a serious, even somber event, this passing of an American institution from one hand to another, still there were handshakes and smiles all around.

That was the last time Zuckerman and I smiled at one another. The "Dear Bob" letter reached my desk barely a week later, on May 7, 1980.

It was short but decidedly unsweet.

In clumsy but easily understandable prose the letter announced that Zuckerman was assuming the title of Chairman of the Board of Editors, which title would be emblazoned at the top of the masthead and separated from the names of the rest of the staff; that he would have an office at the magazine which he intended to occupy several days a week; that he intended to be involved in "all elements" of editorial policy. He would, he said, review all editorial ideas, participate in the hiring of editors and in editorial and story conferences.

Uh-oh! I had just met the real Mort Zuckerman.

Gone was the eager little tycoon in custom-tailored Uriah Heep's clothing who was too busy, and who anyway affected to lack the desire or the expertise to run a magazine. Zuckerman said nothing to me about replacing me as editor in chief, nor did he indicate in any way that he was looking for a replacement. He proceeded to evict one of the top editors and assigned that desirable office to himself, but he did not move into it. His letter obviously was not really what it seemed, a move to take for himself my duties and my authority. I saw it instead as a crude first step toward replacing me by establishing conditions that would impel me to resign. Zuckerman was vain, ambitious, calculating and, as I now had reason to believe, suavely deceitful, but he wasn't stupid: He knew that no one other than a pitiful hack would serve as the *Atlantic*'s nominal editor under the conditions he was specifying.

When I got to my feet after reading the letter, clutching my groin in pain and dripping blood from the dagger beneath the left clavicle, I decided to hold in the clinches until the mind cleared and I could see what Zuckerman did next. To resign would mean to renounce the terms of our contract, something that would make Zuckerman exceedingly happy and relieve him outright of the obviously unpleasant task of keeping his word. So I went about the job as I was obliged to do under a contract which stipulated that for the next several years, should I choose to do so, I would perform "the same functions" I had long performed as the top editor responsible for all final editorial decisions and for superintending the editorial operations of the AMP as well.

Though he carefully hid his movements from me, I learned later that Zuckerman was then already bounding about like a wallaby in heat in search of a new editor in chief. He sought suggestions right and left from highly placed people in the trade like Ben Bradlee of the *Washington Post*. He bounded to Austin, Texas, to dangle a tentative invitation before Bill Broyles, the bright and attractive editor of the *Texas Monthly* (and the man who had assembled most of our special supplement on Texas). He flew with a party of friends to London on the Concorde in order to interview Harold Evans, the hotshot editor of London's *Sunday Times* and *Times*. How many were offered or tantalized with the possibility of being offered the job I never did learn, but I did learn that in some if not all instances Zuckerman told candidates that he was conducting his search with my full knowledge and approval. He gave this same assurance to the man to whom he was finally about to offer the job. What symmetry! Zuckerman's choice happened to be the very person I was going to ask him to bring in as his and my annointed successor.

After leaving Cyrus Vance's State Department, Michael Janeway, partly with my help, had become a major editor under 393

Tom Winship at the *Boston Globe.* Mike had been my strong right hand at the magazine for several years. He had contributed much to the magazine and the press. Also he had developed his own strong notions of what *The Atlantic* should be and how he would edit it, and he obviously had discussed those freely with Zuckerman. Janeway found me by telephone when I was a visiting some friends on Martha's Vineyard and said he was sorry about what was happening.

What *is* happening, Mike? I asked, wondering but suddenly suspecting what he could be apologizing for. Janeway was taken aback by my surprise. When Zuckerman picked him as editor, he said, Mort had assured him that he had told me in advance of his plan to replace me with Janeway. So Janeway had called me in the light of our long association and friendship, intending, I guessed, to thank me for being both understanding and approving of what was going on. Even though I had him in mind as my successor, I was jolted by the discovery that my former chief lieutenant, a protégé, in fact, had been dickering with Zuckerman. As for Janeway, he seemed embarrassed and disturbed. After he hung up, he got in touch with Zuckerman to express his surprise that Zuckerman had not told me, as he vowed he had. Zuckerman was outraged that Janeway had committed such treachery as to tell me what was going on. Negotiations between them came to an abrupt, ill-tempered end.

Now the Chairman of the Board of Editors had to start his search all over again, this time in plain view of his victim. I was tense with shock and anger over the sneak attack. I had never been fired from any job, unless the Herald Trib fiasco counted as a sacking. I had not been without one since I was fifteen years old. Now I was approaching my sixtieth birthday, not exactly prime time for job-seeking. A flickering image appeared before me that I once had laughed at, the image of Edward G. Robinson in the final frames of the movie *Little Caesar.* Crumpled at the foot of a wall, bleeding from a surfeit of fatal wounds, he half-groaned, half-prayed, "Mother of Mercy, is this the end of Rocco?" Rocco, I ruefully reflected, was luckier in at least one respect; I had taken all my slugs in the back.

394   Cold anger, the sort that leaves no room for panic or self-

pity, was my dominant emotion. Much of it was directed at myself for having been so beguiled, so undiscerning, so unsophisticated—all right, so *stupid*—as to fall prey to such blatant duplicity. But there was plenty of anger left over for Zuckerman. I tried to step back from the scene and look at this objectively: I had to concede that there was no question about Zuckerman's right to dump me and install someone else, even himself (Mother of Mercy!), in my job. After all, he owned the joint (though he hadn't yet paid for it). What he didn't have a right to do was to go cravenly behind my back, violate all his promises, and expect me to accept that sort of treatment without a fight.

When Mort realized that he'd been found out, he suggested that we talk the whole thing over like two gentlemen. I could not understand how a man with such a head for figures could calculate that one + zero = two, but I joined him at the Ritz Café to tender my compliments, to wit (but not necessarily in this order) that he was a liar, a deceiver, a moral coward and probably a physical one too, and more pathetic than all that, his inability to behave in a decent way had lost him the chance to bring about a change of command without bloodshed and without unpleasant publicity. Had he been candid with me about his desires he would have known that I was eager to suggest that he bring in the very Mr. Janeway forthwith on the understanding that I'd give over command to him within a year, even sooner. That would allow me a brief time to enjoy the new opportunities I had done so much to bring about and also allow me a graceful exit. "But you didn't have the wit or the guts to deal with me up front," I said.

Mort nodded his head and sighed in what I took to be agreement with that sentiment, but just to make sure, I put it into the present tense: "You don't have the wit or the guts." He sighed again. Then, like the obtuse fellow in the sick joke who says, "All right, Mrs. Lincoln, but how did you like the play?" he said he planned to continue his search and he wanted to tell all candidates that his search had my blessing. I said Nothing doing, not after the scurvy way he'd behaved; what's more, I have a contract. Mort left me with the Ritz check.

Contracts, it seemed, meant little to Zuckerman. The ink was **395** barely dry on the sale documents when he began demanding that Marion Campbell meet with him and discuss reductions in the purchase price. Failing that, he began to mutter ominously to Hite and to me that he was unhappy with the company's financial figures. "With a guy like Zuckerman," said a veteran of the real estate wars, "the signing of the final documents means that the negotiations now begin." As for my contract, it didn't really mean what it said, Zuckerman maintained in a manner so authoritative it suggested much familiarity with the art of getting around written agreements. As he interpreted it, he went on, it allowed him to replace me and assign me to whatever task he chose for me. Again he asked, Why didn't I just lie down and accept a cozy little senior editorship and a back office and help him find my successor? Then we could tell the newspapers that all was sweet and peaceful at *The Atlantic.* No thanks, I said. More than once in our bitter exchanges in person or on the telephone Zuckerman fell into little-boy-like tantrums; his voice would rise and a lisp would creep into his speech. He pleaded with Hite to persuade me to see reason (meaning, keep further dispute from reaching the press). He was "pithed off" by my unreasonableness, he told Garth, "really pithed off." What he seemed or feigned not to understand was that while he had the power and even the legal right as owner to force me out, I wasn't going to help him braid the rope for my own hanging.

A hanging it was. Zuckerman found the man he wanted in William Whitworth, a long-time editor at *The New Yorker,* widely respected by writers and other editors and almost certainly the best of all the many choices he apparently had been considering. Whitworth had been an early choice but resisted until Zuckerman offered him a contract that provided well over double my salary plus tax-free perks and a piece of a future Zuckerman real estate development. With the help of the same expensive lawyers who had helped construct my worthless employment contract I got a separation paper that allowed me or obliged me (I am not sure which) to edit a few more of the magazine issues I was then shaping, giving Whitworth time to get ready, and in return got yet another written promise from Zuckerman, this one adding a few peanuts—some $750 a month—to the small pension I was to receive after sixteen plus years of labor at the Atlantic Monthly Company in return for my departure from the premises.

Inevitably, word of our head-on collision reached the press. Zuckerman could not have been pleased by some of what he read. In my anger at the devious way in which I'd been treated, I did not resist invitations to prick at what I was delighted to discover was Zuckerman's overblown vanity and tissue-thin skin. I tailored Fred Allen's characterization of Hollywood to fit Mort: "All of his integrity would fit into the navel of a flea. And there'd be room left over for a caraway seed and his heart."* I lamented to another reporter that if the estimable custom of dueling were still in practice, one of us would now be dead, Zuckerman from a shot through the heart but more likely Manning from a shot in the back. A lengthy *Washington Post* profile of the new media baron by the writer James Conaway benefitted greatly, I thought, from my well-displayed comment that he was "a liar and a cheat." (The same article attributed to some of my friends the comment that for all his experience in the real world, Manning was exceedingly naive about human nature. I was too chastened to disagree.)

The December 1980 issue of *The Atlantic* was the 177th I had edited, the last of some 22,000 pages containing perhaps 25,000,000 words which, for better or worse, all carried my fingerprints. The circulation had grown to about 335,000 from the approximately 200,000 I had started with. My last Editor's Page was a farewell love letter to those far-flung readers as well as the magazine's contributors and advertisers. "Above all, it has been an honor and an education," it said in part. "An honor to have been able to preach and pout and cavil and kick the can of laughter and sentiment with literally millions of Americans and not a few thousand other inhabitants of this capricious planet. An education to discover from month to

---

*There are two versions of the Allen original: (1) "You can take all the sincerity in Hollywood and stuff it in a flea's navel, along with nine mustard seeds, and still have room for an agent's heart"; and (2) "You can take all the sincerity in Hollywood, place it in the navel of a fruit fly and still have room enough for three caraway seeds and a producer's heart."

month and from one published book to the next, the infinite variety of pleasures, insights, friendships, and provocations that can come to one who works in the realm of ideas, opinions, and literary artistry."

For the first time since I walked into the *Binghamton Press* forty-three years before, I did not know what I was going to do next, but I wasn't going to be allowed to sit around and moan the blues. When an invitation came to spend a semester at the Institute of Politics at Harvard, Maggie urged me to take it as a means of reboxing my compass. The Institute was the yeasty, venturesome part of the young but already ponderous Kennedy School of Government, where bureaucrats are trained to be more bureaucratic. Each semester the Institute brought in a half dozen or so people from government and journalism to mingle with undergraduates and faculty, conduct once-a-week seminars on subjects of their choosing, and, as in the Nieman program, partake of Harvard courses. This was just the right sanctuary: Most of the half-dozen other Fellows had themselves been rudely deposed from their jobs. The good Senator John Culver of Iowa had been upset in the fall election. Three middle-to-high-level officials of the Carter administration had given way to Reagan appointees. A formidable young colonel of the Nigerian Army had been forced into exile by a coup in Lagos. Another was on brief leave as the much put-upon only woman in the New Zealand parliament. The amiable, relaxed camaraderie of fellow *déposeés* was very good medicine, an effective preventative of feeling sorry for oneself or worrying about the future. What is more, the need to find useful things to present at my weekly seminar on the press and public affairs was demanding enough to leave little time for brooding. I do not think my efforts brought much in the way of enlightenment to the undergraduate and graduate students who participated in the seminar, but I learned that teaching can be at least as difficult as journalism and that I probably was not made to be a teacher. So while continuing to finish my fellowship at the Institute I accepted with pleasure an opportunity to return to my trade. I signed on as editor in chief of an ambitious series of copiously illustrated history books dealing with a subject I felt I had come

398

to know something about. The series was called *The Vietnam Experience.*

The Institute of Politics was proving to be an excellent decompression chamber and I was contentedly facing the prospect of this new adventure in the word trade when Mortimer Zuckerman struck again. On April 30, 1981, the day the next installment payments were due, he announced that he was withholding most of the second installment of his debt to *Atlantic* stockholders and would not pay any of the future installments. His reason for not paying the balance of some $2.5 million, he said, was that he had been misled about the financial state of the company. Incredible! Zuckerman, the brilliant moneyman able to read a balance sheet from around a corner, and his minions had known every particle of truth about the condition of the company, including the important fact that it was losing money and would need substantial transfusions. For a pitifully small price he had gotten a magnificent bargain: one of the country's most prestigious magazines, a book publishing operation with several prize-winning authors in its stable and whose backlist alone was worth as much as $2 million over the next ten years,* and two beautifully located town houses worth probably another $2 million. All that and the honor that went with it for only $3,600,000. This was not enough. Now Mort was on the verge of giving cupidity a new dimension.

Where my own rude treatment at the hands of Zuckerman had made me angry at myself for being so naive, this turn of events deepened that feeling to one of shame and guilt. By bringing him into our lives I had jeopardized the holdings, even the livelihoods of every person associated with *The Atlantic.* I'd exposed them to the whims of a man who lived by his own abbreviated version of the Golden Rule: Do others. What if, as now seemed entirely possible, he broke all his other promises and trashed the magazine and the AMP? Sadly I confessed to

*Zuckerman subsequently sold the Atlantic Monthly Press for a price reported in the newspapers to be $3 million. That figure may be exaggerated, but he certainly recouped a substantial amount of what he had contracted to pay for the entire company.

an inquiring writer for *Boston* magazine: "I'll carry guilt for this to my grave."

Next destination was the courtroom, or so we thought. Marion Campbell and the rest of us major stockholders filed suit against Zuckerman, demanding that he pay what he owed. Zuckerman countered with a suit charging us with fraud in what he maintained was misrepresentation of the company's financial condition. Innocently desiring only to serve the public good by preserving a cultural institution, he had been confused and duped by the figures he got from Garth Hite, or so he alleged. He sued for $25,000,000 in damages. I had expected to join Campbell, Hite, and the others in bringing the suit in federal court, but as a Massachusetts citizen I was required to sue in the state court. So I did. We plaintiffs shared a team of attorneys from one of Boston's best law firms, Hill and Barlow. Zuckerman took on one of the town's great white sharks and a small school of his sharklings to handle his side of the case.

We pressed for an early trial, but a trial wasn't really what Zuckerman wanted. His strategy, it quickly became apparent, was to drag out the pretrial proceedings for as long as possible, all the while avoiding payment and probably hoping that even the resources of Marion Campbell, who was paying almost all our legal costs, would not take the strain. Meanwhile, having been angered by the earlier bad press he had received, Zuckerman waged a clever campaign of character assassination, depicting his opponents as calculating defrauders and himself as an innocent victim. At cocktail parties he waved about some old memos Garth Hite had written to our treasurer and circulation manager. They were, in typical Hite fashion, somewhat hyperbolic but altogether proper, telling them to make the company's financial figures look as good as possible. Yet Zuckerman flaunted them as evidence of a cooking of the books, neglecting to point out that in those same memos Hite had sternly ordered that in all their accounting they avoid "anything illegal or unethical." To my surprise and pain, Zuckerman got considerable help from the *New York Times,* a place where I had some friends. So, it appeared, did Zuckerman. The *Times* Sunday magazine ran a lengthy piece that maligned Garth Hite, dismissed with contempt most of the fruit of my sixteen years'

400

labor at the magazine, and in effect gave credence without proof to Zuckerman's spurious argument that he had been defrauded. When I protested and pointed out among other omissions and flaws the dimensions of the great bargain Zuckerman had achieved for himself, the magazine's editor responded that they were irrelevant.

Most offensive was the help Zuckerman got from his good friend Martin Peretz, a charmless, rich-by-marriage ex-radical at Harvard who had bought the honorable old *New Republic* and was converting it from an intelligently liberal into a neo-conservative journal whose several commendable attributes were diluted by its insistence on being a sort of house organ for the state of Israel. In print, Peretz leveled the ugly charge that anti-Semitism was what motivated animus toward Zuckerman on the part of the plaintiffs and as well as other Bostonians and the *Boston Globe* in particular. Even though any who knew my associates and me would know such an accusation to be ridiculous, this charge was especially infuriating, the nastiest in a string of innuendos emanating from the Zuckerman camp.

With the help of a crowded docket and a federal judge who was in no hurry, Zuckerman's and his lawyers' delaying tactics worked wondrously well for them. I felt fortunate to be immersed in my new work, enjoying the company of some thirty-five bright young writers, researchers, and picture editors—three times the staff I'd had at the magazine—as we produced volumes of *The Vietnam Experience* at the rate of six per year. I was amazed at how much there still was to try to understand and to tell about that grim time in our history and its continuing aftershocks. Our target gradually moved upward from twelve volumes. Preoccupied as I was, I still chafed at our failure to get Zuckerman into the courtroom. Months passed. One, two, three years.

Suddenly, it didn't matter anymore. Nothing much mattered at all.

Chapter 23

Out of the Valley and into the Sun

The dark shadow was so small, little larger than a dime on the X-ray film. When Maggie's appetite began diminishing and her weight falling, she at first dismissed expressions of concern. The less time at the table, the more time for reading. After a few weeks, though, she grudgingly complied with the doctor's insistence that she submit to the X-ray machine. The surgeon operated two days before Thanksgiving Day, 1984. He did not really level with us about what he had found, perhaps because nobody can be altogether sure about a prognosis in many cancer cases, perhaps because he knew that Maggie and I would sense the truth soon enough. The colon cancer had gone too far before being detected. She suffered stoically but was miserable in the hospital. Our sons Rick, Brian, and Rob and I brought her home where she could be with us among her beloved paintings and tumbled heaps of books and be nuzzled by our old poodle Jocko. The obscene disease raced to kill her, pushing her in and out of comas, robbing us of time for proper good-byes. At 4:21 one morning I was awakened by a sudden absence of sound; rather, it was the sensation of Maggie's last breath. She had died in my arms. The date was December 26, two days before the fortieth anniversary of our marriage.

402　　　　How unfair, this brutal theft of a good life, of a unique, still vibrant mind. Unfair, unfair! Maggie had never been seriously ill. She came from tough stock. So did I. We were as hardy as had been most of our grandparents, and like them we were going to live and love into our nineties. She would preside autocratically over a weekly salon from her special armchair, like Madame Ouspenskaya in some 1940s film, tapping her gold-headed cane imperiously and dispensing unlimited heaps of caviar to her guests. There would be grandchildren, some great-grandchildren as well to fetch and to recite their homework or listen to their grandmama (she would never be called Grannie or Grandma) read aloud from Yeats or Twain or E. B. White, or perhaps from the book she herself was going to write about women, her ancestors, who went West as pioneers.

She would not have tolerated a religious ceremony or the usual solemn memorial service. Friends and relatives from all over, brother, sister, nieces and nephews, overflowed the comfortable old St. Botolph Club in Boston's Back Bay to exchange happy reminiscences and toast what one of them described as Margaret Manning's "unbelievable dedication to those things that truly matter: honor, personal nobility, compassion, culture, and learning."

That small malignant shadow had grown into a cloud that blocked out the entire sun. For many weeks thereafter, I awoke suddenly each morning at 4:21, confused, desolate, cheated. I wanted to be alone yet could not stand to be so. I was grateful for the presence of those three loving sons and the attentions of dozens of friends. Still, I was gripped by a sensation I had never really experienced before. "I am scared," I told myself. Seeking to provide some means of comfort the young lady who worked closely with me as an assistant in the Vietnam publishing project put into my hands a small book, a pamphlet really, called *A Grief Observed.* It was written by C. S. Lewis after the death of his wife. Its first lines might have been written, though less eloquently, by me:

> No one ever told me that grief felt so like fear. I am not afraid, but the sensation is like being afraid. The same fluttering in the stomach, the same restlessness, the yawning. I keep on swallowing. . . . I find it hard to take in what anyone says. . . . It is so

403

uninteresting. Yet I want the others to be about me. I dread the moments when the house is empty. If only they would talk to one another and not to me. . . .

Like C. S. Lewis, I found grief to be a testing journey through a long winding valley "where any bend may reveal a totally new landscape." I wondered if the sun would ever break through again. I had the three good sons, one lovely daughter-in-law with a second in prospect, and a grandson to help along the way. Self-pity was forbidden in their loving company.

A poker-playing friend who happened to be a psychiatrist recommended that I consult one of his fellow practitioners. "I have no faith in psychiatry," I said. "So what?" said my friend. "Tell him you don't but all you want is to feel better." Then he laid down a jack-high straight to beat my three kings. I took the advice and was pleasantly surprised to discover that I could talk about my sorrows and fears without embarrassment and that just talking with a sensitive man trained to understand was good medicine.

The best therapy of all came from the more than forty years of happy memories. There were plenty of them to draw on, for while Maggie and I of course had had occasion to quarrel and to cry now and then during all those years together, they were mostly years of smiles and laughter. More than once through this slow healing process I was reminded of words from two of her and my favorite American writers. Yes, the golden bowl had broken, Scott Fitzgerald once remarked, but it *was* golden. And Hemingway was right when he said, They can break you, but when it mends you're stronger in the broken place. Cancer had killed a great love affair but not the capacity to love and be loved again.

If there was any doubt of this it was brushed away by the young lady who had called my attention to C. S. Lewis's therapeutic words. Her name was Theresa Slomkowski. She had come to work for me at Boston Publishing Company, where I was editing the books on Vietnam, after a circuitous journey from a small dairy farm in middle Connecticut. The only daughter among the five children of second-generation Polish-American parents, she had to begin earning her own way after high school. At first she was happy to have put school behind her, but while she was working in a secretarial job at a nearby community college her aversion to schoolbooks turned into a desire for a college education. Over nine years she worked days and took night courses. This was a frustratingly slow way to get a college degree, so Miss Slomkowski, endowed with a lifetime supply of true grit, took in hand her two years' worth of slowly accumulated college credits, engineered the requisite student loan, and got herself admitted as the oldest—thirty-five—junior at exclusive Williams College. She majored in English and graduated on schedule in the class of 1982. By the time she walked into my office at the Boston Publishing Company with an enthusiastic recommendation from an employment agency and ordered me to hire her as my secretary, she was a vivacious, extremely attractive blonde of thirty-eight with a world-class smile and an aversion to arriving anywhere on time. "Slomkowski—that's an interesting name," I remarked with a smile. "What was it before you changed it?" She smiled back, but in a way that said "It's all right this time, but just one Polish joke and you'll be floating in the Charles River." She had four strong brothers.

I hired her forthwith, even though I sensed that, as frequently happens in the publishing field, a person that smart and determined really did not want to be a secretary and would seek early promotion to assistant to the editor. It was an excellent decision. Theresa was there to help Maggie as well as me when Maggie took ill and she was there to keep my office from disarray and offer wise counsel in the many months of mourning after Maggie's death.

More and more I looked outward and around me again rather than into the past. I am not sure at what moment it occurred to me that I should change Theresa's name from Slomkowski, but before that happened there was that matter of the unfinished business with Mortimer Zuckerman. More than five years had passed since we filed suit against him. He had long ago abandoned his Beacon Hill mansion for one of the most expensive coop apartments in New York as well as handsome new digs in Washington, and he had graduated from magazine maven to magazine mogul by paying, or promising to **405** pay, almost $170 million for the perennially third-place news-magazine *U.S. News & World Report*. As owner, chairman of the board, and self-designated editor in chief, he'd already gone through two or three putative top editors (handing out reportedly several-digit separation payments on the condition that the late departed would utter no imprecations to the press). But he still hadn't paid out a nickel of the more than $2 million he still owed for *The Atlantic*. The money he owed was inconsequential next to the real issue: His assault on the reputations of a dozen good people had to be exposed as the baseless smear it was.

When Zuckerman's lawyers didn't find ways of engineering delays in the litigation the judge did it for them by way of lassitude if not ineptitude. There was, though, a way to break the logjam and I pressed it with our lawyers. The original strategy had been to move forward with the federal case, brought by multiple plaintiffs, and to assume that the Massachusetts suit brought by a single plaintiff would be determined by the federal verdict. Why not blindside Mort by moving for a quick trial in the Massachusetts court? I had turned sixty-five and therefore under a Massachusetts statute was entitled to a speedy disposition of the case. I savored the prospect of taking on Zuckerman head-to-head in an open courtroom with a platoon or more of reporters filling their notebooks with the story I had to tell. I even spent a few thousand dollars on a public relations man with the single purpose of dramatizing to Zuckerman my eagerness for the confrontation. I suspected that he would not be nearly so eager. It was mighty late in the game to become prescient about Zuckerman, but this time I was. On November 12, the day before the matter of Robert J. Manning v. Mortimer B. Zuckerman was to go on trial in Superior Court, County of Suffolk, before one Judge John L. Murphy, Jr., Zuckerman caved in. His lawyers negotiated with our lawyers a settlement under which Zuckerman would pay me every penny he still owed for my shares of *Atlantic* stock, five years of withheld extra pension payments, plus accumulated interest—a total of just under $430,000. Not exactly cat food.

This was complete capitulation, an admission that Zuckerman's claims of being defrauded were specious. I was euphoric—until I learned the condition attached. The deal would

406

be secret. I would not be allowed to reveal even that there had been a settlement let alone the dimensions of it. I said that such a gag rule was unacceptable. But there was another condition: If I agreed to the gag rule, the Zuckerman camp would agree in writing to proceed to an early trial of the federal suit. Not until that trial was over could any of us reveal that Zuckerman had already in effect capitulated—an exasperating condition. But since the other side's agreement to finally go to trial was a great step forward, our lawyers urged me to accept. I consulted with Marion Campbell; she urged the same. So did Garth Hite, adding the advice that I rush Zuckerman's check to the bank with a high-speed police escort before payment was stopped. I signed the document but with a queasy feeling; that gag order bothered me.

Next day, papers were filed from both sides asking Judge Murphy to dismiss the case. On the morning of November 14 a story in the *New York Times* began, ". . . A five-year-old libel suit by the former editor of the *Atlantic* magazine against its new owner, Mortimer B. Zuckerman, was postponed today, and the judge in the case said he doubted the former editor could win the suit." The story was precisely 180 degrees from the truth.

I couldn't believe it. Another grievous blow from the *Times*. In the opening paragraph alone there were three glaring errors: The suit was not a libel case; the case was being dismissed, not postponed, and the judge had not said "he doubted the former editor could win the suit." The article went on to convey the reporter's own innuendo that Garth Hite's old memos constituted evidence of fraud, and he compounded that sin of bias by maintaining that I had told Zuckerman, which I never had, that the company was losing $100,000 a year when, according to Zuckerman, it was actually losing nine times that. The story quoted the judge as saying that the case "didn't seem like a triable one." The writer of this travesty was a *Times* reporter named Fox Butterfield, whom I vaguely remembered as a rather dour and distant fellow when he was the paper's Boston correspondent. He was presumably not a novice, having also served a stretch as the paper's correspondent in China.

Butterfield when asked to explain the evolution of the story **407** to his superiors admitted that he had not even talked to the judge himself but had accepted the word of a young lady apprentice whose only experience came from work on a college newspaper. Butterfield had telephoned me for comment on the dismissal of the case, though not mentioning that he was going to report that the judge was discounting in advance of any evidence my chances of winning. In responding to Butterfield's inquiry I had been handcuffed to "no comment" by the legal agreement, but a reporter with even limited perception would have been struck by my exceedingly cheerful tone of voice. Later the judge assured my lawyers that he had never said the case "didn't seem like a triable" one. He told the *Boston Globe* that any judge would be stupid to say such a thing before evidence was heard—a statement that was unarguable whatever the judge had or had not said to the young apprentice. That is, if he said it, he *was* stupid.

Puzzlement at this pitiful piece of misreporting in the great newspaper of record was almost as strong as my feeling of outrage. I protested, of course, with angry remonstrances and a letter to the editor which the *Times* did not publish, perhaps finding it too embarrassing, or too ill-tempered for the chaste editorial page. Instead, the paper printed a few days later a brief correction, admitting with what must have been some embarrassment that the case was not a libel action but otherwise letting stand the story's damaging falsity, its inescapable inference that I had been guilty of fraud. Some correction.

At least the logjam was broken. A few months later, after six years of the other side's defensive maneuverings and time-consuming, costly taking of depositions the plaintiffs got Zuckerman into the federal courtroom. To relate in much detail the proceedings that began on March 18, 1987, would be an act of sado-masochism, an act of cruelty against both narrator and reader. The event is worth some attention, however, for what it says about the state of the American system of jurisprudence. Justice has become a sort of commodity, obtainable by those with large sums of money with which to seek it. There is less and less room in the process for a poor person or even one of moderate means, whether he seeks to get redress from a victimizer or to defend himself from bogus claims. For many attorneys it has degenerated into a sort of sport, usually lucrative for those who lose a case as well as those who win it, a game designed, played, and refereed by lawyers, for lawyers, to the financial betterment of lawyers; a contest in which the trophy too often goes to the cleverer, the trickier, the less principled. Even if achieved, justice frequently comes only at brutal cost not just of money but of time and suffering.

The case of Campbell, et al. v. Zuckerman, et al. should never have gone to trial. Having begun, the trial should have been a short one. If Zuckerman and his lawyers had had a real case to present, or if the timid, bewildered-seeming federal judge had taken command of the proceedings, it might well have been. Instead, it droned on and on, a parody out of Dickens's *Bleak House* as written by Franz Kafka with emendations by Baron Münchausen. The opposition's chosen weapon was character assassination. Zuckerman's lead lawyer, using language and gestures to match the overstatement of his haberdashery, carried hyperbole to astral heights. To hear him tell it to the jury, Marion Campbell and those who ran *The Atlantic* for her were consummate swindlers, 1980s embodiments of Samuel Insull, Kruger the Match King, and the entire Teapot Dome gang, with a touch of Lucky Luciano thrown in for flavoring. As for Manning, he was but an "embittered" man with "many personal problems"—this bit of besmirchment delivered with an ominous inflection intended to make the jurors wonder whether the affliction might be dementia praecox, HIV positive, acute alcoholism, a fetish for female orangutans, or a combination of all four.

Zuckerman's lawyer was one smart and nasty gutter-fighter, but he wasn't as smart as he thought he was. He singled out Garth Hite for most of his attack, hectoring, jabbing, trying to find a weakness, some nonexistent smoking gun. He kept Hite on the witness stand for seventeen days, striving to turn him into a villain in the jurors' eyes. That was a serious mistake. What this did instead was to give the jurors more than enough time to see a quiet, imperturbable, honest man with a crystal-clear conscience. Another of the defense team kept our treasurer, Arthur Goodearl, on the stand for another thirteen days, her voice shrilling in exasperation as she tried to pin the label of **409** swindler on that most frugal and moral man. "You were a very tough witness," she complained to him afterward. "All I did was to tell the truth," he told her with a consoling smile. Virtually neutralized by the terms of my own settlement, I was disappointed when allowed only a brief time in the witness chair, a time given mostly to refuting Zuckerman's gross misrepresentation of the preparation and the meaning of a set of hypothetical figures Hite had prepared at Zuckerman's request—that set of "guesstimates" prepared many months before to suggest how the merger of *Harper's* might work financially.

As the Zuckerman lawyers and his helpers substituted innuendo for fact and cowed the judge into occasional odd and disadvantageous rulings, there were moments when we wondered why we had chosen such gentlemanly, almost maddeningly ethical lawyers to represent us. As time went on, though, the triple-play team of Gael Mahony, Michael Greco, and Randolph Tucker methodically countered the exaggerations and misrepresentations while extracting evidence that showed that Zuckerman knew exactly what he was buying, that he had already milked the company for many thousands in tax advantages and, as a matter of fact, hadn't paid a penny of federal income tax for the preceding several years. Both sides spent thousands of dollars on so-called "expert" witnesses who shed little light on the matters in question—the types Garth Hite liked to describe as "people who borrow your watch to tell you the time." For one example, it was never made adequately clear by our "experts"—though our circulation manager, Roy Green, could prove it—that millions of dollars Zuckerman had spent in costly but foolish, ego-driven efforts to puff up the magazine's circulation after he took over the company were represented by Zuckerman's lawyers as unexpected and necessary expenditures for which he should be compensated. Still, in the end the facts spoke more compellingly than the innuendo. When all the testifying was over the jury had a clear view of where the truth lay.

I had hoped that the trial would end by early summer, because a far more important proceeding had been scheduled for July 11, 1987. On that day Theresa Slomkowski and I were **410** married in the chapel of Boston's Holy Cross Cathedral. We came back from a brief honeymoon to receive a handsome wedding present. The federal jury threw out every one of Zuckerman's accusations of fraud, rejected outright his demand for some $10 or $16 or $25 million in damages (he or his lawyers kept changing the figure), and ordered him to pay the money he still owed for *The Atlantic*. It was a resounding verdict, though blemished by the jury's finding that there had been a minor, inadvertent breach of one—not specified—of the long laundry list of warranties that the Chicago lawyer had lavished on Zuckerman in the sale documents. This subtracted a small amount, approximately $157,000 in the final accounting, from Zuckerman's debt.

"Over the years Zuckerman has been 'winning' his case on the Easthampton cocktail circuit and in the pages of the *New York Times,*" I told the newspapers after the verdict. "But now a jury has spoken and he has lost it where it counts, in a court of law. . . . If Mort gracefully accepts the verdict he will have allowed us to have saved him from becoming the richest deadbeat in America." Mort did not accept that advice. He hailed the verdict as "complete vindication" of his fraud charges even though the plain facts said the opposite. So did the checks which after some delay Zuckerman handed over to the victorious plaintiffs.

And so, in an eloquent postscript, did a voice from the jury box. Zuckerman's claim of a great victory persuaded the stubbornly consistent *Times* and perhaps another newspaper or two to report the outcome as a kind of "both sides win" draw instead of the decision it really was. Such misreporting so provoked one of the jurors, Mrs. Lynn E. Freeman, that she ventured to set the record straight for once and all with an extraordinary letter that was printed in the *Boston Globe:*

> . . . After hearing 19 weeks of testimony, reviewing hundreds of documents and deliberating three days, the jury concluded there had been no fraud. The jury did find that certain specific warranties in the purchase and sale agreement had been unintentionally breached by the former Atlantic owners, requiring compensation to Zuckerman.

It was Zuckerman himself who, through his lawyers, charac-   **411** terized this principally as a fraud case in highly dramatic opening and closing statements. It was Zuckerman, then, who "lost" the case according to his own definition. Now, to distract attention from his loss, Zuckerman chooses to redefine the case as one breach of warranty to claim victory.*

The jury did reach a verdict, albeit complex. Yet it seems more and more that the lawyers were the real winners and the taxpayers the real losers (paying for 19 weeks of federal court time), while Zuckerman continues to try the case in the media.

So after seven years, a long, nasty, senseless ordeal was over. Or was it? Zuckerman still owed some small amounts, about $40,000 each, to half a dozen other stockholders of the company. They were loyal employees for whom that kind of money was important. It was only pocket change to Zuckerman. The federal jury's emphatic dismissal of the fraud charges would seem to oblige him to pay those outstanding debts. Not if Zuckerman and his lawyers could find ways to avoid paying. He withheld the payments, challenging those whom he owed either to accept about twenty-five cents on the dollar or sue him or drop dead. One of them, the fine editor Louise Desaulniers who had served *The Atlantic* for most of her adult life, in fact did die (of cancer) without seeing a penny; a few of the others accepted niggardly settlement checks; the rest were still waiting—without high expectations—years later.

For Marion Campbell, who picked up almost all the costs of defending her honor and ours, the bill was at least $3 million, far more than the amount that Zuckerman was obliged finally to pay her. If she had not done so the rest of us would never have been able even to take Zuckerman to court; he would have been allowed, as I saw it, to steal with impunity while his depiction of us as defrauders would have gone unanswered. That is how the system works. Zuckerman's own legal costs were at least $3 million as well, considerably more than the debt he had tried to negate. His wizardry at tax deductions no doubt took

---

*After the trial I talked to Mrs. Freeman at some length and she told me that the jurors did not want to award even this token money to Zuckerman but they reluctantly agreed that the judge's charge obliged them to find a breach of warranty.

care of that expenditure. But then there was the additional cost to him, incalculable but real, in the loss of face and the dishonor he had inflicted on himself.

I, too, had been sullied by the long, degrading experience. For a long time after its culmination I was afflicted by self-demeaning feelings of contempt for the man and a compulsion to divine what would cause him to behave as he did. I got no further than the assumption that simple greed was surely not the explanation, because Zuckerman could have saved several millions by eschewing the lawsuit and made several more by concentrating instead on the money-making potential of the bargain he'd struck for himself. Here, I realized, was a classic case that would require the subject's full cooperation and even then would likely test even the most perceptive head-candler in the psychiatric profession.

My own case was serious enough. For far too long I took unseemly, addictive delight in reading and hearing of the jibes and snickers generated by Zuckerman's activities in the glitzier reaches of New York society and in the condescending salons of Georgetown. They were many to savor. There were the chortles that followed his clarion call in *U.S. News & World Report* for Americans to pay higher income taxes, an exercise in chutzpah committed only a few weeks after it was revealed in court that he himself had paid not a penny of income taxes for years. The plans for a gaudy pair of shadow-casting skyscrapers adjacent to New York's Central Park that summoned to arms against him the likes of Jacqueline Kennedy Onassis, Bill Moyers, and a large cast of other distinguished personages. The cracks behind his back from those he wanted to think of as friends about his sneaking an extra step when he pitched in the much self-celebrated "literary softball game" in the Hamptons. The huge TV satellite dish that blocked the view of an irate Easthampton neighbor and had to be taken down. The plans for an even more controversial Zuckerman office complex that would despoil the land around Thoreau's Walden Pond. The society page photographs showing him with a soppy smile and the latest female attachment, soon to be replaced like the many before. His weekly column in *U.S. News* was usually good for a hearty laugh, bringing to mind the English wit who once said of an- **413** other's work, "I had always thought of cliché as a suburb of Paris until I read his writings."

It began to dawn on me that this preoccupation with the man was not only unbecoming, it was a kind of sickness itself and it had afflicted me for too long. One day, though, I accidentally saw Zuckerman on a TV panel show dealing with foreign affairs, far out of his depth, blinking through his contact lenses and groping for some timely fatuity. As I watched I was suddenly gripped by a spasm of discovery. Behind that forced smile and expensively tailored exterior lived a sad and lonely man. I couldn't hate such a deprived person or even despise him. I just felt sorry for him. I was cured.*

How good it was to walk again in the full sunlight, rancor drained from the system, with a new love by my side, golden memories of the first one in my satchel, and after half a century still engaged in the kind of work I loved. Now that serenity had returned I realized that I had not missed for one day the demands and frustrations of working at *The Atlantic*. It had been time for me to leave; it was the manner of the leaving that had caused the damage.

I could now read the magazine with detachment—and with admiration untainted by bitterness or jealousy. It is still a damn fine magazine, perhaps not quite as adventurous, as risk taking as it ought to be with the ample resources now at its disposal, but extremely well-written and -edited, with a bright, much bigger and better-paid staff, an enviable editorial budget, and a designer who has made it more attractive than the magazine I put out. It deserves a long and prosperous future. These were precisely the conditions I was hoping to assure when I made that fateful lunch date in June of 1979. If this is taken to mean that I am bragging about having helped to assure a healthy future for an American institution, so be it.

We at Boston Publishing Company had already produced the first five volumes of *The Vietnam Experience* history books

---

*Now that I am rid of my preoccupation, I feel uneasy even in recounting the unbecoming intensity of it but do so in keeping with the teaching of old Father Hannon of St. Thomas Aquinas church to the effect that absolution and peace of mind require full confession of one's sins.

when the project was taken on by Time-Life Books, the biggest mail-order book operation in the world, and was proving so successful that the originally scheduled twelve volumes grew to sixteen, then to eighteen and ultimately to twenty-five. Though we produced them at a journalistic clip under pressing deadlines, they were carefully wrought and strikingly illustrated books. Well before the series was completed the books attracted superlative reviews in the *Times* and other major newspapers. We got the glory but Time-Life Books got the profit; that was fair enough because when our little company foundered because of our poor business management and other sought-after backers declined out of fear that Vietnam was "death at the box office," the TLB people took the gamble. At last check, almost 10,000,000 volumes had been bought by just under 2,000,000 subscribers. At $15 per book, that comes to $150,000,000, almost enough to pay the annual salaries and bonuses of the CEOs of three or four money-losing American corporations.

When that editing job was finished in 1988 and time came to say good-bye to the bright young people who had done all the researching and the writing, we all lifted a glass and warmly toasted ourselves for producing in the heat of immediacy a work of history that might stand for years to come. Then I climbed to the figurative roof of a figurative American embassy in Saigon and in a figurative helicopter took leave at last from the tragedy of Vietnam, a drama in which for nearly thirty years I had been by profession and preoccupation a sort of player.

For all my adult life I had lived by deadlines, by the clocks and the calendars of others. Now was the time to work by my own rhythm. I was feeling better and fitter than I'd felt for years, more like my old friend and idol from the West Junior High School library in Binghamton, New York, Sabatini's derring-do Scaramouche, who was "born with the gift of laughter and the sense that the world was mad." For a half century I'd been privileged not only to watch history in the making but to see from inside some of its making, perhaps even to contribute in obscure ways to its shaping. Journalism after all is not exempt from the Heisenberg principle—our very act of examining a phenomenon often has the effect of altering the phenomenon. **415**

And I'd actually been paid to do all this! Considering the length of the time span and the great variety of the challenges, the setbacks and disappointments and traumas have been relatively few. I am now sufficiently mellow to ascribe the worst ones to pilot error, I of course having been the pilot.

Transformation from unindicted co-conspirator to bystander has of course required a considerable amount of adjusting. It is not easy to stop thinking like an editor. For example, I got up early one morning and couldn't find the cold war. Looked everywhere. I knew it had been there the night before, or was it last month or last year? Waking up to it was as natural as brushing the teeth and putting on clothes. For four decades a glowering, seemingly intractable set of circumstances, confrontation between two nuclear-armed Superscorpions in a bottle, had dominated the world, conditioned the thoughts and the deeds of my generation of politicians, journalists, and citizens alike. Now it was over. On another morning I looked out and saw that the Soviet Union was missing. The whole damned empire, crumbled by the "seeds of decay" within, just what forty years earlier George Kennan had predicted would happen. Next thing you know they'll be announcing a cure for cancer and a surefire international mechanism for preventing famine and mass hunger.

Older reflexes may be too atrophied for traveling in new directions, but what an exciting prospect opens for the new generation of politicians, public servants, and journalists as this new horizon spreads before them. Now it should be possible to pursue peace in some way other than the accumulation of terror; get some people working on that. And while they are at it, they might try to bring back the dream, that dream, mawkish perhaps, of a more benign world, poor and middling and rich countries all working together, the vision we young idealists in the United nations pressroom watched dissolve day by day, and some of our idealism with it. The UN, incidentally, now seems to be in the best shape ever, already demonstrating that with the cold war off its back it can really accomplish some of the peacekeeping and wound-healing it was created to do—or so I try to believe. Perhaps, too, the opportunity really has come to put a definite limit on how many more wars the Jews must fight before they are allowed to live securely in their own homeland and can join with Arabs in turning their bloody Middle Eastern deserts, teeming refugee camps, and ruined cities into peaceful gardens.

Such sanguine hopes are difficult to sustain in the face of the sanguinary events (how marvelously perverse is the English vocabulary) paraded before us daily in headlines and on the TV screen—Armenians and Azerbaijanis, Serbs and Croats, Cambodians and Cambodians, all killing each other; the Chinese killing their college students, blacks killing blacks in South Africa (and in assorted American neighborhoods), and just about everybody killing the benighted Kurds. Surgeon General's Warning: Long pent-up ethnic, racial or tribal rivalries can be dangerous to the general health. So can unrelieved economic oppression.

(I can hear someone mutter, "That's a journalist for you, always looking for happy outcomes while he burdens the citizenry with mostly bad news.")

Then there is the immense amount of unfinished business right here at home. The schools, for example. Young people don't even learn to read and write and many are taught less in many colleges than I was taught in Binghamton Central High School in the thirties. I look with anxiety at the unkempt men and women with pathetic sacks of old clothing sleeping on benches only yards from my front door and brood about the rusting factories and unemployment lines that defy the gutsy "can do" spirit of America, and worry about the inequalities and prejudices that mock the notion of liberty and justice for all. Did my generation bring this about?

As they were growing up I often told my sons that bad as the Great Depression was for those of us who endured it, the experience had brought most Americans together, a lot more together than they are now in the nervous, confrontational final years of the twentieth century, one that my old boss Henry Luce had proclaimed to be the American Century. By being born later they had been deprived of the character-building experience of deprivation. Now I am not so sure they have escaped; they might be in for something like deprivation after all, or if not them then their sons and daughters, who will be confronted   **417** with the reckoning being forced on them by us who have preceded them—just as the Great Depression and World War II had been bequeathed by the generation that preceded mine.

("There he goes again, talking only about the gloomy side.")

Yes, but if I had time I'd be happy to join the challenging search for the silver linings, offering what little I might in the way of commentary or providing encouragement for thinkers and communicators who are able to rise above rhetoric and help us toward solutions. There are already more than enough voices, critics, and commentators in newspapers, magazines, and on TV and in the windy corridors of government. Unfortunately, they are at best just building inspectors, like me, when what the world needs are architects. Some will come along, they almost always do, and if we are lucky they will not all be dictators and tyrants.

If I think of something useful I'll pass it along, but don't count on it. I am pretty busy as it is. There is the matter of my grandson, Matthew. He is smart as witch hazel and already a gentleman at eleven years. He has learned early how to spot a phony from a goodly distance and how to cast well from the shore for striped bass and bluefish; now I must help teach him patience.

As for Madeline, granddaughter number one, she is almost four, beautiful, charming, and, as a leading anchorwoman or topflight editor in chief should be, strong-willed. While she prepares to follow a career in journalism like her father and mother, her two grandfathers, and one uncle, I hope she also will take time to become the first talented amateur pianist in the family. There is one particularly beautiful passage, just a few bars of the andante movement of Mozart's Sonata in C Major, Koechel 545, that I will try to help her with, though I never have gotten it right myself.

Granddaughter number two, Mary, cannot yet run for office, being only three, but she has already got the wit, the charm, and the memory for names that make for a winning politician. She even shakes hands like one. I intend to help with the speeches and position papers. I see her as one of the best of the forty women in a future United States Senate. She won't accept the vice-presidential nomination, not if I have anything to do with it.

These are among the most pressing assignments at this moment, though there are enough others on the agenda to keep me working toward more deadlines than I can count. Now and then—when I am not too busy, that is—I wonder what will happen when I get to be old and have to retire. Perhaps I'll write a book. I'll call it *Lucky Bob*.

Index

421